A History of Malaysia

Macmillan Asian Histories Series
D.G.E. Hall: *A History of South-East Asia – 4th Edition*
B.W. Andaya and L.Y. Andaya: *A History of Malaysia*
M. Ricklefs: *A History of Modern Indonesia*

A History of Malaysia

Barbara Watson Andaya

and

Leonard Y. Andaya

MACMILLAN

First published 1982 by
THE MACMILLAN PRESS LTD
Houndmills, Basingstoke, Hampshire RG21 2XS
and London
Companies and representatives
throughout the world

ISBN 0–333–27672–8 (hardcover)
ISBN 0–333–27673–6 (paperback)

A catalogue record for this book is available
from the British Library

Printed in Hong Kong

Reprinted 1985, 1986, 1987, 1988, 1991, 1992

For Elise and Alexis

Contents

Foreword

Although a small country, Malaysia has been given more than its share of attention by foreign scholars especially those from the English-speaking world. Two reasons perhaps account for this. Malaysia, since the mid-nineteenth century, has had a flourishing economy; its society is unique — it is, one might say 'Asia in miniature'.

Writings on the Malay Peninsula, in English, paralleled the growth of British economic interests in the region in the first half of the nineteenth century as it became necessary to introduce the area to the British public. It was at this juncture that what might be considered the first history of the Malay Peninsula, in English, was published — *The Malayan Peninsula Embracing Its History, Manners and Customs of the Inhabitants, Politics, Natural History &c. from its earliest Records* — in 1834. The author (P. J. Begbie), a military officer, devoted much space to a discussion of the Naning War (1831–2) in which he had participated; the book nonetheless dealt rather elaborately with the history as well as various other aspects (including botany) of the Malay States.

T. J. Newbold, another professional soldier, published his *Political and Statistical Accounts of the British Settlements in the Straits of Malacca* in two volumes in 1839. Quite apart from providing a useful political and social history of the Malay states, this work is still considered a mine of information on the contemporary economy of the Straits Settlements and the Peninsula.

The next attempt to write a history of the Malay Peninsula, however, occurred more than fifty years later. Published in 1906, Frank Swettenham's *British Malaya: An Account of the Origin and Progress of British Influence in Malaya* was more an apologia for British colonialism than an exposition of Malay history and society as Begbie's and Newbold's books had been. Indeed Swettenham practically established the framework for Malayan history which remained unquestioned for the next fifty years. It is his view of Malayan history which the modern generation of scholars describe as *Euro-centric*.

Following upon Swettenham's footsteps came R. J. Wilkinson and R. O. Winstedt, two officials considered authorities on Malay culture, literature and history much as Swettenham himself was then revered as an expert on things Malay. Originally interested in the Malays, Wilkinson first wrote his 'History of the Peninsular Malays' as part of a larger project entitled *Papers on Malay Subjects*; it was published in

1908. Subsequently, it was revised and expanded to include the establishment of British political control and was published in 1923 as *A History of the Peninsular Malays with Chapters on Perak and Selangor*. Winstedt was the more prolific of the two. He edited *Malaya: The Straits Settlements and the Federated and Unfederated Malay States* (1923), wrote 'A History of Malaya' (1935) as well as 'A History of Malay Literature' (1939) both in the *Journal of the Malayan Branch of the Royal Asiatic Society*; *Britain and Malaya 1786–1941* (1944); *The Malays: A Cultural History* (1947) and *Malaya and Its History* (1948). Although both Wilkinson and Winstedt were avid students of Malay literature and culture, they, like Swettenham, saw Malayan history largely in political terms and, more specifically, as the story of the conquerors rather than the conquered, the rulers rather than the ruled.

The 1930s, however, saw the appearance of the American, Rupert Emerson, whose valuable work – *Malaysia: A Study in Direct and Indirect Rule* (1937) – elicited from Frank Swettenham the comment that it was 'full of highly contentious writing'. Emerson was less concerned with writing Malaysian history than a critique of Imperialism. Still his book provided a refreshing contrast to those of Winstedt (on Malayan history) if only because he was under no constraint to reveal frankly the motives behind the formulation of colonial policies.

For a period of more than fifty years since the publication of Swettenham's *British Malaya*, Malayan history had been cast in a particular mould, Emerson's *Malaysia* notwithstanding. In making the first attempt to reshape it, K. G. Tregonning (formerly Raffles Professor of History first of the University of Malaya and later the University of Singapore) remarked that for too long Malayan history had been viewed 'from the deck of a foreign ship'. He would like to take Malaya itself 'as my frame of reference, . . . considering the activities of the many peoples in it as my interest'. His book *A History of Modern Malaya* (1964) broke new ground even if Malaysian historians today are of the opinion that it has obvious shortcomings: it is too preoccupied with modern developments and hence completely relegates the indigenous society to a position of obscurity and inconsequence.

In 1969, J. M. Gullick, ex-Malayan Civil Servant and a social anthropologist by training, published a book entitled *Malaysia* which treated the new nation (formed in 1963) not as a unified whole but as three separate entities: Malaya, Singapore and the Borneo Territories. His conceptualization of Malayan history is nonetheless interesting. It does not differ substantially from Tregonning's but his approach is clearly influenced by his social science training. While not neglecting chronology, he provides more than just a political and economic perspective of Malayan history but, like all earlier authors who had ventured to write standard texts on Malayan history, he was unable to furnish an integrated view of the subject and, in particular, to provide a continuous thread linking the Melaka sultanate with the period of modern developments. In this respect, the present work by Leonard and Barbara Andaya is a major triumph.

The writings of Leonard and Barbara Andaya on the eighteenth-century history of the Malay states have, in the past few years, contributed immensely to the enrichment of Malaysian historiography. Using largely Dutch sources and without ignoring indigenous material, they have not only filled long-existing gaps but corrected a number of erroneous dates, speculations and assumptions.

Apart from being an outstanding example of how Malaysian history can be treated as a cohesive whole, the strength of the present work lies in its treatment of the pre-nineteenth century period. Tracing the origin of the Melaka sultanate to its Sumatran roots, Leonard and Barbara Andaya proceed to explain not only the factors which contributed to the growth of that sultanate but also the beginnings of Malay political culture as we know it today. Other authors have tended to see Malay society as of marginal importance for the period 1511—1800 but here the development of the indigenous society is followed through until the nineteenth century which saw the emergence of a more complex society.

For many years historians have doubted the plausibility of writing a standard work on Malayan/Malaysian history which does not depend heavily on the colonial presence as the pivot. Their treatment of Malaysian history (in particular the period 1400—1945) tends to be fragmented. When confronted with the need also to integrate the history of the peninsula with that of Sabah and Sarawak the task appeared to them insurmountable. Admittedly, it is difficult to marry disparate parts but for the historian who is perceptive it is possible to discern common denominators.

Quite apart from having skilfully woven together the entire span of Malaysian history, Leonard and Barbara Andaya have not, unlike previous authors, neglected to discuss education and religion (in particular Islam). Therefore, while the work is comparatively more tightly structured, it is also more comprehensive and the authors have presented a viewpoint which is not only new but more in keeping with current local interpretation of Malaysian history.

September 1981

Khoo Kay Kim
Professor of Malaysian History
Department of History
University of Malaya

Acknowledgements

The authors would like to acknowledge the help of a number of colleagues: Professors Nicholas Tarling and David Lim, Associate Professors Grant Anderson, Warwick Neville and Andrew Pawley, Drs Richard Phillips and John Terrell, and especially Professor Khoo Kay Kim. Our thanks also to Barbara Batt, Freda Christie and Sisilia Tonga who cheerfully and efficiently typed the manuscript, and to Jan Kelly who drew the maps.

Preliminary Note

The new spelling system adopted by Indonesia and Malaysia has been followed for Malay words. The most notable features of this system are the use of 'c' and 'sy' respectively to represent English ch/Dutch tj and English sh/Dutch sj. The spelling of place names follows current practice; for example, Melaka and Kuching.

The spelling of titles in Malaysia has not yet been standardized. In this book most honorifics have been rendered in the new spelling (thus Syah, not Shah), but some states still retain the old form for state titles, for example 'Dato' rather than 'Datuk'. Where relevant this differentiation has been maintained. 'Dato' has also been used when an individual held that title but died before the new spelling was introduced (for example, Dato Onn). Chinese words have been romanized according to the Wade—Giles system since pinyin is not yet widely used in the literature on Malaysia.

All dollar figures quoted are in Straits (later Malayan/Malaysian) dollars or *ringgit*. In the nineteenth century the value of the Straits dollar fluctuated, but in 1904 it was pegged to sterling at the rate of M$1.00 to 2s. 4d. (about US$.40—60 in pre-World War II terms). From 1947 to 1974 M$3.00 was equal to about US$1.00. The *ringgit* has appreciated since 1973 when Malaysia opted out of the Sterling Area and floated the *ringgit* against the US dollar and the British pound. The value of the *ringgit* towards the end of 1981 was approximately M$2.22 to US$1.00.

Throughout the text the term 'Thai' refers to the ethnic group which came to settle in present-day Thailand, as well as to the citizen of that state which was officially decreed as Thailand in June 1939. Before the latter date the various Thai kingdoms are called by their specific names, such as Sukhothai and Ayudhya. The terms 'Siam' and 'Siamese' are used for the Thai kingdom and people reunified under the Chakri dynasty in 1782 until the official name change in 1939.

Abbreviations

ANU	Australian National University
ASA	Association of Southeast Asia
ASEAN	Association of Southeast Asian Nations
BKI	*Bijdragen tot de Taal–, Land– en Volkenkunde* (Journal of the Royal Institute of Linguistics and Anthropology)
CCP	Chinese Communist Party
Cod. Or.	Codex Orientalis
DAP	Democratic Action Party
EIC	English East India Company
FAMA	Federal Agricultural Marketing Authority
FELDA	Federal Land Development Authority
FMS	Federated Malay States
FSGCP	Fort St George Council Papers
FWCP	Fort William Council Papers
Gerakan	Gerakan Rakyat Malaysia (Malaysian People's Movement)
GLU	General Labour Unions
JMBRAS	*Journal of the Malayan* (later *Malaysian*) *Branch of the Royal Asiatic Society*
JSBRAS	*Journal of the Straits Branch of the Royal Asiatic Society*
JSEAH	*Journal of Southeast Asian History*
JSEAS	*Journal of Southeast Asian Studies*
JSS	*Journal of the Siam Society*
KA	Koloniaal Archief (Colonial Archives)
KMT	Kuomintang (Chinese Nationalist Party)
MBRAS	Malaysian Branch of the Royal Asiatic Society
MCA	Malayan Chinese Association
MCP	Malayan Communist Party
MCS	Malayan Civil Service
MIC	Malayan Indian Congress
MPAJA	Malayan Peoples Anti-Japanese Army
MRLA	Malayan Races Liberation Army
NCC	National Consultative Council
NEP	New Economic Policy
OB	Overgekomen Brieven (Incoming Correspondence)
PAP	People's Action Party
PAS	Parti Islam Sa-Melayu (Pan-Malayan Islamic Party)
PETA	Pembela Tanah Air (Defenders of the Fatherland)
PMFTU	Pan-Malayan Federation of Trade Unions

PPP	People's Progressive Party
SFR	Sumatra Factory Records
SITC	Sultan Idris Training College
SSR	Straits Settlements Records
UMNO	United Malays National Organization
UMS	Unfederated Malay States
VBG	*Verhandelingen van het Bataviaasch Genootschap van Kunsten en Wetenschappen* (Proceedings of the Batavian Society for Arts and Sciences)
VOC	Vereenigde Oostindische Compagnie (the United East India Company, i.e. the Dutch East India Company)

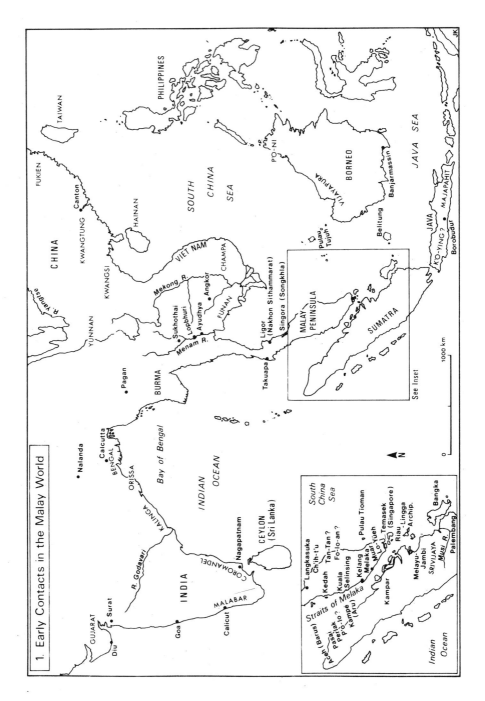

1. Early Contacts in the Malay World

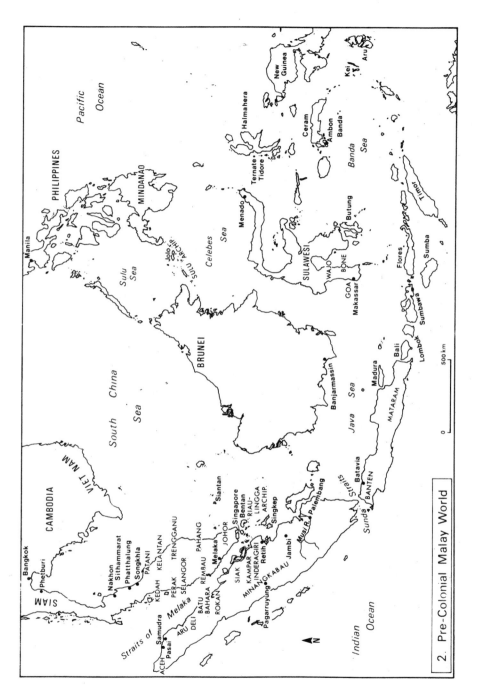

2. Pre-Colonial Malay World

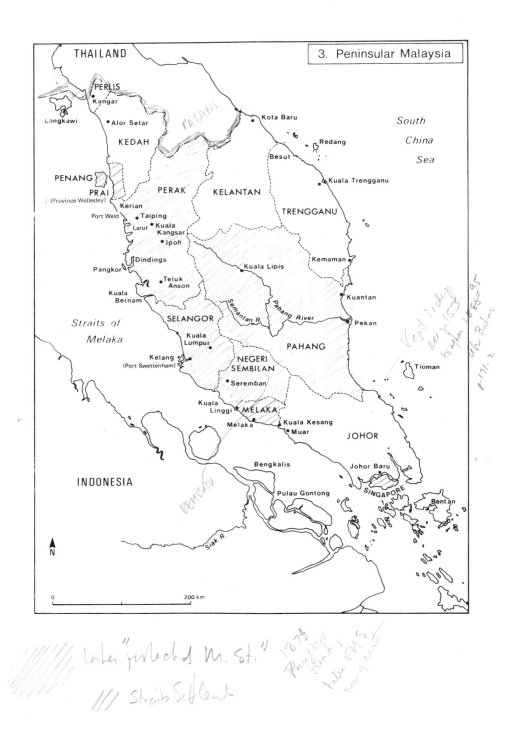

3. Peninsular Malaysia

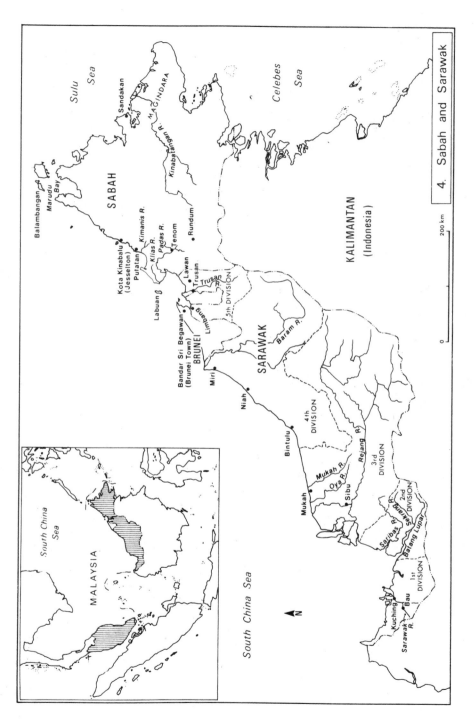

4. Sabah and Sarawak

Introduction: The Environment and Peoples of Malaysia

Formed in 1963, the Federation of Malaysia comprises the long peninsular land mass which separates the Indian Ocean from the South China
Sea, together with the northern quarter of Borneo but excluding the
small state of Brunei. Peninsular Malaysia, covering 131,794 square
kilometres, is made up of eleven states: Perlis, Kedah, Penang, Perak,
Selangor (with the Federal Capital Territory of Kuala Lumpur), Melaka,
Johor, Negeri Sembilan, Pahang, Trengganu and Kelantan. The island
of Singapore, part of Malaysia between 1963 and 1965, is now independent. The Borneo territories, Sabah (formerly British North Borneo)
and Sarawak, together cover roughly 198,000 square kilometres, but
are separated at the closest point from the peninsula by over 650 kilometres. Kota Kinabalu (previously Jesselton), the capital of Sabah, is
864 kilometres from Kuching (Sarawak's capital) and more than
1,600 kilometres from Kuala Lumpur.

The landform of both the peninsula and Borneo is characterized by
coastal plains giving way to a rugged mountainous interior. The spine
of the peninsula is the Main Range, running roughly north—south for
483 kilometres and varying from 914 metres to 2,134 metres above
sea level. A further block of highland, covering most of upper Kelantan,
inland Trengganu and Pahang, includes the peninsula's highest peak,
Gunung Tahan (2,207 metres). Along the west coast from Perlis to
Johor stretches a continuous alluvial plain 960 kilometres long and at
places sixty kilometres wide. Another lowland plain occurs on the east
coast, but this is narrower and interrupted by the Trengganu highlands.
Because the interior mountains have always posed a formidable barrier
to trans-peninsula movement, the focus of settlement has been the
coastal lowlands. Initially political centres were established on the
rivers which have their headwaters in the inland ranges, and it is from
their principal river that most peninsular states derive their name. Of
these the Pahang River (434 kilometres) is the longest.

In Borneo low-lying, often swampy alluvial plains also form a belt
along the coast, narrowing considerably when they reach Sabah where
larger but isolated plains occur in the north and east. Behind these

plains are the foothills leading inland up to a mountainous mass through which runs the border between Malaysia and Indonesian Borneo (Kalimantan). The imposing Mount Kinabalu (4,500 metres) in Sabah is the highest point in Southeast Asia. It is from the highlands of the interior that the great rivers of Borneo flow down to the sea, the largest in Malaysian Borneo being the Rejang in Sarawak and the Kinabatangan in Sabah (560 kilometres).

Both Peninsular Malaysia and the Borneo states lie between 1° and 7° north of the equator. The climate is uniformly warm and humid with temperatures ranging from 25·5°C to 33°C, except at high altitudes where the nights are considerably cooler. The passing of the seasons is not marked by variations in temperature but by changes in rainfall, which in turn are related to the cycle of the monsoonal winds. The northeast monsoon, a steady strong wind sweeping down across the South China Sea, is the dominating air stream during November–January. It then gradually decreases in force, with a transitional period in April–May followed by the southwest monsoon. Another transitional period occurs in October–November, and the whole cycle starts again, once more made apparent by changes in rainfall. Throughout most of Malaysia the rainfall ranges from 2,000 mm to 4,000 mm per annum, although there is considerable variation between different regions. Nowhere is there a true dry season, but in most areas certain periods in the year predictably receive more rainfall. For much of the peninsula and northwest Borneo the wettest season coincides with the northeast monsoon.

Although Malaysian soils are not generally fertile, the heavy rainfall and warm temperatures have provided almost perfect conditions for equatorial rainforests. About 70 per cent of the land is still covered with some form of forestation, much of which is primary jungle, often so inaccessible or at such altitudes that it will probably remain uncleared. A very different vegetation type, but one equally characteristic of the region, is the mangrove swamps. These border the sheltered shores and estuaries along the western coasts of the peninsula and Borneo, sometimes reaching inland for twenty kilometres. Coastlines more exposed to the open sea, like the east coast of the peninsula, are edged by long sandy beaches backed by low heath. Along the plains most of the original forest cover has been removed since the nineteenth century to make way for settlements, road and rail communications, and the development of commercial agriculture and industries.

In 1980, Malaysia's population was almost 13·46 million, of whom about 11·14 million live on the peninsula mainly in the west coast states. The composition of this population remains one of the principal reasons for Malaysia's interest to specialists on Asia. The dominant ethnic group is the Malays, who according to the 1970 census figures comprised 53·2 per cent of Peninsular Malaysia's population and who are largely involved in the bureaucracy or rural agriculture. The contemporary definition of a Malay — one who habitually speaks Malay and who follows the Moslem faith — has readily permitted the inclusion of migrants from elsewhere in the Indonesian archipelago as well as many individuals with an admixture of non-Malay blood.

Besides the Malays, there are other numerically small but historically important indigenous groups in the peninsula. These are the *orang asli* (literally, original people), the aboriginals, who number around 53,000, less than 1 per cent of the population. Around 60 per cent still live in the deep jungle. The *orang asli* are commonly divided into three broad groups: the nomadic hunting and gathering Negritos (recently estimated at 2,000) in the northern and central regions; the semi-nomadic Senoi of the central area, who practise a form of shifting cultivation; and the so-called Jakun of the southern peninsula, often termed proto-Malays, who are increasingly adopting a sedentary farming life.

Among the non-indigenous population, which includes a range of different groups such as Arabs, Armenians, Eurasians and so on, the main communities are the Chinese (35·4 per cent) and the Indians, including individuals of Pakistan, Bangladesh and Sri Lanka origin (10·76 per cent). Both Chinese and Indians are largely descendants from migrants who arrived after the mid-nineteenth century to work in the colonial economy. The Chinese are mainly urban dwellers, being particularly active in the professions and the commercial sector; Indians are prominent on the rubber estates, in the railways department, in the bureaucracy and professions.

When Sarawak and Sabah are taken into account the population picture changes considerably. Categorization of the local peoples, problematic enough on the peninsula, has in Borneo posed enormous difficulties for census makers. Over the years there has been a gradual tendency to reduce categories, and the resulting classification may mask considerable variation in language and lifestyle. At one time in Sabah, for instance, at least thirty-eight different groups were enumerated, but in the publication of the 1980 census only three categories will be listed: *bumiputra* (literally 'sons of the soil' or indigenous peoples), Chinese and others. Previous figures, however, have shown that in Sabah's population (preliminary 1980 census: 1,002,608) Moslems account for more than 38 per cent of the population, including the largest Moslem group, the Bajaus. The dominant non-Moslem group in Sabah is the Kadazan (formerly termed Dusun) who comprise about 30 per cent and like the Murut people of the interior include several different language groupings. In Sarawak (preliminary 1980 census: 1,294,753) the Moslem figure has been given as 25 per cent, which apart from Malays includes a large proportion of Kedayans and Melanaus, groups who have adopted Islam. The non-Moslem indigenes in Sarawak account for approximately 44 per cent of the

population, the largest group being the Ibans ('Sea Dayaks'). In both
Borneo states there are also numerous other indigenous peoples, some
of whom number only a few hundred, some two or three thousand.
Both Sabah and Sarawak include significant Chinese populations
(21 per cent and 30 per cent respectively), roughly divided into urban
Chinese, who are predominantly merchants and middlemen, and rural
Chinese involved in agriculture.

Incorporating this range of humanity under one national flag has
meant that no single group in Malaysia has a total majority. In the
1970 figures Malays numbered 46·8 per cent; Chinese 34·1 per cent;
Indians 9 per cent; Dayaks (including Ibans) 3·7 per cent; Kadazan
1·8 per cent; other native groups 3·2 per cent and others (Eurasians,
Arabs, Thais, Filipinos, Indonesians and so on) 1·4 per cent. These
percentages at present appear stable and although the population
growth is rapid (2·7 per cent per annum) no major shifts are predicted
for the foreseeable future.

Language is seen as an important means of linking the nation together,
and Malay is the national language and the medium of instruction for
schoolchildren. English, however, is widely used, especially among the
élite. There are numerous Chinese dialects, notably from South China
(Hakka, Teochew, Hokkien, Cantonese and Hailam) as well as Mandarin.
Among the Indians Tamil is most common, but numerous other
regional languages from the sub-continent are also spoken. About fifteen different languages can be found among peninsular *orang asli*, while
the linguistic diversity in Borneo makes it a fertile field for research.

The linguistic complexity is matched by the range of religious and
cultural traditions within Malaysian society. The state religion is Islam
and virtually all Malays are Moslem. Although some other indigenous
groups have adopted Islam, most have their own unique perceptions of
the world and how it functions. Some Chinese are Moslem, but the
majority are Christian, Buddhist, Confucianist, Taoist or a combination of these. Hinduism and Christianity are common among Indians,
but a significant number are also Moslem.

Malaysia and Singapore are the only two countries in Southeast
Asia which have held elections at regular intervals since they became
independent. However, Malaysia's racial composition has contributed
to a political structure which seeks to combine some of the main
features of the parliamentary system with the practical realities of the
local situation. The head of state, the Yang Dipertuan Agung, is a
position which rotates among the Sultans of the peninsular states.
Though Malaysia is a federation of states, the Borneo territories have
special rights which were granted when they joined. The governing
National Front is noteworthy because it is based on a coalition of
parties, the most important of which claim to represent the interests of
specific ethnic groups. Occasionally the assumptions and compromises

underlying this structure have been questioned, as in May 1969 when ethnic disturbances broke out. In general, however, Malaysia has successfully held the balance between its different ethnic communities while maintaining an economic growth which is the envy of many of its neighbours. The way in which future governments of Malaysia reconcile the often competing demands of ethnicity and the sharing of economic resources will continue to make this young nation of special interest to scholars in a wide range of disciplines.

The present work surveys Malaysia's rise to a modern state, tracing its development from early times through the period of colonial rule to the creation of an independent nation. It falls naturally into three divisions, which represent significant periods in Malaysian history. Chapters 1–3 examine the social and economic bases of the 'traditional' society which grew up in the Melaka Straits area prior to the nineteenth century. Chapters 4–6 continue the story from the founding of Singapore in 1819, which initiated a new type of economic and political organization that opened the door to far-reaching changes in local society. From 1874, with the imposition of colonial rule, the pace of change was quickened, altering the nature of the traditional Malay polity and necessitating fundamental readjustments in its relations with the outside world. Chapter 7 discusses the modern Malaysian nation as the heir of both the traditional maritime state and the colonial past. The conclusion then attempts to highlight some significant patterns which can be traced in Malaysian history from early times to the present day.

Certain factors have influenced the manner in which this book was written. A primary consideration was the state of research in Malaysian history, where there are still many fields unexplored. The authors have tried to avoid any suggestion that contemporary knowledge permits a consistently detailed and well-rounded account of the past. This is particularly true for the pre-colonial period, despite the continuing research which is unearthing new information and in some cases challenging accepted interpretations. Because the historian is always a tool of his sources, the authors have included several short sections which discuss the available material, mentioning some of the problems it poses and how it has determined the kind of historical writing possible. One of the major difficulties is the dating of events before European records became available in the sixteenth century. Sometimes a date is given on a Sanskrit or Arabic inscription or tombstone, or in the Chinese dynastic annals. Where such evidence is lacking, the precise chronology remains a matter for speculation. It is somewhat disturbing to see how several dates for the early period of Malaysian history, tentatively proposed by past scholars, have over time been accepted in many textbooks as fact. In this work only those dates corroborated by authoritative evidence have been provided.

The organization of the material has inevitably involved a degree of selection, especially in the late nineteenth and twentieth centuries when the amount of information is frequently overwhelming. In determining the weight given to individual topics and events, the authors have tried to assess the relative importance of each in contributing to the present state of Malaysian society. Consideration has also been given to episodes and characters which have retained significance to Malaysians themselves.

As a general text, this book presents an interpretation of the Malaysian past which is reflected in the selection of events and the way in which they are drawn together. It essentially aims at explaining how a number of small maritime trading settlements evolved over nearly two thousand years into an independent nation able to take its place in the world community. The themes discussed in the conclusion suggest some of the continuities which may be discerned when modern Malaysia is viewed in its historical context. What Malaysia is today is not simply an outcome of changes initiated by Western economic influence and eighty years of colonial rule; it is equally an outcome of a much earlier past when cultural, political and economic patterns were established which can still be felt in contemporary Malaysian society. Only with this perspective can one begin to appreciate the process which has contributed both to Malaysia's present problems and to its very considerable achievements.

1

The Heritage of the Past

Until the beginning of the fifteenth century AD, the history of what is now Malaysia is difficult to reconstruct with any real certainty. Because of the lack of information, historians have tended to regard the rise of a great entrepôt, Melaka, on the west coast of the Malay peninsula, as an identifiable starting point for Malay history. There is a consequent inclination to consider the centuries before 1400 — the 'pre-Melakan period' — as being of relatively little importance in the evolution of modern Malaysia. But Melaka's rise from a quiet fishing village to a world-renowned emporium and centre of Malay culture cannot be explained unless one realizes that behind the splendour of its court and the vigour of its commerce lay traditions of government and trade which had evolved over centuries. The story of Malaysia does not therefore begin at Melaka but stretches back deep into the past. An examination of Melaka's heritage provides not only the context essential for an understanding of later events but throws up themes which continue to be relevant as Malaysian history unfolds.

The Reconstruction of Early Malaysian History: Historiographical Considerations

In Malaysia today tangible evidence of the past is far less obvious than in most Southeast Asian countries. There are no great temple complexes such as Angkor in Kampuchea or Borobudur in Java, no impressive array of inscriptions as in Burma's Pagan, no chronological continuity like that provided by the Vietnamese court annals. Painstaking research has unearthed numerous references to the Malay world before 1400 scattered through Indian, Chinese and Arab sources, but the patience and linguistic skills required to exploit these are daunting. The Chinese records are the most promising for a historical reconstruction of the early history of the Malay region, yet they also present the historian with specific problems. Imperial dynastic histories usually devote one section to a description of foreign countries, but these sections were often compiled years later from notes and are thus subject to error. Descriptions by Buddhist pilgrims of their voyages to India, navigational guides for mariners and, in the Ming period (1368—1644), accounts by travellers are also important Chinese sources. But here too questions of chronology and veracity may arise because supposedly eyewitness reports could incorporate much earlier material or be based on second- or third-hand information.

More problematic than the Chinese sources are the Arab travel accounts which purport to contain an accurate picture of far-flung places in the then known world. Until the mid-fourteenth century, however, none of the more frequently quoted authors had ever been to Southeast Asia and their collections often deteriorate into a farrago of highly imaginative sailors' tales, emphasizing the incredible and miraculous.

The use of archaeology to reinforce these written records or assess their reliability also holds out limited possibilities. The rapid decay of most material in a tropical climate means that only the most durable objects of stone or metal have survived. Sometimes the function of these items is unknown because so little of the material culture remains. The written evidence available provides few clues as to the location of early settlements, and many of the most valuable finds have been purely accidental, or have occurred by digging in a location remembered in local legend. Contemporary geography may actually be misleading, for alluvial deposits have considerably altered the shape of some coastlines. Not infrequently discoveries have been made in almost inaccessible jungle or along creeks now virtually uninhabited because of river silting. Occasionally the remains of ocean-going craft have been found several miles inland. But even fairly extensive finds made in the last century, like 'the relics of a Hindoo colony' discovered in Kedah by James Low,[1] were not subjected to the same rigorous investigation which would be employed today. It is unfortunate that the bulk of metal antiquities on the peninsula were unearthed before the introduction of scientific archaeological methods. Epigraphic evidence, too, has been disappointingly sparse, apart from spectacular remains such as the famous Trengganu Stone left by some Moslem ruler in the fourteenth century. In the last two decades considerable progress has been made under the leadership of trained professionals, but the number of experts is lamentably small and real investigation is still in its infancy.

The dearth of information and the problems involved in using available sources have to date provided only tantalizing glimpses of Malaysia's distant past. Even with the combined skills of historians, archaeologists, linguists, anthropologists, art historians and geographers the material does not permit more than a tentative reconstruction of developments in the Malay archipelago before about 1400. Speculation on many aspects of early Malaysian history is still rife and theories currently accepted by scholars could well be overturned should fresh evidence come to light.

The chronology of human habitation in the region is still a matter for conjecture and hypothesis. One of the oldest finds of modern man anywhere in the world, dating from perhaps 35,000 years ago, was discovered in Sarawak's Niah Caves. The human relics which have been unearthed in cave sites on the peninsula are more recent, going back about 10,000 years. At one time it was believed that the Malay archipelago was peopled by 'waves' of migrants from south China, each progressively more advanced. Evidence for this view seemed to lie in the diversity of different groups in the peninsula and Borneo: the small, dark Negrito of the peninsular interior who existed by hunting and gathering appeared to have little in common with the sedentary rice-growing coastal Malay. However, it is now considered more useful to think in terms of a slow filtering of peoples into the archipelago occurring over a vast period of time and combined with continued movement back and forth between islands and along coasts and rivers. The routes by which these peoples came are still speculative. Among the *orang asli*, the Negrito and Senoi speak Mon-Khmer related languages of the Austroasiatic family once found over the whole of the southern Indochinese mainland. The other indigenous languages in modern Malaysia, including Malay, belong to the Austronesian family. Several scholars have suggested that the remote origin of Austronesian-speaking peoples was somewhere in the region of south China, possibly Taiwan. From thence, it has been argued, they gradually dispersed through maritime Southeast Asia and Oceania via the Philippines and eastern Indonesia, reaching the Malay peninsula from western Borneo and more recently Sumatra.[2]

In the slow process of social development and environmental adaptation, variations in language, appearance and culture among these peoples became more marked, as attested by modern anthropological studies in Borneo and the peninsula. But the activities of all communities, from the coast to the deep interior, overlapped to some degree with their neighbours so that no cultural feature was completely unique. In some cases the lifestyle of one linguistic community was virtually indistinguishable from another with which it commonly interacted; in other cases distinct cultural characteristics persisted although the groups might live in close proximity. Even when differences appeared extreme, certain societal traits were shared because in various ways all groups were responding to a similar physical environment and had in common a world-view in which animism and ancestor worship were entwined with a veneration for the forces of fertility. Although the prehistory of the Malay region remains a subject for debate, the links between the indigenous peoples are as an important a line of inquiry as the undisputed differences.

Early Trade and the Products of the Malay Archipelago

A major theme which does emerge as we move from prehistory into the historic period is the importance of trade in shaping the region's history. By the time Melaka was founded around 1400 the Malay archipelago had for hundreds of years been part of a complex trading network stretching from Africa to China. During the first millennium AD the skills of merchants, sailors and suppliers from India, the Arab lands, China and the archipelago had been brought together in a close-knit commercial relationship.

The geographic position of the Malay archipelago was fundamental in this development. Located on the convergence of two major sea routes, it was linked to the great markets of India and China by the annual monsoon wind systems. Although the all-sea route between China and India did not come into use until the fifth century, trading links between India and the Malay world were well established at least two hundred years before that.

A second factor in the growth of trade to and within the Malay archipelago was the richness of its natural resources, which provided a multitude of products for sale or exchange. The most important resource in early times was the jungle-covered landscape itself, since it was the trees of the rainforest which supplied the aromatic woods, resins and rattans for which the Malay world became justly renowned. But while Malays may have been responsible for the eventual sale and distribution of forest products, they were not the principal gatherers. Malay settlement had developed along the rivers and coasts rather than the hinterland, and Malays themselves rarely ventured beyond the fringes of the jungle. To them the forest remained an alien realm, the haunt of demons and spirits which must be propitiated by offerings and warded off by charms.

The jungles were the habitat not of Malays but of the forest dwellers, the ancestors of today's *orang asli*, and it was they who were the major collectors of local products. Fully adapted to forest life, these people did not see their environment as threatening. For them, the thousands of species of trees and plants which make up the primary rainforest were a virtual sea of resources. Generation after generation, each group had come to know its own locality in intimate detail, as studies of a contemporary *orang asli* group, the Temuan, suggest. By late adolescence every Temuan can identify several hundred species of plants from his particular environment, and to move him to a different locality would demand an almost impossible task of re-learning a great number of unfamiliar types.[3] Such specialized knowledge was a vital factor for the trade in forest products because despite the vast array of species, many jungle trees are found only in certain areas and even there in strictly limited numbers. Localities which might otherwise have been considered backwaters could thus assume significance as one of the few sources of a valued product.

The collection process, however, demanded much more than pure identification. The collector had to be attuned to minute clues acquired as part of his cultural upbringing. The aromatic gharu wood, for example, is in fact the diseased core of a particular tree, but only certain signs such as peeling bark and falling leaves betray the presence of the valuable heart. Camphor, which takes the form of small grains inside the tree trunk, must be detected by specific signs like the smell of the wood when chipped. But even more important for the extraction of forest products was the mastery of the magical skills needed to facilitate the search and placate the spirits of the plants concerned. Part of the market value of forest products depended on their rarity and the secrecy which surrounded their collection. Even among jungle dwellers few men could boast the esoteric knowledge indispensable for appeasing the powers of the forest and the life-force inherent in every living creature. According to late-nineteenth-century accounts these beliefs were so ingrained that collectors employed a special language and observed rigid dietary restrictions while gathering certain jungle products.

The available sources do not explain how early forest collectors brought their supplies to the Malay coasts, although it has been suggested that an internal trading network linked the periphery of the jungle with the hinterland. By this means goods were bartered and passed from one group of jungle dwellers to another. Sometimes this traffic went overland along forest tracks but more frequently it was along the rivers, where skilfully paddled rafts and canoes negotiated upstream rapids and the currents in the estuaries. Finally the jungle products were brought to a central collection point which acted as a subsidiary market, and also fed larger ports nearby. Kuala Selinsing, in the Larut area of Perak, apparently served as an intermediary link with neighbouring centres in Kedah and archaeological finds here have been dated as early as the sixth century.

Apart from the wealth of the jungle, the Malay lands were fortunate in being located along a highly mineralized belt reaching from Yunnan in south China to the islands of Bangka and Belitung. The richness of the soil lay not in an ability to support crops but in the metals which it yielded. Like particular trees or plants, the presence of certain metals, base and precious, was to provide opportunities for relatively isolated regions to develop their trading potential. Excavations in northwest Borneo, for example, indicate that from the seventh century the Sarawak Delta, known to the Chinese court only through hearsay, was actively involved in the export of smelted iron and gold to other places within the archipelago.

It may have been for its gold deposits that the Malay peninsula was best known in early times. Although Malaysia and Sumatra are not today considered to be important sources of this metal, the reputation of this region was once sufficient to warrant the appellation 'Golden Khersonese' by early Greek geographers. The tradition of yellow as a royal colour is almost certainly linked with the widespread use of gold for decoration and ornament in early Malay courts.

Less valuable than gold, but far more extensively found, was tin. The world's largest tin fields are located on the Malay peninsula, and the richness of the deposits is apparent when one recalls that even after at least 1,500 years of continuous extraction, tin-mining is still one of Malaysia's foremost industries. It is not known when Malay tin first became desired overseas, but from the fifth century AD it may have been shipped to India to be used in alloys like bronze for the manufacture of religious images. Because the tin was washed down from the granite ranges of the interior and deposited on the coastal river beds and alluvial plains, mining was not a complicated procedure. Even with primitive techniques, it could be a profitable supplement to agriculture and collecting, and the local people could pan tin from nearby rivers without venturing far beyond their settlements. The method of washing tin-bearing soils to extract the tin as well as the simple smelting described by a fifteenth-century Chinese visitor to Melaka had probably remained unchanged for centuries. Sinking shallow shafts to gain access to tin deposits below the surface, mentioned in seventeenth- and eighteenth-century Dutch sources, may have been a relatively recent development.

The hinterland of the Malay areas thus offered minerals and jungle products; equally important was the rich harvest of sea products possible along the coasts and in the oceans. The mangrove forests which border the west coast of the peninsula and the river deltas of western Borneo are as much a specific ecological zone as the rainforest, and those who lived there also selected from a multitude of resources those which were economically profitable. To outsiders the labyrinth of mangroves rooted in alluvial mud and washed by the saltwater tides was as mysterious as the jungle, the haunt of man-eating beasts like the dreaded crocodile. But to the *orang laut*, the 'strand and sea peoples' who made this region their home, the creatures of the mangrove swamps were treated with respect rather than terror. Gliding on dugout canoes along the natural waterways formed by tidal channels and depressions, they sought out from the very limited species here those which had a specific value. Mats could be woven from the leaves of the *nipa* palm, a fermented drink distilled from its fruit; the bark of certain mangrove trees yielded tannin and the timber provided excellent firewood.

Along the east coast of the Malay peninsula where the wave action is more vigorous the shore is edged not with mangroves but with stretches of beach fringed by plants resistant to salt spray and capable of growing in sandy soil. Over time the peoples here had discovered uses for the numerous types of shellfish in the rock pools and could recognize the types of edible seaweed cast up on the sand at low tide. Offshore, plant and animal life was even richer, especially along the coral shelves formed by strong winds and currents as in the Riau-Lingga archipelago and the Pulau Tujuh area in the South China Sea. Here warm shallow waters, rarely more than sixty metres deep, provide an environment ideal for the evolution of a variety of sea life. Along the reef at low tide molluscs and bivalves could be found, with pearl oysters deep in the coral sand bottom. The cowrie shell, widely used as currency before coins became common, was an important product and archaeology has suggested that shells were leaving Malay shores as early as 4,000 years ago. Written Chinese sources provide clear evidence that from at least the fifth century AD tortoiseshell and cowries were a vital component in Malay trade.

Later the list of sea products grew as the Chinese market developed, and came to include such items as the rare black branching coral known to the Malays as *akar bahar* and the famed *tripang* or sea slug, used as an ingredient in Chinese soups and medicinal preparations. Again it was the *orang laut* who could locate with unerring accuracy the desired products. Equipped with an intimate knowledge of local conditions, they could safely navigate their dugouts around the perilous sand banks and coral reefs where an unwary sailor might well founder. Without their swimming and diving skills it would have been impossible to dredge up the shells and corals from the ocean floor. Something of the respect these abilities aroused in China is suggested in a twelfth-century mention of slaves from the Malay lands, that 'variety of wild men from near the sea which can live in water without closing the eyes'.[4]

Thus, from a very early point in historical time, the inhabitants of the Malay world not only came to realize the wealth of the jungles and oceans which surrounded them, but also learned to combine their particular knowledge and skills to exploit the environment. The expanding lists of marketable products, the experimentation which must have preceded any appreciation of new uses for specific plants and animals, and the development of more efficient trapping and collecting techniques, could only have occurred in response to the demands of a lively and growing market. But this market could not be just a local concern, for the potential buyers of camphor and laka-wood, incense and gold, were far away. Furthermore, it was goods from distant lands — cloth, copper and ironware, musical instruments, beads, pottery, glass, drums — which were desired in the Malay region.

e resulting development of an international exchange trade, its changing patterns and its effects on local society provide the key to understanding early Malaysian history.

Indian Influence in 'The Land of Gold'

There is no definite evidence which dates the first Indian voyages across the Bay of Bengal but conservative estimates place the earliest arrivals to Malay shores at least 1,700 years ago. Blown by the westerly winds, shipping made landfall in the isthmian region, north of Kedah, from whence passage down the Straits must have been a logical development. However, although the routes of Indian traders can be reconstructed, it is not known if the products they took back from the Malay archipelago were essentially the same as those in the later China trade. We do not know precisely what early Indian merchants most desired from the Malay areas. Despite vague references to a 'land of gold' which has been linked with the peninsula, Indian sources have yielded little tangible information. There are no Indian navigational guides, lists of products or travellers' itineraries like those from China. Before the extension of maritime communications to China, Indian traders may have been drawn to the Malay region principally in search of gold, aromatic woods like sandalwood, and spices such as cloves.

For indisputable evidence of Malaya's centuries-old relationship with India, which trade initiated and sustained, one must look at the influence of the sub-continent on Malay culture. The growth of trade with India brought the coastal peoples in much of the Malay world into contact with two major religions, Buddhism and Hinduism, and with concepts of political power well established in India.[5] Without the physical testimony of great monuments or inscriptions, it is not possible to discuss the effects of Indian influence in any depth. All one can say is that they were pervasive and long lasting. Seventh-century inscriptions in Old Malay are heavily sanskritized and much of the ritual, vocabulary and notions of kingship still preserved in Malay courts are clearly Indian in origin. Numerous royal genealogies in classical Malay texts, seeking to enhance the royal patron, include genealogical traditions linking his ancestors with the kings of Kalinga, a semi-mythical kingdom once situated on India's east coast. At the village level, too, the Hindu Gods Śiva and Viśnu have become part of a pantheon of supernatural beings, while stories from Indian epics like the *Ramayana* have become an integral part of the Malay cultural heritage.

The process by which early Malay society absorbed many Indian beliefs and made them part of the Malay world-view is equally a matter for speculation. Acceptance was undoubtedly facilitated because the religious concepts which came from India had themselves evolved from a belief system similar to that prevailing in early South-east Asia — a veneration for particular stones, hills and trees regarded as manifestations of the deity of the soil, and a general acceptance of the existence of spirits who must be propitiated in daily life. Malay legends hold no memories of a Hindu or Buddhist 'conversion' like the dramatic depictions of Islam's adoption, nothing that conveys any sense of a cultural watershed. The merging of Indian with Malay proceeded imperceptibly, deepening and enriching an already vital culture. While trade with China in later centuries added materially to the local way of life, introducing a wide range of objects and some technological skills, the relationship with India was in many ways richer, providing for Malay society a more refined and elaborated version of a fundamentally similar religio-political system.

The contact with India stimulated other responses among the peoples of the Malay areas, encouraging them to recognize the rewards which came to those willing to participate in maritime trade. With the refinement of the basic dugout canoe and simple riverine craft, Malay sailors must have become bolder. The range of indigenous nautical terms and the variety of boat types which defy English translation indicate that, while foreign models may have been readily copied or adapted, the acquisition of seafaring skills was primarily a local accomplishment. Indeed, one of the few specifically Indonesian terms in the seventh-century inscriptions in Old Malay found in the Palembang region of Sumatra is *puhavam*, meaning shippers,[6] and the first mention of a Malay vessel making the journey from Sumatra to India comes from the same period.

Early Malay trade with India must also have made apparent the commercial potential of local collecting points. Vessels which came from India on the southwest monsoon were forced to remain in the archipelago for several months until they could sail back with the northeast winds towards the end of the year. During this period they required a place to discharge their cargoes, to refit vessels, replace masts and purchase enough to make a profitable sale on their return. They needed a permanent base where they could obtain credit, lay up surplus and return again the following year. Numerous Malay harbour chiefs in the vicinity of the Straits and even beyond would have been ready to fulfil the requirements of a restapling port in the hopes of reaping the benefits of a growing ocean-borne trade. One of these ports, Ko-Ying, is mentioned in Chinese sources in the third century AD as a terminus port for Indian shipping, and was apparently located somewhere near the Melaka Straits or possibly western Java.

With the development of sea communications between the Malay regions and China from the fifth century AD, the trade with India received further impetus. To service this trade, numerous small settlements began to spring up along the archipelago's principal maritime routes. Excavations at Takuapa on the Kra Isthmus have shown that between the seventh and tenth centuries this was a flourishing entrepôt, connecting the ports of the Indian Ocean and the South China Sea.[7] It was in such coastal ports that the infusion from India was most pronounced and in Takuapa inscriptions and the remains of a temple indicate that the Tamil trading community there was affiliated with a South Indian merchant guild.

As might be expected, most of the other Indianized archaeological discoveries have also been along the west coast of the peninsula which provided a landfall for shipping from India. There have been several finds in Kedah and Prai (Province Wellesley) including fragmentary Indian inscriptions as well as Hindu and Buddhist images. The earliest of these has been attributed to the fourth century. Further pieces of Indian statuary have also been discovered near present-day mining districts of Perak. These include a Buddha image dating from the late fifth or early sixth century resembling the Gupta style of North India (c. AD 319–500) and various Buddha images from the eighth to tenth centuries.

The vitality of the commercial exchange with India meant that the coastal peoples probably had some knowledge of changes in the intellectual and religious environment in the sub-continent. It has been tentatively proposed, for instance, that ritual deposit boxes found in Kedah and the Sarawak Delta bear some relation to the Tantric Buddhism gaining favour in India from around the sixth century. But while receptivity to new ideas became a hallmark of Malay society, there is also very early evidence of adaptation of outside influences to suit the local environment. This is well illustrated in the reconstructed temple of Candi Bukit Batu Pahat in central Kedah, apparently erected to the memory of a deceased ruler or official. Dating perhaps from the tenth century or later, it is a combination of many styles, a mixture of the cults of Śiva, Viṣnu and Mahayana Buddhism in a blend which finds no exact equivalent in India but which exhibits similarities with items from sites in Sumatra and Sarawak, and was obviously meaningful to the local community.

Such adaptation suggests that Malays themselves played an important role in spreading Indian cultural ideas beyond the entrepôts where Indian influence made its greatest impact. It is hard to imagine that a Malay trader who regularly carried cargoes of tin, beeswax, woods and rattans to some collecting point or port, who waited while they were graded and priced, who then purchased another cargo for the homeward trip, would have been untouched by the stories of the foreigners to whom he sold his goods. Although direct ties with India were stronger on the west coast, seventh-century Chinese itineraries testify to the strength of Indian religions in courts along the east coast of the peninsula, and it would seem unrealistic to deny Malay traders a place in the transmission of these new ideas. Local participation in the gradual Indianization process also meant that ideas about the nature of the universe and man's place in it remained basically similar throughout the region. The resemblances between archaeological finds excavated in Kedah, the Sarawak Delta and the east coast of Sumatra suggest that the oceans did serve to link the intervening coasts and that the peoples who lived here remained part of one cultural world.

Chinese Trade and the Rise of Early Malay—Indonesian Entrepôts

Prior to the fifth century Chinese sources contain few references to the Nan Yang, the Southern Ocean, which was the general term used to refer to the Southeast Asian region. Interest in the Malay peninsula probably stemmed initially from Chinese relations with Funan, believed to have been a major kingdom or collection of kingdoms on the Lower Mekong River. From AD 200 it began to extend its influence into the northern Malay peninsula, and Chinese envoys to Funan make vague mention of the '100 kingdoms' which existed to the south. The Chinese may also have been aware of some Indonesian products such as the clove which had appeared on Funanese markets. During this period, however, the foreign goods most desired in China were the luxury items from western Asia which Chinese sources call the 'Persian trade'. Before the fifth century, these goods were carried overland from western Asia to northern China, and only subsequently did the 'Persian trade' begin to use the sea routes.[8]

The reason for this shift to the sea was political events in southern China. In 420 a new dynasty, the Liu Sung (420—78), gained control in southern China but it did not have access to the overland trade route in the north. Furthermore, the Yangtze River area in southern China was becoming more prosperous and could afford to buy luxury items from western Asia. These developments made the participants in the 'Persian trade' look more closely at the possibilities of shipping goods previously sent by land. China itself, however, did not begin to develop ocean-going vessels until the eighth and ninth centuries and it was thus not the Chinese who acted as shippers. It has been argued that, with the incentive of rich profits, 'Persian' goods were taken by sea across the Bay of Bengal to the Malay archipelago and then transhipped in Indonesian and Malay vessels to China. Non-Chinese shipping, including that of the coastal Malays, was therefore vital in bringing valued cargoes to Chinese ports and maintaining trans-Asiatic trading links.

From the fifth century AD onwards the increasing use of the sea to transport goods between western Asia and China created an environment well suited to the rise of ports in numerous places in the Malay archipelago. But those harbours in the Melaka Straits area had a distinct advantage because of their geographical position at the 'end of the monsoons', where all ships had to await the change of winds to continue further or return homeward. Unlike the west coast of Borneo, which was somewhat isolated from the main maritime routes, the Melaka Straits was 'a gullet . . . through which the foreigners' sea and land traffic in either direction must pass'.[9] Moreover, the Straits provided a refuge from the buffeting of the greater oceans beyond. Along the east coast of the peninsula, the seas were unnavigable during the northeast monsoon, but the Straits were so sheltered that they were frequently compared to an inland lake. Even though violent storms, which later European sailors termed 'Sumatras', could spring up, these were confined mainly to the area between Kelang and Selangor and in any event were seasonal and therefore predictable.

The calmness of the Straits waters also facilitated transport of cargoes. Local traders were able to carry goods between Sumatra, the peninsula, and the small islands of the Riau-Lingga archipelago with boats which depended only on paddles and the simplest of mat sails. Jungle products could be brought down to the coast along any of the numerous rivers which disembogue on both sides of the Straits. Many of the tidewater bays and inlets into which these rivers flow could potentially serve as collection and distribution as well as transhipment points. It has been suggested that gradually some local jungle products were drawn into the China trade and accepted as substitutes for 'Persian' frankincense, bdellium and camphor. In time the variety and versatility of marine and jungle produce from the Malay areas assumed great value in China in its own right. When a king of Melaka went to China in 1411 a selection of these local products was considered a fitting gift even for the Emperor.

It is possible that Kan-t'o-li, a toponym occasionally mentioned in fifth- and sixth-century Chinese sources, was the first port in the Straits vicinity to exploit the growing Chinese market for Malay products. Kan-t'o-li has been tentatively located on Sumatra's south-east coast, at the eastern approaches to the Melaka Straits. In this area several species of jungle trees are found which could have provided the resins accepted in China as substitutes for those of India and Persia. It is known that Kan-t'o-li's trade was based not only on the cartage of overseas goods but on the export of forest products, perfumes and drugs for the Chinese market. Because of the advantages of its location and its access to desired items, Kan-t'o-li for a brief period came to dominate other collecting points which were contenders for the position of entrepôt. The suggestion has been made that Kan-t'o-li was a predecessor of the great market of Srivijaya which arose in the Palembang area of southeast Sumatra in the late seventh century.

The mention of Srivijaya brings us to one of the most longstanding controversies in Southeast Asian studies. In 1918 George Coedès published a learned discussion of the kingdom which the T'ang Chinese records (AD 618–906) call Shih-li-fo-shih. Transcribing the Chinese characters as Srivijaya, he located the kingdom in southeast Sumatra on the Musi River in Palembang. For some years now it has been generally accepted that Srivijaya was probably the earliest of the great maritime kingdoms, arising some time in the seventh century and lasting until the end of the thirteenth. It is believed that Srivijaya came to exercise suzerainty over the Melaka Straits, the hundreds of islands which dot the approaches, and the shores on either side. It developed into a mighty emporium which served as a distribution centre for products from India, western Asia and China as well as those from its own empire. Finally, Srivijaya was renowned as a place for the study of Mahayana Buddhism.

The evidence relating to Srivijaya is extremely limited. From the late seventh century comes a description by a Chinese monk, I Ching, written after a period in Srivijaya studying Buddhism, and numerous inscriptions in Old Malay from the Palembang district, Jambi and Bangka. Records of missions from Srivijaya to the Chinese court and notes by Chinese geographers also begin in the late seventh century and, with a break in the ninth century, continue on through to the thirteenth century. The Chinese sources are supplemented by scattered inscriptions invoking the name of Srivijaya in Ligor (present-day Nakhon Sithammarat in southern Thailand) and at Nalanda and Coromandel in India, and by isolated references in Arab writings.

So fragmentary is the evidence and so inconclusive that some scholars, while accepting the existence of Srivijaya, are not convinced that it maintained its hegemony in the Malay world from the seventh to the thirteenth century or even that it was located in Palembang. Although sherds tentatively dated as nine- and tenth-century have been recently collected in the vicinity of Bukit Si Guntang, a hill in Palembang which has always been revered by local society, archaeological excavations have yielded disappointing results. As yet there have been no authenticated finds of Chinese pottery dating earlier than Ming (1368–1644). Sceptics have suggested that 'Srivijaya' as it existed in Palembang may have existed for only the space of a century, that is, for the seventh century when inscriptions are available. One scholar has contended that several products listed by the Chinese as coming from Srivijaya are not necessarily confined to Sumatra but can also be located in Borneo, the peninsula and other southerly regions of Southeast Asia.[10] The argument that Srivijaya was located somewhere in Ligor is also periodically revived, and a study of Arab sources has pointed to the possibility of a capital to the north of Palembang nearer the Straits of Melaka.[11]

Because of the paucity of written sources and the limitations placed on archaeological research, the debate is likely to continue for some time. More important in terms of Malaysian history is O.W. Wolters's contention that a direct line can be traced between Kan-t'o-li, Srivijaya and the type of settlement which grew up in Melaka after 1400. These places, he feels, satisfied the criteria of entrepôt and in that capacity serviced maritime trade in the western archipelago. As an extension of this reasoning, one could suggest that in understanding the foundation of Srivijaya's power we can more readily appreciate what contributed to the prestige not only of Melaka but of the latter's successor kingdom, Johor.

Srivijaya and Its Rivals

From its appearance on the historical scene in the late seventh century, Srivijaya conveys the impression of a state determined to dominate its neighbours. One of the early inscriptions found in Palembang commemorates a mighty expedition of 682 which brought 'victory, power, and wealth' to Srivijaya. Four years later another force was sent against 'Java'. But if Srivijaya was attempting to impose its authority over its neighbours, fragmentary references to blood, battle and victory on several Palembang inscriptions suggest considerable resistance. Nearby, along the southeast coast and towards the interior, there were other ambitious riverine chiefs. Srivijaya was by no means the only port in the archipelago which could attract traders, for the jungle and ocean products which drew merchants there could also be carried to numerous other places. Several of these were also able to offer good anchorage and harbour facilities and had a reputation overseas which may well have predated that of Srivijaya. A place called Melayu, believed to have been located on the Jambi River just north of Palembang, had sent a mission to China in 644, several years earlier than Srivijaya's first mission around 670. But between 672 and 692 Melayu was incorporated into Srivijaya, perhaps by conquest, perhaps by marriage between two ruling families. This prestigious association between Melayu and a great kingdom in Palembang was remembered, albeit dimly, in later Melaka Malay traditions and perhaps provides a clue to the origins of the founders of that kingdom.

T'ang dynasty records also show that across the Melaka Straits other kingdoms had developed. Quite possibly these areas had once been dominated by a larger state in the Cambodian region, such as Funan, but had gained a degree of autonomy when central authority in Cambodia declined about the middle of the sixth century. Their exact positions remain conjectural, since several transcriptions cannot be related to modern Malay place-names, and the location of others must be calculated from the often vague geography of Chinese sources. There is understandably more information about the east coast, which was better known to Chinese travellers. Despite the low prestige of geographical studies in China, sufficient work was undertaken to enable modern historians to sketch a broad outline of the peninsula and eastern archipelago during T'ang times. On the basis of sailing directions and itineraries seven states have been listed in the isthmian region of the peninsula with a possible eighth in Johor.[12]

What were they like, these early kingdoms which shared the same commercial world as Srivijaya but were eventually overshadowed, though not eclipsed, by it? Like Srivijaya, their rulers were clearly aware of the importance of cultivating good relations with China. By the sixth century Langkasuka in the Patani region was sending envoys to the Chinese Emperor, as was Ch'ih-t'u, the 'Red-earth Land' tentatively located in the Kelantan area, and Tan-Tan, which some scholars, again with reservations, place on the east coast somewhere near present-day Trengganu. The Chinese did not by any means regard these places as insignificant. In 607, several decades before we first hear of Srivijaya, the Sui dynasty (AD 590—618) decided to 'open up communication with far-distant lands', and honoured the court of Ch'ih-t'u with an embassy carrying over five thousand gifts. Langkasuka, too, was well known in China as a religious centre, and in the later seventh century several Buddhist monks specifically made voyages there. Chinese records show that these small states could conduct diplomatic affairs with the aplomb of their larger neighbours. When the Chinese envoys entered Ch'ih-t'u waters, a leading court figure whom they called a 'Brahman' was sent to meet them with a fleet of vessels. On their arrival at the upriver capital a month later the king's son himself came down to greet them with all the appropriate presents. The hospitality extended to foreign visitors and missions which was to become a feature of Malay court protocol is clearly evident. The Chinese monk, I Ching, records that Buddhist pilgrims en route to India were treated in Langkasuka 'with the courtesy appropriate to distinguished guests'.[13]

These kingdoms were not mere collecting centres which had sprung up under the leadership of some enterprising chief. They were states which had had time to build up a tradition of government. In the seventh century Langkasuka already claimed an existence of two hundred years, and when the ruler of Ch'ih-t'u gave up the throne in favour of the religious life, the succession passed peacefully to his son. Nor was their territorial control inconsiderable. It reputedly required thirty days to cross Langkasuka from east to west, and the Lion City, the capital of Ch'ih-t'u, was a month's journey inland. From their forested interior came the jungle products which were so prized in the markets abroad, and it was from the trade in items like gold and camphor that these kingdoms drew their wealth. The king of Ch'ih-t'u had thirty ocean-going vessels presumably used to carry cargoes to other countries, and the Chinese envoys sent in 607 were obviously impressed by the richness of the court: 'The king sits on a three-tiered couch, facing north and dressed in rose-coloured cloth, with a chaplet of gold flowers and necklaces of varied jewels. Four damsels attend on his right hand and on his left, and more than a hundred soldiers mount guard.'[14]

These kingdoms also maintained well-ordered governments. Officers of the state were appointed in charge of matters such as criminal law, and in Ch'ih-t'u each settlement had its own district chief. Within the court the king himself would have been expected to carry out his administrative duties, and Chinese envoys specifically recorded that the ruler of Tan-tan held audience twice a day. With the treasury under royal control, the king could both reward the powerful families in the kingdom and keep them in check. As in later Melaka, one of the means of achieving this was to limit the display of wealth. In Ch'ih-t'u, the Sui envoys noted, although the great clans were largely independent of the ruler's authority, they were permitted to wear gold lockets only at his discretion. Even at this early date we thus catch a glimpse of a familiar theme in Malay history — the potential challenge to royal authority from noble families. If a ruler disregarded the code of conduct considered appropriate for kingship, he could not expect to maintain the support of the leading court figures. In Langkasuka one king exiled a popular 'man of virtue', but the latter fled to India and there married an Indian princess. The Chinese envoys were told that shortly afterwards, following the death of the Langkasuka ruler, the chief ministers 'welcomed back the exile and made him king', thus initiating a new dynasty.[15]

These early trading kingdoms along the east coast of the peninsula flourished with the growth of commercial exchange between India and China and within the archipelago. Other ports that sprang up along the maritime route to China are also briefly mentioned in Chinese sources. For example, Lo Yueh, which has been located in Johor, is described in the ninth century as 'a place where traders passing back and forth meet'. In the same period Pulau Tioman, off Pahang, was another well-known port of call. It thus appears that from the seventh century the expansion in maritime communications and the increasing value placed on products from the Malay archipelago created widening commercial opportunities. This impression becomes greater when it is recalled that Chinese sources give only part of the picture. Vijayapura in west Borneo was a major port which apparently coexisted with Srivijaya, yet it did not send envoys to China and therefore attracted scant attention in imperial records. The failure to send missions may merely indicate a healthy local trade and freedom from external or internal threats, so that there was no need to court China's favour. Kedah too receives little mention in Chinese sources except as an embarkation point for India, but the excavation of over thirty archaeological sites there has provided strong evidence of a thriving economy based on agriculture, trade and the distribution of local products. None of these places could have attracted merchants unless they could offer a whole range of facilities which became typical of Malay trading states — a hospitable attitude to foreigners, efficiency in discharging cargoes, desired products available for purchase and an enlightened and co-operative administration.

It is a measure of Srivijaya's achievement that it was able to impose suzerainty over many of these ports, some long-established kingdoms. A stele found in Ligor dated 775 indicates that Srivijaya had by this time extended a loose overlordship to the Malay peninsula. At the beginning of the eleventh century Chinese records note that 'fourteen cities' paid tribute to Srivijaya, which was called the 'uncontested master of the Straits'. It is felt, however, that the nature of this control was not onerous and that local chiefs were left to rule in virtual independence. The question then arises as to why Srivijaya could command such a dominating position, and what its prestige contributes to an understanding of later Malaysian history.

The Bases of Srivijaya's Power

In trying to understand the nature of the Srivijayan state, scholars have again been faced with a paucity of information. It is important to remember that any reconstruction of Srivijaya is of necessity based on disparate and sometimes contradictory evidence, which can often be reconciled only by supposition and informed suggestion. Much of the basic work was done by Coedès, but Wolters has continued piecing together what is known of Srivijaya in an effort to explain why it flourished and why its name disappears from the records in the fourteenth century.[16]

In Wolters's view, Srivijaya owed its initial rise and its later success primarily to the development of a special relationship with successive Chinese emperors. First, it was well placed to benefit from the maritime trading route to China. Located on the path of the northeast monsoon, it held an advantage which other kingdoms could not match as long as ties with China determined a port's international standing. Secondly, the Maharajas of Srivijaya fully understood the value of the tribute system which involved a recognition of China as overlord. Because Chinese emperors until the Southern Sung period (AD 1127–1279) refused to countenance private Chinese trade, overseas goods could be accepted only if they came in the guise of tribute missions. Although other Malay kingdoms were also aware of this, Srivijaya was the most successful in manipulating the system to its benefit. Its rulers were willing to acknowledge China's suzerainty in order to ensure that a profitable trade continued. Between 960 and 983, for instance, no less than eight missions from Srivijaya presented themselves at the imperial court. Nothing was permitted to interfere with the health of this relationship. When the Buddhist pilgrim I Ching arrived at the Srivijayan capital, he was received with due hospitality, but after the ruler realized his visitor came from China his respect doubled. In the following centuries the same pattern continues. In 1003 Srivijayan envoys arrived in China with the flattering information that their ruler had built a temple to pray for the Emperor's well-being. In compliance with their request, the Chinese Emperor then bestowed a title on the temple and presented it with a bell. The prestige acquired by Srivijaya in such an exchange must have been considerable.

Another reason behind Srivijaya's dominance was the ability to maintain a supply of local products for its own market as well as the China trade. Not only was it easily accessible by river from jungle areas in Sumatra and the peninsula, but it also had under its jurisdiction the Riau-Lingga archipelago and the nearby coastal mangroves. In the estuary of the Musi River, which probably remained the Srivijayan port until the eleventh century, one can visualize the dugouts loaded with *nipa* mats, tortoiseshell, beeswax and aromatic woods for which the country was justifiably renowned. A story related in an Arab travel account of the ninth century suggests that the Maharajas fully appreciated their debt to the sea. It was said that the ruler daily propitiated the spirits of the ocean by throwing a gold brick into the water, saying as he did so, 'Look, there lies my treasury.'[17]

In this favourable commercial environment an entrepôt economy would have been readily established. Here, in the lull between the monsoons, exotic cargoes from overseas could be unloaded — pearls, frankincense, rosewater, gardenia flowers, myrrh, amber, silks, brocades. Here local products could be sorted, graded, blended and loaded, with the surplus stored for other buyers. Here could be found the vast array of skills necessary to refit and provision vessels for the voyage home. In sum, Srivijaya could well satisfy the demands of an international market. An Arab source in the early tenth century notes that the bulk of Srivijaya's wealth came from tolls and harbour dues, a testimony to the number of ships it attracted. Two hundred years later Srivijaya was still famous as a place where a merchant could rely on justice, correct commercial behaviour and all the business facilities expected of an entrepôt. When troubles disturbed trade in India and China, Chinese merchants are said to have transferred their activities to Srivijaya. The consistency with which foreigners comment on the vitality of its trade is impressive. As one Chinese official wrote in 1178, '[Srivijaya] is the most important port of call on the sea routes of the foreigners from the countries of Java in the east and the countries of the Arabs and Quilon [on the Malabar coast] in the west; they all pass through it on their way to China.'[18]

Wolters also believes that a basic factor in Srivijaya's strength was the relationship which developed between its rulers and the *orang laut*, the sea and riverine people. Control over the *orang laut* was vital because, released from authority and without proper means of support, they found a living by preying on passing ships. The Malay saying that 'where there are seas there are pirates' did not arise without good reason. The Chinese Buddhist pilgrim Fa Hsien remarked in 413 after a voyage to India that the oceans were 'infested with pirates', and the fear of unexpected attack continued to haunt sailors. One of the most dangerous areas was the southern approach to the Melaka Straits where hundreds of rocky outcrops provided havens for raiding fleets. A Chinese itinerary dated about AD 800 directs mariners' attention to an island to the northeast of Srivijaya where 'many . . . people are robbers and those who sail in ships fear them'.[19]

Srivijaya's great triumph was to control piracy in the surrounding sea by commanding the loyalty of the *orang laut*. Intimately acquainted with the treacherous shoals and sandbars, understanding local wind conditions, they protected Srivijaya's sea lanes from other raiders and thus increased its attractiveness to foreign traders. The *orang laut* were a formidable fighting force, and their paddling skills made them the obvious choice as crews for Srivijaya's fleets and thus the backbone of its navy. The 'Harladj' mentioned in tenth-century Arab sources 'who gave his name to an island and was head of the ruler's army' may have been the predecessor of the Raja Negara, the *orang laut* leader in seventeenth- and eighteenth-century Johor who commanded all the sea people throughout Singapore waters. Living in the islands and coasts off Palembang and Jambi, the *orang laut* could have responded readily to the ruler's call in time of crisis. Of them it was said that 'in facing the enemy and braving death they have not their equal among other nations'. Wolters thus suggests that when the Maharaja of Srivijaya styled himself 'King of the Ocean Lands', it was no meaningless honorific.[20]

Srivijaya's prestige in the area would also have been due to the fact that its rulers had succeeded in creating a society which, by the standards of the time, was cultured and civilized. As a result of its trading connections Srivijaya had become a centre of learning that could hold its own against far older kingdoms. A Chinese source mentions that the people there were skilled mathematicians and were able to calculate the eclipses of the sun and moon. Perhaps the greatest indication of the respect given to scholarship in Srivijaya was the strength of religion. When I Ching went there in 671 he found a community of over a thousand Buddhist monks, and in his own writings he commended the city as a place to study the Buddhist scriptures. With the wealth that trade brought, Srivijayan rulers could sponsor religious studies and maintain religious foundations. One

Maharaja endowed a Taoist temple in Canton while another rebuilt a Buddhist sanctuary in India's great pilgrimage centre of Nalanda. Although the nature of Buddhism in Srivijaya is not totally clear, several different schools, including Tantrism, coexisted. When the history of Buddhism in the archipelago is understood more fully, Srivijaya may assume even more importance as a dissemination point for religious ideas.

A number of factors thus contributed to Srivijaya's emergence as a leading entrepôt in the archipelago, a position which it apparently sustained for six centuries. It was able to maintain this dominance because harbour chiefs along the coasts of Sumatra and the peninsula were willing to accept Srivijaya's overlordship so that they could share in its prosperity and take part in its thriving trade. Such ties could only survive if vassal chiefs recognized that acceptance of a central authority was to their own advantage. But available sources also hint at the underlying tension in the ruler—vassal relationship. Ideally, a chain of command stretched down from the Srivijayan ruler to his chiefs and vassal princes, binding him to his lowest subject. The administration of the realm was based on the concept that loyalty to one's leader was unquestioning, and nowhere was this better exemplified than in the fidelity of the *orang laut*. Nonetheless, despite the great riches which the ruler of Srivijaya had at his disposal and the honours which he could heap on his faithful servants, rewards could not have been a guarantee of unfailing allegiance. It was perhaps to remedy this weakness that *derhaka*, a word found repeatedly in Srivijayan inscriptions and meaning 'treason to the ruler', was adopted from Sanskrit to denote what became a heinous crime. Srivijaya's court may also have propagated the belief in a special force possessed by the ruler, perhaps by invoking the Hindu concept of a god's *sakti* (later expressed by the Arabic term *daulat*). This force would strike down the disobedient vassal, the subject guilty of *derhaka* (treason). Inscriptions of 686 found in Jambi and Bangka are replete with threats against those who betray the ruler and his appointed officials: 'If you behave like a traitor, plotting with those who are in contact with my enemies, or if you spy for the enemy, you will be killed by the curse.' It was possibly, too, the Maharajas of Srivijaya who first built up the idea of the devoted subject willing to die for his lord, which is frequently found in later classical Malay texts. So entrenched was this concept in Srivijayan statecraft that in the thirteenth century the Chinese customs official Chau Ju-kua believed the personal followers of the Maharaja commonly killed themselves when their master died.

The Weakening of Srivijaya's Authority

Srivijaya's commercial and political dominance in the Melaka Straits ultimately depended on its ability to tie a large number of scattered harbours to an acknowledged centre. Neither force nor rewards nor threats of divine retribution could achieve this unless local chiefs recognized that allegiance was in their own interests. As long as they were convinced that a powerful and prosperous capital was to the benefit of all, they remained the Maharaja's loyal vassals and sent their products to be sold in his port. However, the centrifugal forces which remained an enduring problem in Malay society eventually undermined Srivijaya's hold over its dependencies. The natural wealth so freely available, the favourable position of the Malay world on the maritime trading paths, and the profits to be drawn from this commerce made the lure of independence great. From the twelfth century Srivijaya's vassals became increasingly less amenable to its authority.

The basic reason for this seems to have been a weakening in the centre itself. Several seemingly unconnected pieces of evidence suggest a kingdom undergoing severe tensions. Srivijaya's prestige and wealth did not go unopposed by the growing ambitions of Javanese kings. Historians believe that in the mid-ninth century a marriage alliance joined the royal family of Srivijaya with the Sailendra dynasty of central Java. An inscription from Nalanda in India dated about 860 refers to a younger son of the Sailendras who was then ruling in Srivijaya. These ties, however, did not make for continued harmony. In 992 envoys from Srivijaya told the Chinese court that the Javanese had invaded and asked the emperor for protection. In the same year a Javanese mission claimed that the two countries were continually at war, and less than three decades later, in 1016, Srivijaya retaliated in a campaign against Java.

At the same time Srivijaya was also challenged from India, although here again information is fragmentary and therefore conjectural. One brief episode refers to hostility between Srivijaya and the Chola dynasty of southern India (tenth–twelfth centuries), perhaps because of disputes over the passage of trading ships through the Melaka Straits. In about 1025 it is thought that the Chola ruler attacked Srivijaya, capturing the Maharaja himself. Several other states in Sumatra and the Malay peninsula were also raided, including Srivijaya's vassal Kedah. Longstanding results of this were slight, but memories of the conflict with the Cholas may have given rise to accounts of battles waged by mythical Indian kings recounted in the later Melaka court text, the *Sejarah Melayu*.

Between 1079 and 1082 there was another significant development in Srivijaya when the centre of power moved from Palembang to Melayu, customarily located in the Jambi River area. Melayu's reputation was already such that an Arab text dating from around AD 1000 notes travellers bound for China sailed through 'the sea of Melayu' and a Chola inscription calls it 'the ancient Malaiyūr'.[21] Though the implications of the move of the capital to Melayu are unclear, available evidence suggests that it came at a time when Srivijaya's dominance in the Melaka Straits was weakening. From this period it seems that Srivijaya was increasingly compelled to rely on *orang laut* patrols to maintain its hold over passing trade. As one twelfth-century Chinese observer remarked, 'If some foreign ship passing Srivijaya should not enter the port, an armed party will certainly board it and kill the sailors to the last man.'[22] But it also appears that Srivijaya's authority even over the *orang laut* was gradually diminishing and that much wealth was passing into hands other than the Maharaja's. *Orang laut* piracy in the vicinity had made the eastern approaches to the Melaka Straits notorious. At times Srivijaya itself was forced to stretch an iron chain across the harbour to prevent pirates from entering, raising it only to permit the passage of merchant ships. The danger to shipping was greatest in the islands around Singapore which were the homes of several pirating *orang laut* groups. In the words of a Chinese who himself knew the southern seas,

> When junks sail to the western ocean the local barbarians allow them to pass unmolested but when on their return the junks reach the Karimun [islands] . . . of a certainty two or three hundred prahus will put out to attack them for several days. Sometimes the junks are fortunate enough to escape with a favouring wind; otherwise the crews are butchered and the merchandise made off with in quick time.[23]

Malay legends also comment on the increase in piracy at this time, attributing it to *orang laut* raiders sent out by the Javanese minister Gajah Mada (1330—64) to attack Palembang.

In such disturbed times those archipelago ports which could guarantee their sea lanes would have presented a real alternative to Srivijaya. The unlocated Fo-lo-an (possibly Kuala Berang, Trengganu) was purportedly protected from pirate raids by the compassionate Bodhisattva Avaloki-teśvara who sent fierce winds to drive enemies away. It is not surprising that with this reputation traders from Arab lands found Fo-lo-an as attractive a market as its overlord Srivijaya. One important dependency, Kedah, had already demonstrated a desire for greater economic and political freedom. Between the tenth and twelfth centuries commercial activities expanded, possibly due in part to the development of wet rice (*padi*) on Kedah's alluvial plains. Excavations have shown that along the Bujang River there was an established entrepôt engaged in handling foreign wares such as Arab glass and Chinese porcelain. It probably also obtained jungle and marine products from subsidiary collection centres like those in the Larut area of Perak. There may well have been some storage facilities so that the Kedah ports could act as a transhipment centre between monsoons. An eleventh-century Chola inscription mentions 'Kadaram [Kedah] of fierce strength'[24] and even after the devastation of the 1025 Chola raid Kedah was apparently able to make a bid for independence. In 1068 it is believed that Kedah's ruler may have rebelled and that Srivijaya then called in Chola assistance to bring its vassal to heel.

In the twelfth and thirteenth centuries Srivijaya faced a progressively greater challenge from other neighbouring ports and dependencies. A prime factor in the growth of regional trade was changing policies within China. During the Late Sung and Mongol periods (late twelfth to mid-fourteenth centuries) the restrictions which permitted foreign trade only in the guise of tribute missions lapsed. Srivijaya, which had gained recognition of itself as the regional overlord and the rightful bearer of tribute to China, had prospered under the tributary system. Now, however, private Chinese trade flourished. These traders began going to the sources of supply, rather than to the central entrepôt, and therefore fostered the development of the many small but attractive ports within the Malay world which now found it more profitable to buy and sell without reference to Srivijaya. Some of these ports are known through Chinese court records or archaeological excavations, but others have left virtually no concrete evidence behind. Little is known, for instance, of the north Sumatran kingdoms of Po-lo, Barus and Kampé (Aru) which may have posed the most serious challenges to Srivijaya. By the thirteenth century Kampé had proclaimed its independence and like Kedah was sending its own ships to southern India. Further north along Sumatra's coast the kingdoms of Perlak and Pasai were also thriving. During the thirteenth century they were being drawn into the fold of Islam, although the full impact of this would not be felt for another hundred years. Srivijaya's hold over the peninsula was similarly lessening, for a 1230 inscription from the Ligor area makes no mention of its former overlord and presumably represents a local claim to autonomy.

Throughout the Malay world the benefits of economic independence continued to grow as Chinese trade with the Malay world increased. In return for ivory, tortoiseshell, aromatic woods, wax, resins, rattans and tin, Chinese merchants supplied basic items like pottery and luxury goods such as silk and lacquerware. Fourteenth-century Chinese sources comment that all the Malay states along the peninsular east coast 'acknowledged a ruler', indicating a tradition of settled government and stable administration which was an inducement to foreign merchants. Chinese travellers were also struck by the ease with which trade was conducted, the inhabitants' honesty, and the calibre of those in control. One account mentions Trengganu in particular: 'The present ruler is capable, forbids greed and encourages diligence and frugality.' From this report it seems that life there was relatively comfortable: 'The fields are middling to poor, but even the poorest folk have enough food.'[25]

The benefits which came as a result of private Chinese trade were not limited to the Melaka Straits region. Elsewhere other ports were thriving, among them P'o-ni in northwest Borneo. First mentioned by the Chinese in the ninth century, the toponym continues to recur in Chinese sources until the fifteenth century. Some historians have consequently seen P'o-ni as a rendering of 'Brunei'. Although it can probably be regarded as the forerunner of Brunei, 'P'o-ni' is in all likelihood a general term used by the Chinese court to refer collectively to Borneo's northwest coast. Archaeological work near Brunei's present capital suggests a continuous occupancy of the region from T'ang times (618–906) onwards and it probably drew trade away from the Sarawak Delta where pottery findings are virtually all earlier than Ming (1368–1644). By the twelfth century P'o-ni's trade was flourishing and in 1225 Chau Ju-Kua, the Inspector of foreign trade at Canton, depicted it as a state of some territorial power. According to his account, the capital had a population of 10,000 people and the country itself comprised fourteen districts. His informants were clearly impressed by P'o-ni's wealth and fighting power. 'The ruler,' Chau wrote, 'has for his protection over a hundred fighting men and when they have an engagement they carry swords and wear armour.' Court protocol was well established and no Maharaja of Srivijaya could have extended greater hospitality to merchants than did the court of P'o-ni. 'Traders here are treated in high regard,' Chau Ju-kua recorded. From the Chinese this was high praise indeed.[26]

The rise of P'o-ni represents part of a recurring pattern in the Malay archipelago. As trade in the ports of its vassal states and other rival kingdoms expanded, Srivijaya was less able to impose recognition of itself as the region's principal market. Although its prestige as a major entrepôt was still considerable, Srivijaya was under severe pressure. So vulnerable had it become that in 1275 the ruler of the Javanese kingdom of Majapahit, Kertanegara (1268–92), launched an attack against Srivijaya's capital in Jambi and also laid claim to Pahang, a dependency of Srivijaya on the peninsula. From the thirteenth century Java regarded itself as the rightful overlord in southeast Sumatra. But the challenge to Srivijaya did not come only from Java. In the late thirteenth century the chiefs of Ligor in southern Thailand were also extending their control over the northern Malay peninsular states, which then became vassals of the Thai kings of Sukhothai. Thai ambitions became greater after 1351 with the rise of an energetic new kingdom, Ayudhya. Pushing down into the peninsula, the kings of Ayudhya demanded a closer relationship, a more formal mode of homage from their Malay vassals, thus initiating a tradition of tension which was to endure for centuries afterwards.

On the basis of this evidence it is generally accepted that the fourteenth century saw the last gasp of the once mighty Srivijaya, eclipsed by more powerful neighbours. But the evidence also suggests that Srivijaya considered these developments as only a temporary setback and that it was therefore ready to seize any opportunity for reversing its fortunes. The chance came when the first Ming Emperor, T'ai Tsu, came to the throne in 1368. On his accession T'ai Tsu restored the old tributary system and forbade the private trade which had contributed to the growth of Srivijaya's rivals. From 1371 to 1377 both Melayu-Jambi and the old capital at Palembang sought to reassert their former status by sending official missions to take both tribute and cargoes of goods to China. In an attempt to renounce Java's claim to suzerainty, the ruler of Melayu-Jambi in 1377 asked to be invested by China and to become its vassal. The Chinese Emperor agreed because he was unaware that Java now claimed overlordship in southeast Sumatra. The Ming Annals then record how the Javanese prevented the Chinese envoys from reaching Srivijaya by 'enticing' them to Java, where they were killed. Learning of what had happened, Emperor T'ai Tsu was incensed that Srivijaya (meaning both Melayu-Jambi and Palembang) had deceived him. In the Chinese view, Srivijaya had not only defied its Javanese overlord but had flouted Chinese policies which did not favour a proliferation of regional power centres. T'ai Tsu therefore decided to punish this rebellious vassal by refusing to receive further tribute missions.

This reconstruction of events further suggests that the Malays of southeast Sumatra saw their banishment from the imperial court and the consequent loss of trade as unfortunate, but not catastrophic. They fully believed that, given time, the attitude of Chinese emperors would change and that the traditional relations between Srivijaya and China would be restored. In 1391, in an effort to revive Palembang's claims to leadership in the region, the ruler there apparently declared himself independent of Java and overlord of the Malays. This was too much for the Javanese, and they invaded, expelling the rebel. As the records of the Ming dynasty noted in 1397, 'At that time the Javanese had already destroyed San-fo-ch'i . . . [i.e. Srivijaya]. Consequently San-fo-ch'i was a ruined country. Great unrest existed there.' Ten years afterwards, when an official naval expedition from China reached Sumatra, the harbour of Palembang, though still a busy port, was controlled not by Malays but by a Chinese pirate chief.

From Srivijaya to Melaka: Two Differing Accounts

Both Malay and European accounts of Melaka's early years attribute its establishment to a refugee prince from Palembang. But in attempting to understand something of the circumstances surrounding his flight, the historian has again been faced by problems inherent in the sources. This time it is not so much a dearth of information as a conflict between two historical traditions. We now have two exciting, even gripping, versions of Melaka's founding, each of which was a conscious effort to record past events in a coherent form. The difference between them, however, becomes more understandable when we appreciate why each was written.

The first is the *Suma Oriental* (*Complete Treatise of the Orient*), the work of Tomé Pires, a Portuguese apothecary sent to Melaka in 1512 after its conquest by Portugal. Pires was to act as accountant and supervisor of drug purchasing, but he was also regarded as a skilled diplomat of studious tastes and an inquiring mind. After two and a half years in Melaka, during which time he made several trips within the archipelago, Pires had amassed sufficient information to compile his 'complete treatise'. The sixth book, based on Pires's own observations and 'what the majority affirm', deals with Melaka, its origins, administration and trade. Pires intended the *Suma Oriental* to be as far as possible an authentic account of Melaka's history which could serve as a reference book for its new Portuguese masters.[27]

The second source stems from a very different tradition.[28] The *Sejarah Melayu*, the so-called 'Malay Annals', has been handed down in a number of different versions, the earliest of which is now dated from the early seventeenth century. It is clear, however, that many of the stories it contains had been part of Malay culture for generations. The work is generally regarded as the foremost example of classical Malay prose style, a literary masterpiece as well as a Malay perception of the past. Like most other *hikayat* (story, account), it consists of a number of episodes which can stand on their own, strung together like 'a garland of flowers' or 'a necklace of pearls'.[29] The text's stated aim was 'to set forth the genealogy of the Malay rajas and the ceremonial of their courts for the information of [the king's] descendants . . . that they may be conversant with the history and derive profit therefrom . . . ' But the *Sejarah Melayu* does not purport to adhere to a strict chronology or provide a precise rendering of events in the past. It was not written according to the Western conception of a historical document, and to treat it as such is to misunderstand its fundamental aims. Like other Malay court annals, the *Sejarah Melayu* should be regarded as a particular genre of Malay literature whose primary concern was the edification of future generations.

The *Suma Oriental* and the *Sejarah Melayu*, despite their differing purpose, contain a core of similar information concerning the founding of Melaka. Both trace the Melaka line to an individual ruling in Palembang; both mention his special status; both describe his departure for Singapore, where he sets up a settlement. They relate how the settlement was later moved to Muar, about eight kilometres from Melaka, then to Bertam, being finally established at Melaka itself, the site of which was chosen because of a mousedeer's peculiar behaviour. Apart from this basis of shared information, however, the two accounts differ markedly. Pires's narrative is presented in a relatively straightforward manner which to Western ears has a ring of authenticity. Paramesvara, the Palembang prince, leaves Sumatra because he realizes that his standing in 'the neighbouring islands' makes his subserviency to Java intolerable. As a sign of his new status he takes a title which Pires translates as 'The Great Exempt'. Following an invasion by a Javanese army he flees to Singapore with a following that includes thirty *orang laut*. After eight days in Singapore he kills the local chief there, an Ayudhyan vassal, and sets himself up as lord. In Singapore he and his followers eke out a living by growing rice, fishing and piracy, but after five years a force from Ayudhya drives them out and they flee to Muar. After another five years the *orang laut* discover an attractive site for a settlement at Bertam where Paramesvara moves. He rewards his faithful followers with noble titles, and his son marries the daughter of their leader, who then becomes chief minister.

One day this son, Iskandar Syah, is out hunting, but as he approaches Melaka Hill the mousedeer his dogs are chasing suddenly turns on them. Attributing this strange behaviour to the fact that the sea is so close, or to some quality in the hill itself, Iskandar Syah asks his father's permission to settle there. 'And at the said time, he built his house on top of the hill where the Kings of Melaka have had their dwelling and residence until the present time.'

The Malay version, the *Sejarah Melayu*, begins with an impressive genealogy which traces the line of Melaka kings back to Alexander the Great (Iskandar Zul-karnain) who assumes in the text the status of a glorious Moslem king. It follows the fortunes of Raja Iskandar's line in India and the Malay world until three of his descendants miraculously appear on Bukit Si Guntang, a sacred hill in Palembang. Their heavenly descent acknowledged, the princes are hailed by the rulers of Sumatra, and one, Sri Tri Buana, is made ruler of Palembang. After vainly seeking a consort who can cohabit with him, Sri Tri Buana finally weds the daughter of his chief minister, Demang Lebar Daun, who had been Palembang's former ruler. Minister and king then conclude a solemn covenant which ensures that Malays will always remain loyal to their kings, who must repay them by just rule. In due time, in search of a suitable place to build a city, Demang Lebar Daun and Sri Tri Buana leave Palembang. When their fleet arrives at Bentan in the Riau-Lingga archipelago, the Queen there takes Sri Tri Buana as her son.

Some time afterwards, seeking a suitable site for a settlement, Sri Tri Buana sees across the ocean the island of Temasek. With the help of the Queen of Bentan, he establishes a city on Temasek which he calls Singapura, the 'Lion City', after glimpsing a strange beast there,

which he takes to be a lion (*singa*). His descendants rule in Singapura
(Singapore) for another five generations. Under their rule it becomes
a great city which will not accept Java's attempt to impose overlordship and even withstands an assault by the ruler of Majapahit. However, when the fourth king unjustly punishes one of his subjects, con-
travening the contract made between his forebear and Demang Lebar
Daun, Singapore is attacked by swordfish. The attack is repelled by a
stratagem suggested by a child, who in turn is killed by the ruler,
apprehensive of some future challenge. 'But when this boy was executed
the guilt of his blood was laid on Singapore.' The next ruler, Sultan
Iskandar Syah, publicly humiliates the daughter of a treasury official
because he believes the unjustified slanders against her. The wronged
father then invites the Javanese to attack, and this time they are
successful. Sultan Iskandar flees to Muar, but here he is attacked by
monitor lizards; he flees yet again, but his fort collapses; he finally
moves up the coast to a river called Bertam. And as the king is out
hunting one of his hounds is kicked by a white mousedeer. 'And
Sultan Iskandar said, "This is a good place, where even the mousedeer are full of fight!"' Because he was then standing under a *melaka*
tree, he decides that the new settlement should bear that name.

These episodes are related in considerable detail with embellish-
ments that, recited aloud, must have been highly dramatic. Although
it is not difficult to understand why the stories have lived on in Malay
memory, scholars have been puzzled about certain discrepancies between the *Sejarah Melayu* and Pires's account. The Singapore period,
for instance, receives considerable attention in the *Sejarah Melayu* and
is attributed a length of a hundred years, yet no evidence of a great
city such as that it describes has yet been found in any other source.
However, rather than being distracted by the differences in the two
versions, it is more useful to concentrate on the similarities. Above all,
both see Melaka's origins in Palembang, where scholars believe a great
entrepôt called Srivijaya once flourished. Available evidence and
Melaka's subsequent history support the suggestion that its rapid rise
and great self-confidence were due to a direct connection with the
legendary Srivijaya. This link would provide Melaka with the background which it hitherto seemed to lack and which has represented an
unexplained gap in our understanding of the period. The movement
from Palembang to Melaka can then be seen as part of a continuum
with no significant break in the momentum of Malay history.

Melaka's Heritage

This chapter has drawn together some of the scattered evidence
relating to the Malay world before the founding of Melaka about

1400. Far from being merely a prelude to the period of great Malay power, these early centuries established a context which makes later Malaysian history more explicable. The Malay archipelago came to the attention of the outside world because of the great natural wealth of its jungles and oceans. The area was doubly fortunate in being placed midway on the sea route between China and India and linked by a wind system with these two great markets of the early Asian world. But even more importantly, the peoples of the area were ever ready to respond to the demands of international trade. Because the long coast-lines surrounding the Malay archipelago provided many natural harbours which could act as collecting points, rivalry inevitably grew up between different ports vying for trading supremacy. Periodically one would establish itself as a regional entrepôt with the right to command the patronage of foreign merchants. As such a port asserted commercial hegemony, its neighbours had to accept their position as subsidiary collection centres feeding the entrepôt.

The maintenance of this relationship depended on the ability of the centre to hold together a number of scattered harbours by loose politi-cal and economic ties which both vassal and overlord recognized as mutually advantageous. When the vassals began to question the value of the benefits they received, links with the overlord were weakened. The region would then break up into a number of small kingdoms again competing for supremacy until one again succeeded in asserting its pre-eminence. It is this ebb and flow of power which has been called the 'rhythm' of Malay history.[30]

In the continuing contest to gain and maintain hegemony, a port along the Melaka Straits or its approaches had the advantage. Favour-able geographic conditions and the availability of desired products led to the development of Kan-t'o-li, arguably the first important Malay entrepôt, somewhere in southeast Sumatra. Though virtually nothing is known of Kan-t'o-li, it was highly successful in exploiting trade with India and China, and in commercial terms can be regarded as the predecessor of the greatest of the early Malay maritime kingdoms, Srivijaya.

Emerging in the seventh century in southeast Sumatra, Srivijaya was apparently able to maintain its economic and political superiority in the region until about the thirteenth century. Though some claims made on Srivijaya's behalf are still questioned, its fame as an entrepôt is unchallenged. But traders were not drawn only by the ready market in jungle and sea products, or by the exotic goods brought from overseas by foreign merchants; they also appreciated the regulated government and the smooth functioning of commercial transactions. The pros-perity that came to Srivijaya through international trade made possible a refined and cultured society which could hold its own even when compared with the great civilizations of India and China. Such an achievement was not easily forgotten. The honorific Srivijaya may have disappeared from the Malay mind but the memories of a mighty kingdom in Palembang did not. As the *Sejarah Melayu* puts it: 'According to the account we have received, the city of Palembang which has been mentioned was the same as the Palembang of today. Formerly it was a very great city, the like of which was not to be found in the whole country of Andelas [Sumatra].'

It was the Palembang tradition which was Melaka's heritage. To quote the *Sejarah Melayu* once again: 'From below the wind to above the wind Melaka became famous as a very great city, the raja of which was sprung from the line of Sultan Iskandar Zul-karnain [Alexander the Great]; so much so that princes from all countries came to present themselves before [the ruler].'

Melaka knew itself to be no parvenu kingdom; behind its proud boast lay the same assurance which, centuries before, had prompted an unknown Srivijayan ruler to proclaim himself 'sovereign over all the kings in the entire earth'.[31]

2

Melaka and Its Heirs

During the fifteenth century Melaka rose to become, in the words of
Tomé Pires, 'of such importance and profit that it seems to me it has
no equal in the world'.[1] Melaka's great success and its honoured place
in Malay history were not only due, however, to its prosperity and
renown as a trading centre. Building upon an illustrious past, it established a pattern of government and a lifestyle which was emulated by
subsequent Malay kingdoms and became the basis of what was later
termed 'traditional Malay culture and statecraft'. So imposing was the
reputation of Melaka that its successors were in a sense condemned to
the awesome task of attempting to revive the glory of the Malay past.
The trading policies of the Portuguese in the sixteenth century and the
Dutch in the seventeenth placed such restraints on international commerce that it was all but impossible for a Malay emporium in the
tradition of Melaka to re-emerge. But while no Malay kingdom succeeded in re-creating the greatness of Melaka, it remained an inspiration
and a source of strength to all those states which considered themselves
its heirs.

The Sixteenth and Seventeeth Centuries: Historiographical Considerations

Although historians generally agree that Melaka was founded somewhere around 1400, the evidence for its subsequent history remains
scattered. Apart from the two major sources relating to the late
fourteenth and fifteenth centuries, the *Suma Oriental* and the *Sejarah
Melayu*, information for the period of Melaka's greatness is limited to
the occasional mention in Chinese imperial histories and isolated comments in Portuguese sources. This caveat has not, unfortunately,
deterred some historians from attaching precise dates to rulers and
events despite the tenuous nature of some of the evidence. In this
chapter the only dates cited are those which can be corroborated from
a number of sources.

The capture of Melaka in 1511 by the Portuguese meant the sixteenth century Malay world did receive greater Portuguese attention,
and their records consequently become more informative. For this

period the *Sejarah Melayu* also continues to provide material unavailable elsewhere about the fortunes of the refugee Melaka princes
until their descendants eventually establish the kingdom of Johor. But
no extant Malay texts chronicle events from the mid-sixteenth century
to the end of the seventeenth, and here the historian is again forced to
fall back on European accounts. The primary concern of the Portuguese — the numerous wars they waged against Johor and Aceh —
reflects the serious dislocation which occurred after Melaka's fall. Yet
it is hard to believe that these sources have been fully exploited.
Extensive studies of Portuguese archival material by I. A. MacGregor,[2]
though going far in constructing a chronological schema, have made
apparent the need for further research concentrating on the activities
of the Malays themselves.

The arrival of the Dutch in the Malay areas in the late sixteenth and
early seventeenth centuries brought yet another European observer
on the scene, bequeathing documentation that has proved invaluable
to the modern historian. The formation of the Dutch East India Company (VOC) in 1602 was followed in 1619 by the establishment of
Batavia (modern Jakarta) as the seat of the Company's government in
Asia. For the success of VOC trade, Batavia needed to understand the
political as well as the economic policies of native kingdoms, since
only with this information could its vast resources be deployed to
good effect. In order to compile accurate political and economic
detail, Company officials all over Asia were required to submit reports
to Batavia.

In the Malay peninsula the chief VOC outpost was at Melaka,
captured from the Portuguese in 1641. From here missions were regularly sent to the various Malay kingdoms to gather information, while
in Melaka itself traders and Malay envoys kept the Dutch informed
of significant happenings in the area. Letters were also exchanged
with native rulers and officials, providing yet another important
source for historians. Finally, this material was brought together and
summarized by Melaka's Dutch Governor in his monthly missive to
Batavia, with many of the original documents appended for further
perusal by the VOC leaders. It is these sources which form the basis
for reconstructing events in the Malay world during the seventeenth
and eighteenth centuries.

Detailed though the VOC records are, their very nature determines
the kind of historical writing possible for this period of Malaysian
history. They were intended primarily as a means of furthering VOC
commerce, rather than aids to government or records for later administrations. Since a knowledge of politics in local kingdoms was vital for
ensuring the Company's trading profits, the focus of Dutch attention
was the governing classes in the various states. Even then on many
occasions only a minimum of information was considered necessary

for Dutch purposes. It is thus futile to expect the VOC sources to
yield the same kind of data about local society as the colonial records
from the late nineteenth and twentieth centuries. The lack of information concerning the common people is also due to the fact that the
available Malay texts (most of which date from the eighteenth century)
emanate from the courts. They therefore deal almost exclusively with
the ruler, the nobles, and with the people and events which impinged
on court life. Failure to appreciate these fundamental differences
between the nature of modern records and those stemming from
earlier times has led some scholars better acquainted with later Malaysian history to set unattainable goals for their colleagues working in
the earlier period. The first task of a historian of the pre-colonial
era is to piece together information which covers limited subjects and
where possible construct a chronological framework. Only then can he
hope to assess the significance of the material.

In the Tradition of Srivijaya

The previous chapter has described the period of rivalry in the thirteenth and fourteenth centuries when neighbouring ports in the Straits
of Melaka sought to inherit Srivijaya's political and economic status.
These harbours flourished with the patronage of foreign traders, who
no longer found it practicable, profitable, or even safe to conduct
their business at the central marketplace in Srivijaya. Now, with
merchants from both East and West going to ports close to the source
of a particular product, ambitious rulers saw the opportunity of
transforming their estuarine settlements in emulation of great entrepôts
in the past.

An area which never totally relinquished its importance as an alternative port to Srivijaya was northern Sumatra. After the twelfth
century two regions became particularly prominent: Samudra-Pasai,
almost at the northern tip of Sumatra, and Aru, to the south of
Samudra-Pasai, in modern-day Deli. Both states are mentioned in
thirteenth-century Chinese sources, but their prestige increased in the
early fourteenth century after their adoption of Islam. There are
numerous theories debating the reasons for Islam's success here and
elsewhere in the archipelago, but historians generally agree that
proselytization was closely linked to trade, which in this period was
dominated by Moslems from India. Samundra-Pasai's fame as a trading
port is well documented, and preliminary archaeological evidence
suggests that Aru too was probably a prosperous commercial state in
the twelfth and thirteenth centuries.

When Melaka was established at about the turn of the fourteenth
century, therefore, two entrepôts of note already existed in the Straits.
Paramesvara, the founder of Melaka, would have been well aware of

this and consciously set out to surpass both his potential rivals. The selection of a site was of paramount importance for the success of any entrepôt and it was thus with great care that Parameśvara finally made his choice. Situated on the convergence of the sea lanes from India and China, the Melaka harbour was sheltered, free of mangrove swamps, with approaches sufficiently deep to allow large vessels safe passage. There were also connections with the interior, for the Melaka River gave access to a trans-peninsular trade route which went via a portage area known as Penarikan to the Muar-Pahang waterway. This route led to the valuable goldmining areas of Ulu (upriver, inland) Pahang, the wealth of which gave rise to legends which persisted well into the nineteenth century. In addition, Melaka had a pleasant climate and an abundant supply of fresh water. However, the decisive factor in its favour was its naturally defensible position. Problems of security may have led to the earlier abandonment of the Riau-Lingga area and of Muar as possible sites for an entrepôt. Although Muar was a promising trading area, it was more vulnerable to attack than Melaka, where a prominent hill overlooked the estuary. As a further precaution Para-mesvara decided to build his residence upstream from Melaka, at Bertam. Here he could receive ample warning of any impending attack and could then flee to safety in the interior. Although Parameśvara's successors maintained a residence on Melaka Hill, they lived for the most part in Bertam, going to Melaka only to settle disputes or dispense justice. Thus in its early years Melaka proper was the settlement of traders, a market city; the ruler himself was represented there by various nobles concerned with administration and by his *orang laut* retainers and guards.

Once the site had been determined and a settlement founded, Para-meśvara began systematically creating the conditions necessary for the establishment of a major trading centre. An unexpected opportunity arose with the installation of the Ming Emperor Yung-lo in July 1402. Following the same policies as his father, the new Chinese emperor forbade all private commerce overseas, re-established the Bureau of Maritime Trade, and encouraged state trading on a large scale. In early October, in order to proclaim his accession and his policies, envoys were despatched to the Nan Yang ('the Southern Ocean'), the term the Chinese used to designate the Southeast Asian region. Because of the information then available in the imperial court, Samudra was the only port in the Melaka Straits visited by the Chinese mission. How-ever, less then four weeks later, informed of Melaka's existence by some Indian Moslem traders, Emperor Yung-lo immediately sent out a further mission. These envoys arrived in Melaka in the middle of 1404, and on their return in early 1405 brought with them to China the first mission from this new settlement. When the Melaka ambassador was presented to the Chinese court, he appeared with delegations from Samudra and Calicut (southwest India), two older and well-established kingdoms. Further evidence of the emperor's favour was shown by the promulgation of an edict 'appointing' all three rulers as kings. Shortly afterwards another signal honour was bestowed on Melaka when it became the first foreign nation to receive the emperor's inscription. This inscription contained the moral and political philosophy of the Ming dynasty and was to be placed on a hill to the west of Melaka which the emperor designated as its 'State Mountain'.[3]

Behind Emperor Yung-lo's fostering of a special relationship between China and various Asian kingdoms lay his desire to expand Chinese trade overseas under the imperial aegis. But the selection of Melaka for particular favour may be explained by China's need for a convenient trading centre in the Straits somewhere at the 'end of the monsoons'. China's interest in encouraging the development of Melaka in these early years imparted a prestige and respectability to the new entrepôt and a guarantee of protection from the Thais. Nonetheless, along the northern Sumatran coast the kingdom of Aru, located in the region of the former port of Kampé, was still a focus of commercial competition. Aru's lack of success in drawing international trade away from Melaka and Samudra-Pasai led it to initiate attacks on shipping destined for the other two ports. Irritating though this piracy was, it presented no significant threat to the trade of Melaka and thus never seriously jeopardized the sources of Melaka's wealth and power.

Samudra-Pasai remained Melaka's greatest rival for many years. Though increasing numbers of merchants flocked to Melaka under its second ruler, Megat Iskandar Syah, Tomé Pires was told that 'this was not felt in Pase [Pasai] because of the large number of people who were there'. Only towards the latter part of the fifteenth century did Pasai feel the effects of its neighbour's success. 'At this time,' wrote Pires, 'there was a large number of merchants of many nationalities in Malacca [Melaka], and Pase was already beginning to be less great than it had been.'[4]

Melaka's efforts to assert its position in the Straits were thus succeeding. At the very outset its rulers had sought and received vassal status from China, thereby gaining the assurance of protection and respectability. They then took the precaution of acknowledging themselves as vassals of their powerful and much closer neighbours, the Thai kingdom of Ayudhya and Majapahit in Java. The advantages of this move were not purely in terms of protection, for Melaka petitioned its two overlords to send people and foodstuffs to assist in the growth of the new settlement. Undaunted by Pasai's prosperity, an early ruler of Melaka could soon confidently inform Pasai that all its needs could be provided in Melaka's markets.

:asons for Melaka's Success

Melaka continued the well-established traditions of its predecessor, Srivijaya, in ensuring the success of international trade in its port. Laws were codified as part of an efficient legal and administrative machinery which provided a predictability essential for the long-term plans of foreign traders. The justice of Melaka's rulers was exemplified by one Sultan who was described as having greater pleasure in being in the city of Melaka than in going hunting 'so that he could hear and decide about the abuses and tyrannies which Melaka creates on account of its great position and trade'.[5]

Melaka was also admirably equipped to satisfy the physical needs of traders. Underground warehouses, for example, were constructed where merchants could store their goods while awaiting incoming cargoes. Such storage facilities, providing protection against fire, damage or theft, were necessary because it was impossible for the traders from India, China and the eastern archipelago to arrive at the same time, since all sea traffic was governed by the monsoon winds. The period of greatest activity was between December and March when ships would reach Melaka from western Asia and the Far East. Ships from Java and the eastern Indonesian archipelago, on the other hand, appeared later, from May until September. Since these traders, especially those from China and eastern Indonesia, had some time to wait before favourable monsoon winds could aid their homeward journey, warehouse facilities were one of the most vital requirements for any port aspiring to become an international entrepôt.

Another of Melaka's attractions as an entrepôt was its ability to assure the safety of traders within the Straits. The rulers of Melaka, like those of Srivijaya, commanded the allegiance of the fearsome *orang laut* who protected Melaka's clients and wreaked havoc on those of its rivals. This guarantee of safety was an important element in the decision of traders to frequent Melaka in preference to other ports in the Straits.

A new administrative arrangement was introduced in response to the needs of a growing trading community in Melaka. Four Syahbandars, or harbour masters, were appointed, each one representing a group of nations. There was one Syahbandar for the Gujarati alone since they were the most numerous, being estimated at 1,000 in 1509; another Syahbandar was appointed for Indians from southern India and Bengal together with traders from Pegu in Burma and from Pasai; a third for those from Java, Moluccas, Banda, Palembang, Borneo and the Philippines; and a fourth for traders from Champa, China and the Ryukyu Islands (probably including Japanese). Each Syahbandar was required to oversee the affairs of his particular group; to manage the marketplace and the warehouse; maintain a check on weights, measures and coinage; and to adjudicate in disputes between the ships' captains and the merchants. The Melaka ruler was the final arbiter in all quarrels between the different trading communities.

Whenever a ship arrived in port, the ship's captain reported to his particular Syahbandar, who in turn referred him to Melaka's principal minister, the Bendahara. The Syahbander then supplied him with elephants to carry his cargo to a warehouse allotted to him for the temporary storage of his goods. Before trading could be conducted, customs had to be paid in accordance with the value of the merchandise and the area from which a trader came. In addition gifts had to be presented to the ruler, the Bendahara, and the Temenggung (the Melaka official principally involved in the collection of import and export duties), as well as to the appropriate Syahbandar.

A much simpler procedure was used for large ships, especially those from Gujarat in northwest India. A flat 6 per cent of the value of the cargo was paid which eliminated all necessity for separate gift-giving. Once the duties had been paid, the merchandise could be sold. Usually a group of Melaka merchants would reach a price with the ship's captain or the merchants on board, and then the goods would be parcelled out in proportion to the contribution made to the total price. This method disposed of a ship's merchandise quickly and efficiently, and since cargoes were customarily handled in order of arrival, traders could normally depend upon fair and rapid transactions. Speed was highly desirable because merchants were often working against time, aiming to complete their business in order to catch the right monsoon winds back to their homelands. The Malay traders of Melaka then took the goods which they had bought and either sold them in the marketplace, in the booths set up on the bridge and in the streets in front of houses, or else brought them to various parts of the archipelago to barter for other products. It was this middleman role played by the Melaka merchants which served to make Malay the language of trade throughout the archipelago.

Melaka's reputation for security, a well-ordered government and a cosmopolitan marketplace equipped with excellent facilities all attest to the care with which its rulers created the conditions for safe and profitable trade. But these facilities alone would not have automatically attracted traders. A crucial element in Melaka's success as an entrepôt was the dual role it played as the principal collecting centre for cloves from the Moluccas and the nutmeg and mace of the Banda Islands, and as an important redistributing centre for Indian textiles from Gujarat, Coromandel, Malabar and Bengal. Indian cloth was carried mainly by Malay traders from Melaka to various parts of the archipelago and bartered for spices, aromatic woods, sea products, and other exotic items highly prized by traders from both East and West. Without the Indian cloth or the spices,

...aka would have been simply one of a number of other ports in the area specializing in a few local products.

In his *Suma Oriental*, Tomé Pires estimated that 2·4 million cruzados' worth of trade passed through Melaka in 1510. This figure takes on greater significance when compared with the total value of imported goods entering Seville, one of the wealthiest ports in Europe, which at the end of the sixteenth century was reckoned at about four million cruzados.[6] In Melaka, the rich merchants were even reputed to keep their accounts in terms of *bahar* (about 170 kilos) of gold. There was some royal trade, but in terms of the kingdom's total revenue this was eclipsed by the customs levied on trading ships now flocking to its port. At any one time there were upward of two thousand boats lying at anchor in the harbour. By the beginning of the sixteenth century, the population of Melaka, swelled by foreign traders, numbered perhaps as many as 100,000.

Nature of the Melaka State

One of the most impressive achievements of the Melaka court was the formulation of a concept regarding the nature of the state and how it should ideally function. This concept, clearly expressed in the *Sejarah Melayu*, became an integral part of the Malay world view and remained basically unchallenged until the nineteenth century. Even today elements of earlier statecraft can be discerned in modern Malay political relationships and in the functioning of Malay society itself. Although the earliest extant version of the *Sejarah Melayu* comes from the seventeenth century, it is likely that some sections were committed to paper a good two hundred years earlier in the days of Melaka's greatness. These in turn probably reflect traditions of government which arose in a much earlier period, possibly in the court of Srivijaya itself.

For Malays, the structure of government was justified by its intimate ties with the kingdom's origin myths. At the apex of the state was the ruler, who claimed descent from the Palembang prince of Bukit Si Guntang, and through him to Raja Iskandar Zul-karnain ('Alexander of the Two Horns', that is, Alexander the Great). This exalted lineage provided the ruler of Melaka with a status and prestige which neighbouring rulers found difficult to match. To affirm this belief a court tradition arose which, expounded in the *Sejarah Melayu*, provided the apologia for the system of Malay governance. A type of social covenant is described in the following terms:

If any ruler puts a single one of his subjects to shame [*memberi 'aib*], that shall be a sign that his kingdom will be destroyed by Almighty God. Similarly it has been granted by Almighty God to Malay subjects that they shall never be disloyal or treacherous to their rulers, even if their rulers behave evilly or inflict injustice upon them.

In this covenant the special position of the Melaka ruler is emphasized, for he is responsible solely to and can only be punished by Almighty God.

The ruler, according to the *Sejarah Melayu*, stood at the heart of all meaningful activity. It was the ruler with his impeccable ancestry and unique 'Melayu' heritage who brought Melaka the prestige which distinguished it from surrounding states. A philologist has recently suggested that in the *Sejarah Melayu* the term 'Melayu' is used as a mark of distinction reserved exclusively for those descended from Palembang forebears.[7] In both the *Sejarah Melayu* and another Malay epic, the *Hikayat Hang Tuah*,[8] the definition of Melayu is clearly linked to Sumatra and in Pires's early sixteenth-century account 'tana Melayu' (the land of the Malays) is identified with an area near present-day Palembang. Early Chinese sources mention a Melayu believed to have been in the Jambi region, but according to the *Sejarah Melayu* 'Melayu' was the name of a river which flowed near the sacred hill in Palembang called Bukit Si Guntang.[9] One day on the summit of this hill three brothers descended from Iskandar Zul-karnain appeared in a supernatural manner. One of these brothers became the ruler in Palembang and later the ancestor of the Melaka kings. In this context, to be 'Melayu' was to be associated closely with this particular ancestor and his descendants who came to rule in Melaka. So successfully did Melaka's leaders equate the kingdom with 'Melayu' that one Malay text describes how, after a defeat, the people of Melaka fled into the jungle where they became *Jakun*, that is, *orang hulu* or upriver people.[10] Without the mantle of Melaka's prestige, the local inhabitants were undifferentiated from the other non-'Malay' elements in neighbouring areas. So valued were the Melayu rulers of Melaka that when one of them was fleeing from the island of Bentan after a Portuguese attack in 1526, he was assured by his minister that ten countries could be found for him.

The ruling dynasty's association with its sacred Melayu-Palembang origins formed the basis of its exclusiveness, which was further reinforced by the concept of *daulat/derhaka*. So odious was the crime of treason (*derhaka*) that the punishments meted out by the forces of kingship (*daulat*) were often unusual or repugnant, and a storehouse of legends was built up recording the fate of those who had transgressed. In the early nineteenth century Sultan Husain of Singapore was merely repeating a traditional prescription in the *Sejarah Melayu* when he said that a man guilty of *derhaka*, along with his family, would be killed, his house uprooted, and the soil on which it stood thrown into the sea. The need to institutionalize the uniqueness of the Melaka ruling family may have been prompted by the requirements of the new environment. With only a small contingent of Melayu newcomers, its position of authority had to be confirmed and accepted by the majority of the local inhabitants, mainly of *orang laut* and *orang asli* origin. By incorporating these people into the Melayu system of governance and society, the Melayu ruling house could then hope to exercise control over them according to its established conceptions of a people's loyalty towards their rulers. For the local inhabitants the prospects of becoming part of a way of life which would enhance their status *vis-à-vis* their neighbours was sufficiently enticing to attract support for the new ruling class.

The exalted position of the ruler, however, was not licence for arbitrary government. The *Sejarah Melayu* warns that: 'No ruler, however great his wisdom and understanding, shall prosper or succeed in doing justice unless he consults with those in authority under him. For rulers are like fire and their ministers are like firewood and fire needs wood to produce a flame.' Wise ministers were essential if the ruler were to fulfil his illustrious role, for they were the practical administrators of government. By faithfully executing their duties, the ministers helped dissociate the ruler from the mundane tasks of government so that his more sacred function within the society could be preserved untarnished. The ministers and the rulers had specific complementary functions, and both were expected to respect the division between them. As one minister in the *Sejarah Melayu* explained: 'What we think should be done we do, for the ruler is not concerned with the difficulties we administrators encounter, he only takes account of the good results we achieve.'

An examination of the *Sejarah Melayu* in conjunction with other sources, particularly Tomé Pires's *Suma Oriental*, conveys some idea of how this ideal concept functioned in practice. The most important minister in Melaka was the Bendahara, the highest official with whom foreign traders dealt and arbiter in disputes between Malays and foreigners or among Malays themselves. The original Bendahara, though a noble, was not of royal birth. But as time passed the Bendahara family married into Melaka's ruling house and came to wield great power, frequently acting as kingmaker. Nonetheless, in theory the Bendahara, like the lowest commoner, was subject to the strictures governing the relationship between ruler and ruled. The *Sejarah Melayu* thus presents the ideal picture of a powerful Bendahara who refused to commit treason against the ruler, despite being unjustly accused; only God Almighty, the text reminded Malays, could punish a wicked king.

According to the *Sejarah Melayu*, the next prominent official in Melaka was the Penghulu Bendahari, who was head of all the Syahbandars and controlled all state revenues. In addition, he was responsible for the ruler's servants and clerks. The third-ranking official in the Melaka hierarchy was the Temenggung, who later became more important than the Penghulu Bendahari and was considered to be the Bendahara-designate. His principal concern was Melaka's security, and he was therefore in charge of the police and acted as Chief Magistrate. Following the Temenggung was the Laksamana, the military counterpart of the Bendahara. He headed the military administration and was commander of the ruler's bodyguard. Since the most effective arm of Melaka's forces was the navy, the post of Laksamana became equated with the leader of the fleets. These four ministers were the most prominent in the Melaka period.

Below them were various titled nobles whose positions stemmed from their territorial holdings or from a privileged association with the royal family. Little is known about individual functions, but it is apparent that Melaka rulers considered these men worthy of consultation in any important decision affecting the people. A meeting of the nobles constituted a form of council or assembly (*mesyuarat bicara* — meeting for discussion) in which all views could be heard and then a decision taken by consensus (*muafakat*). It was this collective decision-making process which normally prevented arbitrary acts by a ruler and guaranteed that a resolution taken would be faithfully implemented. Although there were ways in which shrewd rulers or nobles could circumvent decisions made by the council, in most cases this form of government, which was found in all later Malay states, functioned well.

The success of *muafakat* is the more impressive because the ruling élite in Melaka contained many men of wealth, ambition and ability. The ruler was by no means the only recipient of the riches which flowed into the coffers of the Melaka court. Indeed, the Malay word commonly used for a noble in Melaka, *orang kaya*, simply means 'rich man'. Malay officials such as the Bendahara and Temenggung were presented with princely sums through the traditional practice of submitting a certain percentage of a cargo's value in gifts. One Bendahara was so successful in acquiring riches through patronage and trade that according to the *Sejarah Melayu* he would often have his chest of gold brought to him and allow each of the children in his household to take a handful as a plaything.

As the noble class gained increasing wealth from customs and their own private trade, it became necessary to reinforce the ruler's place at the apex of the state. To accentuate his distinctiveness in relation to his nobles, certain royal privileges were instituted. The colour yellow was reserved for the exclusive use of royalty; white umbrellas were to be used only by rulers and yellow umbrellas only by princes; gold anklets could be worn only by royalty; no one, 'however rich he might be', could wear gold unless it had been presented to him by the ruler, in which case it could then be worn 'in perpetuity'; 'enclosed verandahs, pillars that hung down not reaching to the ground, posts that went right up to the roofbeam, or summerhouses' were the preserve of royalty; only royalty could have windows and reception cabins on boats; and no commoner could have a metal casing on the sheath of his kris.[11] Such visible manifestations of the unique position of the ruler were a continual reminder to Melaka nobles of their rightful place in the hierarchy.

At times, however, even these royal privileges were insufficient to deter a powerful official from aspiring to greater authority and prestige. The possibility of a successful challenge to the ruler was always present. One of the Bendaharas mentioned in the *Sejarah Melayu* was 'so clever in his handling of foreigners and skilled in conciliating the good will of the populace' that masters of ships bound for Melaka would invoke a prayer before weighing anchor which concluded: 'May we reach Melaka safely and see Pisang Jeram, the stream of Bukit China, and Bendahara Sri Maharaja.'[12] Such rich and famous men could attract a large following, and in the Southeast Asian context followers have always meant strength. During the reign of the last Melaka ruler, accusations that the Bendahara intended to usurp the throne seemed eminently credible. So convinced was the ruler of his minister's treachery that he ordered the Bendahara put to death.

In the relationship between the ruler and his nobles, the wealth of international trade was thus a mixed blessing; while it enriched the ruler, it also swelled the coffers of the local aristocracy and provided them with the means to oppose royal authority. Not surprisingly, Malay court traditions stress the power of sovereignty vested in the ruler and the dire retribution visited upon those committing treason. Reinforced by rigid sumptuary laws, these traditions became part of the mystique which surrounded the Melaka rulers descended from the Palembang line. For many years they served to discourage would-be usurpers, or to compel them to mask their activities by outwardly acknowledging the formal relationships which tradition dictated.

The ruler's commoner subjects formed the largest group in Melaka society. Despite their humble status, the *Sejarah Melayu* regards them with respect, echoing the traditional concern for manpower in the lightly populated lands of Southeast Asia. In the words of this text, 'subjects are like roots and the ruler is like the tree; without roots the tree cannot stand upright; so is it with rulers and their subjects'. The ruler is only one part, albeit the outward and brilliant manifestation, of a unity in which all the people have their appropriate niche and carry out their individual tasks.

Unfortunately, available sources present only fragmentary evidence regarding the actual life of the common people in Melaka. The most that can be established is that they gained their livelihood from agriculture and fishing, and that they rendered their services to the ruler in times of war and during major celebrations. The sources do suggest, however, that Melaka's commoner population in the early stages was divided between the newcomers from Sumatra and the original inhabitants of the Melaka area. When Paramesvara appeared in Melaka with his following, including a group of *orang laut*, there was already a small fishing village at the site. It therefore appears that Melaka's original population must have included a number of local people, among whom would have been the *orang asli* and *orang laut*.

The incorporation of the aboriginal population from neighbouring coastal and riverine areas into the hierarchical structure of the Melaka kingdom would not have entailed great disruption in their existing way of life. For several thousand years forest dwellers had been collecting jungle products which had come to play a vital role in Asian trade. Those groups living at the fringe of the jungle and along the coasts would have been influenced by centuries of trading contacts with the outside world long before Melaka's founding. Dealing with coastal traders would have entailed a degree of hierarchical command structure to ensure that barter and exchange took place smoothly. It could be argued, therefore, that when the Melayu newcomers arrived with an established system of social and political ranks, there were already *orang asli* groups in the Melaka region to whom such concepts would have been familiar. This familiarity may have hastened their decision to become associated with the new kingdom as a means of enhancing their social and economic position in relation to other groups in the area. Even up to the beginning of this century the Jakun, an *orang asli* group, were considered by the people in the hinterland of Melaka as the original lords of the soil.

The new rulers of Melaka would have found the *orang asli* a ready source of vital manpower which could be harnessed to the kingdom's interests. Although never populous, their knowledge of the jungle and ability to deliver the forest products valued in international trade would have encouraged the new Melaka rulers to incorporate them as Melayu subjects. Indeed, when referring to the common people of Melaka, who must have included a large percentage of local *orang asli*, the *Sejarah Melayu* calls them *hamba Melayu*, the 'subjects of the Melayu'.

The early association which must have grown up between the Melayu and *orang asli* found a place in Malay legends and literature. The *Hikayat Hang Tuah*, a text incorporating many Malay oral traditions, mentions a mythical queen of Melaka who flees into the jungle to escape from the Portuguese. She then becomes a member of one of the northern *orang asli* groups, the Batek. In another episode, the hero of the story, Hang Tuah, retreats upriver to Perak where he is accepted as ruler by another *orang asli* people, the *orang biduanda* (literally, palace servants). Although the latter group are now referred to as *orang Temuan*, the older terminology may give some hint as to their relations with the Malay-dominated centre. The effects of this continued contact is suggested in a nineteenth-century Malay account of Pahang, which mentions that some of the aboriginal groups who had strong trading ties with the Malays had begun to emulate their speech and dress.[13] An indication of early *orang asli* perceptions of the Melaka dynasty is suggested in modern Johor, where some Jakun still regard the Johor ruler with great respect and consider that Malay culture imparts special insights into spiritual and religious matters.

The willingness of *orang laut* to become associated with the new kingdom would have equally been a great advantage to Melaka. Their relatively large numbers in the Straits and their naval power rendered them a desirable ally for any lord aspiring to political hegemony in the area. Furthermore, their cargoes of sea products, transported to Melaka's market, were acknowledged as being vitally important in attracting the traders who were to become the source of Melaka's wealth. Parameśvara tightened his links with the *orang laut* by bringing their leaders into the political hierarchy and, via judicious marriages, into the royal family itself. For hundreds of years the *orang laut* devotion to the Melayu rulers of Melaka was a crucial factor in the kingdom's preservation and prosperity.

Melaka's Territorial Expansion

The increased revenue from trade transformed Melaka from an insignificant backwater into a bustling international emporium with political ambitions. Under Parameśvara (died 1413/14), Melaka had comprised the small settlement at the port itself and the royal residence upriver at Bertam. During the reign of Parameśvara's successor, Megat Iskandar Syah (died 1423/24), Melaka's boundaries expanded to include all lands between Kuala Linggi and Kuala Kesang (the borders of the modern Melaka State). However, it was then still much smaller in size than its principal competitor, Pasai. Melaka's territorial expansion resumed three reigns later under Sultan Muzaffar Syah (died *circa* 1459), who incorporated the Dindings, Selangor, Muar, Singapore and Bentan into the kingdom. Pahang, which fourteenth-century Chinese sources depict as a thriving port on the peninsula's east coast, was similarly forced to acknowledge Melaka's suzerainty. Muzaffar was also the first Melaka ruler to attempt to impose authority over both shores of the Melaka Straits. Inderagiri and Kampar, two east coast Sumatra kingdoms which controlled access to the rich pepper and gold of the Minangkabau interior, became Melaka's vassals. They, like the other vassal states, recognized the potential benefits in acknowledging as overlord a wealthy state which would then be predisposed to extend its bounty (*kurnia*) to its dependencies. As long as the relationship with Melaka was perceived as advantageous, its vassal states generally remained quiescent.

Sultan Mansur Syah (died 1477) added Bernam and Perak on the Malay peninsula to the Melaka kingdom, while Siak on Sumatra's east coast became another vassal area. Pahang, Kampar and Inderagiri had attempted to assert their independence but were subdued, and one of Mansur's sons was placed over Pahang as ruler. On succeeding his father Mansur, Sultan Alauddin Riayat Syah (died 1488) extended the conquests southward 'to the many islands belonging to the Celates [*orang laut*]', that is, the Riau-Lingga archipelagoes. By the reign of Melaka's last ruler, Sultan Mahmud Syah (1488–1530), the kingdom had grown to include Pahang, the west coast of the Malay peninsula from Perak to Johor, Singapore, the Riau-Lingga archipelagoes, and much of east coast Sumatra. So powerful had Melaka become and so assured of its strength that Mahmud rejected the overlordship of both Ayudhya and the weakened kingdom of Majapahit while continuing to acknowledge the more distant and less obtrusive suzerainty of China.

Melaka's control in the area, however, was never as complete as that credited to Srivijaya at the height of its power. The northern Malay states of Patani, Kelantan, Trengganu and Kedah still acknowedged Ayudhya's overlordship, and only towards the end of the fifteenth century was Melaka's influence felt there. Even on the opposite side of the Straits the suzerainty of Melaka was incomplete. Pasai, though suffering from Melaka's increased international trade, was still an independent port able to satisfy foreign traders, and Aru too retained its autonomy. With both Pasai and Aru continuing to exercise freedom of action in local waters, and Ayudhya still a major threat on its borders, Melaka never really succeeded, as had Srivijaya, in making the Straits its private lake.

Islam and the Spread of Melaka Culture

Melaka's territorial ambitions may have been checked, but its cultural influence spread beyond the immediate vicinity of the Straits throughout the Malay—Indonesian archipelago. A principal factor in the transmission of its culture was its association with Islam. By the ninth century Arab traders knew a large part of Southeast Asia but appeared to have neglected this area in favour of the lucrative China trade. Although Arab sources mention the northwest and east coasts of Sumatra, the Melaka Straits down to Palembang, Johor, part of the Riau-Lingga archipelago and Pulau Tioman, there is no hint of organized Arab trade with these areas until the mid-tenth century. This period provides the only clue of a Moslem trading colony in a place called Kalah, located tentatively somewhere in the northern part of the Malay peninsula. As one might expect, isolated evidence of this

Moslem contact is scattered through the western archipelago, such as a Moslem tombstone in Grisek (east Java) bearing the date 475 AH (AD 1082) or 495 AH (AD 1101). However, the first accepted evidence of local Moslem activity is Marco Polo's account of 1292 which mentions that the town of Perlak in northern Sumatra was Moslem.

By the thirteenth century trade to Southeast Asia by the Arabs was all but superseded by that of their Moslem brethren from India, and it is to them that the spread of Islam through the archipelago is generally attributed. Although the ongoing debate as to which Indian group was responsible for the conversion of island Southeast Asia may never be resolved, the direct relationship between trade and the spread of Islam is little denied. After the fall of Baghdad and the destruction of the Abbasid Caliphate by the Mongols in 1258, the spice route from the east through the Persian Gulf up to the Levantine coast and thence to northern Europe was effectively closed. A new route now went from the east to India, then to Aden in Southern Arabia, through the Red Sea up to Alexandria and thence northward. Since the Caliph in Egypt refused any but Moslem shipping through Alexandria, the Moslem ports of Cambay, Surat, and Diu in Gujarat province (northwest India) acquired great importance as transhipment centres for spices. In addition to the thousand or so Gujarati merchants resident in Melaka, there were about three to four thousand others always en route between this port and those in Gujarat.[14] Growing demand for Eastern spices by a prosperous Renaissance Europe and the cessation from the fourteenth century of direct Chinese trade to India brought the Gujarati merchants into great prominence as intermediaries in the spice trade. Their sizeable numbers in Melaka, the major mart in the Malay—Indonesian archipelago, facilitated the work of Moslem missionaries in spreading the ideas of Islam to Melaka and elsewhere in the region.

But the Gujarati did not have the exclusive trade to Southeast Asia. There were substantial numbers of other Indian traders from the Malabar and Coromandel Coasts in South India, as well as from Bengal in northeast India. All these groups at one time or another would have played their part in familiarizing the island peoples of Southeast Asia with Islam, not necessarily with any of its dogma but with attitudes, values and a way of life.

The manner in which Islam, once brought to the shores of Southeast Asia through the trading connection, took root within a particular society is still a matter of speculation. The impressive flourishing in sixteenth- and seventeenth-century Aceh in north Sumatra of the ideas of Sufism, a mystic stream of Islam which at various periods in its history verged on heterodoxy, has given rise to the suggestion that Sufism was the vehicle by which Islam became the religion of the archipelago. Sufism's ability to incorporate a number of pre-Islamic beliefs and its moderate spiritual demands are seen as positive factors in its acceptance. However, although the Sufi connection can be established for Aceh, parts of Java and even South Sulawesi, this has not yet been the case for the Malay peninsula in the Melaka period. While there appear to be hints of Sufi theology in the *Sejarah Melayu*, these may represent a seventeenth-century interpolation of ideas borrowed from Aceh and not necessarily demonstrate any strong familiarity with Sufi doctrine.[15] It is therefore premature to claim that one method or one particular school of Islam would have found uniform acceptance throughout the varied societies in the archipelago. In the absence of further research, one can only state that Moslem traders, principally from India, were responsible for familiarizing local societies, including Melaka, with Islam as a way of life, but the process by which the society became Moslem is still unknown.

Once Melaka had embraced Islam some time in the early fifteenth century, the kingdom became transformed. The *Sejarah Melayu* rightly sees the acceptance of Islam as a watershed in Melaka's history, an inspired event which confirmed the kingdom's superior status. But is seems clear that, while the doctrinal simplicity of the new religion and its stress on the individual worth of all men were appealing, the temporal benefits were equally apparent. Melaka's rulers had only to look across the Straits to see an object lesson in the advantages of adopting the new religion. Pasai had accepted Islam towards the end of the thirteenth century and had consequently been favoured by large numbers of Moslem Indian traders. Its prosperity had demonstrated that any port which succeeded in obtaining the patronage of these Moslem Indian cloth merchants could be certain of attracting all other merchants since Indian textiles were the basic item of trade. Was it the hope of emulating Pasai's success, one wonders, which prompted a local ruler in Trengganu some time in the fourteenth century to embrace Islam? The famous Trengganu Stone which he set up, with its inscription enjoining obedience to Allah's word and to his law, is considered to be the oldest Malay text in the Arabic script.

There were, moreover, other less tangible benefits to be gained from adherence to Islam. A Moslem prince, regardless of where he ruled, was a member of a great Islamic community (*ummat*) which included the fabled Rum (Turkey) and Mogul India. Islam also provided a new ideology which strengthened kingship by depicting a Moslem ruler as 'the Shadow of God Upon the Earth' and by making him the head of a religious hierarchy extending to the village level. These advantages, propagated by Moslem preachers, were readily understood in Melaka and may help to explain the decision of one of its earliest rulers to embrace the new faith. According to both the *Sejarah Melayu* and the *Suma Oriental*, this decision was made with the encouragement of the ruler of Pasai.

As Melaka expanded territorially, it persuaded or compelled its vassals in the Straits area to accept Islam. But its growing prestige and commercial success also stood as an example which reinforced the process of Islamization in the archipelago. Local traders who brought their products for sale in Melaka markets would have witnessed Islam at work and seen the added status accruing from the new titles and pretensions assumed by the Melaka 'Sultan' and his nobles. Such changes would have been reported to their own courts which, eager to emulate the wealthy Melaka court, would have been receptive to proselytizing efforts by Moslem missionaries. Undoubtedly some rulers were sincerely attracted by the doctrine of the new faith, but other less spiritually inclined princes would have recognized the practical advantages that had earlier appealed to the Melaka court. Perhaps the deciding argument would have been the assurance that Moslem traders from India and Melaka would favour their ports because of the protection they could expect from a fellow Moslem and because of the presence of a mosque where they could worship without interference.

Throughout the fifteenth century Melaka's reputation as a commercial and religious centre established it as the yardstick by which other Moslem kingdoms in the archipelago were measured. Its literature, style of government, music, dance, dress, games, titles and even *pantun*,[16] all of which were distinctively Melaka Malay, were consciously imitated. But the clearest evidence of Melaka's influence is undoubtedly the widespread use of Malay as the language of numerous courts ranging from Aceh in the west to Ternate in the east. As one sixteenth-century Portuguese observer remarked, 'Though the heathens [on Sumatra's east coast] differ from one another in their languages, almost all of them speak Malayo de Malaca [Melakan Malay] because it is the language most used in the whole region'.[17] So identified was language with the entire gamut of Malay culture that the word *bahasa* (literally, language) came to subsume correct behaviour, appropriate speech and knowledge of Malay custom or *adat*.

Nonetheless, the spread of Malay culture, like the development of Melaka itself, should be viewed in perspective. The Malay cultural heritage did not originate in the fifteenth century, and neither Melaka's great reputation nor the ubiquity of its traders fully explains Malay influence in the Indonesian archipelago. It is more revealing to look beyond Melaka to the period of Srivijaya's dominance in the Straits. Scholars have noted that the oldest evidence of the Malay language is found in four seventh-century inscriptions from the Srivijaya period found in Palembang and Bangka. It would appear, therefore, that the language of government and the court of Srivijaya was an early version of the Malay spoken in Melaka. Malay legends of Melaka's founding by a Palembang prince give further weight to the argument that its language and culture were based upon that which flourished in the centres of kingly power in Srivijaya. The spread of Malay culture thus built upon a much earlier tradition. Because of its prestige and commanding position, Srivijaya's cultural influence would have been disseminated throughout its extensive though loosely governed empire. Smaller kingdoms would have adopted Srivijaya's lead, including the use of an early form of Malay as the language of the élite.

Melaka's main contribution to this ongoing Malay court culture was the incorporation of Islamic ideas. Though Islam had been promoted earlier by Samudra-Pasai, the new religion became so closely identified with Malay society in Melaka that to become Moslem, it was said, was to *masuk Melayu*, 'to enter [the fold of the] Melayu'. Preserved and enriched in Melaka, Srivijaya's language and culture thus continued to establish standards among areas formerly under Srivijaya's influence. Aru, for instance, had originated as a Batak state but by the mid-fifteenth century had adopted many of the trappings of a Malay kingdom, including the use of Malay titles for its officials. It had become Moslem, although the *Sejarah Melayu* is quick to point out that the people of Aru could not read the Koran. At the height of Melaka's power in the fifteenth century, Malay culture spread eastwards beyond the Straits even to areas which had never known the control of Srivijaya and were far beyond Melaka's political sway. But Melaka's period of greatness was already drawing to an end with the arrival of the Portuguese in Asia.

The Portuguese Conquest of Melaka

Fifteenth-century Portugal was unique in Europe in having suffered no debilitating internal strife. Freed from civil wars and major intrigues, the Portuguese rulers beginning with Infante Dom Enrique, better known as Prince Henry the Navigator (1394—1460), initiated a number of reconnaissance missions both by land and sea. The fifteenth century thus became known as Portugal's Age of Discovery. The motivation for Portuguese expansion beyond their tiny kingdom to the far corners of the globe represented a mixture of different aims: an anti-Moslem crusading spirit; a hope for Guinea gold; a search for the mythical priest—king Prester John ruling over a powerful kingdom in 'the Indies'; and a desire for Asian spices.

Only with the accession to the throne of Dom Joao II in 1481 did the Portuguese crown become seriously interested in obtaining Asian spices. Up to this time it had been content, as were the other European kingdoms, in receiving its Asian spices from the Venetians, who in turn obtained them from the Moslem Mameluke empire in Egypt and Syria. The reason for Dom Joao's change of attitude is unknown, but to investigate the possibilities of this trade he sent an agent overland to the Persian Gulf area and the east coast of Africa. It is doubt-ful, however, that the agent's report of 1490–1 ever reached Portugal because when Vasco Da Gama arrived by sea in Calicut on the west coast of India in 1498, he was unprepared for the sophistication of trade there. Informed of Vasco da Gama's feat, Portugal announced that it intended to divert the Asian spice trade away from the Moslems by establishing a new spice route around the Cape of Good Hope.

It was with this avowed aim that the Portuguese came to Asia. The principal architect of Portuguese expansion in Asia was Afonso de Albuquerque, who became the second Portuguese governor or viceroy of the *Estado da India*, Portugal's Asian empire. During his tenure of office (1509–15) Albuquerque sought to dominate the key points in the Moslem trading network through which Asian spices reached Europe. Towards this end he seized the island of Goa off the west coast of India in 1510, Melaka in 1511, and Hormuz, at the mouth of the Persian Gulf, in 1515.

Melaka, as the collecting point for the valuable spices of the Moluc-cas, was a prime target of the Portuguese. Albuquerque personally led an expedition against Melaka which succeeded in capturing the city on 10 August 1511, after little more than a month's siege. Beset by palace factionalism and daunted by superior Portuguese firepower, the Malays posed little resistance. Sultan Mahmud Syah and his son Sultan Ahmad Syah, who was ruling at the time of the attack, both fled into the interior. When it became apparent that the Portuguese had no intention of abandoning Melaka, the rulers went their separate ways to Muar and then to Pahang, eventually settling on the island of Bentan in the Riau-Lingga archipelago. A short time later Sultan Ahmad was murdered at the instigation of his father, who then resumed the throne.

Sultan Mahmud's choice of Bentan as the location for a new capital was a well-calculated move. According to the *Sejarah Melayu* the island was considered a friendly area, and it was also the home of one of the largest *orang laut* groups in the Riau-Lingga archipelagoes. With their support Sultan Mahmud hoped to oust the Portuguese from Melaka. Though this goal was never attained, the *orang laut* did make possible the re-establishment of Sultan Mahmud's court and the resumption of trade at the new site. Its success led to a Portuguese punitive expedition which destroyed Bentan in 1526. But, as in the past, the *orang laut* were summoned to fetch the ruler and to begin once again the entire process of restoration.

With *orang laut* assistance Sultan Mahmud Syah escaped the destruc-tion of Bentan by the Portuguese in 1526 and fled to Kampar in east coast Sumatra where he died. He was succeeded by his son, Sultan Alauddin Riayat Syah, who married the sister of Pahang's ruler and then established his royal residence at Pekan Tua in the upper reaches of the Johor River some time between 1530 and 1536. He therefore became the first of the Melaka dynasty to rule in what became known as the kingdom of Johor.

Brunei and Perak: Two Typical Responses to the Fall of 'Melayu' Melaka

The fall of Melaka to the Portuguese in 1511 has usually been seen as the end of a chapter in Malay history. But although it came as a considerable shock to Malays, it was simply another episode in the changing fortunes of entrepôt states in the western half of the Indonesian archipelago. As with Srivijaya in the past, there was a temporary dislocation of the centre of the kingdom but it quickly reconstituted itself under a new name in another part of its extensive territories. The only real change was the entry of the Portuguese as a power seeking in the tradition of the area to become the dominant entrepôt in the Straits. During the period of readjustment, the more ambitious and powerful of the states in the archipelago sought to inherit the mantle of power bequeathed by Srivijaya and Melaka, whereas the smaller kingdoms were preoccupied with asserting their independence and assuring their survival in a time of uncertainty.

Representative of the first type of response was Brunei, on the northwest coast of Borneo, which had a long maritime tradition. In earlier centuries two kingdoms had arisen in the same area: the first known from its reconstructed Chinese toponym as Vijayapura, and the other simply called by the Chinese toponym, P'o-ni. The northwest coast was an ideal landfall for trading ships participating in the China trade, and Chinese sources indicate that it had been frequently visited by Chinese travellers and sailors at least since the fifth century. Traders bound for China who came north on the southwest monsoon could harbour here before proceeding on to Chinese ports. From China itself, ships followed a route to the Vietnam coast and then sailed with the northeast monsoon southward to the western Indonesian archipelago or across to the northwest coast of Borneo. Chinese traders who had gone to the northern part of the Philippine Islands and had moved southward to obtain cargoes of exotic products from the Sulu archipelago would then go to the northwest coast of Borneo. Following the completion of their transactions, they would return to China or set sail to other parts of Southeast Asia on the appropriate monsoon winds.

In the early fifteenth century, P'o-ni appears to have been an independent state of some consequence. Envoys were exchanged with China, and in 1405 P'o-ni, like Melaka, became one of only four countries to receive an imperial inscription for the State Mountain. In a special ceremony the ruler of P'o-ni was invested as king with 'a seal, a commission and silks of various colours'. Relations between P'o-ni and China remained fairly regular until the end of the fifteenth century. Although there is still some debate as to P'o-ni's location, the consensus of scholarly opinion sees it as the predecessor of the six-teenth-century kingdom called 'Brunei'. Having long been a part of the international trading network, Brunei was frequented by Moslem merchants and would therefore have come in contact with Islamic teachings. The flight of many Moslem traders and perhaps even some Malay officials from Melaka after its conquest by the Portuguese in 1511 would have laid the groundwork for Brunei's conversion. Its ruler finally adopted Islam some time between 1514 and 1521. The association between Melayu culture and Islam brought Brunei within the ambience of the Melayu world, although it is possible that its early rulers were ethnically more closely related to the Bisayas and Muruts of Borneo than to peninsular Malays. According to Brunei tradition, it was around this period that the Sultan of 'Johor' (that is, Melaka) presented the Brunei court with various items to form part of its royal regalia and granted it rights over certain rivers along the northwest coast.

Islam brought prestige, a new loyal religious hierarchy, and increased trade to the Brunei Sultans, all of which had been experienced earlier by other archipelago rulers. But Islam also brought its dangers. In 1521, when the survivors of an expedition led by the Spanish explorer Ferdinand Magellan arrived in Brunei, they were impressed by the splendour of the court and by evidence that its influence extended northward to Luzon in northern Philippines. The establishment of a Spanish post in Cebu in 1565 signalled the beginning of Moslem—Christian rivalry for control in the northern area of the archipelago.

After the Spaniards conquered Moslem Manila in 1571, they directed their attention southward. The task was more formidable in the south because of the possibility that Brunei would afford protection and support to weaker Moslem rulers in the area. The ruler of Sulu, for example, was a vassal of Brunei and had himself originated from that kingdom. In 1578, however, the Spaniards successfully attacked Brunei and installed two officials as puppet rulers. What they found there confirmed earlier sixteenth-century Spanish reports of Brunei's importance. Traders from China, Vietnam, Cambodia, Ayudhya, Patani, Pahang, Java, the Moluccas, Mindanao, Sumatra and elsewhere frequented the ports, while Brunei's religious and commercial links with the southern areas of the Philippines was found to be equally strong.

Another unforeseen difficulty was European susceptibility to tropical disease. Among the Spaniards Brunei acquired a reputation for being unhealthy, and despite their wish to colonize the area the Brunei post was soon abandoned. Their campaigns here did, however, have far-reaching consequences, for they provided Sulu with an opportunity to assert its independence from Brunei. While the latter kingdom revived, maintaining an independent but cautious relationship with Spanish Manila, its political hegemony had been severely curtailed and was now limited to the regions of northern Borneo. Only its position as a vital link in the northern trade route to the Spice Islands assured it a source of revenue and hence the hope of re-establishing its former strength in the area.

The subsequent history of Brunei and northern Borneo in the seventeenth century became closely linked to that of Sulu. Their fortunes had been interwoven even earlier since these adjoining areas together produced the exotic sea and jungle products in demand by traders, especially those from China. During Brunei's period of dominance in the area, it became the central collecting point for these valued items and thus the focus of international trade. Sulu later came to challenge Brunei's position, and in the seventeenth century attained the upper hand by intervening in a succession dispute in Brunei. In return for supporting the successful claimant, Sulu obtained suzerainty over the territories north of Brunei Bay. These concessions, which were soon disputed by later Brunei rulers, comprised almost half of Brunei's territories on Borneo. More importantly, they consisted of the coastal waters and the areas along the Marudu, Magindara and Tirun Rivers in northeast Borneo which yielded the forest and sea products so much desired by foreign traders. By the eighteenth century the growing economic and political strength of Sulu was clearly seen in the allegiance it could now command from many of the *orang laut* groups formerly responsive to the Brunei court. Brunei, which had initially seized the opportunity to become a dominant entrepôt with the fall of Melaka in 1511, had now been eclipsed by its northern neighbour.

Another typical response to the fall of Melayu Melaka is exemplified by the kingdom of Perak. Like many other smaller kingdoms in the Malay world with little or no pretensions to regional overlordship, it sought only to preserve its independence and security after the demise of the major power in the area. Tin deposits along the Beruas and the Perak Rivers had made Perak much coveted by both Ayudhya and Melaka in the fifteenth century. But Perak's prominence in the Malay world was due not only to its vast deposits of tin but also to the fact that the founder of its royal house was a direct descendant of the Melaka line. Sultan Muzaffar Syah, the first ruler of the newly established kingdom of Perak, was a son of Sultan Mahmud Syah, the last ruler of Melaka. Muzaffar had been designated *Raja Muda*, or Heir-Apparent, by his father in Melaka, but in later years the latter had favoured a younger son of another wife whom he accorded the title *Sultan Muda*. This Sultan Muda then succeeded his father and became Sultan Alauddin Riayat Syah, the first ruler of Johor. The elder prince,

Raja Muzaffar, left Melaka and went first to Siak and then to Kelang where he was noticed by a trader from Perak. According to the *Sejarah Melayu*, it was the latter who brought Muzaffar to Perak and installed him as ruler.

This event marked a significant change in Perak's status. No longer was it merely one of the western territories (*rantau barat*) on the fringes of the Melaka empire; it was now a respectable kingdom ruled by a prince from the prestigious Melaka dynasty. Perak could thus take its place among more established states in the area, confident in its enhanced position as a sovereign kingdom in its own right. The founding of Perak also signified a further extension of Melayu culture, for the reign of Sultan Muzaffar Syah (1528?–1549?) brought to Perak not only members of the Melaka court, but also its customs and traditions. Muzaffar's court, established some eighty kilometres from the mouth of the Perak River, was organized in the image of Melaka. A major chief from Selangor was invited to become his Bendahara, and Sultan Muzaffar and his son Mansur are credited with creating a hierarchy of chiefs of varying ranks for the whole kingdom, generally reflecting that which had existed in Melaka. The influence of Melaka continued under its second ruler, Sultan Mansur Syah (1549?–1577?) who had been raised in the Johor court and had been sent back to Perak to rule after his father's death. As part of his policy of extending Perak's boundaries into the mountainous interior, Mansur established his capital further upstream not far from modern-day Kuala Kangsar.

Slowly wealth began to flow into the new kingdom. By the second half of the sixteenth century, Perak was able to profit from an increased demand for tin from the European traders now slowly filtering into Southeast Asia via the Cape of Good Hope. Tin was not only sent back to Europe but also used as a medium of exchange for the inter-Asian trade. Europeans and Indians began going directly to Perak to obtain this product, encouraging a more extensive mining of the rich alluvial tin deposits along the Perak River and its tributaries. As the market expanded, more people were attracted to Perak to participate in the tin mining and to share the state's newly found prosperity. In the early sixteenth century Perak had been a tiny settlement of about two hundred people, but a hundred years later it had grown to a kingdom of some standing with a population numbering more than five thousand.

Perak, however, never harboured any ambitions for economic and political hegemony in the Straits of Melaka. Its relatively small population was scattered over a vast expanse of territory and its many inaccessible settlements along the numerous tributaries of the Perak River made control from the centre a difficult task. Since some of the richest tin veins were located in the remote upriver areas, opposition to the ruler from interior chiefs able to avoid royal tolls and retain revenue for themselves was a perpetual problem. Furthermore, Perak remained basically a collecting point for local products, notably tin, and its rulers never aspired to the status of an international entrepôt like Portuguese Melaka, Johor, or the newly emergent Aceh in north Sumatra.

The weakness of Perak was always a lure to stronger powers, and from the late sixteenth century it fell under the control of Aceh. After Melaka's fall Aceh, like Brunei, had reaped the benefit of Moslem trade. It soon developed into a wealthy kingdom, able to sponsor Islamic scholars whose erudition was famous throughout the Moslem world. In 1575 it attacked Perak and, according to one Perak source, Sultan Mansur's widow and her children were brought to Aceh and her eldest son taken as a husband by the queen of Aceh. Four years later he succeeded to the throne of Aceh and sent his younger brother back to Perak to become installed as ruler there.

Relations between Aceh and Perak remained amicable until the early seventeenth century, when Perak's decision to allow the Portuguese to establish a factory and thus gain direct access to the tin supplies met with the disapproval of Aceh's powerful ruler, Sultan Iskandar Muda (1607–36). Indeed, the quarrels between Sultan Iskandar Muda and the Portuguese came to involve a number of the Malay states. Beginning in 1620 Iskandar Muda launched a series of attacks on Deli, Kedah, Perak, Johor and Pahang, wreaking havoc on these lands. The Sultan of Kedah fled to Perlis where he placed himself under the protection of the Ayudhya ruler. His country and capital city were ravished and some 7,000 people brought as slaves to Aceh. A similar fate was experienced by other Malay areas, so that at one time, according to a European observer, there were in Aceh some 22,000 slaves captured in these invasions. Of this number only about 1,500 survived their ordeal.[18]

After Iskandar's death in 1636, Aceh relinquished its hold over its peninsular conquests, except for Perak. Only after Aceh's failure to take Portuguese Melaka in 1626 and its massive naval defeat by Portuguese forces in 1629 did Perak seek to reject Aceh's overlordship. The ruler of Perak soon began to make overtures to the Dutch East India Company (VOC) which, founded in 1602, was rapidly eclipsing the Portuguese as the major European power in the area. However, despite arrangements reached between the VOC and Perak's nominal overlord, Aceh, the Dutch found it difficult to maintain control over the tin trade.

Association with the Dutch held little attraction for many Malay nobles in Perak, who saw the monopoly contracts which the Company attempted to impose as an infringement of their independence. At the same time, however, a small faction within the court was increasingly pressing for a Dutch fort in Perak as a guarantee against the ambitious

Ayudhya ruler, Narai (1657—88), whose demands were already being felt in Kedah. Rumours of an imminent Thai invasion in 1674 and 1677 made Perak more receptive to the re-establishment of a Dutch fort on Pangkor Island, opposite the Dinding River. But as soon as the danger from the north diminished, the old hostility against commercial restrictions introduced by the Dutch once again surfaced. In 1685 and again in 1689 attacks were made on the Dutch and their employees, and consequently the VOC withdrew its garrison. It says much for the lure of Perak's tin that the VOC was still willing to negotiate another treaty. However, it proved impossible to reach agreement with the Perak nobles, and for another fifty years any ties with the Dutch were virtually severed.

Despite the continuing opposition from some Perak nobles who resisted attempts to curtail their lucrative tin trade, the more perceptive court members realized the necessity of a strong ally if a weak state were to maintain its independence and survive as more ambitious powers struggled for dominance. In the late seventeenth century this was particularly true; Aceh may no longer have presented a threat, but to the north the Thais were a source of recurring anxiety.

Thai Influence in the Malay States

Historians believe that the presence of Thai-speaking peoples in the Malay peninsula is a relatively recent occurrence. Beginning perhaps about the seventh century, the Thais slowly trickled southwards from their homelands between the upper part of the Mekong River and the tributaries of the Menam River. Though originating from the same general area, they followed different routes and settled in widely scattered areas. These Thai settlements formed the nucleus of the independent kingdoms such as Ayudhya and Sukhothai which were to emerge in later centuries.

During the thirteenth century princely leaders and their followers came from an early Thai state at Phetburi to clear forests, establish ricefields and form organized communities in the southern peninsula. According to one version of the *Ligor Chronicle*,[19] the Thais then began moving further south, incorporating areas inhabited by Malay-speaking peoples. Two descendants of the Phetburi royal family who became lords of one southern region were responsible for appointing Malays to govern the Malay lands now under Thai control. Among the places mentioned in this chronicle are Pahang, Kelantan, Patani and Kedah. Ligor or Nakhon Sithammarat became the major Thai centre in the south through which Ayudhya was able to supervise its Malay vassals. In the early sixteenth century Pires speaks of the 'viceroy' of Ligor who controlled territories from Ayudhya to the Malay peninsula, including Pahang, Trengganu and Patani, 'all [of which] have lords like kings, some of them Moors [Moslems], some of them heathen'. Each area was required to send about 600 grammes of gold as tribute, the collections being supervised by two Ligor officials. Although Pires also mentions Kelantan, local Kelantan tradition suggests that in this period it consisted of two countries. Historians have inferred that the chiefs west of the Kelantan River offered allegiance to Patani, and those east of the river to Trengganu.[20]

From this early period, therefore, Ligor came to exercise a very particular form of control over the northern Malay states. A principal reason was its favourable strategic and economic position. In the second half of the thirteenth century, Ligor had already developed into the maritime outlet for the Sukhothai kingdom and was thus well-placed for any Thai penetration into the Malay peninsula. So serious were incursions from Ligor into the Malay areas in the thirteenth century that Srivijaya sought the Chinese Emperor's intercession to prevent further Thai aggression. By the mid-fourteenth century, however, Ligor had acknowledged its vassal status to Ayudhya, now the dominant Thai power, whose overlordship of many Malay areas became an established fact. In turn, Ayudhya's ambitions initiated a long period of rivalry with Melaka and its successor kingdom Johor concerning hegemony in the peninsular region. Melaka was at first willing to recognize Ayudhya's suzerainty in order to obtain both protection against more powerful rivals in the Straits and trade from its wealthy Thai overlord. But although Ayudhya had granted Melaka vassal status, it was apprehensive about the prospects of a new entrepôt in the Straits which could well challenge its own ambitions of becoming a major international trading port. In the early fifteenth century Moslem merchants from the West were already going directly to Ayudhya, auguring well for its commercial future. Delayed by its political manoeuvres against Sukothai, Ayudhya finally launched an attack against Melaka in the mid-fifteenth century in an effort to destroy this budding emporium.

Both Thai and Malay sources mention a major Thai campaign which, according to the *Sejarah Melayu*, was under the command of a provincial lord who led his troops overland through Pahang and across the Penarikan route to Muar. It seems reasonable to accept the *Sejarah Melayu*'s assertion that the Thais were repulsed, especially since Thai chronicles, though precisely dating the expedition at 1455–6, are silent on the outcome. Nonetheless, Thai aspirations to overlordship in the southern peninsula were not forgotten. An Ayudhyan Palatine Law of 1468 alludes to the campaign to justify its allegation of suzerainty over Melaka.[21] Periodically in later centuries ambitious Thai kings such as Narai (1657–88) and Rama I (1782–1809) revived the old claims.

Ayudhya dispatched no further expeditions to the peninsula for some years because of its increasing involvement in the affairs of Sukhothai. For the greater part of the fifteenth century these two kingdoms were locked in a struggle for hegemony in the Thai-speaking world and could not disperse their scarce resources in a prolonged campaign so far from home. Only during the reign of Sultan Mahmud Syah, the last ruler of Melaka, did the Thais again intervene in the Malay states, seemingly in response to what they saw as Melaka's arrogant defiance. Shortly after his accession, Sultan Mahmud attacked Kelantan, one of Ayudhya's vassals, and brought three of its princesses back to Melaka. The assault on Ayudhya's overlordship apparently did not stop at Kelantan, for the *Ligor Chronicle* mentions an attack in 1497 from 'Ujung Tanah', a term later used for Johor but in this context obviously referring to Melaka.

Other Malay states which recognized the overlordship of Ayudhya appear to have noted Sultan Mahmud's ambitions and taken appropriate action for their own preservation. According to the *Sejarah Melayu*, a Thai prince defeated a Malay ruler of Patani and became a Moslem in fulfilment of his vow to embrace Islam if given the victory. He then selected a new site for his capital and went to Melaka where he acknowledged Melaka's suzerainty and received in turn from its ruler the 'drums of sovereignty'[22] and the title Sultan Ahmad Syah. The Sultan of Kedah likewise requested and received the drums of sovereignty from Sultan Mahmud Syah of Melaka, as well as the traditional robes of honour reserved for individuals the ruler favoured. When the Sultan of Pahang died, his successor was installed by a Melaka official sent especially to supervise the beating of the drums of sovereignty during the ceremony.

Despite Ayudhya's preoccupation with Sukhothai, it could not ignore these challenges in the south and retaliated through the medium of its vassal ruler at Ligor. The *Ligor Chronicle* records that in 1500 a Thai force penetrated as far south as Kelantan but soon retreated via Patani because of rumours of yet another invasion of Ligor by Ujung Tanah (that is, Melaka).[23] The *Sejarah Melayu* also records an attack by Ligor on the northeast states which occurred some time prior to the first appearance of the Portuguese in Melaka in 1509. This may have been the same expedition mentioned in the *Ligor Chronicle*, but according to the Malay version the Thai army went beyond Kelantan to Pahang. No further mention is made of Thai involvement in the Malay peninsula until 1535, some twenty-five years after the fall of Melaka. In that year, says the *Ligor Chronicle*, the 'enemy' again came from Ujung Tanah. The enemy, now clearly meaning Johor, would have come from the new capital in the upper reaches of the Johor River which was destroyed by the Portuguese later that same year.

Ayudhya's continued expansion down the isthmus in the first half of the sixteenth century had thus impinged upon areas considered to belong properly within the sphere of the powerful kingdom of Johor, the self-proclaimed heir to all that Melaka, and Srivijaya before it, represented. Although Johor was unable immediately to challenge Ayudhya's extension of suzerainty over Pahang because of Portuguese harassment, its ties with Pahang remained close, particularly since several past rulers of Pahang had been princes from the prestigious Melaka dynasty. In the late sixteenth century Johor was again in a position to reassert its overlordship over Pahang because of Ayudhya's preoccupation with the threat from the Burmese kingdom of Taunngu. In 1564 and 1569 Ayudhya was defeated by Taunngu, and for the rest of the sixteenth century it was subject to repeated invasions from both Taunngu and Cambodia.

Ayudhya's wars with its two neighbours diverted attention from the Malay vassals, with predictable results. Patani, the dominant Malay state in the north, seized the opportunity to attack the weaker Kelantan and extend its own territory. Only with the accession of Narai (1657–88) as ruler of Ayudhya were the Thais able to reimpose their former suzerainty over the northern Malay kingdoms.

A powerful and prestigious Ayudhya was able to protect its Malay vassals from outside attack and raise the status of small Malay kingdoms. However, this association had its price. A strong Ayudhya was far less willing to tolerate defiance by a Malay ruler and was more likely to challenge its own traditional enemies — Burma, Cambodia and Vietnam. Prolonged warfare meant that Ayudhya's vassal states, whether in Lower Burma, Laos or the Malay peninsula, were expected to demonstrate their loyalty by willingly dispatching men, food and weapons to service Ayudhya's large armies. Even in times of peace the tribute demanded by Ayudhya was considerable. Submitted triennially, this tribute was known collectively as the *bunga mas dan perak*, 'the gold and silver flowers'. It consisted of two small trees, fashioned from gold and silver, and standing about a metre high. An eyewitness account in the early twentieth century describes the creation of the gold and silver trees, faithful replicas even to the birds in their branches, and attests the meticulous workmanship involved in these works of art. Accompanying the trees were other costly gifts, weapons, cloth and slaves for both the ruler of Ayudhya and the provincial governor at Ligor, who was in charge of escorting the tribute to the Thai capital. Although the value of the *bunga mas* in earlier times is uncertain, nineteenth-century evidence notes that its total worth was in the vicinity of a thousand Spanish dollars.

The necessary funds for the *bunga mas* were raised by the imposition of a poll tax, which local chiefs, both Malay and Thai, at times abused to enrich their own coffers. But even prompt payment of the *bunga mas* did not relieve the Malay states of their vassal obligations. Ligor, Ayudhya's principal administrative centre in the south, could and did demand burdensome corvée duties and tributary gifts. In 1821, for example, an English envoy to the Thai court remarked that Kelantan, Patani, Kedah and even Pahang had contributed to the cost of constructing a great Buddhist reliquary in Ligor. Thus, while Malay court chronicles gloss over the deep resentment which Thai over-lordship aroused among the peasants, it is small wonder that at the village level tales abound of the greed of Thai kings.

Little is known of the origin of the *bunga mas dan perak*, or its precise significance. Trengganu Malays attribute the first sending of the golden flowers to the late eighteenth century when the royal merchant suggested this as a suitable present for the Thai king. In Kelantan, too, the custom appears relatively recent, and a Thai chronicle notes that tribute had only been sent regularly since the early nineteenth century.[24] In Kedah and Patani, however, it had become an established custom at least by the seventeenth century. According to one legend recounted in a Kedah court text, the *Hikayat Marong Mahawangsa*,[25] the royal families of Kedah and *negeri Siam* (that is, Ayudhya) had in the past been closely related and the *bunga mas* had been originally sent as a gift from the Kedah court intended as a plaything for a Thai prince. But whereas Ayudhya saw the dispatch of the *bunga mas* as Malay recognition of its suzerainty, a seventeenth-century Kedah ruler claimed that it was a demonstration of friendship and alliance rather than an acknowledgement of vassal status. When Ayudhya was weak, some Malay kings delayed sending the *bunga mas*, perhaps for several years. But at the first sign of a revival of Thai power, missions were quickly dispatched with the *bunga mas* for their overlord. This unique practice was only ended with the extension of British control over most of the northern Malay states in 1909.

The great strength of the Thai–Malay relationship was the mutual understanding that, however onerous Thai demands might be, the Malays would be left to conduct their own affairs and be treated with the respect due to independent kings, not simply provincial governors. In 1645 when the Kedah ruler was uncharacteristically summoned several times to Ayudhya, he feigned illness and did not go. It would have been humiliating for a Malay ruler to have submitted to the pros-tration ceremony customary at the Thai court and demanded of all other vassals. But rather than sending an army to punish the Kedah ruler, the king of Ayudhya found an acceptable solution by sending a statue of himself to Kedah with instructions that the entire court should pay it homage twice daily.[26]

Ayudhya was thus willing to allow Malay kings to rule with mini-mum interference as long as they duly submitted their tribute. This

factor, combined with their distance from the Thai capital, allowed
Ayudhya's Malay vassals considerable political flexibility. In effect,
they were able to operate within two distinct geo-political spheres,
each with different sets of rules. One sphere was that of Ayudhya,
where certain obligations were demanded in return for protection and
patronage. As Malay culture developed and expanded, however, the
Thai milieu became increasingly alien, concerned with a diplomacy
where the Malay vassal remained peripheral to the overlord's central
priorities. The other sphere was that of the Malay world itself, where
Malay kingdoms conducted their affairs as independent states vying
with one another for greater prestige in the area. For Ayudhya's Malay
vassals, this was always the environment of real importance. Ayudhya,
like China in earlier centuries, belonged to another realm and, like a
powerful spirit, had to be appeased so that the more immediate world
could function with greater harmony.

The complexities involved in being linked to two cultural worlds
are well illustrated in the history of Patani. The gradual extension of
Thai control here in the eighteenth and nineteenth centuries, and
international recognition of its incorporation into Siam proper in
1909, often lead modern historians to overlook Patani's traditional
role as a leader in Malay resistance to Thai overlordship. During the
latter part of the sixteenth century Patani had been relatively free
from Thai restraints and developed into an important trading centre,
drawing considerable wealth from local commerce in pepper, gold and
foodstuffs. Unchallenged by any other Malay kingdom, Patani was
able to assume a prominent place in Malay affairs. Aceh was only
slowly becoming a major power in the Straits, and Johor was effectively checked by the Portuguese in Melaka. Through marriage between
a Patani princess and a Pahang ruler, Patani became increasingly involved with Pahang and through Pahang with Johor. By 1620 marriage
alliances and practical politics had pushed Patani to attempt a balance
between the influence of Ayudhya and Johor by endeavouring to
maintain friendly relations with both. In 1628, however, the outbreak
of disturbances in Ayudhya coincided with threats of an invasion by
Aceh. In this situation Patani's court decided to link its fortunes firmly
with Johor. Raja Ungu, queen of Patani (1623–35), refused to use the
Thai title *Phra-cao*, as had been customary among her predecessors.
She provoked Ayudhya by marrying her daughter Raja Kuning to the
ruler of Johor, although the princess's former husband, a Thai officer
(probably the eldest son of the governor of Ligor), was apparently still
alive. When a Thai prince, Prasat Thong, usurped the throne of Ayudhya in 1630, Patani openly defied its overlord and attacked Ligor
and Phattalung. Ayudhya did not react immediately to these challenges
because it was already preoccupied with its troubles with Cambodia,
Burma, and the Japanese community in Ayudhya itself. Finally in

1634 a Thai punitive expedition of some 30,000 troops was sent, whereupon Patani sought and received help from the Malay kingdoms in the south, including fifty ships and 5,000 men from Johor and Pahang. Patani and its Malay allies succeeded in repulsing the invaders, but another Thai expedition was under way when Raja Ungu died. Her successor prudently sought the mediation of the ruler of Kedah in order to bring about a reconciliation with Ayudhya. Prasat Thong accepted this peace offer, and subsequently Patani resumed its *bunga mas dan perak* tribute to Ayudhya, while its new ruler, Raja Kuning, once again assumed the Thai title *Phra-cao*.

At the same time, Patani's ties with the Malay world were undergoing some strain, despite Raja Kuning's marriage to the Johor ruler's younger brother. The increasing arrogation of power by the Johor prince and his entourage aroused much disaffection in the Patani court and eventually in 1645 led to a massacre of many of the Johor people, including the prince's mother. A mission of reconciliation sent to Johor by Patani towards the end of that year averted war, but relations between the two states remained cool.

Patani's history exemplifies the dilemma faced by the northern Malay states. The very independence which the nature of Thai overlordship permitted them often tempted Malay rulers to repudiate some of their vassal obligations, in turn incurring harsh retribution. The relationship between Thai and Malay kingdoms was thus never static, but was constantly undergoing reassessment according to the circumstances of the moment. But the northern Malay states during this period were never able to conduct their affairs with the independence and confidence of the other Malay kingdoms further south. Johor, for example, was able to seize opportunities as they presented themselves in the Malay world and in the seventeenth century became one of the most powerful states in the Straits of Melaka.

The Dutch and Johor's Ascendancy

Johor's position in the Malay world gradually improved in almost direct proportion to the growing importance of the Dutch in these waters. The appearance of the first Dutch trading ships at Banten in west Java towards the end of the sixteenth century was part of an expanding Dutch trade in the 1590s to the Mediterranean, the Levant, the South Atlantic and the Indian Ocean. The profits gained from the sale of pepper obtained at Banten spurred the development of a number of trading companies in the various Dutch port cities. But it soon became evident that the rivalry among these companies was hurting trade, and in 1602 they were amalgamated into the United Netherlands Chartered East India Company, often referred to as the VOC (Vereenigde Oostindische Compagnie). In its charter the VOC was given wide-ranging sovereign powers, such as the right to enter into treaties and alliances, wage war, levy troops, erect forts and appoint governors and judicial officers. These powers, coupled with a substantial operating capital and the blessings of the Dutch government leaders, many of whom were Company directors as well, made the VOC a formidable organization in Asia. In the last quarter of the seventeenth century the Company was further strengthened by its decision to retain part of its profits in Asia, which was used judiciously at selected times and places to ensure a continuing maximization of returns on various commercial ventures. Overseeing this vast trading empire in Asia was the VOC's Supreme Government composed of the Governor-General and the Council of The Indies based in Batavia (present-day Jakarta). Founded in 1619, Batavia became the nerve centre of the VOC in Asia, assimilating reports from various outposts and factories and making decisions based on the interests of the Dutch trading network as a whole rather than on the immediate concerns of any individual area.

From the first contact with the Dutch in the beginning of the seventeenth century, Johor saw them as a potential ally against its two most hated enemies, Aceh and the Portuguese. Johor had suffered devastating raids throughout the sixteenth century by these powers, both of whom aspired to dominate economic and political affairs in the Straits of Melaka. From the very beginning of their relationship, the VOC and Johor quickly realized their mutual benefits in co-operating against their common enemies.

A change of fortune for Johor began in 1636 with the death of Aceh's aggressive ruler, Sultan Iskandar Muda, and with the VOC decision to seek the assistance of Johor in an assault on the Portuguese citadel at Melaka. The siege of Melaka commenced in August 1640 and was successfully ended in January 1641. Although Johor's forces did not participate in any major fighting, they played an important supporting role in transporting material, constructing batteries and trenches, preventing the enemy from fleeing into the jungle and, most importantly, in lifting sagging Dutch morale at a very crucial time during the siege. In 1643 the Dutch Governor-General Antonio van Diemen, writing to the VOC Directors, clearly expressed this sense of indebtedness: 'We must continue to remember that the Johor people contributed substantially towards the conquest of Melaka. Without their help we would never have become master of that strong place.'[27]

In acknowledgement of this assistance, the Dutch granted Johor certain trading privileges at Melaka which were denied all other local kingdoms. The Dutch also assured Johor of protection against its great rival, Aceh. Through Dutch mediation Johor and Aceh signed a peace treaty in 1641 in which the two powers agreed that 'each occupy his own kingdom . . . and all hostile actions be stopped'. By this treaty and the conquest of Melaka, Johor was freed from Portuguese and ιcehnese threats which had plagued it for more than a century. Shortly afterwards a bolder Johor removed Aceh's presence from Pahang and again reasserted its control there. With renewed vigour and a revived sense of purpose, Johor sought to regain its former status in the Malay world. Attracted by the greater variety of goods and cheaper prices, traders flocked to Johor, while Dutch Melaka soon became simply one of a number of archipelago ports helping to fuel the bustling Johor entrepôt. Dutch officials in Melaka continually begged Batavia to destroy Johor so that Melaka's trade could revive but their pleas were rejected. The VOC leaders had already decided to make Batavia the centre of all economic operations in the Company's vast Asian trading network. Melaka's task was henceforth to be a guardpost protecting shipping through the Straits and not an international emporium as it had been in the past.

Johor soon realized that the VOC's wider interests would override Melaka's parochial concerns. It therefore began to send missions directly to Batavia whenever there was a difference of opinion with Dutch officials in Melaka. In Batavia its envoys subtly indicated that any Dutch punitive measures against Johor would result in the flight of the court and re-establishment at another site, probably in the islands among its *orang laut* subjects. From here the *orang laut* would be sent to harass all ships passing through the Straits and to divert them from Dutch ports. Batavia considered this prospect with dismay and therefore often sided with Johor at the expense of Melaka.

Johor's revival was due in part to the benefits accruing from its alliance with the Dutch. To a far greater extent, however, Johor owed its recovery to the services of two powerful ministerial families, those of the Bendahara and the Laksamana. The influence wielded by individual ministers has been noted previously in Malay Melaka. According to ideal prescriptions of Malay statecraft, the ruler remained above the mundane affairs of state, leaving his ministers to carry out the practical duties of administration. By adhering to this model, the position of the ministers as mediators between the ruler and the outside world allowed great scope for personal aggrandizement. In periods of crisis in the kingdom, ministers frequently assumed considerable authority. In the *Sejarah Melayu*, probably commissioned by a Melaka Bendahara, the activities of the Bendahara overshadow all other ministers. Nonetheless, the importance of the Laksamana's office cannot be ignored, especially in times of war, for it was he who commanded the *orang laut* fleets so vital for the defence of the kingdom. The closeness of the Laksamana—*orang laut* association is suggested by the legend that Hang Tuah, the most famous Laksamana in Malay folklore, was himself of *orang laut* background.

The Laksamana family rose to prominence in the sixteenth century during the dislocation resulting from the Portuguese conquest of

Melaka. Johor, Melaka's direct heir, was forced repeatedly to move its capitals in the face of attacks from Aceh and the Portuguese. Led by the Laksamana, the *orang laut* were responsible for establishing Johor's ruler at a new site and then redirecting trade to its port. In so doing, they ensured the preservation of the kingdom and the international trade which was its lifeblood. Not surprisingly, many of the new capitals chosen were among the islands of the Riau-Lingga archipelagoes in the *orang laut* heartland. Under these circumstances, the Laksamana's duties became far more vital to the kingdom than those of the Bendahara.

The individual perhaps most responsible for Johor's rise in the seventeenth century was Laksamana Tun Abdul Jamil, who succeeded his father some time in the 1640s. The opportunity to serve his kingdom while furthering his own ambitions came with the destruction of Johor by Jambi in 1673. Sultan Abdul Jalil (1623–77) took refuge in Pahang, but instructed the Laksamana to re-establish the kingdom. It was the Laksamana, therefore, working from a secure base among Johor's *orang laut* in Riau, who succeeded in wreaking vengeance on Jambi, restoring Johor's status in the Malay world, and establishing his family in the most influential positions in the kingdom.

Nonetheless, the wars with Jambi had taken their toll, for the razing of Johor's capital weakened its authority over its dependencies. This trend was most apparent among the Minangkabau settlements of Naning, Sungai Ujung and Rembau, whose origins may date from the early years of the Melaka kingdom. Over the years, however, they had developed a system of government distinct from that in Minangkabau and had accepted Melaka and then Johor as their overlord. In 1641 the Dutch had assumed control over Naning in Melaka's hinterland, but in 1677 all three territories had rejected the authority of their respective overlords. Their leaders requested and received a representative from their spiritual Minangkabau overlord at Pagarruyung in the mountains of Central Sumatra to rule the three settlements as one entity. This representative was known as Raja Ibrahim, and he claimed to possess many of the supernatural attributes associated with his Pagarruyung lord. For Malays the creation of the new Minangkabau grouping further increased the regard in which they were already held. As one English trader later remarked, 'Malays consider the Minangkabau to have the character of great sorcerers, who by their spells can tame wild tigers and make them carry them whither they order on their backs.'[28] But it was the Dutch who felt the real impact of Minangkabau solidarity as Raja Ibrahim called for a unified front against the VOC. For the first time in the history of the Minangkabau settlements on the Malay peninsula, a broad-based Minangkabau movement had appeared, one which was now directed against the alien Europeans.

Rumours of Raja Ibrahim's plans were taken seriously in Melaka and Johor because in recent years the movement of Minangkabaus to the east coast of Sumatra had increased markedly. Ten years earlier, in 1667, the Dutch had forcibly removed Aceh's control over both east and west coast Sumatra. As a result, the long-bridled traders in the Sumatran interior began transporting their goods down the rivers which originated in the uplands of the Minangkabau interior and flowed eastward out to the Melaka Straits. Foreign traders were now frequenting ports along the Siak, Rokan, Kampar and Inderagiri Rivers in order to buy gold, pepper and tin from the Minangkabau traders. Within a short time large numbers of Minangkabaus, attracted by the renewed possibilities of trade with the outside world, started to move eastward into the *rantau* (areas of Minangkabau settlement outside the Minangkabau heartland in central Sumatra). Some even crossed the Straits and joined their compatriots already established in the areas of Sungai Ujung, Naning and Rembau.

The growing migration of Minangkabaus to the Straits region in the second half of the seventeenth century also coincided with a renewed vigour within the Pagarruyung court due to VOC victories against Aceh. With both the east and west coasts of Sumatra freed from Aceh's control, Pagarruyung's spiritual influence over its subjects was restored. During the late seventeenth and early eighteenth centuries, Pagarruyung was often invoked by Minangkabau leaders to impart legitimacy to their cause and attract support from all Minangkabau in the *rantau*.

Raja Ibrahim, the most successful of a succession of such leaders, appealed to the Minangkabau of Rembau, Sungai Ujung and Naning on the basis of their common culture and overlord in Pagarruyung. At the same time another Minangkabau ruler in upriver Inderagiri was urging his people to rise against the Dutch. However, the two Minangkabau causes never became united, and Raja Ibrahim was forced to broaden his appeal. He therefore called for all fellow Moslems to combine against the infidel Dutch, hoping to attract the support of Bugis and Makassar settlers in Kelang. But the summons of Islam proved insufficient to overcome the Bugis/Makassar suspicion of the Minangkabau. In the event, even the latter did not support Raja Ibrahim wholeheartedly, and in 1678 he was murdered, apparently by a Bugis in the pay of some people from Rembau. With Raja Ibrahim's death, any possibility of a coalition between the Minangkabau settlements on the Malay peninsula faded, and shortly afterwards they reverted to their Malay and Dutch overlords. Only in the late eighteenth century did another effort to form a Minangkabau confederation finally succeed.

Although the Bugis and Makassar settlements had not responded to Raja Ibrahim's call for a holy war (*jihad*), the Dutch were concerned at the increasing numbers of Bugis/Makassar migrants from South Sulawesi fleeing from the civil wars in their homeland. When the VOC combined with some Bugis lords from the kingdoms of Bone and

Soppeng to defeat neighbouring Goa in 1669, there was a wave of refugees from the vanquished kingdom and its allies. Wars continued to plague South Sulawesi for the next decade, and the unrelenting overlordship of the Bugis prince Arung Palakka and the VOC further contributed to a steady outflow of people seeking refuge. Moving westwards, bands of Bugis and Makassar refugees led by some prince or noble began settling in Java, Jambi and Palembang. Here they frequently came into conflict with local authorities, and subsequently Bugis leaders preferred uninhabited lands where they could be guaranteed a certain amount of autonomy. The southwest and east coasts of Borneo and the sparsely populated but economically valuable tin areas of Selangor, Kelang and Linggi on the peninsula suited them admirably, and it was here that pockets of Bugis/Makassar settlements began to grow.

In the late seventeenth century, Johor had become the pre-eminent power in the Straits and felt little threatened by the small Bugis and Makassar communities which had sprung up in its peninsular dependencies. Through the perseverance of the skilled Laksamana, it had succeeded in wreaking vengeance on Jambi and restoring Johor's trade and prestige in the Malay world. So powerful had the Laksamana become that Sultan Ibrahim, who succeeded Sultan Abdul Jalil in 1677, was wary of his influence. Accordingly, the new ruler initiated steps to curtail the Laksamana's authority by encouraging other nobles to take a more active role in the kingdom's affairs. Only Ibrahim's unexpected death in 1685 prevented a potentially dangerous confrontation with the Laksamana. When the five-year-old ruler, Sultan Mahmud Syah, came to the throne, the Laksamana's family was securely ensconced in power. The young ruler sat on the lap of his mother, the Laksamana's daughter, and was surrounded by the Laksamana and his six sons, who all held important posts in the kingdom.

The Laksamana family appeared unassailable, but its strength was dependent on its ability to demonstrate that it was governing on behalf and with the blessings of the ruler. Sultan Ibrahim's death, under extremely suspicious circumstances, eliminated the only potential challenge to the influence of the Laksamanas for nearly a century. The succession of a child ruler under the tutelage of the Laksamana family seemed to reinforce its position as guardian and yet servant of the king. But the other nobles and the Bendahara family understood full well the reasons for the influence of the Laksamana and took measures to undermine it. One fateful day they snatched away the young ruler, breaking the association between him and the Laksamana and demonstrating to the *orang laut* that the supposedly all-powerful minister no longer had royal sanction. This move was sufficient to draw the *orang laut* away from the Laksamana to the camp of the plotting Bendahara and nobles. Within a day the Laksamana family had to flee to safety, bereft of their armed following and the authority which they had so long wielded. Though some of the Laksamana's sons escaped to Patani, the Laksamana himself died fighting.

The demise of the Laksamana family saw the restoration of established roles within Johor. The offices formerly held by the Laksamana's sons once again reverted to the nobles, while the Bendahara assumed his traditional position as the principal minister of the kingdom and rightful role as regent for the young ruler. During this regency period, Sultan Mahmud remained quietly in the background. But with the death of the Bendahara towards the end of the century and with Sultan Mahmud's coming of age in 1695, there were noticeable changes in Johor. The new Bendahara, Tun Abdul Jalil, was unable either to control the excesses of Sultan Mahmud and the atrocities he committed against his subjects, or to direct royal attention to matters of government. With no leadership from the capital, the *orang laut* began to prey on passing ships for their own profit. The lack of security in the Straits and the absence of leadership in Johor led to a sharp decline in Johor's international trade. Fearing further cruel or unpredictable actions by Sultan Mahmud, and resenting their loss of revenue as trade in Johor's ports dwindled, the nobles finally felt impelled to act.

The nobles' decision to end the life of Sultan Mahmud was made with deliberation and yet with apprehension. Despite the Sultan's cruel and unjust deeds, court traditions firmly upheld the view that only God Almighty could punish rulers, especially those descended from the Palembang—Melaka dynastic line. But as Sultan Mahmud, borne on a servant's shoulders, passed through the market on the way to the mosque, one of the nobles stabbed him. No sooner had he fallen to the ground than he was set upon by the other plotters and killed. This regicide in 1699 undermined a very basic assumption about the relationship between Malay rulers and their subjects, and also severed the crucial allegiance which the *orang laut* had personally given to all previous rulers of the Melaka dynasty.

From the establishment of Malay Melaka at the beginning of the fifteenth century till the regicide of Johor's Sultan Mahmud in 1699, the Malay kingdoms had acted and reacted to various external stimuli very much in the tradition of Srivijaya and earlier kingdoms along the Straits of Melaka. Attracting international commerce was crucial for the continuing well-being and lifestyle of such kingdoms, and hence the whole governmental apparatus and rationale for rule were created to assure the smooth functioning of trade. The memories of a mighty kingdom in Palembang served as an inspiration to Melaka and to other kingdoms striving to inherit the mantle of principal overlord and emporium in the Straits. Melaka's founders appeared to have been well versed in the requirements of an entrepôt, prompting one scholar to remark that 'Melaka was founded as, rather than developed into, a trading port'.[29]

With Melaka's fall to the Portuguese in 1511, the situation again reverted to that which followed the demise of Srivijaya. The more powerful kingdoms sought to establish their own entrepôts, while the smaller states enjoyed a period of political and economic independence rarely possible under a strong regional overlord. Unlike the earlier period, however, there were now two new actors on the scene: the Portuguese and the Dutch, both seeking to dominate trade in the area. Despite considerable power exercised by these two newcomers, they were unable by the end of the seventeenth centure to monopolize trade in the same way as had Melaka and Srivijaya before them. Yet their restrictive practices, plus the restraints placed on the Malay states by their belligerent Thai neighbours, served to prevent the rise of another Malay kingdom which could emulate its great predecessors. Johor could legitimately claim to be the direct link to Melaka and did succeed for a time in becoming a port of importance. However, the regicide in 1699 changed the nature of power in Johor and made it vulnerable to new external pressures which came to redirect the entire course of Malay history in the eighteenth century.

3

The Demise of the Malay Entrepôt State, 1699–1819

The decline in Johor's standing in the Malay world after the events of 1699 led to the rise of a number of newly independent states, several of which had once been part of the old Johor empire. No kingdom emerged immediately as a dominant force in the Straits, able to maintain a degree of order in regional trade and politics. Without an acknowledged overlord, individual states now had greater freedom in seeking their own political and economic goals. To nineteenth-century observers, however, a situation where various rulers were attempting to assert their independence or supremacy appeared 'chaotic' and symptomatic of the 'decay' besetting the Malay world. It was therefore with the claim of 'restoring order' to the area that the British came to justify their intervention in Malay affairs. But an examination of events in the Malay world in the eighteenth century indicates that such rationalization ignores the cyclical pattern of alternating unity and fragmentation which had characterized Malay—Indonesian commerce and politics for well over a thousand years.

The Eighteenth Century: Historiographical Considerations

The primary source material for the eighteenth century, both European and Malay, is unevenly distributed, and some areas are particularly ill-served. The history of the east coast peninsular states may never be adequately reconstructed because of the sporadic nature of European trading records and the paucity of relevant Malay texts from this area. Events in what is now Sabah and Sarawak are even more obscure. Court dynastic lists from Brunei, the nominal overlord in the area, and isolated commentaries by Western visitors convey only a broad outline of developments. In the early eighteenth century the Spanish renewed their efforts to subdue and Christianize the southern Philippines, but were never successful. The rising economic and political power in the northern Borneo region was the Sultanate of Sulu, which continued to expand in response to both the Spanish advance and to Brunei's decline. Conflicts between the Brunei ruler and some of his nobles had earlier resulted in Sulu's control over the northeast coast of modern Sabah, while Brunei itself slowly relinquished authority over the Bajaus, the local sea people, and lapsed into a collection of riverine territories ruled by semi-autonomous chiefs. The inadequacy of written sources from northwest Borneo in this period has frustrated historians, who have only recently begun to appreciate the value of indigenous oral material like the chanted genealogies of the Sarawak Ibans.[1]

Turning to Johor and the west coast of the peninsula, we find that there the historical sources stem from a very different tradition. The basic chronology is still provided by the VOC records, supplemented towards the end of the century by those from the English East India Company (EIC). There are also several works written in Malay. Frequent reference will be made to the *Tuhfat al-Nafis* (*The Precious Gift*), written in the mid-nineteenth century by Raja Ali Haji, a Riau prince of Bugis descent whose aim was to explain the relationship between his Bugis forebears 'and the kings of Johor and Sumatra'. Another text from Siak, which has been called the *Siak Chronicle*, gives a different view of events as perceived by the Minangkabau Malays of east Sumatra. Added to these are notebooks of daily happenings in the Johor court, collections of treaties signed with the Dutch, and compilations of customary laws. In the eighteenth century one Perak ruler commissioned a court work, the *Misa Melayu*, and fragments of texts and recorded legends have also survived from Selangor and Kedah. Certainly many valuable manuscripts have been lost, but enough remains for the modern historian to discuss the history of Johor and the west coast during this period with some confidence.

The Consequences of Regicide in Johor

One striking feature is the degree to which so many of these sources, whether indigenous or European, confirm the shattering effects of Sultan Mahmud's murder in late July or August 1699. A hundred years afterwards a Dutchman was told that Malays considered Mahmud the last direct descendant of Raja Iskandar Zul-karnain (Alexander the Great) and Sri Tri Buana, one of the princes who had miraculously appeared on Bukit Si Guntang in Palembang. He was therefore remembered as Sultan Berdarah Putih, the King of the White Blood, to distinguish him from his successors who lacked this same evidence of true royalty. Even a nineteenth-century Thai chronicle considers the death of Mahmud to be a momentous event, for after that 'his lineage disappeared and was never heard of again'.[2]

At the time, eyewitnesses informed the Dutch that the assassination had been carried out by a group of nobles, which included the Bendahara. Malay histories single out the individual responsible for the fatal blow, a man called Megat Sri Rama whose pregnant wife had been disembowelled at Sultan Mahmud's orders. But though contemporary European accounts corroborate Malay texts in describing the Johor ruler as a vindictive sadist, Malays found the regicide difficult to condone; it was, after all, *derhaka*, treason, which merited the most terrible of punishments. According to the *Siak Chronicle*, Megat Sri Rama was struck on the foot by the ruler's spear. Because of *daulat*, the spiritual powers associated with kingship, grass began to sprout in the wound and for four years Megat Sri Rama suffered agony before he finally died. The text goes on to describe how one of the nobles denounces those guilty of murder and delivers an impassioned speech, reiterating a subject's duties and the obedience he owes his lord. But his words go unheeded, and he is killed. The most vehement condemnation of the regicide came from the rulers of Palembang and Perak, who shared with the kings of Melaka–Johor a common tradition of descent from the sacred princes of Bukit Si Guntang. They appealed to the VOC to wreak vengance upon those responsible for this heinous crime, but to no avail.

The gravity of the deed was accentuated because the assassinated Sultan Mahmud had no direct heirs, thus enabling the conspirators to appoint a new ruler. In September 1699 the Bendahara was chosen as ruler of Johor with the title Sultan Abdul Jalil Syah. Some texts attempt to justify this by pointing out that the kings and Bendaharas of Johor had intermarried and that custom decreed a Bendahara should succeed if there were no suitable royal princes. Other manuscripts invoke the Islamic ruling that it is permissible to depose an insane ruler. But Malay society, imbued for centuries with concepts of the divine status of the kings of Bukit Si Guntang, could not easily accept the changed order. Nowhere was the animosity towards the new regime greater than among the *orang laut* whose role in Melaka and Johor had been traditionally linked to their special relationship with the ruling dynasty. Several groups now claimed that 'there were no more descendants of the old royal house [that is, of Bukit Si Guntang] and therefore there could no longer be a ruler of Johor'. Others said publicly that they would rather serve the Sultan of Palembang than a usurper, and there were even rumours of an *orang laut* invasion of Johor. But despite their initial revulsion, most *orang laut* groups realized that they would have to reconcile themselves to the new regime or be excluded from the influential association they had maintained with the Melaka–Johor kingdom for over three hundred years. Although the majority of *orang laut* eventually resumed their former functions under the Bendahara dynasty, their ties with it were always tenuous.

Elsewhere in Johor territory the legitimacy of the Bendahara line was also challenged. In the ensuing years continuous revolts disturbed the peace along the east coast of Sumatra, in Deli, Rokan, Batu Bahara

[handwritten marginalia: K + R / au cities / r maies / in Rembau?]

and Inderagiri, and in Johor's peninsular dependencies of Selangor, Kelang and Rembau. Inevitably this disturbed situation discouraged commerce, and VOC officials noted with pleasure the degree to which Dutch Melaka had benefited from traders seeking an alternative market.

Added to these internal troubles came news of Ayudhya's advance down the peninsula in 1709. Temporarily halted at Patani, the Thai army invaded Johor's dependency of Trengganu in the following year. Johor made preparations for a possible attack, but fortunately Ayudhya's forces were withdrawn and deployed eastwards because of Vietnamese incursions into Cambodia. Nonetheless, Ayudhya remained a potential danger and the new regime in Johor was thus confronted with the task of rebuilding a state which was divided from within and threatened from without. One of the first steps it took under the dynamic leadership of Sultan Abdul Jalil's brother, the Raja Muda, was to move the capital away from the Johor River to the island of Riau, the home of those *orang laut* groups who had returned to serve the new regime. Here the Raja Muda began to re-create an entrepôt, exploiting Johor's privileged status with the Dutch, a result of their 1641 alliance, to divert trade away from Melaka. VOC officials looked with envy towards the port of Riau, which was crowded with 'Moors, Armenians, English, Danes, Portuguese and other nations'. In the words of the *Tuhfat al-Nafis*, 'Johor prospered, and was famed not only for the refinement of its customs, but also for its culture [*bahasa*]'.[3]

Johor's ability to revive an entrepôt economy so rapidly in the wake of regicide is a tribute to not only the determination of its leaders but to its long experience in international trade. Situated at the strategic crossroads of maritime traffic, the Riau harbour offered the same attractive environment that had drawn trade in the past — an international market, good portage and stapling facilities, readily available credit, and an administration which welcomed foreign merchants. Like so many earlier ports, Johor's new capital at Riau also became an important Islamic centre, with scholars from Gujarat and the Arab world expounding religious precepts to the faithful. For the first two decades of its existence, therefore, the Bendahara dynasty conducted itself according to established traditions and appeared no different from its predecessors. In other circumstances, Johor's increasing wealth and prestige as a centre of Malay–Moslem culture might have compensated for the manner in which the new regime had gained power. But the enormity of the crime of *derhaka* had opened deep wounds within the kingdom which no riches or status, however great, could heal. This crack in the façade of unity and well-being was unfortunately quickly detected and exploited with momentous consequences by two migrant groups in the area: the Bugis of South Sulawesi and the Minangkabau of Sumatra.

Bugis Influence in the Malay States

The eighteenth century has often been called 'the Bugis period' of Malay history. As we have seen, Bugis and other South Sulawesi groups had been arriving in the Malay areas since the last quarter of the seventeenth century. Leaving South Sulawesi in the wake of protracted civil wars, they had attempted unsuccessfully to settle in such places as Sumbawa, Lombok, Bali and Java. Conflicts with local authorities led to further Bugis migrations westwards in search of areas which would be free from the exactions of an overlord. Relatively unpopulated and lightly governed areas in Sumatra and the Malay peninsula provided an ideal refuge. During the late seventeenth century a number of Bugis settlements had sprung up along the west coast of the peninsula in the Johor dependencies of Selangor, Linggi and Kelang.

The Dutch in Melaka indiscriminately grouped these migrants together, ignoring the fact that they were from different tribes (*suku*) and kingdoms, and were sometimes mutual enemies. Quarrels among their leaders were by no means rare, and they were never the monolithic force depicted by both European and Malay observers. But in time the Bugis did develop a remarkable cohesion and an intense loyalty to their cultural heritage, a natural response when Malay society challenged their position in the Malay world. New waves of migrants from South Sulawesi and frequent contacts with the homeland helped the Bugis sustain a pride in their identity still found in Malaysia among those of Bugis descent.

At first Malay kingdoms did not regard the Bugis as a threat, since they could be an asset to rulers aspiring to greater economic and political power. Bugis navigational and commercial skills were highly valued, for the widely flung Bugis trading connections stretched from the Spice Islands across the Indonesian archipelago and beyond. As Francis Light, the founder of Penang, wrote in 1794, 'They are the best merchants among the eastern islands... The great value of their cargoes ... make their arrival wished for by all the mercantile people.'[4] Bugis patronage of a port could be a key to its success.

The Bugis appeared equally useful as fighting men, a commodity always in great demand in the Malay world. Their renown as formidable warriors, their awe-inspiring chants and war dances, and their chain mail armour, injected a new element into the conduct of warfare in the area. The support of Bugis mercenaries in conflicts between Malay princes could in many cases help tip the balance in one combatant's favour. In the later seventeenth century, for instance, one Kedah prince declared that with 'two ships and three or four hundred Bugis he could set himself up as king of Kedah'[5] and in 1710 the Raja Muda of Johor employed Bugis troops to help suppress a revolt in

Batu Bahara. The Dutch too recognized the fighting skills of Bugis warriors and they were an important component in the VOC's armies.

An alliance with a Bugis migrant leader could thus make a significant contribution to the economic and political strength of a Malay ruler. As time went on, however, the very presence of these semi-autonomous communities raised fundamental questions about their acceptance of the traditional ruler—subject relationship which lay at the heart of the Malay polity. Although the Bugis paid a nominal allegiance to their Malay overlord, they were governed by their own Bugis leaders. Initially they were able to exist on the periphery of Malay society, but as the migrant Bugis communities expanded this separate existence was no longer possible.

The first event to test the Bugis relationship to a Malay king occurred in 1715 following a succession dispute in Kedah. The details are not altogether clear, but it seems that a younger brother of the Kedah ruler recruited the assistance of the Selangor Bugis, promising them a certain quantity of tin for their services should he be the victor. When the prince failed to fulfil his promise, the Bugis responded by invading Kedah, razing the countryside and seizing a great deal of booty. Malay custom decreed that in such a case half the spoils of war should be surrendered to the overlord, in this case Johor. Conflicts developed after the Bugis refused to comply, not because they denied the ruler's right to a share, but because in their homelands Bugis were traditionally required to give up only a tenth. An angry Raja Muda, acting on behalf of the Johor ruler, immediately sent troops to attack the Bugis strongholds of Selangor and Linggi, but this force was soon repelled.

This Bugis refusal to bow to Johor's demands was only one of several revolts against the new regime which had broken out in Johor territories since Mahmud's death in 1699. This particular confrontation was significant, however, first because it was based on a cultural misunderstanding, and secondly because it demonstrated that Johor's armies, though numerically superior, were no match for the Bugis. Campaigns continued for another two years and invariably Johor's forces were defeated. The Raja Muda was finally forced to acknowledge that he no longer wielded any authority over the Bugis areas in Selangor.

The unsuccessful wars fought by Johor and its loss of the Bugis-occupied territories on the peninsula were but the prelude to further developments which divided not only Johor but the entire Malay world. In 1717 a certain Raja Kecil appeared in Siak, one of Johor's outlying territories in east coast Sumatra, claiming to be the son posthumously born of Sultan Mahmud, assassinated in 1699. Far from being dismissed as pure fabrication, many Johor subjects seized on Raja Kecil's claim as the long-awaited sign for the renewal of Johor's fortunes and the restoration of its former strength and prestige. The kingdom had been riven with hatred and distrust following the 1699 regicide and now was facing defiance from its Bugis subjects. The claims of Raja Kecil raised widespread hopes that the rightful dynasty would return and harmony would again prevail. The *orang laut* flocked to Raja Kecil in their hundreds, accepting him as the miraculously preserved son of their murdered lord, a prince of the old Melayu line come to avenge his father's death. With the Minangkabau spiritual overlord in Pagar-ruyung providing his blessing to Raja Kecil, the latter's claim was also cloaked with a legitimacy Malays appreciated. According to Malay tradition, the kings of Minangkabau were descended from one of the princes who had appeared on Bukit Si Guntang, and therefore shared similar origins with those who came to rule in Melaka.

Raja Kecil appeared in the Riau River in early 1718 with a large Minangkabau force and was met in battle by the Johor fleet. But in the initial encounter between them the *orang laut*, who formed the backbone of the Johor navy, deserted to Raja Kecil and were joined by a number of other prominent Johor nobles. With all resistance overcome, Raja Kecil was able to capture the Johor capital on Riau and proclaim himself ruler. He then married one of the daughters of Sultan Abdul Jalil, whom he demoted to his former position of Benda-hara. The latter, finding this new situation intolerable, fled to Treng-ganu where he set up an alternative court composed of local nobles as well as others from Pahang and Kelantan.

There were now three loci of power in the Malay world: Raja Kecil in Riau, Sultan Abdul Jalil on the peninsular east coast, and the Bugis in Selangor and Linggi. Ultimately, however, it was the Bugis who were to emerge triumphant. Raja Kecil lost much support not only by inexplicably killing some of the principal *orang laut* leaders but also by having Sultan Abdul Jalil murdered. He then proceeded to attack the Bugis in a number of sea battles in which his opponents' mastery of maritime warfare became obvious. As the *Tuhfat al-Nafis* explains, many of Raja Kecil's men were from the Minangkabau interior, accus-tomed to river paddling rather than the ocean. Their actual fighting ability could not match that of the Bugis, and the latter were soon able to force Raja Kecil out and become masters of Johor.

The Bugis leaders realized the need to re-establish a measure of royal authority in Johor as a focus for Malay loyalty. As outsiders they would be unacceptable, and so in 1721 they installed as ruler the twenty-year-old prince Sulaiman, son of the assassinated Sultan Abdul Jalil. By this act they laid the grounds for the later Bugis 'justifying myth' — that is, that they had been recruited by Sulaiman and had come to his assistance when he was abandoned by other Malay kings. Having had no part in Sultan Mahmud's murder, and without the same cultural abhorrence of *derhaka* as Malays, the Bugis found no difficulty in giving Sulaiman their support. But the guilt of Sulaiman's father was still fresh in the mind of many Malays, who also realized that

Sulaiman now had little influence in Johor. The Bugis had all assumed exalted titles and one, Daeng Marewa, had even been named Yang Dipertuan Muda (shortened by the Bugis to Yamtuan Muda). In Malay states this title, roughly meaning 'junior ruler', was traditionally given to the heir to the throne. Daeng Marewa had then married the virgin widow of the murdered Sultan Mahmud. It was, moreover, apparent that Sulaiman himself resented his position as a figurehead. A little over a year after Daeng Marewa's installation Sulaiman wrote to the Governor of Melaka asking to be 'rescued' from the Bugis. The extent to which he had been deprived of all effective power is aptly summed up in an eighteenth-century Bugis chronicle from Johor. 'The Yang Dipertuan Besar [that is, Sultan Sulaiman] is to be like a woman. When food is given to him, he may eat; and the Yang Dipertuan Muda is like her man. Should any question arise, it is he who is to decide it.'[6] Even allowing for the anti-Bugis attitudes often expressed in Dutch reports from Melaka, it is clear that Bugis influence rapidly extended to all areas of government. A Dutch Governor writing in the mid-eighteenth century described Sultan Sulaiman as 'a puppet, who must dance to the piping of the Yamtuan Muda and his Bugis following'.[7]

While the Bugis were consolidating their hold in Riau-Johor, they were subject to periodic attacks from Raja Kecil from his base in Siak. But the Bugis managed to maintain their position, eventually forcing Raja Kecil to abandon any hopes of recovering the kingdom. Meanwhile, leadership of the Bugis in Riau-Johor came under the control of a small group of closely related men. In 1728 when the Bugis prince Daeng Marewa died, the post of Yamtuan Muda passed without opposition to his brother, Daeng Cellak (1728–45). Gradually other contending Bugis factions in the Malay peninsula were pushed aside, despite their efforts to withstand those in power in Riau. In Linggi, Topassarai, an uncle of the queen of Bone in Sulawesi, had attempted to strengthen his position by assuming the title of Sultan. In 1732 he even offered the VOC all Linggi's tin if it would support his bid for power. Another prince from the kingdom of Wajo, also in Sulawesi, joined Raja Kecil's son, Raja Alam, in an effort to assert authority over Selangor. Through the 1730s the battlelines between different Bugis groups moved back and forth contending for control of the rich tin areas of Selangor, Kelang and Linggi. By 1743 these were all firmly in the hands of the Riau Bugis, with Selangor itself regarded as the appanage of the Yamtuan Muda family.

In less than three decades after Mahmud's death the nature of power in Johor had once more been radically changed. Not only had the Sultan himself lost any real authority; the Malay nobles found that unless they were willing to co-operate with the Bugis leaders they too had little influence in government affairs. In sum, it was probably the *orang laut* who were most affected. From the days of Palembang they had always held a privileged and valued place not only in the actual economy but also in the administration of the realm. Honoured with titles, entrusted with duties such as leadership of the war fleet and guardianship of the ruler's chambers, they had now found themselves replaced by the Bugis seamen whose navigational and fighting skills quickly made redundant most services the *orang laut* could render. The only area in which they still played a vital role was in the procurement of sea products. Even more significant was the fact that the *orang laut* no longer had a specific focus of loyalty. Some followed Raja Kecil to Siak, but others could not accept a move away from their familiar haunts in the Riau-Lingga archipelagoes to the alien mangrove swamps of east Sumatra. Among the latter group some again submitted to the new Johor dynasty, and a court notebook records numerous occasions when Sulaiman personally sailed out to encourage the *orang laut* to return. Yet others simply retreated to islands like Siantan in the South China Sea and, bereft of their former functions, took to raiding passing ships outside the authority of any court. For all *orang laut*, however, their proud and ancient status had gone. Whereas the founder of Melaka had been pleased to marry his son to the daughter of an *orang laut* chief, at the beginning of the nineteenth century a Malay writer described them as filthy, repellent, little better than animals.

The changes which had taken place in Johor meant that there was no longer the same reason for Malays to ascribe to its rulers a special status because of their descent from a semi-divine prince who had appeared on Bukit Si Guntang in Palembang. The new dynasty's direct links with the old Melaka line had been forever severed, weakening Johor's formerly exalted status among Malay kingdoms. The Malay world by the 1750s was in some ways reminiscent of other periods like the early seventh or fourteenth centuries, when the direction of an overlord was lacking and a number of states had the opportunity to assert their own individuality. Although the loosening of ties with a central authority has led some to describe the period as one of 'fragmentation', this process did not necessarily entail a loss of morale or purpose, as is apparent from a closer examination of developments outside Johor.

Developments in the Peninsula outside Riau-Johor

Though the sequence of events in other Malay states during the first half of the eighteenth century is not as well documented as in Johor, it is obvious that for some this was a significant period in their history. At the time of Mahmud's murder Trengganu had no fleets and only five hundred fighting men, but it had a well-established reputation as a supplier of pepper to junks from China and *perahu* from the eastern archipelago. Trengganu's status as one of Johor's more valuable dependencies was enhanced in 1718 when Sultan Abdul Jalil fled there from Riau to escape further humiliation at the hands of Raja Kecil. Setting up his own court in defiance of Raja Kecil, Sultan Abdul Jalil distributed many titles among local nobles, bringing Trengganu into the centre of Johor politics and giving its chiefs a greater sense of participation in Malay affairs. Trengganu continued to receive the attention of the Johor court even after the Bugis were established on Riau. It may have been to strengthen Trengganu's ties with Johor that Zainal Abidin, a brother of the late Sultan Abdul Jalil, was installed as the first ruler of Trengganu in 1722. Following his death eleven years later, his youngest son, Raja Mansur, was taken under the protection of Sultan Sulaiman of Johor. Raja Mansur was brought up in the Johor court and later married Sulaiman's daughter. When the young prince came of age in 1741, Sulaiman installed him as Trengganu's second ruler.

Little is known of events within Trengganu during this period. The sources focus primarily on the activities of Sultan Mansur (1741–93) who lived on Riau from 1750 to 1760, leaving Trengganu's administration in the hands of his uncle. We can infer something, however, about Sultan Mansur himself. As a king of impeccable Malay pedigree who was both cousin and son-in-law to the Johor king and whose mother was a Patani princess, Sultan Mansur was implacably hostile to the Bugis arrogation of power in Riau-Johor. During his ten years' residence on Riau he led Malay opposition to the Bugis, staunchly defending the interests of what he called 'the Malay nation'. Even after his return to Trengganu in 1760 he actively sought to unite all Malays against the Bugis.

At the same time, Sultan Mansur obviously had personal ambitions for a greater role in Malay politics. At one stage he was intent on assuming the throne of Johor itself and wresting it from Bugis control. At home, he extended his influence northwards into weak and divided Kelantan, which he attacked in 1764. Initially he attempted to support Kelantan princes as his representatives but after continuing resistance he eventually installed his own son, married to a Kelantan princess, as Kelantan's ruler.

The effectiveness of Sultan Mansur's government depended on strong central control, for the possibility of opposition from chiefs in the isolated areas of Besut and Kemaman, or in the interior region, was always present. Contemporary European accounts praise Sultan Mansur's well-ordered administration and the respect in which his subjects held him, and his personal stamp on Trengganu's history is attested by the legends about him which still survive. Even as a child, it is said, he demonstrated remarkable powers. According to one story, a learned man of religion officiating at Sultan Mansur's birth predicted that he would be a famous ruler who would rid the seas of pirates. Had it not been for the renewed Thai threat after 1782, Trengganu might conceivably have moved to fill the political vacuum left when Johor lost its position of leadership.

With the rise to power of another dominating and equally long-lived ruler, Sultan Muhammad Jiwa (died 1779), Kedah also took a more active part in Malay affairs. Events immediately prior to his reign are impossible to reconstruct in detail, but it is apparent that civil war in Kedah had been endemic since the late seventeenth century. The confusion of these decades is reflected in the conflicting accounts found in Dutch and Malay sources. Both the *Tuhfat al-Nafis* and the *Siak Chronicle* mention a prolonged war between the king and his younger brother, while VOC sources record actually two major conflicts, one in 1715 involving the Bugis and another in 1723–4 which drew in both Bugis and Minangkabau. It is unclear whether the protagonists were the same on both occasions, for neither Dutch nor Malay sources give their names. It is reasonable to assume that Sultan Muhammad Jiwa played a prominent role in the second war, for some time around the middle of the eighteenth century he emerged from the background of civil strife to become ruler of Kedah. A coin minted in his reign has been found with the Moslem date 1154 (1741–2 A.D.), although the precise year of his accession is unknown. It seems that his victory was not easily won, and he may, as the *Tuhfat* claims, have initially relied on Bugis arms. The internal conflicts in Kedah at the beginning of his reign presaged the periodic outbreak of short-lived rebellions led by rival princes which are briefly mentioned in VOC records.

Despite undercurrents of opposition, Sultan Muhammad managed to retain control of his throne until his death. He is remembered in Kedah tradition as a hero in the classical Malay image, a man of great courage who in his youth journeyed to Palembang, Java and India with a learned teacher. Returning in triumph to Kedah, he reputedly established customary and Islamic law codes, organized an administrative hierarchy, and laid the basis for organized government. European sources depict him as a man of independent mind who, in order to maintain an open port, persistently refused to sign a commercial contract with the Dutch. With its direct trading links to India, Kedah's economy thrived, supported by its brisk trade in pepper and its exports of rice in a rice-deficient peninsula. Nineteenth century Kedah Malays remembered how Sultan Muhammad Jiwa was also able to alleviate the burden of tribute to Ayudhya by reducing the amount of gold used in the *bunga mas* and limiting the accompanying presents. His independent policies were probably encouraged by Ayudhya's weakness. Occupied by protracted wars with Burma, Thai kings did not press their claims to overlordship in the northern Malay states until the 1770s.

In Perak the 1699 regicide in Johor served to enhance the status of Perak's ruling house which, as a Perak text implies, could now be regarded as the sole heir to old Melaka. But Perak could never lay claim to the same wealth, power and prestige possessed by either Melaka or Johor. The kingdom was torn by civil war in the first four decades of the eighteenth century, with rival princes supported by different chiefs hoping to seize the throne and thus gain control of revenue from the lucrative tin trade. These quarrels were complicated by the ambitions of the Selangor Bugis and the Minangkabau. Both groups were willing to assist one or another of the warring factions in order to extend their influence into Perak. In 1743 dissatisfied Perak chiefs allied with the Selangor Bugis to oust the reigning Perak ruler, Sultan Muzaffar (died 1752). In his place they installed the Raja Muda, who was in reality manipulated by his son, the dominating Raja Iskandar.

In the wake of this conflict, Perak was effectively divided into two. Retreating inland, Sultan Muzaffar retained control over the *ulu* (up-river) districts, leaving the lower reaches of the Perak River to Raja Iskandar. Attempting to reassert his position, Sultan Muzaffar recruited Minangkabau help but he still could not dislodge Raja Iskandar and his Selangor Bugis allies. With Muzaffar denied access to the sea, and Iskandar unable to reach the tin-bearing highlands, both sides reached a reluctant reconciliation. Yet Sultan Muzaffar remained adamantly opposed to Iskandar's eventual succession as ruler and therefore secretly contacted the VOC. In return for a VOC tin monopoly in Perak, Muzzaffar wanted Dutch assurance that his daughter and Raja Kecil's son, who were betrothed, should accede to the Perak throne after his own death. It was on this understanding that a contract was signed in 1746, permitting the Dutch to construct a lodge and maintain a small garrison in lower Perak to supervise tin deliveries. From the outset the contract was under fire from Perak chiefs and princes wishing to sell their tin for higher prices elsewhere. However, the majority of the court valued the prestige and protection which came from Dutch friendship. Despite recurring tensions in VOC–Perak relations, such as the threat by one ruler in 1773 to join with Selangor, the alliance endured until the British assumed control of Melaka in 1795.

A major benficiary of the Dutch alliance was Raja Iskandar himself. When Raja Kecil's son fell from favour, Raja Iskandar married Sultan Muzaffar's daughter and was reinstated in royal favour. Although he had initially opposed the contract, he decided to renew it after his accession in 1752. His reign was a time of unprecedented peace in Perak, for the VOC alliance guaranteed protection from outside attack and strengthened the ruler's hand against potential rivals. Sultan Iskandar was also able to take advantage of opportunities provided by the prosperity from uninterrupted trade. He travelled widely throughout Perak, appointing his personal representatives in isolated areas like Larut and Kuala Kangsar and giving the kingdom a sense of royal authority it had never before known. A major development in his reign was a shift of power away from the ministers to the royal princes. It was Sultan Iskandar who made the position of Bendahara a prerogative of the prince third in line to the throne rather than of a noble family. The sources also suggest that such actions were not undertaken lightly and that Sultan Iskandar saw himself as part of the continuum of Malay history. The court text he commissioned, the *Misa Melayu*, tells the story of his rule but it was obviously modelled on accounts of great rulers in the past like the king of Aceh, Iskandar Muda (1607–36). Even Sultan Iskandar's adoption of the honorific Iskandar Zul-karnain (Alexander the Great) was a reminder that Perak kings claimed descent from the princes of Bukit Si Guntang. His reign stands out as a high point in Perak history and in Perak today is still remembered as a *zaman mas*, a golden age.

The importance of leadership in providing a focus for government becomes apparent in Perak's history after Iskandar's death in 1765. The two brothers who succeeded him in turn were not of his calibre and under them the challenge to royal power resurfaced. Now princes and even the principal ministers became involved in the smuggling of tin, bypassing not only the Dutch monopoly but also royal tolls.

More telling examples of the effects of weak rule are found in Patani and Kelantan, where the eighteenth century could well be regarded as a period of fragmentation. From about 1688 a dynasty originating from Kelantan ruled Patani, but factional disputes continued to undermine stable government, driving away the traders who had formerly brought Patani such wealth. Conflicts worsened as differing royal groups sought to curry favour in Ayudhya or to gain assistance from one of the Thai governors in the southern provinces. By 1730 central control had collapsed, the gravity of the situation eliciting a terse comment in the *Hikayat Patani*: 'Patani has been in great confusion and its people suffer from many ills, while rules and customs are no longer observed.'[8] Despite a proud sense of being Malay, Patani at the end of the eighteenth century was in no position to withstand the revitalized and belligerent Siam, successor to Ayudhya.

In Kelantan too there were continuing problems of leadership. For the greater part of the seventeenth century Kelantan was divided into small districts controlled by chiefs. In about 1730 a move towards greater unity was made when a royal family with strong Patani connections attempted to extend its rule over the state. But rebellions persisted, and even though the exploits of individual princes are recalled in Kelantan legends the country was ill-prepared to deal with the threat of invasion. In 1746, when a Thai attack was believed to be imminent, a Riau text notes the arrival of envoys from Kelantan requesting Riau-Johor's assistance. Any temporary unity this impending danger might have brought to Kelantan was soon dispelled when the renewal of Burmese power in 1752 under the Konbaung dynasty diverted Thai attention. Continual warring amongst Kelantan's princes coincided with incursions from Patani chiefs to the north, making outside intervention almost inevitable. In 1764 Sultan Mansur of Trengganu, allied with a force from Siak, launched what was probably the first of several campaigns into Kelantan. Subsequently he installed his protégé, a Kelantan prince named Long Yunus, as Raja Muda. His own son, married to a daughter of Long Yunus, was made ruler of Kelantan.[9] This occurred some time before Sultan Mansur's death in 1793, and not until 1800 did a local prince with the aid of Chinese from one of the mining settlements oust the Trengganu faction. He then assumed the throne as Sultan Muhammad I (ca. 1800–37). A Chinese description from the 1780s indicates that the local economy, based largely on gold-mining, was not markedly affected by the conflicts within the ruling class. Nonetheless, Kelantan's political history during most of the eighteenth century is an example of the vulnerability of a state caught up in continuing internal strife.

Economic and Political Challenges in the Eighteenth Century

Economically, the eighteenth century is more appropriately regarded as a time of new opportunities and challenges rather than of decline. The prospects for international trade had rarely been better. In 1729 the Chinese emperor lifted the oft-flouted prohibitions against junk traffic with Southeast Asian ports, and the expanding China trade reflected the great demand for forest and marine products from the Nan Yang. The revenue Malay rulers derived from the China trade is evident in the numerous royal monopolies, ranging from rattans to the more exotic birds' nests used in Chinese soups.

Trade with China was made even more profitable because of the growing European participation, primarily due to the popularity of Chinese tea in Europe. By the beginning of the eighteenth century tea, like coffee, had become a social beverage and the demand seemed almost insatiable. Europeans had difficulty in acquiring sufficient quantities of tea because they found Chinese merchants uninterested in the goods Europe could offer in exchange. Silver was naturally acceptable, but this was a heavy drain on bullion. Another solution was to transport cargoes of Indian cloth and opium to the Malay world, and barter these for tin and spices, which were valued items on the China market. The Malay world had long been an important transhipment area, but to Europeans in the eighteenth century it became a linchpin in the valuable China tea trade.

Europeans preferred to deal in tin and spices because, unlike the Chinese, they did not have sufficient specialized knowledge to select high quality cargoes of forest and marine products. Furthermore, Malay tin was preferred in China to that from England since it was more malleable and could be beaten to the fine foil required for lining tea chests and for ritual burning. With large quantities of tin available, especially in the west coast peninsular states, virtually every estuary from Kedah down to Singapore was a potential supply point for passing European traders seeking to overcome the VOC's monopoly treaties with the tin-producing states of Perak, Rembau and, across the Straits, Palembang.

Malay pepper also had a high reputation abroad and became another important item in European trade with China. Because the Dutch monopolized trade with the Spice Islands, the pepper of Borneo and the peninsula was one of the few spices available outside the sphere of VOC control. Kedah, with access to the 'pepper island' (Pulau Lada) of Langkawi, had long been an important source of the spice for traders coming from India. Trengganu pepper was especially favoured in China, being considered superior to any other in the archipelago and cheaper than that from Malabar. Not surprisingly, both Sultan Muhammad Jiwa of Kedah and Sultan Mansur Syah of Trengganu actively sponsored trading ventures, sending out cargoes of pepper on their own ships.

The expanding international market stimulated a widening search for fresh sources of tin and gold, the most valuable of the local products. In Rembau in 1769, for instance, gold mines were opened, while a contemporary Chinese work entitled *Hai-lu* (*Record of the Seas*) mentions several gold-producing settlements in the Kelantan and Pahang interior, accessible only by braving treacherous rapids and swift-flowing mountain streams. During the latter half of the century major tin lodes were also discovered on the island of Singkep in the Lingga archipelago, on the Perak—Patani border, in Larut, and elsewhere in Perak and Selangor. Throughout this period one has the impression that slowly but inexorably hitherto little frequented areas are becoming known as sources of some valued product.

But developing economic opportunities often opened the door to unforeseen political and social problems, especially in terms of royal authority. As settlement fanned out to develop natural resources in the hinterland, Malay rulers encountered in a more urgent form the whole question of territorial control. Many of the valuable gold mines and rich tin lodes of the isolated mountain regions were located in areas between states where forest dwellers moved freely back and forth and where only legend established the limits of control. When the economies of neighbouring states began to expand in response to growing commerce, disputes over territory inevitably arose. Malay rulers were entitled to a percentage of profits from mining or agriculture, and it was therefore important that any claim to territory be publicly recognized. A longstanding conflict, for instance, arose between Perak and Kedah regarding ownership of the Kerian River, a valuable tin area, and it was not settled in Perak's favour until the middle of the nineteenth century.

Obviously it was not sufficient merely to claim suzerainty over large tracts of land, especially if these were far removed from the royal residence. Effective territorial control demanded a stable administration and officials who would loyally represent a ruler they might not see for a year at a time. On the calibre of these district chiefs could hang the allegiance of an entire local population which in terms of manpower was an economic resource as valuable as the richest tin mine. In Kedah alone, the collection of birds' nests from Langkawi was said to require a thousand *perahu* and 4,500 men annually. Elephant trapping in the northern states involved huge numbers of men to clear the jungle for an enclosure, drive the animals towards it, and subsequently tame them. A useful measure of the manpower required simply to build an elephant enclosure is suggested by the eighteenth-century *Hai-lu*'s account of elephant trapping in Trengganu; the text mentions the necessity of 'clearing out the big trees in a ten-mile [16-km] circle and building a fence around this area'.[10]

It was of prime importance for a Malay ruler to harness these human resources. Economic expansion, therefore, was normally closely followed by extension of political authority aimed at tying distant settlements more closely to the centre. Malay and Dutch records from Perak contain a detailed and probably typical account of the appointment of *ulu* chiefs who, entrusted with wide administrative powers, were also charged with the general supervision of local tin collections. Ties between *orang asli* and Malays may have been tightening during this period as Malays became increasingly active as middlemen in the transport of jungle products. In Selangor, says the *Hai-lu*, mountain aborigines were 'controlled by the king of the country' and took their goods to trade with the Malays; according to the same text, contacts between some *orang asli* and Malays in Kelantan were such that the former were even prepared to bring their disputes to the ruler for adjudication.

Undoubtedly, in most cases local administration functioned smoothly, but the tension between the centre and periphery which recurred in the archipelago on a wider scale was also prevalent in smaller territorial units. Local revenues, frequently considerable, made it possible for an ambitious chief to acquire a fair degree of independence, and geographical distance enabled him to virtually ignore the existence of his suzerain. As a result, the potential foci of allegiance for the peoples of the Malay world multiplied. An *orang laut* headman of an island like Siantan could essentially operate as an autonomous chief, while in northwest Borneo nobles could oppose the Brunei ruler with impunity, especially as royal authority in districts where property was inherited (*tulin*) was strictly limited.

The difficulties involved in asserting central control were compounded in border areas where inhabitants had traditionally learned to reconcile the often conflicting demands of two masters. As links with local centres became stronger, such compromises were less feasible, and border disputes were commonly expressed in terms of regional rivalries — Patani men against those of Kedah, Kelantan against Trengganu. The recognition of a shared cultural Malay identity with its roots in the Melaka kingdom did not mean that regional differences were less strongly felt. It was not necessarily easy, therefore, for a Malay ruler to impose his political authority over an area where the population saw him as an outsider. Thus in 1764, when Sultan Mansur of Trengganu invaded Kelantan, he purportedly said that he had not come as a conqueror but to place 'a prince of Kelantan' on the throne. In Perak, after a district head from Patani usurped control over lucrative tin mines near the northern border, Sultan Alauddin (1774–92) explained that he himself could do nothing because the person involved was 'not a Perak man but from Patani'. By the same token, the lengthy correspondence about piracy carried on between the Dutch and Malay rulers often hinged on the origins of the raiders themselves, for only thus could they be brought to justice.

There were always those who disclaimed association with any court, and such individuals posed particular difficulties. A feature of the Malay world during this period is the number of wandering *anak raja* (sons of princes) who for various reasons rejected the authority of their rulers. Too numerous to be absorbed into the court administration, the extensive royal offspring resulting from the custom of polygamy had been an endemic problem in Malay courts. In the eighteenth century they attracted greater attention because widespread succession disputes, especially in Siak and Kedah, led to a marked increase in dispossessed *anak raja*. In this situation, a longstanding custom in Malay courts suffered serious abuse. For generations it had been accepted that princes unable to support themselves on the ruler's bounty (*kurnia*) could take to sea raiding, while observing royal guidelines as to what ships they could attack and where. Now, however, many princes were roaming the seas as independent pirates. In the eighteenth century the growing *orang laut* piracy, which had been an indirect consequence of the Johor regicide in 1699, was augmented by the raiding of undisciplined *anak raja* beyond the reach of a responsible ruler. Their activities did not stop at piracy, and many were ready to act as the focus for other discontented elements. They and their followers were ripe for conspiracy or revolt. Previously such princes could have found few allies willing to risk men and arms on some dubious adventure, and rarely were rebellions against an established ruler successful. What now made these fugitive princes a far greater threat was the Bugis who, as in Kedah and Perak, could be enticed to lend their fighting skills in return for promises of material and/or political rewards.

The eighteenth century thus presented Malay states with economic opportunities, yet at the same time also witnessed the proliferation of challenges to political authority that often defied solution. But one continuing feature was still the strength of Melayu culture which, despite regional variations, bound the Malay states of the peninsula and east Sumatra together. The individual experiences of each Malay area had inevitably meant local adaptations of customs, dress and dialect, but such differences were still incorporated in the concept of Malayness. Whatever the difficulties faced by Malay rulers in exercising political control over other Malays, there was at least a shared language, religion, belief system and an acceptance of the traditions governing ruler–subject relations. This did not exist in the same way for non-Malays who, in response to expanding economic prospects, were now much more evident in the region.

The Growing Influence of Non-Malay Groups in the Peninsula

Most Malay states had a growing Indian population, many of whom were Moslem traders from the Coromandel Coast. Among them were men who moved easily between the two cultures and the case of an Indian trader mentioned in the *Misa Melayu* who had 'one wife in India and one in Perak' was by no means uncommon. Some of these traders were incorporated into Malay courts, taking up influential intermediary positions such as scribe or interpreter and thus serving to reinforce the key role of Indians in Malay commerce. In several states, and especially Kedah, the wealthy Indian community formed a powerful faction whose interests were not always in accord with those of the ruler.

Another influential group was the Arabs, particularly those from the Hadramaut. They traded extensively in the archipelago where they were granted special commercial privileges because they were of the same race as the Prophet. Towards the end of the century a part-Arab, Sayid Ali, even became ruler of Siak. Europeans viewed Arab influence with concern, and in 1750 a Dutch Governor of Melaka complained at the extent to which they had penetrated Malay society. He would probably have agreed with a later comment by Francis Light that the

Arabs were 'unwilling to yield to any authority . . . good friends and very dangerous enemies'.[11]

Economic opportunities in the Malay states also attracted large numbers of migrant Chinese, swelling the small existing Chinese communities, some of whom could date their predecessors to the Melaka period. They had intermarried with Malays, producing a mixed Sino-Malay or Baba society with its own distinct characteristics, the Chinese in Melaka being a prime example. The Chinese communities each had their own Kapitan China, appointed by the Dutch in Melaka and elsewhere by the Malay rulers. Though control generally presented no problem, the seeds of change can be seen as Chinese migration increased, their settlements became larger, and newcomers moved into occupations formerly dominated by Malays. In earlier times most Chinese migrants had been traders or shopkeepers, but now there was a growing emphasis on miners and agriculturalists. Trengganu's pepper plantations were by the middle of the century largely in the hands of Chinese who, according to a Thai chronicle, had been encouraged to settle there by the ruler. In the 1730s Daeng Cellak, the second Yam-tuan Muda, brought Chinese coolies to Riau to develop gambier, a tanning agent also used in medication. The gambier plantations there became almost totally a Chinese concern. Large numbers of Chinese had come to Riau after the Chinese uprising in Batavia in 1740, and forty years later the population included at least 4,000 Teochew and 1,000 Hokkien. Elsewhere the Chinese population was also growing. The *Hai-lu* notes that in Kelantan there were Chinese gold miners from Kwangtung and traders and pepper growers from Fukien, while English reports from the same period mention a settlement of Chinese pepper planters in Brunei. In Selangor, Fukien and Kwangtung settlers worked in tin mines, and from 1777 the ruler of Perak and the Dutch collaborated in recruiting indentured Chinese labourers from Melaka to exploit newly discovered tin fields. It was not long before these Chinese miners themselves introduced innovations in mining and smelting techniques which were to give them a tight grip on the industry in later years. Already there were complaints by Europeans of the secret society and clan rivalries which became enmeshed with Malay politics in the nineteenth century.

The Minangkabau were yet another group to respond to the economic opportunities in the Malay peninsula in the eighteenth century. There were already sizeable settlements of Minangkabau who in earlier centuries had selected the peninsula as an area for *merantau*, the Minangkabau practice of temporary or permanent residence abroad for a spiritual or economic purpose. The focus of their migration remained the *rantau* districts of Naning, Sungai Ujung and particularly Rembau. This was the nucleus of what later came to be called Negeri Sembilan, the Nine Lands.[12] Until ceded to the Dutch in 1758, Rembau remained in theory under Johor, but in fact only paid nominal allegiance to its Malay overlord. Despite the renewal of an ancient contract between the Minangkabau ruler in Pagarruyung and Johor in 1725–6, in which the former relinquished authority over his subjects in the *rantau* areas, the Minangkabau settlements on the Malay peninsula retained strong cultural links with their homeland in Sumatra. A loose affiliation bound the peninsular Minangkabau communities together, but there is little information in Dutch sources about the development of their varying political systems, which were superimposed on a complex social system based on matrilineal descent. The customs associated with matrilineality were known as *adat parapatih* (Malayized to *adat perpatih*), while those practices more closely related to Islamic laws of inheritance and succession, particularly with regard to royalty, were codified in the *adat katumanggungan* (Malayized to *adat temenggung*). Within the Minangkabau states themselves the strong influence of the clans (*suku*) meant that rivalry for leadership was often bitter. After Raja Hadil of Rembau died in 1778, the territorial heads and clan leaders attempted to govern 'Rembau' (then meaning much of present-day Negeri Sembilan) jointly, but by 1780 hostilities between two factions over the choice of a new Dato Penghulu had broken out. The disruption to the tin deliveries was so great that, notwithstanding their reluctance to interfere, the Dutch in their role as overlord felt compelled to send an investigative mission. At one point the Melaka governor even contemplated persuading some Minangkabau prince from Sumatra to come to Rembau as ruler to ensure greater co-operation there. More research into Dutch records is needed to establish whether the Sultan Ahmad ibni Raja Bayang elected as paramount ruler in 1785 was from Sumatra or locally born. As yet no individual has emerged in VOC sources who can be definitely identified with the legendary Raja Melewar, popularly believed to have been installed in 1773 as the first ruler of Negeri Sembilan. But it is perhaps premature to suggest that this folk hero arose from myths surrounding Daeng Marewa, the first Bugis Yamtuan Muda (1721–8), despite the similarity in names.[13] Some future study may trace in detail the process by which the Minangkabau areas on the peninsula became so politically distinct that by the end of the eighteenth century there was no way in which the former relationship with their Johor sovereign could have been reforged.

In the same period the Bugis in Selangor broke away from Johor and set up an independent state. During the 1730s the Riau Bugis had asserted control in Selangor and had made it the special appanage of the acknowledged heir to the Yamtuan Muda post. From 1740 to 1760, when relations between Malays and Bugis in Riau were often extremely tense, Selangor was a convenient place of retreat where local Bugis welcomed their compatriots from Riau. By the middle of the century Selangor's administration had taken on a character of its own, with a form of government which borrowed certain aspects from South Sulawesi. Considerable power lay with a small group of nobles, the *orang tua* or elders, resembling the *Hadat* or governing council of the Bugis state of Bone rather than the large assembly of nobles as in other Malay states. The office of Suliwatang, which in the Bugis homelands was a military title, became in Selangor a senior position of great influence.

In 1745, when Yamtuan Muda Daeng Cellak died, his son Raja Lumu was designated as Selangor's future ruler, but during his minority a Regent was appointed. For nearly two decades, until Raja Lumu came of age, this Regent and the Suliwatang controlled Selangor's affairs. In 1766, together with his nobles, Raja Lumu took the momentous step of declaring Selangor independent of Riau-Johor. To signify his independence, the new ruler, now called Sultan Salehuddin (1766–82), requested the sanction of the Sultan of Perak, acknowledged to be a descendant of the old Melaka line. The Perak ruler then presented him with the Malay mark of royalty, the *nobat* or drum of sovereignty, to signify his new status. Selangor had by no means set aside its Bugis cultural heritage, but its leaders had clearly seen the need to reach some accommodation with the Malay environment of which they now formed a part.

Despite the persistence of enmity among the Bugis, Malays and Minangkabaus, the distinction between their ruling classes became increasingly blurred. Migrant groups gradually adopted Malay, and Malay titles were used rather than Bugis or Minangkabau honorifics. This merging was reinforced because from time to time political alliances sealed by marriage were made among the three groups. The intricacies of the blood ties which had developed a generation after the Bugis installation in Riau in 1721 are well illustrated in Siak. Because Raja Kecil and several Bugis leaders had married daughters of Sultan Abdul Jalil of Johor, they were, though sworn enemies, also brothers-in-law. Raja Kecil later established his own dynasty in Siak, but after his death some time in the 1740s the throne was disputed between his two sons, each of whom could draw on differing sources of support. One, Raja Alam, could appeal to the Bugis through his marriage to the sister of Daeng Kamboja, the Bugis Yamtuan Muda from 1745 to 1777. Raja Alam also retained links with the old following of his father, Raja Kecil, and was able to appeal not only to the Minangkabau of east coast Sumatra and Rembau, but also to several *orang laut* groups. Raja Muhammad, Raja Kecil's other son, was more closely associated with the Malays because his mother was Sultan Sulaiman's sister. Inevitably, these bonds of blood and marriage conflicted with the obligations imposed by other alliances.

Extensive intermarriage meant that the conflicts in the area cannot be characterized as simply one ethnic group versus another. Some Riau Malays like the Temenggung had acquired Bugis relations through marriage and therefore felt bonds of loyalty pulling them in opposing directions. Nor was Malay leadership in complete agreement. Although Sultan Mansur Syah of Trengganu saw a sharp division between Bugis and Malays, several Malay nobles were willing to seek accommodation with the Bugis because they resented Sultan Mansur's arrogation of power in Riau and the influence of Trengganu Malays at court. During his residence in Riau from 1750 to 1760, Sultan Mansur dominated the Assembly of Nobles, taking unilateral actions which ignored long-standing precedent that all government decisions should be the result of *muafakat*, consultation between the chiefs and senior ministers. Discontented Riau nobles found allies among the Bugis leaders who believed that the second Yamtuan Muda, Daeng Cellak, who died in 1745, had been poisoned by Sultan Mansur.

Expansion of Bugis Influence

The marriage ties linking the Bugis and several Malay leaders notwithstanding, in Riau the struggle for power was still in fact perceived as one between two distinct cultural groups. The most public reminder was the formal oath of loyalty sworn on the death of any Malay ruler or Bugis Yamtuan Muda. During the ceremony every member of the court had to decide whether he would swear as a Bugis or as a Malay, and those of mixed blood thus openly made known their allegiance. The very oath itself, which solemnly spelt out dire punishments for any Bugis or Malay who harmed each other, revived memories of how the Bugis had become part of the Johor polity. During the 1750s the *Tuhfat al-Nafis* graphically describes how *fitnah* (malicious rumour) ran rampant, thrusting the two groups even further apart. This estrangement was not confined to Johor, for Malays elsewhere were increasingly resentful of the rapidly expanding Bugis influence. In the words of Sultan Muhammad Jiwa of Kedah: 'Riau, Johor, Selangor and Kelang [were] formerly governed by Malay kings and are inhabited by Malays . . . the Bugis came and settled at Riau and from thence to Selangor and from Selangor to Kelang. From what pretensions the Bugis derive their authority in these areas we know not.'[14]

A crisis was reached in 1754 when the entire Bugis community left Riau for Linggi. In the wake of this development, Malays must have been shocked to see how heavily Johor's economy had come to depend on Bugis commercial acumen. Dutch sources note the 'desolation' of Riau, the total lack of trade, while the *Tuhfat al-Nafis* describes in more human terms the pitiful attempts of the *orang laut* to fend off starvation. It was therefore in a mood of desperation that Sultan Sulaiman, with Sultan Mansur's urging, signed a treaty with the

Dutch in 1756 promising them toll-free trade throughout Johor and reiterating an earlier offer to cede Siak to the VOC if the Dutch would help him bring all the territory occupied by Bugis and Minangkabau 'under his authority again'. Naturally such a move aroused the anger of the self-exiled Bugis in Linggi, and they too began making military preparations.

A confrontation between the Bugis and the Dutch in the region had long been threatening. Melaka governors never ceased to blame the Bugis for the VOC's declining trade, consistently repeating their belief that treaties made with the Bugis of Sulawesi did not apply to the 'pirates and riffraff' who had made their way to the Malay world. If VOC officials in Batavia had been willing to give material support, Melaka would have undoubtedly moved to oust the Bugis as early as 1711. When in 1756 Sultan Sulaiman of Riau-Johor promised substantial economic benefits if the Bugis were driven out and agreed to assist the Dutch with fleets from Riau, Trengganu and Siak, the Melaka government was able to draw up plans for an open attack on the Bugis strongholds. While preparations were being made, however, the Bugis Yamtuan Muda, Daeng Kamboja, seized the initiative and laid siege to Melaka, burning houses in the suburbs and even raiding into the town itself. The inadequacy of Melaka's defences was embarrassingly obvious, and Dutch reports describe with awe the Bugis military equipment and their stockades, the largest of which could hold up to 2,000 men. Only in mid-1757, with the arrival of a Dutch fleet, was Melaka able to make plans to avenge its humiliation. In December an attack on Linggi was launched, catching the Bugis off guard. Daeng Kamboja then agreed to become a signatory to a peace treaty by which Johor ceded suzerainty over Kelang, Rembau and Linggi to the VOC with the stipulation that there was to be no interference in Islamic practices. The Bugis, for their part, promised to acknowledge Dutch authority and to recognize the ruler of Johor as their sovereign. Sultan Mansur of Trengganu, however, would have willingly seen the implementation of stronger measures to control his enemies. Though basically opposed to a monopoly treaty with the Dutch, he even expressed his willingness in 1759 to grant the VOC all Trengganu's pepper if they would help oust the Bugis from Johor territories and grant Riau protection from any Bugis attack. Negotiations abruptly broke down when the VOC decided that the commercial inducements he offered would be insufficient compensation for the costs such a campaign would involve. Besides, even in Riau, Malay support for continuing the confrontation was vanishing. Trade there had deteriorated to such an extent after the Bugis departure that one influential faction felt it was crucial to persuade them to return. In 1760, when Sultan Mansur Syah was absent in Trengganu,

the principal nobles took the opportunity of bringing about a reconciliation with the Bugis.

Following the return of the Bugis leaders to Riau, several factors
guaranteed that they would not only regain but intensify their former
influence in Johor. First, Sultan Mansur decided to remain in Trengganu, where the government had suffered during his ten years in Johor.
Secondly, in 1760 Sultan Sulaiman died and was followed in rapid
succession by his son and elder grandson. The Bugis then nominated
as king a small boy, Mahmud, also Sulaiman's grandson, whose mother
was a daughter of Daeng Cellak. Thirdly, several Malay nobles were
willing to co-operate with the Bugis, and the Temenggung and his
father-in-law Daeng Kamboja were named as joint Regents for the
young ruler. It was not long before the Malay component of this
partnership was submerged, so that Daeng Kamboja could rightly
term himself 'Yang Dipertuan Muda, who occupies the throne of
Johor and Pahang and all their dependencies'. Dutch comments at
this time confirm the reality of Bugis power in Riau which 'increases
from day to day, the Malays no longer having any influence in the
government'.[15]

English–Dutch Rivalry and the Impact on Malay Trade

Two years after Melaka's near capture by the Bugis, questions about
the VOC's military preparedness were again raised. In 1759 Raja
Muhammad, Raja Kecil's son and ruler of the new VOC possession
of Siak, routed the Dutch post on Pulau Gontong, an island at the
mouth of the Siak River. Not until 1761 were the Dutch able to
mount a punitive expedition which avenged the massacre and placed
Raja Muhammad's brother Alam on the Siak throne, ignoring his past
alliance with the Bugis. This was to be the last active Dutch campaign
in the Malay world until 1784. The decade before 1760 had seen the
VOC deeply and uncharacteristically involved in Malay politics, prepared to take the part of any ruler who held out sufficiently enticing
economic offers. But the Dutch were to find that they had gained
little by their activities, and they now stood to benefit by a continuance of the *status quo*. From 1760 permission was granted for
Melaka to dispose of surplus tin in direct sales to passing ships, and the
town's finances showed a noticeable improvement as the revenue
collected from duties and tolls increased.

Despite the improvement in Melaka's trading figures, the growing
weakness of the VOC as a whole was slowly becoming obvious to
Malays. Hamstrung by financial difficulties and problems in VOC
organization, Dutch administrators faced almost impossible odds in
any attempt to keep pace with rising prices. By the middle of the

century officials were publicly commenting on the 'disadvantageous aspect' of the VOC's fortunes. A contemporary observer compared the VOC to a man infected with a creeping disease which, if not cured in time, would prove fatal. The erosion of its trade was so marked that during the 1750s new measures had been introduced to force ships to dock at Melaka or Batavia. Particular efforts were made to prohibit 'smuggling', the secret transport of goods from places governed by Dutch monopoly contracts to areas outside VOC control. Naturally, Malays everywhere resented the increasing restrictions on trade, especially the diversion of Chinese junks to Batavia. In the past the dubious economic benefits derived from a contract with the VOC were balanced by the recognition throughout the Malay world of Dutch prestige and military superiority. The attacks on Melaka and Pulau Gontong brought even this assumption into question.

Malay awareness of Dutch decline was heightened by the increasing presence of their major competitors, the English private 'country' traders.[16] At a time when official English interest in the Malay world was minimal, these men had formed close associations with Malay courts. They sometimes acted as advisers on political and military matters and were often on intimate terms with the ruler. Speaking fluent Malay and sometimes related to local Malays through liaisons with their womenfolk, the influence of such traders was considerable. Although Malays still viewed the Netherlands as the most powerful European state, they were becoming conscious of England's mounting prestige. The English were able to gain a dominating commercial position over other Europeans in the Malay areas for several reasons. First, by the middle of the eighteenth century the English East India Company had gained a tighter control over the cloth-producing areas of India. With access to steady supplies of cloth, English traders were able to squeeze out most of their Indian rivals in the vital piece-goods trade.

Secondly, the English also controlled the principal poppy growing areas of India and could thus dominate the supply of opium to Southeast Asia and China. Malays had been smoking opium mixed with tobacco since the seventeenth century, when the Dutch began importing the drug into the area. A hundred years later their consumption had reached such heights that the Governor of Melaka could tell his superiors that 'the people of Rembau, Selangor and Perak, like other natives, cannot live without opium', while Chinese accounts show that east coast Malays were equally addicted. No entrepôt could compete in this new economic environment unless it had ready supplies of opium, and in 1786 Francis Light was to recommend the import of large quantities of the drug to Penang specifically to attract merchants.

Thirdly, through improved maritime techniques English shipping was fast overtaking that of other Europeans. As early as 1714 the English navy was larger and better administered than any other in Europe, and England was also superior in skills such as ship-building and cartography. Whereas in 1754 the Dutch had to postpone a mission to Trengganu because available maps were totally inadequate, British sea captains, though relative newcomers to the area, had by 1788 charted the east coast sufficiently well for maps to be used as a guide for navigation. The eighteenth century saw the development of the great India-built East Indiamen, which in the 1780s averaged 600 to 800 tonnes and were capable of transporting extremely large cargoes.

Finally, English country traders had no compunction about selling armaments, which had been strictly forbidden by the VOC. It is significant, for instance, that when a French crew went ashore to trade in Trengganu in 1763, they took 'two cases of muskets, two cases of opium, and some knives'. English adventurers were also willing to trade their knowledge of the manufacture of gunpowder and cannon and thus exploit the Malay desire for acquisition of arms denied them by VOC policies.

The growing numbers of English traders added to the importance of those ports free of Dutch control along the maritime routes to China. There was now an even greater need for places to refit vessels and buy up supplies for the trip to Canton, and with this new impetus, Kedah, Selangor and Trengganu continued to flourish. The greatest beneficiary, however, was undoubtedly Bugis-controlled Riau, which one English country trader called 'the key to the Straits'. Here vessels from Cambodia, Siam, China, Vietnam and all over the archipelago, including the Bugis homelands, flocked to trade. Riau now became an integral part of an extensive Bugis trading community which stretched like a giant web across the entire region. It was Bugis ships which made Riau a principal point of exchange for smuggled spices from the eastern archipelago. In Riau too could be found all the features typical of a Malay entrepôt. There were the various items in demand in the China market, such as forest and ocean products, tin, pepper and locally grown gambier which were readily bartered for cloth and opium. Duties were low and cargoes could be discharged or stored easily. Traders also reported that there was little need to extend credit, a common practice in smaller ports with less access to funds. Looking back in later years, says the *Tuhfat al-Nafis*, old people simply said, 'those days in Riau were good'.

The similarity between Riau under the Bugis and earlier Malay entrepôts like seventeenth-century Johor, Melaka and the legendary Srivijaya was not limited to trade. Like its predecessors, Riau's fame as a centre for religious scholarship continued. Moslem scholars from India and the Islamic heartlands were maintained in special religious hostels, while devotees of Sufism, the mysticism at the margin of orthodox Islam, could seek initiation into one of the many *tarikat* or brotherhoods which flourished on Riau.

There was, however, one significant difference between Riau and the great ports of former days. Although a Malay king ruled in Riau, effective control was no longer in Malay hands but in those of outsiders.

The Curtailment of Bugis Power and the Decline of Riau

In Trengganu, Sultan Mansur found the Bugis prosperity particularly galling. Although he had returned home, he did not forget his campaign to oust the Bugis from Riau even without VOC support. For a time he hoped to achieve his goal by allying with Raja Kecil's grandson, Raja Ismail, to whom he gave his daughter in marriage in 1765. Two years later a fleet under Raja Ismail left to attack Riau. Remembering the events of 1699 in Johor, several *orang laut* groups, especially those from Singapore, flocked to Raja Ismail's cause, but the Bugis successfully drove them off and Raja Ismail was forced to return to Sumatra.

The abortive Malay attack on Riau came at a time when, for a brief period, a chink appeared in the Bugis armour. Following the installation of Sultan Salehuddin of Selangor in 1766 and his declaration of independence, a rift developed between the Selangor and Riau Bugis. Daeng Kamboja, the Yamtuan Muda, was furious at Selangor's defiance of its overlord, and for a few years Malays witnessed a return to the Bugis divisions which had characterized the early years of the eighteenth century. The alienation between Selangor and Riau in turn made Sultan Salehuddin anxious to strengthen his ties with his Malay neighbours. He entered into an alliance with Kedah, which was sealed by a betrothal between his daughter and Tunku Abdullah, son of Sultan Muhammad Jiwa. By this arrangement Selangor hoped for respectability and acceptance among Malay rulers by establishing a *berbisan* relationship (that is, one between those whose children wed) with an acknowledged Malay leader. Sultan Muhammad Jiwa, for his part, hoped to guarantee assistance for Kedah should Burmese forces, already deep into Ayudhya's territory, move down the peninsula. He also hoped that Tunku Abdullah's new relatives would eventually ensure his succession to the Kedah throne in the face of claims from several other princes. A few days after Ayudhya fell to the Burmese in April 1767, the wedding between the Kedah prince and his Selangor bride took place.

The Thai recovery, however, was rapid. In December 1767 a provincial governor, Phaya Taksin, was crowned king and soon demanded the traditional token of submission, the 'gold and silver flowers' (*bunga mas dan perak*) from Ayudhya's former Malay vassals. Although Malays resented the fact that Taksin was a usurper, a man of inglorious genealogy, they could hardly refuse to comply. Sultan Mansur of Trengganu had even been told to expect annual raids. Kedah was particularly vulnerable because its alliance with Selangor had lasted less than three years, and it was now bereft of allies. Both VOC records and Bugis texts mention the announcement of a divorce in 1769, which Bugis historians attribute to Sultan Salehuddin's anger at his son-in-law's prolonged absences in Kedah.

Bugis resentment at this slight led to the mending of the rift between Riau and Selangor through the mediation of Raja Haji, son of Daeng Cellak and brother of the ruler of Selangor. He was a charismatic adventurer whose exploits had become legendary and who even in his own lifetime was regarded as imbued with magic power, often associated with saints (*keramat*). Under his leadership the Bugis of Selangor and Riau soon demonstrated how quickly they could avenge wounded pride, and in 1770 they formed a secret alliance with some of the discontented Kedah princes opposed to Tunku Abdullah's succession. Their consequent attack on Kedah later the same year was brief, for the Bugis found greater opposition than they had expected. When they retreated in early 1771 Sultan Muhammad Jiwa was still in power. Nonetheless, they so devastated Kedah that it was to be many years before it showed signs of returning to its former prosperity.

Once again a single incident served to highlight the Bugis–Malay enmity which permeated Malay politics of the period. Neither Sultan Muhammad Jiwa nor his son, the future Sultan Abdullah (1779–1802), ever forgot what the Bugis had done. In alliance with Sultan Mansur of Trengganu, they were determined to make yet another effort to drive the Bugis out of the Malay world. According to this new plan, Selangor and Riau-Johor would be invaded and Raja Ismail of Siak would then be installed as ruler in the latter kingdom. Sultan Muhammad Jiwa later declared that 'the whole coast of Malaya and Sumatra would be well pleased to see Raja Ismail on the throne of Riau as he was descended from all their ancient kings'.[17] For a short period it appeared that he might have found an ally in the English East India Company (EIC), to whom he promised the cession of the coast near Kuala Kedah in return for support in an attack on Selangor. However, when it became clear that any assistance the English could give would be insufficient, Sultan Muhammad Jiwa refused to continue the association, and in the middle of 1772 the English post in Kedah was withdrawn. When it also became obvious that Raja Ismail was more interested in returning to Siak than in setting himself up in Riau, talk of a Malay invasion was quietly dropped.

The short-lived association between Kedah and the EIC in 1770–1 is noteworthy because it represented part of the ongoing English quest for a place on the China sea route which would also give them access to Malay products. Riau and the Redang Islands, off Trengganu, had already been considered but tentative English approaches to the Malay rulers concerned had been inconclusive. In 1759 the English discovered the existence of an eastern sea route to China, which enabled ships to reach Canton even when the adverse monsoon was far advanced. As a result, English interest in the Borneo region grew. By an agreement in 1762 with the Sultan of Sulu, the EIC acquired the island of Balambangan, off Borneo's northern coast, as a trading post. In 1773 a factory was established there but was abandoned two years later following an attack by Sulu raiders. Efforts in 1774 to reach an agreement with Brunei which would provide access to local pepper supplies proved no more successful than the negotiations with Kedah.

For Sultan Muhammad Jiwa of Kedah, the collapse of his brief alliance with the English meant the loss not only of a potential ally against the Bugis but the end of his plans for an attack on Bugis-controlled Selangor and Riau. The eventual elimination of the Bugis as a serious threat in the region can be attributed not to Malay action but indirectly to the deteriorating relations between England and the Netherlands. During the last two decades of the century political events in Europe helped pull the VOC back sharply into Malay affairs. In 1780 the British declared war on the Dutch Republic to prevent its joining the Russian-sponsored League of Armed Neutrality. To VOC employees in Asia the news of war in Europe seemed merely an extension of the long years of bitter commercial rivalry between British and Dutch traders in the Asian areas. What became known as the fourth Anglo-Dutch War (1780–4) intensified this rivalry and led to unexpected developments in the Malay world. In 1782 the Dutch Governor of Melaka, hearing that a British merchant vessel was in Riau's harbour, had the ship seized. Raja Haji, who had succeeded as Yamtuan Muda in Riau-Johor in 1777, angrily protested but also demanded half the confiscated cargo. When this was denied, he immediately began massing troops from Selangor, Riau and Rembau, and rumours of an impending assault on Melaka, possibly with English help, circulated wildly. Although a Dutch fleet was dispatched to lay siege to Riau, its performance was mediocre and an attempted landing in January 1784 failed miserably. Two weeks afterwards, despite efforts at mediation by the ruler of Perak, Raja Haji and his allies attacked Melaka.

At first the Dutch governor fully expected he would reap the benefits of Malay–Bugis hostility and be able to rally the assistance of neighbouring Malay kings. Most did send letters of encouragement, but the two from whom Melaka had expected most, Kedah and Trengganu, were themselves occupied with preparations for a possible confrontation with the reunified Thai kingdom of Siam. The only Malay state which actually dispatched ships and men was Siak, but because the prince in command, a nephew of the Sultan of Siak, was a notorious former pirate, the Governor was wary of placing too great a reliance on his loyalty. In any event, the Siak fleet did not reach Melaka in time to repel the Bugis forces which placed the town under siege for five weary months. Had it not been for the arrival of a large Dutch squadron and the death of Raja Haji in a skirmish, Melaka would almost certainly have fallen to the Bugis.

For a short time after the relief of Melaka, the VOC was able to press home its military advantage. A fleet was quickly sent to capture Riau, and by the end of 1784 Sultan Mahmud of Riau-Johor had signed a treaty in which he formally announced his 'eternal gratitude' to the Dutch who had freed him from 'the Bugis yoke'. Riau-Johor was to become a Dutch vassal state, a *leenrijk*, where Malays would rule only at the VOC's pleasure. All Bugis except those actually born in Riau were expelled, and the Dutch stipulated that no Bugis was ever again to hold the position of Yamtuan Muda. Control of all trade was placed firmly in VOC hands. In the face of the Dutch victory over Riau, the Selangor ruler, Sultan Ibrahim (1782–1826), fled to Pahang, and the VOC immediately sent a force to claim Selangor. The ruler of Siak was rewarded for his services by being placed in control of Selangor, which was now subject to Dutch sovereignty.

As a result of these developments, the VOC came to exert greater territorial control in the Straits and peninsular states than ever before. Naning had been a VOC possession for more than a century with its chief required to accept a Dutch-appointed head 'without demur'; Siak, Rembau, Kelang and Linggi had been ceded by Riau-Johor in the 1750s; now the VOC had become the lord not only of Selangor but of the entire kingdom of Riau-Johor, from Sumatra to Pahang. But if any Dutchman had entertained visions of a new trading empire under VOC control, he would have been quickly brought back to reality. The last decade of the eighteenth century saw the VOC slide rapidly into bankruptcy, a major factor being the settlement with Britain in 1784 which permitted free navigation in the eastern seas. As Dutch seaborne trade faced unprecedented competition, the VOC position as overlord in Selangor and Riau was also called into question. In Selangor, the rule of the Siak princes proved totally unsatisfactory, and when Sultan Ibrahim returned overland from Pahang with a large band of followers, he easily persuaded most of the Selangor district chiefs to join him. In June 1785 his forces overran the Dutch defences at the mouth of the Selangor River, forcing the occupants to flee. Although the subsequent Dutch blockade had disastrous effects on Selangor's economy, Sultan Ibrahim would not surrender, and in 1786 the Dutch reluctantly concluded a treaty, reinstating him as their *leenman* or vassal.

In Riau, the challenge to the Dutch was much greater. Sultan Mahmud, contrary to Dutch expectations, did not prove a grateful recipient of Dutch favours, especially when further measures were introduced which made the VOC Resident the virtual ruler of Riau. Resentful and humiliated, Sultan Mahmud in 1787 recruited the assistance of a fleet of Sulu raiders, who had begun to appear in Malay waters and whom Malays generally termed 'Ilanun'. With Malay co-operation, the Ilanun fleets entered the Riau River by stealth and overcame the Dutch garrison, who escaped by ship to Melaka. When Ilanun demands for rewards and fear of Dutch reprisals became too great, Sultan Mahmud fled to Pahang. For another eight years he remained a wandering exile. Except for the Chinese, Riau was depopulated, the Malays having followed Sultan Mahmud to Pahang and Trengganu, and the Bugis having dispersed to Selangor, Siantan and Borneo. The catastrophic effects of these years when there was no Malay ruler and when the economy was moribund ended any hopes that Riau might once again assume its former position in the Malay world.

The Resurgence of the Thais and the Establishment of Penang

Other important shifts of power were occurring in the northern Malay states. In 1782 a dynamic general in the Thai army, Chakri, subsequently known as Rama I (1782–1809), seized the throne and established a new dynasty at Bangkok. This revitalized kingdom of Siam resumed hostilities against the Thais' traditional enemy Burma with renewed vigour. But whenever the Thai army was assembled, it boded ill for the Malay vassals who were required to contribute their quota of men and weapons. The northern Malay rulers therefore waited apprehensively for indications of what their new overlord would require. The demands surpassed their worst expectations. Siam not only ordered greater material assistance than ever before, but also commanded that the rulers of Kedah, Patani, Kelantan and Trengganu leave their capitals and make personal obeisance in Siam. The Malays were outraged: 'from time immemorial' such a thing had never been asked. The sending of money, supplies, men and arms was as much as any overlord should properly demand. No Malay ruler should be required to prostrate himself before the Siamese king as Thai court protocol in Siam required. Every Malay would have been familiar with the story of how Hang Tuah, the legendary hero of Melaka, had refused to crawl on his hands and knees when visiting Ayudhya because this was totally opposed to the dignity of a Malay subject. How then could a king accept such humiliation? Sultan Abdullah of Kedah sidestepped the issue by sending his brother-in-law and son in his stead; Sultan Mansur dispatched a Portuguese envoy to placate the Siamese king while continuing his negotiations with Goa and Macao for a Portuguese post in Trengganu. The ruler of Patani flatly refused, returning 'a very rude answer', and suffered the most terrible consequences. Patani, it was said, was razed by the Siamese, 'all the men, children and old women . . . [being] tied and thrown upon the ground and then trampled to death by elephants'.[18] But unrest continued in Patani, and after two major rebellions in 1791 and 1795 Rama I deposed the ruler and divided the state into seven jurisdictions under the control of the southern Thai province of Songkhla (Singora).

It is not surprising that Malay rulers initially looked with hope towards the English, whose representatives, the country traders, had been specifically advised 'to conciliate the esteem and affection of the natives and to teach them to look up to the English as their friends and protectors'. Little wonder, too, that Sultan Abdullah of Kedah, pressured by Burmese demands as well as Siamese, offered to lease Penang to the EIC. He hoped by this means to gain protection against possible attacks from Siam or Burma and from any future uprisings by his own relatives. In August 1786 Francis Light, a country trader entrusted with the negotiations, took formal possession of Penang in the name of King George III of England.

For Malays, the establishment of Penang transformed the EIC into a territorial power with an obvious stake in the security of the area. Only a year after its founding all Malay rulers of standing had written to Light in an effort to gauge English willingness to lend them material aid. Perak saw the British as a potential ally against the Bugis of Selangor; Trengganu and Kedah hoped for assistance against the continuing demands of Siam; Sultan Ibrahim of Selangor, Sultan Mahmud of Riau-Johor, and the new Bugis Yamtuan Muda, the exiled Raja Ali, all anticipated support against the Dutch.

Disenchantment, however, quickly set in. Whatever verbal promises Light may have made, whatever hopes he may have encouraged, it soon became clear that his superiors were as unwilling as the Dutch to enter into any contract which might in the future involve them in warfare with another power, whether Siam or the Netherlands. Sultan Mansur of Trengganu, having failed in his efforts to gain Portuguese help, now found that the most the EIC was willing to offer was a post with twelve men. In Kedah, Sultan Abdullah discovered that the compensation he was to receive in return for the British occupation of Penang was far less than he had been led to expect. The sense of disillusion was complete. In the words of the Kedah chiefs, 'Now these English will not submit to the King's demand, therefore we have written to the English to go away from Pulau Penang in the name of peace, for when they first came it was with a good name'.[19] When Sultan Abdullah's efforts to effect a financial settlement with Light failed, he recruited some Ilanun raiders already present in the Straits and attacked Penang in March 1791.

The attack itself, while unsuccessful, is intriguing because for the first time since the Minangkabau-led movements of the late seventeenth century there was some effort to rise above ethnic divisions and to forge a unity based not on a sense of being Malay but on being Moslem. In writing to the native population of Penang to arouse support, the Kedah nobles addressed themselves to 'all Moslems, that is, Bugis, Acehnese, men of Minangkabau, Malays and Chulias [Indians from Coromandel] who dwell at Pulau Penang . . . God will assist us and our Lord Muhammad the Guardian of the Moslems and the last of all the Prophets'.[20] The following month the British attacked the Kedah placements on the shore opposite Penang, dispersing the Kedah forces and removing the immediate threat to the island. The British occupation of Penang was subsequently confirmed in a treaty with Kedah in 1791.

Britain's supremacy in the area seemed total when, in 1795, it assumed direct control of several VOC possessions in the Malay Indonesian archipelago. This move was part of a general policy intended to prevent any Dutch possession in Asia falling into French hands after Napoleon conquered the Netherlands in January 1795. After the Dutch Stadthouder fled to England, he requested the British government to take control of Dutch territories in the East until his restoration to power in the Netherlands. Technically speaking, therefore, Melaka remained Dutch, but the subtleties of the European situation were lost on Malays, who could not understand why the 'Kompeni Wolanda', the Dutch Company, which had existed for so many years had capitulated without a struggle. With their base in Penang, the British had no interest in reviving Melaka's position, nor in encouraging the development of an entrepôt at Riau. Even though the Dutch and English acquiesced in Sultan Mahmud's return in 1795, Riau-Johor's claim to leadership had gone. Riau itself was poor, a commercial backwater, and as the *Siak Chronicle* shows, there were still those who remembered that not only was Mahmud half Bugis, but also that he 'was not descended from the line of Sultan Iskandar Zul-karnain, but from the Bendahara who committed *derhaka* against the ruler of Johor'.[21] Now the epitome of commercial success was represented not by a Malay port but by the British town of Penang. In his reminiscences, one Chinese merchant later recalled how 'the English called in traders and it gradually became more prosperous. The clothing, food and houses there [were] all magnificent, and horses and carriages [were] used for travelling.'[22] In 1800 the ruler of Kedah also leased the district of Prai (Province Wellesley) on the coast opposite Penang to the EIC in return for an increased pension.

The Demise of the Malay Entrepôt State

The legacy of generations of hostility and division, combined with economic weakness, meant that in Riau Sultan Mahmud could exert little influence over his chiefs or principal ministers. The Bendahara in Pahang and the Temenggung at Singapore became to all appearances independent rulers. Numerous Malay leaders, notably the Temenggung, desperately in need of an income which Riau-Johor could no longer provide, financed and equipped *orang laut* raids as a source of revenue. It was in fact the prevalence of piracy that prompted some Englishmen to write of the Malay kingdoms in terms of 'decay'. They blamed the Dutch monopoly treaties which, by disrupting traditional trading patterns, had weakened Malay states and caused a breakdown of authority on the oceans. However, other reasons also contributed to the increase in *orang laut* and *anak raja* piracy. First, the ties between Johor and many *orang laut* groups had been irrevocably damaged after the regicide of 1699, and this had been compounded by the weakening of central control in Riau after 1784. Secondly, succession disputes, especially in Kedah and Siak, had led to a rise in the number of pirating princes operating outside the restraints of any court. Thirdly, since the 1790s a different type of raiding had come to exist to-gether with the plundering of the *orang laut* and *anak raja* of the Malay world. Requiring virtually unlimited supplies of manpower to service the lucrative China trade, the chiefs of the Sulu Sultanate were now raiding throughout the archipelago specifically for slaves. Their raids along the Borneo coast had become so frequent that the pepper plantations lay untended and junks no longer called there. Regularly with the northeast monsoon they surged out into Malay waters, even establishing a permanent base at Retih, on the east Sumatran coast. Throughout the archipelago coastal settlements came to dread the 'pirate season', the *musim Ilanun*.

From the end of the eighteenth century continuing disputes over succession racked the Malay world. Perak, disrupted after 1792 by battles between contending heirs and without the protective mantle provided by the VOC contract, was a tempting lure to ambitious neighbours. In 1804 forces from Selangor attacked and for some years occupied the downstream area. The withdrawal of Selangor did not end Perak's troubles, for Bangkok and its provincial government in Ligor revived Thai claims to suzerainty. In 1814 when the Perak ruler flatly refused to send tribute to Bangkok, invoking his proud descent from Bukit Si Guntang, Siam ordered its vassal, Kedah, to invade. Troops from Kedah moved into Perak in 1816, and three years later Perak acknowledged the overlordship of Siam. In Kedah itself succession disputes took a different turn. One prince, seeking support for his bid for the throne, turned in 1803 to Bangkok. He was duly installed as Sultan Ahmad (1803–21, 1842–5) with the deposed ruler being made Raja of Perlis, but at a price. In addition to the traditional levies of men and supplies demanded by its Siamese overlord, Kedah was now expected to act as its agent when force was required in the peninsula. Even in the Minangkabau states of later Negeri Sembilan struggles between branches of the ruling families pitted faction against faction.

Though conflicts within the Malay states were extensive, it was events in the kingdom of Riau-Johor which were to have the most far-reaching ramifications. The last years of Sultan Mahmud's life had been relatively peaceful, and in the words of a Malay account, 'in justice, equity and mercy he cherished all his people'.[23] Nonetheless, it is also clear that the old Bugis—Malay conflicts simmered, even after the reinstatement of a Bugis Yamtuan Muda in Riau in 1804. Neighbouring princes were all too ready to take up the quarrel on the side of one or another party, and there was thus no possibility of any succession dispute remaining purely an internal affair. This became apparent in 1812 when Sultan Mahmud died leaving two sons, both born of commoner mothers. The Bugis faction, led by the Yamtuan Muda, favoured the younger, Raja Abdul Rahman; while the Malays, under the Bendahara of Pahang and the Temenggung, supported the elder, Raja Husain. In 1818 the Dutch signed a treaty with Abdul Rahman recognizing him as Sultan in return for the re-establishment of the Dutch post on Riau.

The Dutch action was a bald challenge for those Englishmen who were convinced that Britain must control the maritime route to China. Sir Thomas Stamford Raffles, the greatest exponent of this view, had strongly opposed the return of Dutch possessions in the East after the Napoleonic wars. Britain, he felt, was destined to take on the role of overlord in the archipelago in the tradition of great kingdoms of earlier times. Raffles was convinced of the need to establish a British entrepôt somewhere in the region which could become another staging post along the maritime route to China. Previous hopes of developing an entrepôt in the Borneo area had failed when Balambangan, re-established in 1803, was abandoned two years later. However, another opportunity came when Raffles was ordered to set up a post in the southern approaches to the Melaka Straits. Raffles had hoped to use Riau, but found the Dutch already entrenched there. An alternative site was soon found. On 30 January 1819 Raffles signed a treaty with the Temenggung of Riau-Johor, the territorial chief of Singapore, which gave the British the right to establish a factory on the island.

Singapore had an abundance of drinking water, a natural sheltered harbour and was conveniently placed as a centre for trade with China and the eastern archipelago. All it needed to fulfil the classic role of a Straits entrepôt in the tradition of Srivijaya and Melaka was a ruler. To impart legality to the rights he had acquired on Singapore, Raffles recognized Husain, elder son of Sultan Mahmud, as the legitimate successor in Riau-Johor. On 6 February 1819 a financial settlement was made and a formal treaty signed with 'Sultan Husain Syah of

Johor', together with the Temenggung. Four months afterwards the new ruler took up residence in Singapore in his own settlement, known as Kampung Gelam. Both he and the Temenggung continued to live in Singapore, although in 1824 they formally agreed to give up their authority there in return for a pension. But without the regalia and the backing of the Riau-Johor court, which remained with his younger brother in Riau, Sultan Husain could never claim any great prestige among Malays. In practical matters he was always eclipsed by the more dominating Temenggung, whom the British saw as the stronger of the two. Although the Temenggung traded his 'rights' over Singapore for allowances and later a pension, his status had not diminished but had on the contrary been enhanced by his association with Raffles and the new European power in the area. Sultan Husain, on the other hand, was treated by the British as 'a legal necessity' and with the passing of time faded into the background.[24]

While there are identifiable continuities between Singapore and previous entrepôts, its founding does usher in a new period in Malay history because it confirmed the dominance of British commercial interests in the region. This process had begun in 1786 with the establishment of Penang, but although Penang was founded, like Singapore, on the principles of free trade, it did not make the same impact. In the latter part of the eighteenth century the British still had to contend with the Dutch, whose prestige, even when the VOC was crumbling, was still great. Furthermore, Penang was not on one of the major routes between China and the archipelago. Though its trade flourished, it was generally focused on the region of the Straits and southern Thailand rather than drawing shipping from all over the island world. When Java was taken by the British in 1811 during the Napoleonic Wars (1795–1815) to prevent its falling to the French, Batavia was opened to country traders and its position as the dominant centre in the archipelago was strengthened. All this was changed after 1819. Singapore was better sited than Penang and its free trade policies drew commerce away from Batavia, where the Dutch, returning in 1816, had reimposed their old tariff restrictions. Moreover, the great days of the Netherlands were past; Singapore, by contrast, was linked to the growing industrial power and prestige of Britain, which in the nineteenth century came to eclipse all other nations. As a contemporary Chinese traveller, marvelling at Singapore's prosperity, remarked: 'There has never been a country as powerful as England.'[25]

In terms of Malay history, Singapore signalled the end of the entrepôt under Malay rule or even, as Riau, functioning under Malay auspices. With two British ports, Penang and Singapore, in the area there was now no need for British traders or Chinese junks to frequent Malay harbours. As the nineteenth century progressed, the economies of the Malay states gradually became more linked with those of the British settlements. Ties between Malay states and a central entrepôt were centuries old. But a port such as Singapore, controlled by Europeans and maintained primarily for their benefit, was different from any others which had previously existed in the area. Its impact on Malay history was to reflect that difference. The musings of Raffles's Malay scribe capture something of this sense of change:

> Singapore at that time was like the sun when it has just risen, waxing stronger and stronger as it gets higher and higher . . . I am astonished to see how markedly the world is changing. A new world is being created, the old world destroyed. The very jungle becomes a settled district and elsewhere a settlement reverts to jungle. . . [26]

In many ways one could argue that the eighteenth century was a low point in Malay history. The murder of Mahmud of Johor in 1699 set in motion a chain of events which resulted in the usurpation of effective power in that kingdom first by Minangkabaus from Sumatra and then by Bugis from Sulawesi. But Bugis attempts to expand their power in the peninsula brought them into conflict with the VOC. A final major battle between them in 1784 ended for ever any possibility of Bugis dominance in the area. The beginning of the nineteenth century saw Riau-Johor's hopes of commercial revival dashed by the founding of a British entrepôt at Singapore in 1819. No Malay kingdom succeeded in challenging this new port, nor in re-establishing the tradition of Malay commercial hegemony in the Straits. Many of the Malay states were preoccupied with succession disputes and wars which increased in intensity and complexity as outsiders became involved. Siam was quick to exploit the situation and within a short time reasserted Thai overlordship in the northern Malay kingdoms.

But the picture is not as bleak as the broad outline of events might indicate. The history of individual states shows that for some the eighteenth century could be remembered with pride. Trengganu and Selangor were formally established as independent kingdoms; other states, like Kedah and Perak, threw up their share of able leaders. A shadow of the great economic developments of later years is discernible as both Malays and newcomers moved to take advantage of changing international trade and the growing demand for Malay products, especially for the China trade. The very concept of what 'Melayu' signified had broadened far beyond the narrow definition of Melaka's early days. The language and culture of the Riau-Johor court was still held up as a model, but 'Malayness' had grown to incorporate the whole range of regional variations from Patani to east

Sumatra. In a difficult period the Malay world did not stagnate and the legacy of past achievements was still honoured. However, transition to the changed political and economic environment of the nineteenth century required time, and it was one of the ironies of history that this is precisely what Western imperialism could least afford to give.

4

A 'New World Is Created', 1819-74

The most colourful description of life in the new British settlement of
Singapore is contained in the *Hikayat Abdullah* (*The Story of Abdullah*)
which is the autobiography of the noted teacher of Malay who was
also scribe to Stamford Raffles. One of Abdullah's main concerns is
the change brought about by the European presence, 'the destruction
of the old world and the creation of a new'. He is understandably less
interested in the historical continuities which, despite the overriding
sense of change, can still be discerned. The very readiness of Malay
rulers to establish links with British officials in Singapore and Penang
was in keeping with previous Malay diplomacy. Like the Dutch and
Portuguese, the British simply represented a new and powerful element
whose friendship was desirable. Nor was Singapore's commercial success
unprecedented. In the tradition of earlier entrepôts such as Melaka
and Johor, its prosperity owed much to its unrivalled geographic position, to which was added the attraction of free trade in an age when
tariffs and protection were almost universal. The initial acceptance of
the British was also aided by the fact that the areas involved — Penang,
Singapore, Province Wellesley and Melaka — had not been forcibly
taken from any Malay power and at least the trappings of legality surrounded their transfer. Well before the Anglo-Dutch Treaty of 1824,
the British appeared the legitimate heirs to the prestige formerly
accorded the VOC. Melaka continued under British rule from 1795,
except for a brief period of Dutch control from 1818 until 1824, and
Munshi Abdullah remembered how those people of Dutch extraction
'changed their customs and language, their clothing and habits of their
race, men and women alike copying English ways of life'.[1]

It is not 'change' as such which makes the nineteenth century of
special significance. The Malay world had, after all, been absorbing
and responding to outside influences for hundreds of years. What
characterizes this period is rather the pace of change, itself part of a
global phenomenon. 'The world,' as one Englishman wrote in 1864,
'moves faster and faster.'[2] The Malay archipelago, always sensitive to
the shifts of international trade, was now caught up by far-reaching
economic and political forces which were drawing Europe and Asia
ever closer. Developments such as the expansion of Western technology,

the tightening relationship between European government and commerce, and the shrinking of distance through improved communications began to transform the nature of Malay society. The nineteenth century saw the establishment of political boundaries which became the basis of modern Malaysia, the strengthening of the role of the Malay peninsula as a supplier of raw materials, and growing socio-economic distinctions between the major ethnic groups. These developments helped define the central concerns of the colonial and independent governments of Malaya/Malaysia well into the twentieth century.

The Nineteenth Century: Historiographical Considerations

In the historiography of Malaysia, the nineteenth century enters a new phase. The principal sources are no longer the commercial reports of European trading companies but those of the local British administration, concerned as much with the problems of governing as with revenue. The work of amateur historians, Europeans interested in the Malay past, also becomes an indispensable source of data. Employed in some official capacity, these men usually had considerable experience in the area and their publications include a mass of detail on many aspects of Malay life. Several such studies contain useful statistics, and the most frequently cited are those for population. However, while the figures for the Straits Settlements are probably reasonably accurate, those for the Malay states must be treated as estimates until 1891, when the first official census was carried out.[3]

As the century progresses, the information available in newspapers, personal reminiscences, contemporary journals and official documents becomes more extensive and more reliable, although allowances must always be made for imperialistic bias particularly in the period of high colonialism after 1874. A hundred years have elapsed since many of these documents were first compiled, but historians are still discovering in them material which furthers an understanding of how modern Malaysia developed.

Another important source is the various writings in Malay, which in the nineteenth century was passing through a transitional phase. Chronicles in the classical literary style persisted, but now personal accounts were reaching a wider audience through lithographing and vernacular publishing houses. Later in the century Malay newspapers and journals, freed from the conventions governing court literature, began circulating among a small reading public concentrated in the towns. In addition, efforts were made, usually by British civil servants, to record the vast corpus of Malay village legends and stories which continue to provide insights into the ways Malays perceived their past.

This large body of source material does not by any means imply that all the historian's questions can be answered. British records are far more useful for the west coast of the peninsula, where political and commercial interests became more entrenched, than for the east coast. Glaring gaps still remain in our knowledge of vital subjects such as developments in Malay Islam and the life of the Malay peasant. Undoubtedly local studies undertaken by Malaysians themselves have much to contribute in the field of oral history, but the systematic organization of such material demands specific techniques not always considered part of the historian's training. Nonetheless, the relatively greater amount of material available makes historical reconstruction in the nineteenth century more practicable than in earlier periods.

Relations between Siam and the Northern Malay States

In the early nineteenth century the Malay view of the British as a potential friend assumed particular importance because the Thais had once again begun to push southwards into the peninsula. The reassertion of Thai overlordship after 1782 was the more onerous owing to the relative freedom the northern Malay states had enjoyed during the mid-eighteenth century. As Sultan Mansur Syah of Trengganu had put it, 'The previous king was content when I sent him the *bunga mas dan perak*, but the present King [Rama I, 1782–1809] thinks only of ruining me.'[4] The end of the wars between Siam and Burma after 1810 brought no respite from Bangkok's demands and in 1819 Kedah, acting under Siamese orders, helped reduce Perak to vassal status. Continuing Thai aggression here was largely due to the ambitions of Ligor, whose traditional autonomy was sufficiently great for its governor to declare himself king after the destruction of Ayudhya by the Burmese in 1767. In 1811 a new governor had been appointed whose status was so high that some European visitors assumed Ligor was not a province but an independent vassal of Bangkok. In its administration of Kedah and Kelantan, however, Ligor had a rival in the other major Siamese provincial centre, Songkhla (Singora), which was responsible for Trengganu and Patani. The Ligor governor, jealously guarding his prestige, was extremely sensitive to anything which undermined his own standing. According to one account, he was particularly annoyed when Sultan Ahmad of Kedah (1803–21, 1842–5), his presumed subordinate, was awarded the superior title of Chau Phaya[5] by the Siamese king as a reward for assistance in the campaigns against Burma.

The animosity of the Ligor governor was a potential danger for Kedah. Although Bangkok assumed general responsibility for any moves in the south, the Siamese administrators in the southern provinces had great influence in formulating policy and were given considerable freedom in its execution. The Ligor family had powerful relatives at court, and in 1820 the governor's accusation that Sultan Ahmad refused to recognize his authority and was conspiring with the Burmese coincided with other allegations of misgovernment from a rival Kedah prince. Bangkok's mood was evident in the attitude of the future Rama III, who had been accorded wide-ranging powers owing to his father's ill-health. Suspicious of British aims in the region and determined to maintain Siam's hold in the strategically important peninsula, the prince would not countenance any suggestion of disloyalty. A Siamese fleet was made ready and in November 1821 the invasion of Kedah began. The Siamese were met by a strong Malay force, but when the Kedah Laksamana and Temenggung were killed and the Bendahara captured, Malay resistance collapsed. Hoping to receive British help, Sultan Ahmad fled to Penang where his plight aroused some sympathy among the white community, particularly as British commercial interests in Kedah appeared endangered. However, although loud voices were raised locally in support of intervention, the EIC government in India persistently refused to condone any confrontation with Siam, regarding such a prospect as 'an evil of very serious magnitude'.[6] The question of Kedah's future was made more problematic by Bangkok's appointment of two sons of the Ligor Governor as administrators and by the proximity of Sultan Ahmad. Reluctantly maintained in Penang by the British, his presence provided Kedah Malays with a focus for conspiracies directed against Siamese rule.

Bangkok rewarded the Ligor governor for his part in the subjection of Kedah by bestowing on him the Chau Phaya title in 1822.[7] Two years later Rama III ascended the throne fully prepared to continue the expansionist policies he had pursued as Prince Regent. The Malay rulers liable to be directly affected made clear their apprehension. Already in 1822 Kelantan had unsuccessfully petitioned the British to be accepted as a vassal state. Perak, which had expelled the occupying Siamese with Selangor's help, was in 1825 again reduced to a Siamese vassal under Ligor's control. Appealing to Penang for assistance, the Perak ruler expressed his feelings simply: 'I am afraid, for this country is part of the same continent as Siam.'[8] It seemed that a further extension of Siamese influence into Selangor would soon follow.

This possibility finally aroused the British authorities in India to respond to appeals from the Governor of Penang. Although EIC officials were anxious to avoid direct conflict, they agreed that some kind of agreement was necessary to exclude Siam from Perak and Selangor, where prospects for English investment in the tin trade seemed bright. In 1826 the Military Secretary at Penang, Henry Burney, was sent to Bangkok. After lengthy discussions a treaty was concluded by which Siam agreed not to attack either Perak or Selangor, with the provision that the Perak ruler could, if he wished, send the *bunga mas dan perak* to Bangkok. But although Kedah was clearly acknowledged to be 'a territory subject to Siam', the English wording of the Anglo-Siamese Treaty left the status of Kelantan and Trengganu ambiguous. Burney was careful to guarantee British trade there, for Singapore's commercial links with Kelantan and Trengganu had alerted Straits business interests to the attractiveness of the east coast. The populations of Kelantan and Trengganu were estimated as being higher than other Malay states, and until the mid-nineteenth century the east coast economy, based on trade and agriculture, outstripped that of the western states. While no British military involvement was permitted in Kelantan and Trengganu 'on any pretext whatever', the treaty did not formally recognize Siamese overlordship. Even at the time, British policy makers realized the advantage of such an omission if British 'protection' were to be eventually extended over the peninsula. But this ambiguity only existed in European eyes. From Bangkok's point of view, Kelantan and Trengganu were vassal states who acknowledged their tributary status by sending the *bunga mas dan perak* every three years.

In Perak, where Ligor's interests had always been greater than Bangkok's, the ties with Siam were also severed in 1826. Captain James Low was sent to Perak by the Penang authorities and on his own initiative concluded a treaty by which the EIC recognized Perak's sovereignty and promised help in case of attack. Although the Governor-General in Calcutta refused to ratify this agreement, it was never explicitly abrogated and thus allowed the continuation of a vague relationship between Perak and the British. With Penang's encouragement the Perak ruler formed a new administration free of any pro-Ligor officials and publicly announced that he would no longer send the gold and silver flowers to Bangkok.

Among the other northern Malay states, the experience of Thai overlordship undoubtedly helped sharpen the sense of being Malay. For centuries Malay rulers in Kedah and Patani had fretted against the sending of tribute, seizing the opportunity of weak Thai rule to ignore their overlord's claims. It was to such troublesome areas, which were an important source of manpower and rice, that powerful Thai kings sent their invading armies. The suffering experienced by Malays at Thai hands left its mark in folk memory. Stories of carnage, looting and rape had become so closely associated with Thai armies that the first reports of Siam's advance on Kedah in 1821 were sufficient to cause a terrified flight of refugees to the safety of English protection in Penang and Province Wellesley. Such punitive expeditions served to widen the gulf between the Thai overlord and the Malay vassals. However, the centuries of contact between the two cultures was nonetheless reflected in the northern Malay states, where a distinctive Malay culture emerged which owed much to the Thai. This influence was the more obvious because the court language and culture of Riau-Johor were still regarded as being 'pure' Malay. Munshi Abdullah in his travel accounts thus contrasted the dialect of Kedah, Kelantan and Trengganu with 'the Malay language' and drew a distinction between *joget Melayu* and the Thai-influenced dances of Kelantan.[9]

Despite regional differences, those Malays living under Thai suzerainty still remained firmly rooted in the Malay world and shared a common heritage with their southern brethren. They too acknowledged the same traditions, the same set of norms governing interpersonal relations subsumed in the word *bahasa* (language, etiquette), the same perception of the world and above all the same adherence to the faith of Islam. The degree to which Siam's Malay vassals relied upon their sense of being Malay to maintain the distinction between them and their overlord is seen in the *Hikayat Sri Kelantan*'s description of the king of Siam as 'an infidel [who] does not know correct behaviour [*bahasa*]'.[10]

In the nineteenth century the role of religion in shaping Malay relations with outsiders, and particularly Siam, took on a new character because of a marked change in Islam's doctrinal mood. In 1803 a puritanical sect, the Wahabi, had succeeded in capturing Mecca, and the wider Moslem community reverberated to their call for a purification of the faith and a return to the Koran's basic teachings. Another feature of this reforming wave was the increased stress on Islam as a militant religion and on religious teachers as both spiritual and temporal leaders. In the archipelago the impact of such doctrines was apparently first felt in Minangkabau, but their influence soon extended to the peninsula. Several important Islamic works had been translated into Malay and became a means by which the reformist teachings spread. Another medium for propagating Wahabi ideas was the influential *tarikat*, the mystical Sufi brotherhoods.[11] Some of the most prestigious, like the Naksyabandiyyah, which had been influential in the region since the early seventeenth century, were quick to respond to Wahabi condemnations of moral decay and embarked on a process of self-purification.

The new resurgence in religious militancy with its call for Islamic unity was particularly appealing in Kedah after the Siamese conquest. The efforts by Sultan Ahmad and other *anak raja* to regain possession of Kedah took on the character of a holy war (*jihad*) against a regime which was not only non-Malay but *kafir* (infidel). For nearly two decades Kedah princes and Islamic leaders joined in a resistance to the Siamese which held the attention of Malays everywhere. Moslem merchants in the Straits Settlements and even some Europeans lent covert support, and it was probably about this time that the Penang-based Red Flag society was formed as a rallying point for Islamic opposition. In 1831, Tunku Kudin, Sultan Ahmad's half-Arab nephew, actually succeeded in capturing Kedah and held it for six months before Siamese rule was reinstated. Anxious to maintain friendly relations with Bangkok, the Penang government had already run a naval blockade to prevent supplies reaching what were described as Malay 'pirates', and Sultan Ahmad was forcibly moved to Melaka to discourage further resistance. In 1838, however, another Kedah prince expelled the Siamese from Kedah, and Malay forces pushed northwards to Patani and Singora, sacking Buddhist pagodas as they went. Supported by Penang's blockade of the Kedah coast, the Siamese were able to reassert their control of Kedah and Patani in a few months.

The intensity of anti-Siamese feeling in Kedah caused Bangkok some concern. When the Ligor governor died in 1839 the authority of his sons was reduced and Muang Saiburi (Kedah) was divided into four regions — Setul, Perlis, Kabang Pasu and Kedah proper (the last two being combined in 1859). Each of these was governed by a Malay chief who was simultaneously a Siamese official, his appointment dependent on his willingness to work with Bangkok. In 1842, following pressure from British officials anxious to see peace in Kedah, Sultan Ahmad was restored to his throne but died three years later. The legacy of the conflict between Kedah and Siam remained. Kedah's population loss was substantial, and although refugees trickled back the previously thriving economy was not fully restored until the 1870s. Furthermore, the influence of both Penang and Siam, if either cared to exert it, had been considerably strengthened. In 1848 Penang invoked Low's 1826 engagement with Perak, forcing Sultan Ahmad's successor to transfer the disputed border district of Kerian to Perak. But at the same time the Kedah court so feared Bangkok's wrath that it refused to cede to Penang another small district adjoining Province Wellesley. The subsequent development of a strongly centralized Malay government in Kedah and its friendly relations with Bangkok could not disguise the reality of Siamese suzerainty.

Bangkok's ability to enforce the installation of co-operative rulers was also apparent in Trengganu and Kelantan where there had similarly been rumblings of discontent against the Siamese overlord. Rulers in both states sent troops to assist a Patani uprising in 1832 and provided a place of refuge for the fugitives from avenging Siamese forces. Yet after witnessing Patani's total subjection by Siam neither Sultan could realistically contemplate renewed resistance. A further argument for appeasing Bangkok was the assurance of support against rival claimants to the throne. These considerations moved Sultan Muhammad I of Kelantan (ca. 1800—37) to reaffirm his loyalty as a vassal to his Siamese overlord and pay a substantial indemnity, thus enabling him to survive the Patani crisis. On his death a civil war broke out, but another Siamese-backed prince, Sultan Muhammad II (1838—86) was eventually

restored as ruler. His long reign was due not only to his strong person
control but to the support of Bangkok, a powerful deterrent to other
contenders for the throne.

The situation in Trengganu, too, illustrates the readiness of Siam to
manipulate local politics. Unlike his neighbour, the Trengganu ruler
had been reluctant to make his peace after his involvement with Patani,
and Bangkok took advantage of a succession dispute to unseat him.
Another claimant to the throne, Baginda Umar (1839−76), then living
on the island of Lingga, was encouraged to return to Trengganu. With
only a small force he succeeded in seizing power and exiling the former
ruler to Kelantan.

With Malay rulers acknowledging Siamese control, and with King
Mongkut of Siam (Rama IV, 1851−68) and his son Chulalongkorn
(Rama V, 1868−1910) desiring peace, Siamese−Malay relations from
the mid-nineteenth century onward improved markedly. Provided a
Malay vassal recognized his obligations, and conditions in the state
were stable, Siamese interference in internal affairs was minimal.
Malay rulers of talent and ambition were able to exploit their situation,
creating legends which assured them a place in Malay history. Baginda
Umar of Trengganu is remembered as a devout ruler, a man of exceptional ability who devoted his energies to the promotion of trade and
ordered government. According to local memories, he lessened the
possibility of chiefly challenge by making village administration
directly answerable to himself. He also travelled extensively within
the state, extending his authority over outlying areas like Kemaman
and supervising the prospecting of tin and gold in the interior. So free
was his reign of Siamese intervention that he was later erroneously
believed to have refrained from sending the *bunga mas*.[12]

The nineteenth century was a formative period in the history of the
northern Malay states. Previously, Thai control on the peninsula had
waxed and waned in proportion to the strength of successive Thai
kingdoms, but the 1826 treaty placed Siam's Malay vassals within an
internationally recognized and far less flexible sphere of influence.
They now had little choice but to continue to acknowledge Siamese
overlordship. It was clear, as Governor Ord of Singapore remarked in
1868, that the Siamese 'assumed the right to act for the [Malay] Rajas
without asking their consent and that they anticipated no difficulty or
defection on the part of these rulers'. The traditional Malay policy of
countering Thai strength by enlisting a powerful ally was rendered
ineffective because of the 1826 treaty signed between Siam and Britain,
both of whom were anxious to preserve peace in the peninsula. Thus
in 1867 when Singapore merchants complained of restrictions to trade
in Kelantan, the Siamese government quickly took steps to ensure the
compliance of its Malay vassal. Two years later, Baginda Umar sent a

deputation to London petitioning Britain to extend formal protection to Trengganu without apparently realizing the futility of such a gesture in the face of Siamese—British accommodation.

The Creation of New Political Units in the Peninsula

In British policy elsewhere in the Malay world the 'sphere of influence' concept remained a cornerstone of diplomacy, serving to limit the commercial or political ambitions of rival powers but avoiding the expense of establishing further outposts of empire. However, while British officials in Penang and Singapore regarded Siam with disquiet, in London the principal concern was the possible expansion of other European nations, notably France, into the archipelago. One response to this was the Anglo-Dutch Treaty of 1824. Setting aside centuries of history without a qualm, Britain and the Netherlands agreed to partition the Malay world through the Melaka Straits. By so doing they irrevocably divided the Riau-Johor kingdom and arbitrarily severed the cultural unity of east coast Sumatra and the peninsula. Islands south of Singapore, including Java and Sumatra, were to remain the preserve of the Dutch, who for their part would not seek to set up any settlement on the peninsula. No mention was made of Borneo, but the implications of this were not apparent for another generation.

The Treaty of 1824 provided the rationale for the later colonial division down the Melaka Straits and is thus the basis for the contemporary boundary between Indonesia and Malaysia. At the time, the British government had no intention of any territorial expansion beyond the existing settlements; indeed, the aim of guarding Britain's interests while avoiding direct commitment was to dominate imperial policy for the greater part of the century. This policy was persistently challenged by men on the spot who pressed for a furtherance of British political control in order to guarantee trade. The most vocal exponent of this view, Stamford Raffles, died in 1826 but his writings continued to inspire other Englishmen with a vision of Empire. The interaction of these opposing views is apparent in the wording of almost every treaty concluded by Britain relating to the region. Whether it was with a small Malay state or a major power, these were carefully phrased to minimize involvement while keeping open the possibility of an extension of interests in the future. In 1826 Singapore, Melaka, Penang and Province Wellesley were formed into a single administrative unit called the Straits Settlements which remained under the control of British authorities in India until 1867, when it was transferred to the Colonial Office. It was to become the base whence British influence was gradually extended throughout the peninsula.

The formation of the Straits Settlements coincided with a period of expanding trade and a growing population in all three ports. In Singapore alone Chinese migration pushed the population, estimated at 10,000 in 1824, to nearly 18,000 five years later, and in 1832 Singapore replaced Penang as the capital of the Straits Settlements. But this rapid development did not herald British movement into the peninsula, as some vociferous empire builders had hoped. The debates continued between those who proclaimed the benefits to be gained from commercial exploitation with official British protection, and those who maintained that further involvement would be disastrous. The first test of these differing views came in 1831 in Naning. The energetic Governor of the Straits Settlements, Robert Fullerton, considered Naning part of Melaka and attempted to impose Melaka's land and judicial system and to collect a full tenth of local revenue to which Melaka was in theory entitled by earlier VOC treaties. The British move met strong opposition from a local *penghulu* (district head), Abdul Said, who saw British demands as a deliberate humiliation. In the tradition of Malay folk heroes Abdul Said was credited with supernatural abilities, and he even invoked the powers of the rulers of ancient Melaka by adopting titles once used by them. His resistance to the British, however, was not simply that of Malay against outsider. The affair was complicated because many of the Malays involved were also caught up in another local dispute concerning the installation of a Yang Dipertuan Besar over Sungai Ujung, Johol, Naning and Rembau. A decisive point in the outcome of the conflict came when powerful chiefs, anxious to obtain support in the succession quarrel, defected to the British side. Despite the final British victory, the year-long Naning War aroused strong criticism in London because of the expense entailed and the dubious rewards. To officials in Singapore, Naning remained a sensitive reminder of the complexity of Malay politics and the unforeseen dangers of involvement in Malay affairs.

The arguments of those who opposed any further acquisition of territory gained further ammunition in 1833 when the EIC lost the monopoly of the China trade which had hitherto alleviated the costs of maintaining the Straits Settlements. Like the VOC a century before, the EIC found itself in possession of strategically valuable ports that were not self-supporting and were a drain on financial resources. There was thus no temptation to embark on any further extension of territorial control. If Sultan Husain, created Sultan of Singapore by Raffles, had been a more impressive figure he might well have been able to form a new centre of power as a rival to the old kingdom of Riau-Johor. He was, however, a pathetic personality who proved incapable of arousing the admiration of either British or Malays. Living in obscurity in Melaka, he appeared, remarked Munshi Abdullah scornfully, 'like a tiger without teeth'.

The situation was otherwise with the Riau-Johor ministers. During the latter part of the eighteenth century the independence of the

Bendahara family and its hold over its appanage of Pahang had markedly increased. Bendahara Ali (1806–57) was quick to perceive the possibilities created by the division of the Riau-Johor kingdom and European anxiety to sever links between the peninsula and Dutch-controlled Riau. At first he refused to acknowledge Sultan Husain on the grounds that his principal allegiance was to Riau-Johor, but as time passed he became aware of the advantages of the changed situation brought about by the Anglo-Dutch Treaty. The Riau-Johor court could no longer become involved in Pahang affairs without incurring European displeasure, and in effect the Bendahara was able to conduct himself as an independent king. By 1853 he was sufficiently confident to declare his autonomy, and in 1881 his son, with the support of the Pahang chiefs, assumed the title of Sultan. The nineteenth-century *Hikayat Pahang*, written in the classical Malay court style, serves not merely to glorify and legitimize this new royal house, but to demonstrate Pahang's status as a distinct political unit.

But the greatest beneficiary of the new boundaries established by the English and the Dutch in 1824 was undoubtedly Riau-Johor's Temenggung family, who prospered as Singapore grew. When Sultan Husain died in 1835 no influential voice was raised in support of the succession of his son Ali, then a child of ten. The Governor of Singapore in fact commented that now 'no reason exists for the recognition of a mere titular prince'. Political wrangles about Ali's status continued, but in 1855 it was finally agreed that he could be installed as Sultan of peninsular Johor but with authority only in the small area of Muar. All administrative powers in Johor proper would be ceded to the more energetic Temenggung Ibrahim (1841–61), whose father had been instrumental in the acquisition of Singapore. Although British officials regarded Ibrahim with some misgivings because of his reputation as a pirate, he was still the best candidate for paramount chief. Gradually the Temenggung came to realize the benefits which would accrue to him personally by co-operating with the Singapore government, and with general British approval he governed mainland Johor until his death. The links with Riau gradually weakened or were ignored and by 1885 the position of the Temenggung family was so secure that Ibrahim's son, Abu Bakar, was able to take on the title of Sultan. In so doing he, like Bendahara Ali, formalized an independence from Riau which had effectively existed for over sixty years. The Anglo-Dutch Treaty of 1824 thus indirectly opened the way for the emergence of modern Johor and Pahang as independent states.

The Creation of New Political Units in Borneo

There were other areas on the periphery of the Malay world where the weakening of central authority also created opportunities for ambitious men. The Anglo-Dutch Treaty did not mention Borneo and thus left its relation to the Dutch and British spheres of influence ambiguous. The Dutch had signed treaties with several small sultanates in southeast and southwest Borneo, but had not made any move up the northwest coast where the hold of the Brunei court was purely nominal. Because Batavia was reluctant to assume the financial burden of further expansion, the British were not yet seriously concerned about a Dutch challenge in this area. In any event, for the first half of the century British policy was firmly wedded to the EIC's view that 'trade, not territory' was the goal east of the Melaka Straits. The likelihood of future involvement in the Borneo region became much greater from the 1840s after Sarawak developed as an identifiable political unit.

Sarawak, until the mid-nineteenth century a dependency of Brunei, owes its inception as a state to the ambition of a middle-class English adventurer, James Brooke (1803–68). Brought up in India, Brooke was fascinated by life in the East and was also imbued with Raffles's dream of a benevolent English administration which protected the trader while fostering native welfare. Like Raffles, Brooke's attention was particularly caught by Borneo which seemed to hold out the promise of adventure, a place where his dreams of 'reforming' Malay states might become reality. Arriving in Singapore in 1839 *en route* to northern Borneo, Brooke was entrusted with a message from the Singapore Governor to the Raja Muda of Brunei. When he reached Borneo, Brooke found the Raja Muda struggling to preserve a semblance of authority over Malay chiefs in the Sarawak River area whose independence had grown as Brunei's power declined. The rebellion was still in progress when Brooke returned to Sarawak a year later. As a reward for assisting the Raja Muda to suppress the uprising, and in return for an annual payment of £500, Brooke induced the Brunei Sultan to grant him as a personal fief the area later known as the First Division. Accorded the title Raja of Sarawak in 1841, Brooke set up his capital on the coast at Kuching, a small Malay village, and established a dynasty of 'white rajas' which was to rule Sarawak until World War II.

In a remarkably short space of time Brooke was able to consolidate his authority along the Sarawak River. He pardoned rebellious Brunei Malay chiefs and gave them positions of some administrative authority, while at the same time limiting their power. The interior tribal people of the First Division, the so-called Land Dayaks, were generally willing to accept the new order and presented Brooke with no real opposition. When he attempted to press his authority into the Batang Lupar, Saribas and Sekrang River areas, the home of the 'Sea Dayaks' or Ibans, he faced greater problems. Here authority was fragmented and localized, usually vested in Malay or Arab/Malay chiefs established along the rivers. Their effective power rested on the ability to extract revenue from passing trade and to organize Iban groups to defend their interests against rival claimants. The importance of headhunting in Iban culture and their love of travel and warfare prompted the more aggressive groups to join Malays in expeditions against coastal villages and shipping. Iban traditions also fostered continuous retaliatory raiding between different Iban communities. By classifying virtually all Iban raiding as piracy, Brooke was able to justify the extension of his control into Iban territory where he exploited local rivalries to gain Iban allies. With their help he put down other Ibans who opposed him.

The Brooke campaign against 'piracy' was to play a vital part in extending the territory under Sarawak's control. In 1846 a major campaign was launched on Iban communities along the Saribas, Rejang and Sekrang Rivers. In one engagement a squadron of four British ships and 2,500 Iban recruits in seventy *perahu* killed around 800 'pirating' Ibans. Throughout the 1840s and 1850s Brooke's authority in areas nominally subject to Brunei was evident in the European-manned forts along the Batang Lupar, Saribas and Sekrang Rivers. Combined with the enforced resettlement of nearby Malay communities, these forts denied Ibans access both to the sea and to the Malay leadership which had formerly provided a basis for raiding. Brunei proved willing to accept the expansion of Sarawak authority in return for annual 'cession' payments. In 1853 Brunei formally transferred to Raja Brooke the major Iban-occupied districts of what later became the Second and Third Divisions in return for an annual payment of $1,500.

A recurring question in the first two decades of Brooke rule was the relationship of the White Rajas to Britain. Though London persistently refused to grant James Brooke a formal protectorate, the informal connection between Sarawak and British interests was indisputable. Even before the establishment of the Brooke regime, businessmen in the Straits Settlements had been anxious to seek closer economic ties with Borneo, for the potential profits were already apparent, and native maritime trade between Borneo and Singapore was well established. Merchants in the Straits Settlements naturally assumed that the rule of a European would open the door to business enterprise in Sarawak. The Brookes, however, actively discouraged Western commercial activities, fearing that uncontrolled developments would undermine the indigenous way of life and perhaps their own authority. Despite hostile reaction from Singapore merchants and a rapidly depleting treasury, James Brooke continued to maintain his stance even when reduced to considering financial assistance from Dutch, Belgian or French sources. When loans were advanced by a wealthy English heiress, James finally rejected ideas of soliciting foreign help, and during the rule of the second raja, Charles (1868–1917), the financial situation did improve. But though local smallholders were encouraged, it was Sarawak's trade with Singapore which remained the mainstay of its economy.

On a political level, too, the informal links between Britain and Sarawak could not be ignored. However strained relations with Sarawak might become, officials in London acted on the assumption that they were Englishmen dealing with an Englishman. The Dutch suspicion of Sarawak as simply an extension of the British Empire was not totally unjustified. Brooke rule had coincided with suggestions in Britain that some measures should be taken to prevent another power gaining any foothold in northwest Borneo. The White Raja came to be seen as a possible means by which British domination of an important trade route to China could be secured. In 1846 the British government officially informed the Netherlands that although there were as yet no plans to colonize the area, Britain reserved the right to do so. The following year a treaty was concluded with Brunei, stipulating that all concessions of territory had to receive British approval. By the same treaty Brunei ceded Labuan off the Brunei coast to Britain as a coaling station for steamships and, it was hoped, as a future centre for regional trade.

It is unlikely that the peoples of the Borneo area ever really distinguished between the Brooke regime and the British Government. The Royal Navy assisted James Brooke in suppressing piracy and in establishing his personal control over some of the coastal areas; he was knighted and made the first governor of Labuan; and he acted as British Agent to the Brunei court until 1853. Even in later years, when adverse publicity attached to his anti-piracy campaign had led to a lessening of British support for Brooke, he was still able to draw benefits from his links with London. In 1860 the Governor of Labuan took up the case of a Brunei noble who attempted to deny Sarawak traders entry to the sago rivers of the Mukah region, which was in Brunei territory. The British government, however, adopted a neutral attitude and its non-intervention enabled Brooke to annex valuable sago-producing areas of Mukah and Oya and the territory comprising the Third Division for an annual payment of $4,500.

During the last years of James Brooke's life the value of Sarawak in maintaining a British sphere of influence became more apparent. Dutch authority was expanding in southwest Borneo and there was also a growing apprehension of intrusion by France, the United States or Germany. The presence of an English raja in Sarawak seemed particularly advantageous as France moved to consolidate its position in Vietnam and thus dominate another flank of the sea route to China. Despite years of uncertainty about the precise relationship between Sarawak and Britain, the latter after 1863 effectively recognized Brooke's independence from Brunei, to the extent at least of appointing a consul to Kuching.

The association between Britain and the Brookes did help to reinforce the connection between northwest Borneo and the Malay peninsula. With only a minority of Malays in its varied and scattered population, the Borneo coast had always been on the periphery of the Malay world, and in the *Sejarah Melayu* Brunei had been described as a *negeri asing*, a foreign country. Yet legends of links with Johor were found not only in the Brunei court but among the Bajau, the local sea people, and a text from east Sumatra probably written in the early nineteenth century calls the Borneo kingdoms 'Malay countries' (*negeri Melayu*).[13] The use of 'Malay' as a general term for Moslems in mid-nineteenth-century Sarawak may have been strengthened by Brooke usage. Though the people the Brookes termed Malays were genetically more closely related to other Borneo groups such as Bisayas or Ibans, they were distinguished by their Islamic faith. The consequent propensity to view them in the same way as peninsular Malays was increased because the creation of the Brooke dynasty meant Sarawak was linked, albeit loosely, with the British presence in the Straits Settlements and later the peninsular states. In the words of the second Raja, 'Wherever the Sarawak flag is planted, there English interests will be paramount.'

The Brooke style of government, the personal nature of authority and the opposition to major change, helped establish a unique identity for Sarawak. Nonetheless, some aspects were shared with the later colonial administrations in the peninsular Malay states. A fundamental characteristic in common was the tendency to view the population in terms of ethnic communities. The Brookes divided the range of linguistic and cultural groups in Sarawak into three basic categories, each with distinct roles. 'Malays' were to be discouraged from participating in trade, which the Brookes considered incompatible with their prescribed function of assisting in Sarawak's administration. If not involved in the administration, Malays should be farmers and small-holders. To fill the economic gap, Chinese migration should be encouraged and the Chinese would then trade, cultivate or mine. Finally, the Ibans would serve as Sarawak's fighting forces under the Raja's personal command. The personal relationship Charles Brooke fostered with the Ibans and their specific niche in the administration went far towards creating a feeling of 'Ibanness' in place of the customary fragmentation between longhouse communities.

Another feature characteristic of both Sarawak and the later colonial administrations on the peninsula was the incorporation of native officers into the government while retaining almost all real authority in white hands. The linchpin of Sarawak's government was the White Raja, who at monthly meetings discussed policies and government action with his Supreme Council, which, formed in 1855, included several leading Kuching Malay chiefs. Decisions were then relayed to the European Residents, who were required to be fluent in Malay and sometimes Iban. They in turn presided over their own divisional council and passed down orders to their European District Officers and Native Officers. The latter were normally Malay chiefs who continued to exercise authority in their own region and served as liaison with the headmen of different ethnic communities. The headmen represented their people in any dealings with the Raja or his officers. In 1867 Charles created the Council Negeri, comprising Iban leaders as well as senior European and Malay officials. It had only vague consultative powers but did become an instrument by which policy could be discussed and explained. If Brooke administration did not train the local peoples for self-government, it did foster some notion of allegiance to a central authority alongside the traditional identification with a longhouse, a family group or a river system.

The mid-nineteenth century also saw the first hesitant steps towards the eventual incorporation of present-day Sabah into the Malaysian rather than the Philippine political orbit. Some British officials felt that the northern tip of Borneo, where authority was ill-defined and overlordship claimed by both Brunei and the Sulu sultanate, might provide a means by which Spain would extend her territory southwards. In 1861 the British consul at the Brunei court was even prepared to predict the eventual eclipse of British interests in Borneo unless definite action were taken. Although reiteration of Sulu's independence was the extent to which London would go, this declaration was important because it implicitly denied Spanish authority over Sulu and thus set aside any rights which Spain through Sulu might assert along Borneo's north coast. In 1865 the British government demonstrated a more positive interest in northern Borneo when it learned that the American Consul in Brunei had leased a large tract of land there. Later that year the American Trading Company established a settlement on the Kimanis River, about ninety-six kilometres from Brunei Town. British enquiries in Washington, however, confirmed that the United States was not officially involved and in any event the American settlement was abandoned in November 1866, while the American consulate in Brunei was withdrawn two years later. By 1868, when James Brooke died, there was a tacit understanding in London that Britain, with a minimum amount of commitment, had yet made clear her interests in the northern Borneo area which was now included in the British 'sphere of influence'.

By the middle of the nineteenth century, the Malay world, whether viewed from Bangkok, London, The Hague or Singapore, could be seen as a varied assortment of colonies, vassal states, 'spheres of influence' and independent kingdoms. To a historian the outlines of modern Malaysia are slowly becoming identifiable. At the time the effects of the new alignments were experienced most keenly by Malay rulers, whose family ties represented loyalties which could rarely be contained within precise political boundaries. In 1837, for instance, the Sultan of Riau felt obliged to lend assistance to his cousin, Baginda Umar, in the latter's bid to return to power in Trengganu. These plans were quickly squashed by the Dutch, who feared British reaction to any encroachment over the 'boundaries' established by the Anglo-Dutch Treaty of 1824.

For the majority of peoples in the Malay world the political regroupings as such were not as significant as the social and economic changes which, however imperceptible, were beginning to impinge on their lives. Long before the formal imposition of colonial rule the Western presence had begun to affect the patterns of traditional society, and in this sense justified Munshi Abdullah's perception of a 'new world'.

The Campaign against Piracy

In their desire to safeguard the vital seaborne trade centred on Singapore, the Straits Settlements government placed great emphasis on the elimination of piracy in the region. They were thus pitting themselves against a Malay tradition which had created a distinct cultural niche for pirating activities. As noted in earlier chapters, piracy in the Malay world had played a varied role, whether as a means of forcing trade into local ports or as a source of income for impoverished but ambitious princes. Much of this heritage lingered on into the nineteenth century. The plundering and the savagery of pirate attacks did not detract from the respect accorded a successful raider. Stories abound of local heroes in buccaneering escapades, and the prestige of one *orang laut* group from the island of Galang rested mainly on their reputation as pirates. Sultan Husain of Singapore could thus speak with confidence when he assured Raffles that 'piracy brings no disgrace'.

From the end of the eighteenth century, however, the nature of piratical activity had begun to change. The breakdown in centralized Malay authority in the region and the participation of so many local princes and chiefs removed whatever restraints had existed in the past. The Riau court seemed unwilling or unable to control piracy in neighbouring waters and its authority over *orang laut* in the British sphere was substantially lessened after 1824. To a greater extent than before, *orang laut* piracy had become simply a variation in seasonal occupation. Many *orang laut* groups had attached themselves to Malay chiefs who, in return for a percentage of the profits, helped outfit fleets and supplied the *orang laut* with provisions. From February to early May the latter were principally occupied in collecting sea products for the China trade, but with the southwest monsoon in June they began to move up the Melaka Straits, attacking passing vessels and particularly native craft. In addition, new elements had appeared in the Malay piracy pattern. There was a seasonal raiding fanning out from the Borneo coasts and the Sulu sultanate in search not only of booty but of slaves, preying on shipping along the 2,400 kilometres of ocean between Singapore and Canton. Even more significant than European indictments is the fact that the two major Malay texts of the period, the *Hikayat Abdullah* and the *Tuhfat al-Nafis*, both agree on the unprecedented piracy in the early nineteenth century.

In the past the VOC had waged a wearying and unsuccessful battle against piracy, but had never possessed the means to make any lasting impact. From 1824 the perennial campaign assumed another dimension when the Anglo-Dutch Treaty pledged European co-operation. Although anti-piracy patrols were not co-ordinated effectively until 1835, the combination of European resources, albeit short-lived, was to have far-reaching results. The British and Dutch not only had the advantage of steam-powered gunboats and superior artillery; they were also determined to stamp out a practice which they felt was incompatible with 'civilized' government and of inestimable harm to maritime trade.

A major step in the elimination of piracy came when the Europeans realized the necessity of gaining support from Malay chiefs who were sponsoring local piracy. One of the principal objects of British attention was Temenggung Ibrahim of Johor. Like his father, he had used his authority over a number of *orang laut* groups to organize pirate expeditions in return for a share of the booty. Constantly under pressure from the Singapore government, Temenggung Ibrahim was eventually persuaded to lend his support to the campaign. His changed attitude seems primarily due to his recognition of the benefits of maintaining British approval in his effort to strengthen his hold over mainland Johor and enhance his standing among other Malays. From the 1840s, he, like the leaders of Riau, was probably sending out his own boats to patrol neighbouring waters, joining the small British force which from 1837 was stationed in the Straits. These patrols often met fierce resistance, but the combination of persuasion and force was effective against both *orang laut* and the more formidable Sulu raiders. By the 1870s piracy in peninsular waters had been effectively eradicated.

The eventual success of the protracted European campaign had far-reaching effects on many of the archipelago's maritime peoples. It dealt a severe blow to Malay chiefs for whom piracy was an important source of revenue which enabled them to retain a large following, an acknowledged index of power in the Malay world. It was now much less possible for a member of the ruling class whose fortunes had reached a low ebb to 'seek his fortune' at sea while waiting a chance to make a bid for power. In another sense, the elimination of 'pirates' was also a means of putting down any resistance to Europeans or any authority they supported. Because piracy was regarded as a legitimate way of obtaining revenue, prestigious leaders in the archipelago were frequently involved in raiding activities. It was thus all too easy to see a man like Tunku Kudin, who led Malay resistance against the Siamese in 1831, as a 'pirate' who deserved punishment. Accusations of 'piracy' to justify often savage attacks on pockets of opposition were most clearly demonstrated along the Borneo coasts. Some of the greatest heroes of Iban culture are the nineteenth century leaders who, as 'pirates' and 'rebels' resisted the Brooke advance and the anti-piracy patrols of European ships.[14]

The campaign against piracy may also have been a factor in the declining proportion of native shipping in the overall trade of Singapore. In 1829–30, 23 per cent of this trade was carried by native *perahu*, and 77 per cent by square-rigged vessels; by 1865–6 the figures were 8 per cent and 92 per cent respectively.[15] Quite frequently, as the Straits Settlements Governor, Robert Fullerton, remarked in 1828, a man could be both a trader and a pirate as the occasion warranted, and we have seen that for many *orang laut*, 'piracy' represented merely a change in their seasonal occupation. The European attacks on 'pirates' involved immediate pursuit and shelling of suspected native vessels and the complete destruction of any settlement believed to be a pirate lair. Some abuse of these tactics was undoubtedly encouraged by the monetary payments for pirates killed, captured or present during an engagement which Britain authorized between 1825 and 1850. In the space of a few years during the 1840s, Royal Navy and EIC ships received over £42,000 for actions against piracy. Perhaps not surprisingly, the main Singapore newspaper commented on the decline in native trade between Singapore and Borneo caused by the 'war-like operations' of British gunboats. The experience of one *orang laut*, recorded in the *Tuhfat al-Nafis*, eloquently sums up the bewilderment of a people who were the hapless victims of European determination to safeguard commerce in the region: 'An English warship fired on me, and my *perahu* was smashed to smithereens by bullets as big as husked coconuts.'[16]

Some of the dislocation which must have occurred in the lives of many sea people, for whom trading and raiding had coexisted as part of a cultural heritage, has been documented in Sabah during the late nineteenth century. Here specific policies of taxation, licensing and resettlement instituted by the British North Borneo Company finally forced the Bajau community to move to the land to seek other forms of subsistence and thus brought about lasting changes in Bajau society.[17] The elimination of piracy undoubtedly made the seas safer, but it also came at a time when native shipping was facing increased competition from Chinese, Indian and Arab as well as European seaborne trade. The introduction of steamships in the 1840s foreshadowed the gradual decline of all sail-powered traffic, and even the great fleets of the Bugis became a thing of the past. Maritime trade had always been the life blood of the Malays, the basis of the pre-colonial economy. By the mid-nineteenth century Malay and *orang laut* participation in this seaborne trade had been all but eliminated. In the Singapore region the *orang laut* were fast disappearing as an identifiable group, while in the opinion of contemporary observers Malays were hawkers rather than traders. 'Their one day of glory,' remarks a modern scholar, 'was the New Year's sports [in Singapore] when the Malays and *orang laut* in boats of their own design invariably triumphed over European, Chinese, Bugis and all other competitors.'[18]

Changing Patterns of Trade in the Malay States

The far-reaching impact of the Western presence on regional trading patterns was disguised to some extent because of the expanding trade with China. Although Raffles had originally hoped that Singapore would become a conduit for channelling British goods, especially textiles, to China, his hopes remained unrealized. What attracted Chinese traders to Singapore was still what the British called 'Straits produce', the marine and forest products such as camphor, beeswax, dragon's blood (a resinous gum from the rattan palm), birds' nests, *agar-agar* (seaweed), and so on, which had established the reputation of the Malay world in centuries past. Initially, the trade in Straits produce was given a new stimulus by the growing number of junks arriving in Singapore. For over a hundred years direct trade between China and the Malay world had been limited by VOC demands that all junks make straight for Batavia. The attractiveness of Singapore's free port, however, was quickly recognized by Chinese merchants. In 1821 four large junks docked in Singapore; in 1856—7 the number was as high as 143.[19]

All over the archipelago the demands of the China market encouraged the gathering of local products and closer co-operation between the collector and middleman. During a trip to Pahang Munshi Abdullah in 1838 saw Jakun not only bringing resins, rattans and aromatic wood to trade with Malays but also working in Malay gold mines. In an effort to tap reserves of manpower, Malay rulers may have encouraged *orang asli* headmen to associate more closely with Malay government. In 1844, for example, Bendahara Ali of Pahang appointed a headman as his representative over all *orang asli* in the Endau River area in southern Pahang, while Temenggung Ibrahim of Johor posted agents at numerous aboriginal settlements to supervise forest collection. Gathering forest products also provided a livelihood for numerous *orang laut* groups, especially in the Singapore area, who had been relocated on land and forced to abandon many of their maritime activities. One such group was the *suku* Galang, among the most prestigious of the *orang laut*, who previously had a reputation of being fearsome pirates. In 1837, after the anti-piracy campaign was under way, they asked the Temenggung of Johor if they might settle in Singapore under his protection. They then participated in forest gathering as had many *orang laut* groups before them.

But despite the impressive growth of the China trade, the percentage of overall trade was slowly shifting in favour of Europe. In 1848–9 Britain and Continental Europe account for 16 per cent of Singapore's total trading revenues as against 19 per cent for China; by 1868–9 the figures were 25 per cent and 12 per cent respectively.[20] A reflection of these trends can be discerned in the trade in local products as European industrial development found new uses for the natural resources of the Malay region. Antimony, for example, had only a limited market in parts of the eastern archipelago, where it was used for painting decorations on cloth; in Europe, however, it was in great demand as a component in certain alloys. Deposits had been found in Sarawak in 1824, and Malay chiefs using Dayak labour were quick to open mines and exploit the profits offered by Singapore's prices. So associated was antimony with the region that Malays termed it *batu Sarawak* (Sarawak stone), and Sarawak remained Europe's main source of antimony until the end of the century.

A more dramatic instance of the influence of Europe on the trade in local products was the meteoric rise in the market for gutta percha, previously regarded by Malays simply as one of a number of rubber-like forest resins. Gutta percha's importance rose in the 1840s when Europeans, noting that Malays used it to manufacture buggy whips, realized the potential of a product which could be moulded into any shape by heating and would harden on cooling. With the development of submarine telegraphy, gutta percha was also found to be the only substance which protected cables under water. A Malay chief with access to large tracts of jungle where gutta percha trees grew and with the ability to attract the services of *orang asli* collectors could thus prosper. Temenggung Ibrahim found his monopoly of gutta percha in Johor a welcome substitute for income previously obtained through piracy, and under his leadership the skills of Malays and *orang asli* were combined to bring once again a valued forest product to port. Elsewhere in the Malay world the response to the gutta percha boom was similar. Though the headiness of the early days died as supplies were depleted, gutta percha continued to be an important source of revenue for many Malaysians until it was superseded by other rubber-like products towards the turn of the century.

Nonetheless, the collecting of forest and marine products could not expand indefinitely to meet increased demands. For centuries part of their very value had lain in their scarcity and their limited natural occurrence in certain areas of the jungle. No forest product was cultivated, and collection was attended by strict adherence to certain prescribed formulae which would appease the spirits of the items being gathered. It was also believed that the spirits would be angry if the quantities gathered were too great. With the rising profits in Singapore, many of the age-old strictures were ignored by the Malay middlemen who bartered with the *orang asli* and who stood to gain from greater sales of Straits produce. The recruitment of larger numbers of *orang asli* collectors and the increased demands of Malay middlemen placed in jeopardy the delicate balance which for hundreds of years had allowed harvesting to proceed without endangering the ecology of the jungle. Towards the end of the century, as far away as Sarawak, the Kenyahs of the Baram River area complained that Iban incursions into their territory were denuding the country of jungle produce. The fate of gutta percha was a sobering example of the new strains on the environment. Though it is possible to tap gutta percha resin without damaging the tree, the process was extremely slow and it became common practice to cut the tree down and bleed the trunk at regular intervals by ringing. Even by what has been called a 'predatory' method, ten full-grown trees were still needed to supply enough resin to make one *pikul* (about 62·5 kg) of gutta percha. With the commercial market for gutta percha, the wholesale destruction of trees went on unchecked and in many areas of the peninsula, notably Singapore and Johor, gutta trees virtually disappeared.[21]

The problems of locating specific jungle products, the intermittent nature of collection, and the dependency on a personal relationship between collector and middleman imposed obvious restraints on the future of forest collection as a revenue earner. Because it remained largely in indigenous hands and continued to function along traditional lines it was not an attractive field for investment. Singapore merchants, both Chinese and British, were anxious to find profitable avenues for capital investment which would complement their trading activities and offset losses. They were therefore looking for activities where the injection of finance would guarantee expansion and good returns. In the opinion of Straits business interests, the only really potentially rewarding areas for investment, able to service both the China trade and the growing markets in Europe, were commercial agriculture and tin mining. It was here that they turned their attention.

Chinese Domination of Commercial Agriculture and Mining

In the early years of the nineteenth century Europeans in the Straits Settlements had embarked on some experimental plantation agriculture, hoping to exploit the European market. Coffee, cotton, tea, tobacco and spices had all been planted but none had yielded the anticipated profits. Chinese agriculturalists, on the other hand, had greater success. It was they who pioneered sugar planting in Province Wellesley and thus encouraged later efforts by Europeans. Chinese achievements were most apparent in their three favoured crops —

tapioca, (especially in the Melaka area), pepper and gambier. There was a steady demand for tapioca in flake, pearl or flour form and, like gambier, it ensured rapid returns because of the relatively short life cycle. Pepper was seasonal and slower to mature but it could be combined profitably with gambier which was harvested the year round. Gambier acted as a cover for the pepper vine and also helped reduce erosion, while the residue remaining after the gambier leaves had been boiled in preparation for processing could be used as fertilizer. Chinese migrants had already developed extensive pepper and gambier estates in Singapore by the mid-1830s, initially feeding the China trade but increasingly drawing their profits from Europe. In Britain gambier was widely used in dyeing and in the tanning of leather in pre-plastic days, and the attraction for investors was enhanced after the abolition of duties on gambier in 1834.

Profits from tin also increased. Until the 1850s the principal markets for Malay tin were still India and China, but with the expansion of British tin plate manufacturing and the repeal in 1853 of all duties on tin imported into Britain, sales there leapt ahead. The technological advance of the steamship meant that Singapore and London were now only five weeks apart by sea, and after the opening of the Suez Canal in 1869 the passage was reduced even further. The continuing improvement in communications enabled Straits merchants to take greater advantage of favourable prices in England and Europe.

Chinese participation in plantation agriculture and mining was already apparent in the eighteenth century, and in the nineteenth they came to dominate production in these two industries. Many arguments have been advanced to explain the displacement of Malays in the local economy during this period. Inherent cultural attitudes may well have been a contributing factor, since although Malays had traditionally been noted as energetic traders, they seemed unwilling to work for wages on estates or in mines. But there were other more specific reasons for the tightening Chinese economic hold in the mid-nineteenth century, such as an available labour force, ready capital and an effective business organization.

In the first place, the pool of Chinese manpower in the region was rapidly increasing. By 1827 the Chinese were the largest single community in Singapore, and by 1845 they formed more than half its population. In a less spectacular fashion, the same pattern was repeated in urban centres elsewhere. Kuching, a Malay village in 1840, had by the end of the century become a predominantly Chinese town. Active encouragement was given to this migration by both the Straits Settlements and the Sarawak governments, for Chinese energy and enterprise were widely acknowledged. A Chinese community was also valuable because it provided the European administration with a guaranteed source of revenue through taxes levied on opium, pork, pawnbroking and the sale of spirits. The administration itself was freed from the burden of collecting taxes since this was rented out to other Chinese, either an individual or a syndicate. As Francis Light had perceptively remarked in 1794, 'The Chinese . . . are the only people of the east from whom a revenue may be raised without expense and extraordinary efforts of government.'[22]

Unsettled conditions in South China, and especially the outbreak of the Taiping rebellion in 1851, acted as a stimulus to migration, mainly from the southeast provinces of Kwangtung, Fukien and Kwangsi. As a consequence, the Chinese population in the nineteenth-century Malay areas comprised five major speech groups: Teochew and Cantonese from Kwangtung; Hokkien from Fukien; Hakka from the mountain areas of Kwangtung, Kwangsi and Fukien; and Hainanese from the island of Hainan. Some paid their own passage, bribing local officials in order to bypass Manchu restrictions against emigration, but the majority came under the iniquitous credit ticket system. Sometimes voluntarily, sometimes compelled, the *singkeh* (new man) bound himself to a Chinese employer in return for his passage from China. Enduring the appalling conditions of shipboard existence, these men were put ashore in Singapore to become a key ingredient in the labour force in the urban centres, the agricultural estates and the peninsular tin mines. Until they had worked off their term of service they received no wages apart from maintenance, but after this they were in theory free to choose another occupation or find a different employer.

The Chinese who came to the Malay world were intent on one thing: to escape the life of grinding poverty they had known at home. The hopeful could always point to successful merchants like the famous Hoo Ah Kay, more commonly known as Whampoa after his birthplace. A Cantonese who had migrated to Singapore in 1830 as a youth of fifteen, Whampoa later made his fortune in business and land speculation. As one of the few Singapore Chinese able to speak fluent English, he was able to mix socially with Europeans and even acted as Russian vice-consul. Although only a minute percentage of the Chinese migrants could ever hope to attain such wealth, the lure of riches continued to draw them in their thousands. Demographic changes rapidly extended beyond the Straits Settlements to the Malay states. In the 1830s the small Chinese mining communities scattered through the peninsula rarely numbered more than five hundred; by 1870 there were about 10,000 miners in Sungai Ujung alone. Even on the east coast, where the rise in the Chinese population was far less dramatic, migration continued steadily.

Though most *singkeh* were already accustomed to harsh conditions and backbreaking work, the rigours of existence on the edge of the jungle and the depredations of tropical disease took their toll, the death rate in some areas being estimated at 50 per cent. Those who survived exhibited a competitive spirit and determination to succeed which could not but affect the pace of change in the Malay world. It was the Chinese whose experimentation revealed many of the potentialities and limitations of the Malaysian economic environment.

A second factor in Chinese dominance of planting and mining was their access to the capital necessary for development on any substantial scale. This was especially apparent in tin mining where Malay chiefs were unable to fund the extraction of tin from deeper veins as surface deposits were gradually exhausted. It became common for a Malay wishing to open a tin mine to borrow the necessary money from a Chinese merchant in the Straits, and to recruit Chinese labour and management to work the mine. The tin was then sold back to the creditor at a fixed sum, usually considerably below the market value. Initially, much of the capital was supplied by the Baba Chinese society of Melaka and Penang, men whose wealth was acquired from land speculation, trading profits and their position as revenue farmers (collectors of taxes for the Straits government). Most maintained residences and business houses in Singapore, were well acquainted with the local situation, knew Malay and a little English, and could draw on years of experience in dealing with a European administration. It was not long, however, before the Baba Chinese were challenged by successful migrants, among whom Whampoa was a prime example.

What set both Baba and migrant apart from traditional Malay traders was their access to credit, either supplied from their own resources or from wealthy European merchant firms in the Straits Settlements. Over the centuries outsiders had often commented on the lack of liquid capital even among rich Malays. Available funds were usually expended quickly on an open display of wealth and on the maintenance of a large following, the cultural indices of a great man. The inability of most Malays to call on reserves for immediate investment was to have obvious effects even where Malay interests were well established. In Sarawak, Malays in the Mukah River area had been extracting sago for generations. They found it impossible, however, to compete with local Chinese who were able to process their own sago using modern equipment bought with credit obtained from Singapore merchants.

The Chinese also had a concept of business organization which gave them a further advantage in comparison with Malays. Their expertise is clearly seen in the *kongsi*, an association of individuals from the same dialect group and the same area of China who held shares in a co-operative venture. In South China elements of the *kongsi* system had been in existence from the fifteenth century, but refinements had been introduced over the years, especially in the copper mining areas of Yunnan. In the Yunnan *kongsi* organization, a man with capital brought together a group of men from the same clan or dialect group who, whether managers or wage labourers, were willing to share in the gain or loss of a common endeavour. It was this experience and this tradition, characterized by a sense of group cohesiveness and brotherhood, which the Chinese introduced to the Malay world. An added strength of the *kongsi* system was its ties to other major commercial centres of Southeast Asia, a network that was unfettered by political boundaries. Thus the extensive gold mining settlements of Bau on the upper Sarawak River, already well established when Brooke arrived, had been founded by a Hakka *kongsi* which was a branch of a much larger parent body in Dutch West Borneo. By the early nineteenth century the *kongsi* in Dutch West Borneo had developed into a highly sophisticated organization with central and district branches, each comprising an ordered hierarchy of clerks, overseers, accountants, inspectors and labourers.

Chinese—Malay Relations

With a ready pool of labour, access to capital and a business organization to absorb temporary losses, the Chinese position in a rapidly changing economy was secure. There were, of course, some perceptive Malays who were able to take advantage of the new resources the Chinese represented and to work with them in a true partnership. One of these was Raja Juma'at, son of a Riau prince, who had been granted the district of Lukut by Sultan Muhammad of Selangor (1826—57) in 1846. Because of his disciplined government, Chinese merchants in Melaka were willing to advance capital for the development of mines in Lukut in return for a share of the profits. One of Raja Juma'at's backers was Chee Yam Chuan, a fifth-generation Baba Chinese who was head of Melaka's Hokkien community. A genuine trust seems to have existed between these two men, and Raja Juma'at's son, Raja Bot, lived with Chee in Melaka for some time, acting as his business intermediary with other Malays. In 1849 Raja Juma'at's brother, Raja Abdullah, also borrowed large sums of money from Chee Yam Chuan and other Melaka merchants to open up mines in Kelang, granted to him by Sultan Muhammad. The success of these mines at Ampang and Kuala Lumpur soon attracted other Chinese traders and shopkeepers, so that before long the isolated jungle settlement became a small town.

The best example of Malay co-operation with Chinese investors and labourers was undoubtedly in Johor, where Temenggung Ibrahim encouraged the extensive Chinese cultivation of pepper and gambier plantations. From the mid-1840s Chinese began moving to Johor as the estates in Singapore were exhausted, but by controlling the system of land grants Ibrahim was able to maintain active Malay involvement in Chinese economic enterprises. In the system he devised, a Chinese headman, called the *kangchu* ('lord of the river'), was placed in charge of each river where plantations were developed. He received a written authorization, initially similar to the old *surat kuasa* or letter of authority given to a Malay *penghulu* (district headman). This document empowered him to open up plantations, supervise cultivation and act as a revenue farmer. The last-mentioned privilege, the right to collect taxes, was potentially even more lucrative than agriculture.

Ibrahim's son, Abu Bakar (1862—95), further refined the *kangchu* system. The *surat sungai* (river documents) he issued became more closely modelled on a European-style contract, and they were usually given to individual merchants resident in Singapore or to a *kongsi* made up of a group of businessmen. The *kangchu* now became simply the manager for the absentee holder of the *surat sungai*. The Chinese community in Johor was responsible to a Kapitan China, but ultimate authority was still vested in the Temenggung, who could at any time withdraw his support from a *kangchu* or a Kapitan. Abu Bakar was aware of the importance of good relations with the Chinese. In the 1860s when no British official was proficient in any Chinese dialect, Johor had at least one able Malay administrator who could speak Teochew and write characters. Two Chinese were members of Abu Bakar's 24-member advisory council while prominent Malays in his bureaucracy were shareholders in some of the *kongsi*. By the mid-nineteenth century the results of Johor's policy were evident in the expansion of plantation agriculture and the increase in the Chinese population. When Temenggung Ibrahim took office Johor was covered with jungle, and the settlement was limited to scattered Malay villages along the rivers. In the 1860s there were 1,200 gambier and pepper plantations in Johor, employing about 15,000 labourers. Ten years later, though an estimated 100,000 Chinese were living in Johor, friction with the Malay government was rare. A major factor in this situation was the restraints placed on Chinese secret societies. Only one, the Ghee Hin, was permitted to operate in Johor, and until it was disbanded in 1916 a close association was maintained with the Malay government.[23]

Johor's control over the Chinese, however, was exceptional. On the whole, Malay rulers were content to let the Chinese community exist outside centralized control as long as the revenue due to the local authority was paid. Chinese investors in the Straits soon found it more efficient simply to advance finance directly to the mineworkers, bypassing the local Malay chief. This trend was to have far-reaching effects. First, it hastened the rate at which Chinese tightened their grasp of economic resources; secondly, the independence of the Chinese settlements undermined the authority of the Malay chiefs and hence their ability to maintain order. This development was rendered more serious by divisions within the local Chinese society. Rivalries and hostilities between dialect and clan groups were imported from China and formed the basis for quarrels among migrants in the Malay world. Troubles, for instance, often involved Hakka, whose forebears had originated in the mountain areas of South China and who were frequently ridiculed by other Chinese for their distinctive customs and language. In Sarawak, where Hakka dominated the mining industry but where most Kuching Chinese were Hokkien, Teochew or Cantonese, such cultural differences were to have significant effects on local politics.

Dialect divisions were accentuated since they roughly corresponded to differences in occupation. The Cantonese dominated mining and crafts, while the Hokkien and Teochew were agriculturalists, small shopkeepers and boatmen. But even the affinity between Hokkien and Teochew in occupation, speech and customs was undermined because the Hokkien community was more prominent in urban Baba society and had closer links with Europeans. Chinese of the same surname or clan but speaking different dialects also clung to their own dialect group. To complicate the picture further, other rifts were introduced by the conversion of some Chinese to Christianity and by the rivalries between old Chinese communities and more recent arrivals.

The absorption of the Chinese into the existing Malay political and social system was hindered by the so-called 'secret societies'. In China these organizations had begun as a form of mutual-aid society with all the trappings of a quasi-religious group. From the seventeenth century they assumed a political role as well, advocating the overthrow of the foreign Manchu dynasty in China. When the Chinese migrants came to the Malay world, societies based on clan or dialect associations appeared to be an indispensable organization affording protection and assistance in an alien and often hostile environment. They were also of fundamental importance in maintaining links with China and in preserving Chinese values and culture. Although such societies had existed earlier in Dutch Melaka, they were strictly controlled and appeared to have limited their activity to mutual aid ceremonies and rituals related to ancestor worship. There is no record of any open Chinese defiance of Dutch rule and, with members drawn from the highest strata of the local Chinese community, the Melaka societies were more in the nature of exclusive clubs. In Penang and Singapore, however, where the immigrant community was larger and where there was no long-established tradition of leadership, the societies from the beginning had a reputation for fomenting dissent.

By 1825 there were at least three *hui* (societies) in the Straits Settlements: the Ghee Hin, the Ho Seng and the Hai San, which may all have been offshoots of the Triad Society in China. Other societies mushroomed, and their complexity makes generalizations difficult. Though termed secret, they often operated openly apart from matters connected with oaths and ritual. Some societies were small and exclusive, others numbered thousands and could even include Malays, Portuguese, Indians or Jawi Peranakan (Indian/Malay). Sometimes local chapters were controlled by one speech group, or even a clan, but leadership could pass into different hands with the passage of time. Nor was each society a united and monolithic group. The possible permutations are illustrated by the Singapore Ghee Hin, which had five subdivisions corresponding to each of the major dialect groups. The Hakka Ghee Hin in Singapore was further split along clan lines. Chinese from one area and one speech group might well divide their allegiance. In one mining area of Selangor, Hakka from Kah Yeng Chew (a prefecture in Kwangtung) belonged to three different societies. However, a feature common to all the societies was their covert but strong relationship with the Chinese business community. A society was often virtually synonymous with a *kongsi*, and most *hui* were wealthy because the members included successful businessmen. Added to this was the more sinister aspect of extortion, blackmail and control of gambling and prostitution which brought the societies into such disrepute and provided an umbrella for the criminal elements among them.

Because of the recruitment, sometimes forcible, of all new arrivals into one of the secret societies, they gained a dominating position in most areas where Chinese settled. While they could provide the migrant with assistance in a strange land and a cultural retreat, they could equally demand his services in any capacity, particularly in the recurring conflicts with rival societies. In a monotonous and exacting life it was not uncommon for thousands of men to be sworn foes because of an isolated dispute involving only a few society members over a woman, or rights to a watercourse, or because of some event as far away as Rangoon or Saigon.

Very little in their culture equipped the Malays to deal with this kind of independent organization. Traditionally Malay rulers dealt with the Chinese as a whole through the Kapitan China, normally a man of standing among both Malays and his own people. For its part, the Chinese community had in the past recognized the right of the Malay Sultan, in consultation with the Kapitan, to adjudicate disputes. As the Chinese population expanded in the nineteenth century these customs no longer applied. Usually the Kapitan China was himself a leading member of a secret society and subject to loyalties and obligations to his own *hui*. This was a major change in the nature of a post which had previously functioned as an extension of the Malay court hierarchy. Furthermore, the growth and increasing diversity within the Chinese population required more than one individual to represent their interests. In Sungai Ujung in the early 1870s, for instance, there were at least five different Chinese headmen.[24] No longer was it possible for the Malay Sultans to exercise the same authority over the proliferating numbers of Chinese headmen as they had done in the past with a single acknowledged Chinese leader.

With the competing interests of dialect, clan, *kongsi* and secret societies, only a rare Kapitan could have exerted authority over all Chinese in his area. Kapitan Yap Ah Loy, who was to oversee the development of the tin mines in the Kuala Lumpur region, was one such figure. A Hakka, he was in 1868 elected Kapitan by the headmen of local Hakka, Cantonese and Hokkien groups, and confirmed in his position by the Sultan of Selangor. Even Yap Ah Loy, for all his prestige, could not ultimately prevent quarrels erupting between different Hakka clans. The Kapitan system was also vulnerable because no rules governed succession to the Kapitan post. As the economic rewards for control over a district became greater, conflicts among the Chinese became more frequent. Now the death of a Kapitan could herald the outbreak of a prolonged power struggle between opposing Chinese groups.

The potential threat of the secret societies to established government was evident in the street fights between *hui* in Singapore and Penang, and in the rioting which often erupted when some unpopular law was promulgated. In Sarawak the Brooke regime was nearly driven out in 1857 by the *hui* which had officially been outlawed. Hakka Chinese from the mining settlement of Bau attacked Kuching, reducing it to ashes, in an effort to assert their economic independence from Raja Brooke. The latter's ability to recruit help from a British steamship in the vicinity, from Cantonese and Teochew of Kuching, from Sarawak Malays, and above all from his Iban levies enabled him to suppress the uprising. Strong leadership was a decisive factor in this success, but at least in the British view it was precisely this element which was most lacking in several Malay states. The need to establish law and order became a celebrated rationale for British involvement in the peninsula.

Malay Conflicts and Straits Settlements Involvement

For much of the nineteenth century Raffles's arguments about the 'decay' of Malay society were implicitly accepted among Europeans in the Straits Settlements. Nowhere did this decay seem better demonstrated than in the civil wars which divided so many peninsular states. But though quarrels over succession and territorial rights were particularly widespread in this period, they were by no means uncommon in earlier times. They could even be said to have played a purifying role in traditional politics. Normally Malay conflicts did not entail great loss of life and were exercises in insult and skirmish rather than full-scale battle. The outcome brought a rearrangement of the power structure at the top rather than a change in the policy or style of government. The typical civil war threw up a powerful man who commanded the loyalty of most influential chiefs, and a period of fighting was then followed by a relatively stable reign.

The ultimate victor in Malay wars was usually one who could rally the strongest or most prestigious allies. In previous centuries ambitious *anak raja* had bought the assistance of Portuguese, Minangkabau, Thai, Bugis or Dutch with promises of future rewards should victory be attained. Nineteenth-century diplomacy, however, had lessened the possibility of gaining support from powerful nations in the region. First, the treaties of 1824 and 1826 restrained Siam and the colonial Dutch government at Batavia from interference in the British sphere of influence. Secondly, the English East India Company and, after its demise in 1858, the British government, was adamantly opposed to any involvement in Malay quarrels. It was considered vital to keep any Malay dispute a local matter so that it did not have repercussions in neighbouring spheres of influence. Britain believed its trade and investment in the area could be adequately safeguarded without any formal commitment to a Malay prince.

The application of this policy can be seen in the Pahang Civil War (1858—63). In many ways it was a classic Malay conflict. Two brothers, Mutahir and Ahmad, both sons of Bendahara Ali, disputed the succession when their father died. In the customary manner, both princes sought to recruit support. Mutahir became allied with Temenggung Ibrahim of Johor, while Ahmad was able to obtain support from Sultan Ali of Muar and from Rembau, Trengganu and Kelantan. Sultan Mahmud of Riau, who had been deposed by the Dutch in 1857 but still claimed to have inherited the rights of Riau-Johor along the east coast, was also associated with Ahmad. In former times such a dispute might well have drawn in rulers throughout the peninsula and east coast Sumatra. Now the Singapore government, anxious to localize the Pahang conflict, at first forbade Ibrahim to lend Mutahir direct assistance. It was understandably disturbed to hear that Sultan Mahmud of Riau had gained Siam's sympathy. After a trip to Bangkok in 1861 Mahmud arrived in Trengganu escorted by a Siamese ship, and there were widespread rumours that he might be installed as ruler in Pahang or Trengganu. Fears of increased Siamese influence on the east coast and pressures from Singapore merchants who had invested in Pahang finally convinced Governor O. Cavenagh (1859—67) to support Mutahir's claim. In November 1862, as a warning to Bangkok and to force Sultan Mahmud to leave, Cavenagh ordered a warship to shell Kuala Trengganu.

This episode did not signal the installation of Mutahir as Bendahara in Pahang, for an outraged British government considered Cavenagh's action far too extreme. Prevented from taking further steps which would directly involve Britain, Cavenagh could only encourage the alliance between Mutahir and Singapore's friend, the new Johor Temenggung Abu Bakar. Despite military assistance from Johor, Mutahir could not defeat Ahmad. The latter, supported by powerful Pahang chiefs, gained-from his links with ex-Sultan Mahmud who could still arouse memories of loyalty to Riau-Johor. In 1863 Ahmad successfully invaded Pahang from his Trengganu base. Shortly afterwards Mutahir and his son both died, and Ahmad then became Bendahara. He lost no time in making his peace with Singapore, where the government was pleased simply to see order restored. As Governor Blundell (1855—9) had earlier remarked, 'It matters not who rules [Pahang], but it is of importance that its trade and general prosperity should not be destroyed.'[25]

Though Malay diplomatic traditions always favoured an ever-widening alliance system, the Pahang conflict had been successfully contained. The most powerful European states in the region — Britain and the Netherlands — were unwilling to be directly drawn into local quarrels, and Siam's influence had been effectively confined to the northern peninsula. On the west coast, however, there were many other potential sources of support for ambitious princes. Not only was the Chinese community large, but it was already divided into society and clan factions which were often bitter enemies. Furthermore, Straits Settlements investment in the tin mines was considerable, and the merchants concerned were naturally anxious that the Malay prince who gained power should be amenable to further economic development. These factors had played a relatively minor role in Pahang, where less extensive tin deposits had attracted only limited Chinese migration and outside capital. But in Perak, Selangor and Negeri Sembilan, as Malay chiefs fought for political control to ensure their prestige and revenue, Chinese mining groups and Straits merchants alike were determined that the victorious Malay faction should favour their particular interests. Solicited by one or another Malay leader, the Chinese clans and societies contributed money, supplies, arms and fighting men, while in the Straits Settlements both British and Chinese merchants gave financial backing.

The extent of local non-Malay involvement made the character of nineteenth-century Malay conflicts on the west coast different from those of the past. The supply of funds from the Straits and the pool of fighting men among the Chinese groups prolonged quarrels in a manner hitherto impossible. Because of the numerous vested interests, any Malay disputes in the tin producing states had ramifications stretching far beyond the local issue itself. As the fighting became more widespread through the 1860s and early 1870s, the Straits government was subject to increasing pressure from various lobbies, ranging from individual merchants and shareholders in important companies to English legal firms employed by Chinese secret societies. Through public meetings, the press, petitions and personal connections these interest groups argued that Britain must take steps in the Malay states to create a climate more conducive to investment and trade.

The leader of the mercantile community and the most outspoken advocate of British intervention was W. H. Read (1819–1909). Connected with several leading Singapore companies, he was President of the Singapore Chamber of Commerce and senior non-official member of the Legislative Council. He also had longstanding business connections with several Malay states. Read's partner, Tan Kim Cheng (1829–92), was a noted Singapore-born Hokkien merchant whose commercial interests extended throughout the peninsular states as far as Saigon and Bangkok. This partnership was to play a crucial role in the complex events leading to British intervention in the west coast states in 1874.

The core of the civil wars in the tin areas was the continuing struggles between members of the Malay ruling class.[26] In the Negeri Sembilan confederacy this had a long history. The death in 1824 of the Yang Dipertuan Besar, a prince brought from Minangkabau, initiated a decade of rivalry among contending heirs. Another prince from Minangkabau attempted to assume the office in 1826 but failed, leaving the field open for further fighting among local princes. These prolonged conflicts meant repeated blockades of river traffic as chiefs attempted to extend their control of revenue or levy new customs duties. Hostilities were most pronounced between the Dato Kelana, the territorial chief of Sungai Ujung, and the Dato Bandar, who controlled the middle reaches of the Linggi River. Their quarrels severely hampered Melaka's economy, which was dependent on the tin trade from Sungai Ujung and Linggi. In 1857 the Singapore Governor even despatched an expedition to destroy toll stations erected along the Linggi River, but the effects were shortlived. Local trade received a further setback when Chinese–Malay violence erupted in 1860 after the Dato Kelana attempted to increase taxes imposed on the Chinese community. The pattern of succession disputes, wars and disrupted trade was repeated in 1869 after another Yang Dipertuan Besar died. Under pressure from Straits merchants, the Singapore Government began considering the appointment of a British agent in Linggi to act 'as a referee upon all matters appertaining to the commerce between our merchants and the native traders'.[27]

In Selangor the seeds of conflict were sown during the reign of the ineffectual Sultan Muhammad (1826–57). In 1849 or 1850 he transferred control of the rich tin area of Kelang, previously held by his own son, to Raja Abdullah, brother of Raja Juma'at of Lukut. Raja Mahdi, Sultan Muhammad's grandson, had expected to receive Kelang as his appanage and never reconciled himself to its loss. In other parts of Selangor enterprising *anak raja* were also carving out lucrative holdings, drawing their income from levies made on goods passing along their river and from a share in the profits of Chinese-worked tin mines. By the time Abdul Samad (1859–93) came to the throne, Selangor was effectively divided into five different territories, corresponding to each of the major river systems – Lukut, Kelang, Langat, Bernam and Selangor proper. The princes controlling these districts were prepared to use force to counter any attempt to undermine their authority or wealth.

In 1866 the head of Kelang, Raja Abdullah, granted the Read–Tan syndicate the tax farms in his district in return for 20 per cent of the profits. The following year Raja Mahdi, whose father had once ruled Kelang, disputed the payment of taxes to the Read–Tan group. Fighting broke out and soon Raja Mahdi succeeded in establishing himself in Kelang. However, the Selangor ruler, Sultan Abdul Samad, saw Raja Mahdi's refusal to remit revenues as rank defiance. The Sultan recruited the support of his son-in-law, a Kedah prince called Tengku Kudin (Ziauddin) who had no appanage of his own and was therefore interested in gaining control of Kelang. Meanwhile, Abdullah had died but Kudin found an ally in Abdullah's son, Ismail, who also had ambitions of regaining hold over Kelang.

Like rival Malay princes in centuries past, both sides sought to marshal their allies, forming alliances with local chiefs, leaders of migrant communities and adventurers who could call on large supplies of manpower. The presence of rival Chinese clans and societies in Selangor offered the possibility of further extending these alliances. The Hakka community in Selangor was already split by quarrels between two major clans, the Fui Chew and the Kah Yeng Chew, each linked with separate secret societies. The noted Kapitan Yap Ah Loy, leader of the Fui Chew, was a member of the Hai San while most of the Kah Yeng Chew belonged to the Ghee Hin society. From the end of 1869 Yap Ah Loy and the Fui Chew supported Tengku Kudin; their rivals, the Kah Yeng Chew, joined forces with Raja Mahdi's supporters.

By 1871 the search for powerful allies had gone further, as Raja Mahdi turned to Maharaja Abu Bakar of Johor and Tengku Kudin looked to Rembau and his relations in Kedah. Influential interests in the Straits Settlements had also been drawn in. In order to strengthen their position Raja Mahdi and Raja Ismail obtained financial support from Chinese merchants in Melaka, while Tengku Kudin borrowed money from several Singapore financiers. Notable among his creditors was the Read—Tan Kim Cheng syndicate, which had earlier leased the Kelang revenue farms. Another was James Guthrie Davidson, whose family had developed the powerful merchant firm of Guthrie & Co. and who was himself a well-known lawyer and Secretary of the Singapore Chamber of Commerce. What had begun as a quarrel over territorial rights in Kelang now touched the nerve centre of economic and political influence in the Straits Settlements.

During the first stages of the war the two sides seemed evenly matched, but the Tengku Kudin/Raja Ismail alliance eventually gained the advantage. In March 1870 Tengku Kudin captured Kelang and the retreating Raja Mahdi then established himself at the mouth of the Selangor River. Through personal connections in Singapore, Tengku Kudin was able to convince the Straits authorities that his rule in Kelang would encourage peaceful trade. The capture of a Penang Chinese merchant vessel at Kuala Selangor seemed convincing evidence of Raja Mahdi's piracy, and he was forcibly driven out by British troops who had come to seek restitution. In 1871 the Colonial Secretary, J. W. W. Birch, visited the Selangor capital at Langat and officially promised future support to Kudin, formally acknowledging his position as Sultan Abdul Samad's 'viceroy' in Selangor and lending him a British man-of-war to enforce his position.

By throwing its weight behind Kudin, the Singapore government had stepped beyond London's policy of non-intervention and in so doing had prevented the expected dénouement in a traditional civil war. The local British authorities, like the Dutch before them, had been drawn inexorably into Malay politics as they came to believe that only an amenable ruler could assure the continuing profitability of trade. Kudin was not liked by the Selangor chiefs and could not have maintained his position without continued outside help. By 1872 the war had already swung back in Mahdi's favour, but Governor Ord (1867—73) encouraged offers of help from the Bendahara of Pahang. With Pahang's assistance the Kelang and Selangor rivers were by the end of 1873 again under Kudin's control. The outcome of the Selangor wars demonstrated to Malays that even an unpopular or weak prince could gain power with British assistance. This lesson was quickly learned and applied by other Malay factions in the internal disputes which beset Perak.

Here quarrels over succession were also longstanding. A system of rotating the rulership between three different branches of the royal family, instituted at the beginning of the century, had been intended to prevent disputes but had never functioned perfectly. Problems were bound to arise if a prince were for any reason unacceptable as a ruler. Although the dearth of sources makes reconstruction of events in the

1850s difficult, it is clear that the system was undergoing strain. Sultan Abdullah (1851—7) faced a serious challenge from other princes, led by the Raja Muda. He then appealed to Singapore, an admissible recourse because of Low's (unratified) treaty in 1826 which had assured Perak of British protection. This move apparently checked the rebellious faction, and when Sultan Abdullah died in 1857 the Raja Muda was duly installed as Sultan. The chiefs, however, refused to appoint Sultan Abdullah's son, Raja Yusuf, to the third royal position of Bendahara because he had opposed many of them in the recent conflict. He was also likely to be an autocratic ruler when his turn came to succeed. Instead, a prince of lesser birth, Raja Ismail, was chosen as Bendahara, leaving Yusuf resentful and humiliated.

The enmity of several princes was cause enough for hostility within the ruling class, but in Perak the ambitions of powerful chiefs further increased the possibility of conflict. Aided by geographical isolation and with access to extensive tin deposits, they could maintain themselves economically and become independent of royal authority. The district of Larut, separated from Perak proper by a range of hills, became a particular trouble spot. In 1848 Long Ja'afar, the territorial chief of Larut, had invited Chinese miners to develop the tin deposits there. When he died in 1858 his son, Ngah Ibrahim, inherited Larut's considerable wealth as well as its large Chinese population. The majority of these were Chen Seng Hakka who were members of the Hai San. Fighting broke out in 1861 when another Hakka group from the Fui Chew clan, most of whom were Ghee Hin adherents, attempted to gain control of a watercourse feeding the mines of both factions. Since each group had strong ties to societies and business interests in Penang, and since many Larut Chinese claimed to be British subjects from the Straits Settlements, it was impossible to confine the quarrel to Larut. Penang merchants were also eager to influence the outcome of the disputes, seeing their rewards not only in tin mines but in domination of the Larut opium farms.

Initially, the group backed by the Hai San succeeded in expelling its rivals, but the Ghee Hin faction drew on its Penang connections, persuading the Penang government into forcing compensation from Perak for the loss of their mines. A British gun boat was consequently sent to blockade the Larut River. Ngah Ibrahim then paid the amount demanded from his considerable tin revenue. In 1863 the Perak ruler rewarded him with the title of Orang Kaya Menteri and confirmed his authority over Larut.

Feuding between the hostile Chinese groups simmered after this episode, but soon boiled over again because of the favouritism shown by Ngah Ibrahim to the Chen Seng Hakka and their allies. It even seems likely that he had become a member of their supporting society, the Hai San. By 1865 the Ghee Hin group had been forced out of Larut, but the fighting spread into the rest of Perak. Serious riots also erupted in Penang in 1867, the involved alliances between different clans and societies reflecting the complexities of local Chinese politics. At the height of the struggles in Larut, one side consisted largely of Fui Chew Hakkas and San Neng Cantonese from the 'Four Districts' (Si Kwan) region of southwest Kwangtung who belonged to the Ghee Hin and Ho Hup Seah societies; while the other side was comprised mainly of Chen Seng Hakka from the 'Five Districts' (Go Kwan) who were members of the Hai San society. By 1870 the Ghee Hin grouping had become sufficiently strong to move back into Larut again, and although the Hai San formed an alliance with two other societies, the Penang-based Hokkien Toh Peh Keng and the Ho Seng, the conflict in 1872–3 was still unresolved.

The protracted fighting between the Chinese in Larut soon became deeply enmeshed in the festering succession quarrels in Perak itself. For several years deteriorating relations between members of the ruling class had threatened to bring about civil war, and matters finally came to a head after the death of Sultan Ali (1865–71). Raja Muda Abdullah was the obvious candidate for succession, but he did not appear at the funeral where custom dictated the election should take place. In his continued absence the chiefs elected Bendahara Raja Ismail as ruler. Ismail's genealogy was less prestigious than Abdullah's, and he had already been passed over twice for the office of Raja Muda. Now, however, he had the advantage of support from powerful members of the ruling class. Foremost among these was Ngah Ibrahim, who had quarrelled with Abdullah some years earlier and who himself had aspirations towards the position of ruler. In the following months Raja Abdullah enlisted the help of the Ghee Hin, while Ngah Ibrahim vacillated between several Chinese societies, finally opting for his old friends, the Hai San, in late 1872. In the same year Raja Abdullah openly assumed the title of Sultan, to which he claimed a greater right than Ismail. He could justifiably argue that this claim, if recognized, gave him the state's revenues and resources to bestow as he wished. Having failed to arouse official British interest, he approached Tan Kim Cheng, W. H. Read's partner and a member of the Ghee Hin, and offered him the Larut tax farms in return for assistance.

The Debate on 'Civilization'

Raja Abdullah's decision to solicit Tan Kim Cheng's aid came at a time when the Straits merchants were as never before convinced of the need for British intervention in the peninsula. In the late 1860s tin prices in Britain had risen dramatically, a trend stimulated when the the opening of the Suez Canal in 1869 further shortened the voyage to

Europe. The commercial community in the Straits Settlements were adamant that the disturbances in the Malay states endangered not only trade and capital investment, but also inhibited future economic opportunities. Whipped up by the editorials of influential newspapers, public opinion in the Straits was agreed that drastic changes were necessary to halt the 'decay' in Malay society. The transferral of the Straits Settlements from the India to the Colonial Office in 1867 had not brought any change in the official policy of non-intervention, and it seemed clear that Britain would never countenance outright annexation. However, it might be more amenable to the notion of some kind of British agent whose advice would encourage a Malay ruler to govern in a 'civilized' manner, creating an environment in which commerce could thrive.

The acceptance by Malay rulers of 'civilization' was the keynote of this proposal, first put forward by Straits merchants in 1871. 'Civilization' naturally meant the adoption of English law, English government and, as far as possible, an English way of life. It was felt that no prince could do better than model his rule after that represented by a 'superior' culture. Indeed, in the Malay states several examples could be cited of princes who had established good relations with Straits merchants and officials, and in so doing had bettered their own position. Raja Juma'at of Lukut (died 1864) had become a close friend of the Resident Councillor of Melaka, who acted as guardian for Raja Juma'at's son during a period of English schooling in Melaka. He worked closely with the Straits government, donating land for the construction of a lighthouse, co-operating in the campaign against piracy and helping to apprehend fugitive criminals. Under Raja Juma'at's rule Lukut had appeared a model state, and his willingness to 'introduce our modes of government' raised him high in British esteem. 'Raja Juma'at', said the Governor of Singapore, was 'perhaps the most intelligent of the Malay chiefs and one moreover who has invariably shown a disposition to cultivate our alliance and to be guided by our advice'.[28] The ability of Tengku Kudin of Kelang to rally support in Penang and Singapore was equally due to his willingness to adopt English ways. After taking control of Kelang in 1871 he made some efforts to reorganize the administration, even giving the streets English names. His desire to foster a 'civilized' reputation in the Straits Settlements is suggested by his ostentatious sherry drinking and the pack of dogs he maintained in defiance of Islamic prohibitions. The benefits both he and his English friends drew from their association were obvious. In 1873 Tengku Kudin used his influence in Selangor to grant to the Singapore Tin Mining Company concessions to exploit most of the state's undeveloped mining land. Both J. G. Davidson and W. H. Read were closely linked to this company.

To many Malay princes it would have seemed that the cultivation of

Western acquaintances and the adoption of a European style of living would make the difference between political success and relegation to the backwaters of power. The prime example of the advantages accruing to a ruler who had received the stamp of British approval was undoubtedly Abu Bakar of Johor, son of Temenggung Ibrahim, who had taken office in 1862. Educated at a mission school in Singapore and speaking English well, Abu Bakar became a leading figure in Singapore society. He was a hospitable host, who not only followed horse racing but could hold his own in such civilized pastimes as billiards and cricket. 'In his tastes and habits,' wrote Abu Bakar's friend, Governor Ord, 'he is an English gentlemen.' Abu Bakar made several trips abroad and was received by a number of monarchs, notably Queen Victoria and the Emperor of Japan. In 1866 the flourishing port on the northern shore of the Johor Strait was renamed 'Johor Baru' ('New Johor') and made the state capital, and the royal residence there equipped with every European comfort. The administration of Johor likewise assumed a form familiar to a Western observer. Abu Bakar was advised by a council, which included two Chinese, and the state was drawn up into administrative divisions. The Johor bureaucracy was built around an elite of loyal and able Malays, most of whom were descended from the old Riau–Johor nobility. Appointed as Abu Bakar's representatives throughout the state, these men successfully combined English notions of a 'modern' civil servant with the best features of traditional Malay government. By the 1870s Johor's administration comprised numerous departments, among which were land and public works. There were also a functioning treasury, judicial system, police force and some secular education. In short, Johor so resembled a Western-style government that Ord considered Abu Bakar 'the only raja in the whole peninsula or adjoining states who rules in accordance with the practice of civilized nations'.[29]

A major reason for the generally high opinion of Abu Bakar was his willingness to see Johor operate as an economic extension of Singapore. He went out of his way to attract investment by Singapore merchants and employed English lawyers to minimize the legal differences between Johor and the Straits Settlements. On the very few occasions when Abu Bakar attempted to assert Johor's economic independence from Singapore, he was subjected to such pressure that he eventually capitulated.

For most of his reign, Abu Bakar epitomized the kind of Malay ruler who would best serve British interests, leaving Singapore with no convincing justification for extending control into Johor. Abu Bakar was fully aware of his delicate relationship with the Singapore authorities, and his skilful political manoeuvring and innovations at all levels of government enabled Johor to retain its sovereignty. His achievement is a tribute not only to his personal ability but to the heritage of his own forebears who had also skilfully adapted to changed situations to assure the continuing viability of the Johor kingdom. In 1868 the Riau court recognized Abu Bakar's success when it granted him the right to assume the title Maharaja, once used by the rulers of Melaka.

Abu Bakar, however, was not without his critics in contemporary Malay society. His influence in Singapore and London, and acceptance in European circles, aroused disapproval from some Malay rulers who took exception to his favoured position. It was not easily forgotten that his father had been simply Temenggung, and Abu Bakar's apparent efforts to stake out a claim as heir to the status of the old Johor kingdom did arouse resentment. The announcement in 1885 that he was henceforth to be termed Sultan was an occasion for caustic comment, and one *pantun* of the period was a pointed jibe at Abu Bakar's pretensions:

A gaudy lantern is bound in rattan
The kris is in a wooden sheath
The Temenggung has become a Sultan
Through his royal forebears the Bugis.[30]

Abu Bakar's position raised new and disturbing questions concerning the relationship between 'civilization' as it was defined by the West, and what it was to be a Malay. The adoption of much that was foreign to Malay custom had certainly contributed to Abu Bakar's achievements, as it had to those of other princes like Tengku Kudin and Raja Juma'at. But how far could an individual go along this road without jeopardizing his 'Malayness'? The clearest articulation of this problem came from Riau, long a centre of Islamic scholarship and still regarded as the arbiter of Malay culture. Court writings expressed concern at the decline of traditional custom, especially among the youth, and urged Malays to maintain the purity of their language by eliminating accretions which had crept in through association with other races. To the Islamic-educated élite, the growing foreign incursions appeared a direct threat not only to their religion but to Malay culture itself. The respected scholar, Raja Ali Haji, was openly critical of Malays who dressed in the European or Chinese manner, 'wearing trousers, socks, shoes, so that at night one would not know they were Malay'.[31]

Such discussions gained additional stimulus during the second half of the nineteenth century because everywhere Islam seemed to be retreating before the advance of the Christian West. Debates in the Islamic heartlands about the current state of the Faith assumed a new immediacy for Malays as improved communications, notably the Suez Canal, made the pilgrimage to Mecca easier. Malay newspapers, journals and religious teachers fostered the view that self-strengthening and reform within Islam was the only solution to the Western challenge. The Moslem community could undoubtedly learn from Western technology, but to adopt Western values unquestioningly would undermine the health of Islam and strike at the essence of Malay culture.

Differing styles of government among Malay rulers mirror various perceptions of the appropriate roads towards the goal of a strong and self-reliant state. In Kedah, Kelantan and Trengganu the nineteenth century saw religious bureaucracies developing in response to royal encouragement, and an expansion of Islamic education. Johor during the same period presents something of a contrast. Abu Bakar, a product of a Christian mission education, set up a school in 1865 but it was based on an English-type syllabus rather than the Arabic grammar, logic and Koran reading of the Islamic schools. In 1863, at a time when Baginda Umar in Trengganu was laying the basis for an expansion of the Islamic judicial system governed by *Syariah* law, Abu Bakar wrote to the Singapore Governor to say that he had revised the Islamic code, making it 'more conformable to European ideas'.[32] Yet despite the very real differences between these two approaches to government, the aim was the same: the maintenance of meaningful Malay political control when it was apparent that economic initiatives were passing into alien hands.

The Pangkor Treaty

Until the 1870s the full impact of the Western presence was kept at bay. Despite the continual petitions and memoranda from the Straits merchant community, London remained adamant that there was to be no further British involvement at an official level. At this point, however, commercial interests in the Straits discovered a source of ammunition which was far more effective than complaints about Malay government and Chinese fighting. They began to realize the potential of exploiting London's fear of the intrusion of another power, particularly Germany, into the peninsula. So effective was this approach that the mood in London showed a marked change.

In November 1873 a new Governor, Andrew Clarke, took up his duties with the impression that he could act on his own initiative to settle disputes between Chinese secret societies and among Malay princes, even to the point of appointing a British officer in the Malay states. Briefed on his arrival by W. H. Read, Clarke came to the conclusion that the assertion of British control was the only possible solution. His first step was to arrange a cease-fire between the Chinese factions fighting in Larut and to request the leading Perak Malays to meet him on Pangkor Island off the Perak coast in order to settle the succession question. In the meantime, Raja Abdullah, still hoping to be recognized as Sultan of Perak, had followed the advice of his business associates, Read and Tan Kim Cheng. He had written to Clarke inviting him to send a Resident to Perak and asking in return for recognition as Sultan. It was this offer which resulted in the well-known Pangkor Treaty of 20 January 1874, which recognized Abdullah as Sultan in return for his agreement to accept a British Resident whose advice 'must be asked and acted upon on all questions other than those touching Malay religion and custom'. Not the least of Abdullah's virtues in Penang's eyes was his apparent predisposition to rule 'in an English fashion'; whereas his principal rival, Sultan Ismail, was dismissed as an 'impracticable Malay of the old school' known to be suspicious of British policy.[33]

While the Pangkor Treaty accelerated the process of British involvement in the affairs of the peninsular states, the initial impetus had come from the establishment of Singapore in 1819 which opened a new phase in Malay history. Singapore was unique not just because it had been founded by the European nation destined to build the greatest empire that the world had yet seen, but because it would become an important instrument of that imperial expansion. Singapore's founding initiated a new kind of diplomacy in the region, reflecting the mood of the imperial age. Colonies might be, in Disraeli's oft-quoted phrase, 'a millstone round our necks', but there was a continuing growth of informal European empires of trade, investment and influence. The Malay world was divided among Siam, Britain and the Netherlands, and the new boundaries fixed by international agreement. Singapore, the central point of this redrawn map, was from the first envisaged as a great trading port which would further the commerce of its British rulers. Britain's increasing interest in the area inevitably affected the lifestyle of the local inhabitants. The campaign against piracy made the seas safer for trade, but disrupted the pattern of life of countless maritime peoples. Steamships improved communications, but posed stiff and often fatal competition to native shipping. The ties with Europe opened up new markets, but those who benefited were principally Europeans and the ever-increasing migrant Chinese population. Most traditional forest and sea products of the Malay peninsula were not sufficiently profitable to entice outside capital investment. Instead, European and Chinese investors encouraged new commercial crops and more intensive mining of tin, especially along the west coast of the peninsula. As financial backers of several Malay princes and as investors in the Malay states, Straits merchants became intimately involved in peninsular affairs. When continuing fighting among Malays and Chinese threatened local trade, their lobbying for a greater British supervisory role intensified. The letter from Sultan Abdullah was the 'key to the door' which in 1874 finally led to political intervention.

The British presence in the nineteenth century brought the peoples of the Malay world into contact with a self-confident culture, convinced of its superiority and its 'civilized' status. The success of Johor's rulers, entailing a partial adoption of this culture, raised the still-debated question of what constitutes 'Malayness'. Could Malay society incorporate the advantages of Western civilization without jeopardizing the centuries-old Melayu heritage? With the beginning of colonial rule, this question was to assume a new urgency.

5

The Making of 'British' Malaya, 1874-1919

Although commonly accepted as a convenient means of demarcating the beginning of Malaysia's colonial period, the Pangkor Treaty does not signify a radical change in British imperial policy. Governor Andrew Clarke may have concluded the treaty on his own initiative, but it did not cause great consternation in the Colonial Office, where the possible appointment of a British agent in the western Malay states had been under discussion for some time. Nor does the Pangkor Treaty stand as a clear break between two different phases of economic development. Despite the expectations of the commercial community in the Straits Settlements, European enterprise was only slowly established in the peninsula. Chinese predominance in the Malay economy continued in both tin mining and most forms of plantation agriculture, and not until the 1890s did the initiative pass to Europeans.

The significance of the Pangkor Treaty lies in the fact that it represented a turning point in the formal relationship between Britain and the Malay states. Arguments for and against expansion of British control had been tossed back and forth since Singapore's founding, but once the Pangkor Treaty had been concluded it essentially became a question of how and when British rule would be extended across the entire peninsula. Over a period of about fifty years British authority, whether represented by governor, agent, resident or adviser, was to be formalized in several separate administrative units which became known by the deceptively unified term 'British Malaya'.

The Extension of British Control

Governor Clarke was quick to seize the long-awaited opportunity provided by the signing of the Pangkor Treaty in January 1874. In Larut, where fighting had been most extensive and the tin trade most disrupted, the former commander of Menteri Ngah Ibrahim's forces, a colourful adventurer called Captain Speedy, was installed as Assistant Resident. Three commissioners, including Frank Swettenham, a young civil servant qualified in Malay, and William Pickering, who was fluent in Chinese, were dispatched to Larut to supervise the dismantling of the Chinese stockades, organize the return of women captured in the fighting, and resolve the disputes over mines and watercourses which had fuelled the conflicts. In early November, pending his official posting as Adviser, Singapore's colonial secretary, J. W. W. Birch, took up residence on the Lower Perak River.

Meanwhile, Clarke was ready to exploit the unusually amenable mood in London in order to extend British influence in Selangor. A case of 'piracy' on the Langat River in August 1874 gave him the justification he needed to suggest to Sultan Abdul Samad that Swetten-ham live at the royal capital, Langat, as Assistant Resident. Although no formal treaty was concluded, Tengku Kudin's financial associate, J. G. Davidson, who was already assisting in the administration of Kelang, was officially appointed as Resident of Selangor. A final posting was made in Sungai Ujung, where Clarke gave the newly appointed Dato Kelana, the territorial chief, 'the protection of the British Government' as well as arms and ammunition. In return, the Dato Kelana promised to keep the Linggi River open to trade and to charge reasonable duties. This association with the British gave the Dato Kelana a decided advantage over his rival, the Dato Bandar, who had come to be regarded as the Kelana's equal. Fighting between the two factions had been protracted, but now, in an ensuing quarrel between them, the Dato Kelana unilaterally hoisted the British flag and asked for troops to reinforce his position and an officer to live with him. In granting both requests, British control was effectively extended in Sungai Ujung, despite the lack of any formal treaty. How-ever, the use of arms to strengthen an unpopular Dato Kelana not only upset the political balance between this office and the Dato Bandar; it left behind a sense of insult and resentment which was not easily appeased.

By the beginning of 1875, the first steps had thus been taken in the development of what came to be called the residential system. It is striking how ill-prepared the British were for the role they had assumed. Only some time after the meeting at Pangkor, for example, did Swetten-ham learn of the existence of Raja Yusuf who would have succeeded to the Perak throne in 1857 and 1865 had it not been for his un-popularity with the Malay chiefs. If the men on the spot were often surprised by some new disclosure, it was immeasurably more difficult for decision-makers in London to conceive of what Malaya was like. To them, the way in which Malay culture was intertwined with its politics was a continual puzzle. As one exasperated official in London sighed in 1878, 'Malay modes of election, Malay customs as to inherit-ance and relationship and purity of blood etc. are incomprehensible to us.'[1]

In 1875 there was no long-term plan as to how the British should proceed, and the difficulties which developed were almost inevitable in view of the lack of thought which had gone into the precise nature of 'intervention'. There had as yet been no formulation of the specific duties of a Resident or a clear statement of the way in which he would 'advise'. It is doubtful whether Perak Malays fully understood that the British conceived of powers far more extensive than the purely commercial role of the Dutch Resident in Perak eighty years earlier. One Malay version of the Pangkor Treaty, which may be a copy of the original,[2] speaks not only of advice (*nasihat*) from the Resident but of discussion (*bicara*). Malays would have been justified in assuming that decision-making would continue to be collective, following the same process as in their traditional *mesyuarat bicara* (meetings for discussion). In these assemblies a general consensus was necessary before any action could be taken, and this was reached only after debates which might continue for several days. It was not possible for a Malay ruler to impose his will arbitrarily on his court or his chiefs, since the *enforcement* of obedience was beyond royal powers. The Pangkor Treaty, however, presupposed not only that the ruler himself would be receptive to the Resident's 'advice', and would help to implement any measure he advocated, but that he had the ability to ensure acceptance by his court. In the most peaceful situation this would not necessarily have been the case, and now the Residents also had to deal with the aftermath of years of hostility between members of the ruling class. In Perak, despite Birch's efforts to effect a reconciliation, Sultan Ismail refused to sign the treaty and he, like Raja Yusuf, the third claimant to the throne, was supported by his own coterie of chiefs. Repeatedly in their dealings with the Dutch in past centuries, Perak rulers had insisted that the approval of the assembly was required to make any contract binding. By refusing to sign the Treaty several prominent Perak chiefs were denying its legality.

In cultural terms, moreover, the Pangkor Treaty drew distinctions which were meaningless to Malays but which continued to emerge as contentious issues in British–Malay relations. 'Religion and custom' was to be excluded from British control, but 'the general administration of the country' would be conducted in accordance with the Resident's advice. Yet religion and precedent were the fundamental and frequently the only justification for Malay political action. The division between religious and secular so clear-cut to Europeans was simply an alien concept to Malays. Perhaps the most problematic area involved the raising of revenue. According to Article X of the Treaty, the 'collection and control' of revenue was to be regulated by the Resident. Though resentment at the levying of tolls or taxes by an overlord was nothing new, the nineteenth century had seen a widespread tendency to ignore royal prerogatives as district chiefs and princes established centres of economic independence. These men were understandably hostile to the notion of a central treasury which paid out salaries and was subject to the Resident's control. In 1858 the Selangor princes had already rejected proposals for a centrally controlled treasury put forward by Raja Juma'at of Lukut. In 1874 the threat to a much valued independence was heightened because now the state revenues would be under non-Malay authority, The chiefs, realizing full well that the promised salary could always be withheld from those who failed to please, were not willing to surrender their right to collect taxes in exchange for placement on a 'civil list'.

When the Malays agreed to the Pangkor Treaty, they unwittingly became drawn into certain established British practices contrary to their own. In addition to revenue collection there was also the question of slavery, which after a long and acrimonious battle had finally been abolished throughout the British Empire in 1833. The Pangkor Treaty made no reference to slavery, but it was regarded by Straits Settlements authorities as repugnant to the 'civilized' government they proposed to initiate. Verbal instructions given by Clarke to Davidson, Resident of Selangor, specifically stated that 'no slavery could be permitted to exist in any state under British protection'.[3] Given this adamancy, it was inevitable that difficulties should arise because in the Malay world the human resources represented by slaves were as important to the status of a ruler or chief as revenue itself. In Perak the issue of slavery was more apparent than in Selangor because the Perak ruling class was considerably larger. In Perak slaves and debt bondsmen numbered an estimated 3,000 in a total Malay population of perhaps 50,000 (approximately 6 per cent).[4]

Europeans tended to define such slavery in Western terms and to see slaves as an undifferentiated group of people condemned to lives of unrelenting misery. But among Malays, slaves were generally divided into two classes: slaves in the Western sense, and debt bondsmen. The latter type of slavery served a particular function in Malay society. Debt slavery usually occurred when an individual voluntarily 'mortgaged' himself in return for some financial assistance from his creditor, frequently his ruler or chief. In times of hardship, after a bad harvest or when a trading venture had failed, debt bondage might be the only means for a peasant to raise finances. If after a prescribed time he was unable to redeem the debt, he was absorbed into the creditor's household. He was then obliged to carry out any order the lord might give until the debt was paid. Through debt bondage chiefs and rulers gained followers to increase their status and an economic asset which could be transferred, if need be, to some other creditor.

Such distinctions in the practice of slavery in the Malay states were largely ignored by the newly appointed British Residents, who were all unanimous in their condemnation of slavery. Admittedly the lot of many, especially the women, was indeed deplorable. Slaves proper were often subject to rank exploitation because they were non-

Moslem *orang asli* and were therefore considered outside the pale of the Melayu. Among the debt slaves there were also cases of cruelty and other abuses; a chief, for example, might not mistreat his debt slaves but simply refuse to accept payment when the debt fell due. But because slavery was so bound up with a chief's prestige, British inquiries into alleged mistreatment aroused considerable resentment among Malay nobles. Sultan Abdul Samad of Selangor was so incensed by the intrusive questions that he refused pointblank to permit his slaves to be counted.

As Clarke realized, the questions of revenue collection and the abolition of slavery were potentially explosive. To challenge established custom would obviously demand Residents with sensitivity and discernment who were knowledgeable about Malay society. The difficulty in finding men sufficiently fluent in Malay to take up the new postings is a sobering comment on the lack of British interaction with Malays since the founding of Singapore in 1819. However, the newly created Straits Civil Service had established language requirements and one of its products, Frank Swettenham, spoke good Malay. He quickly succeeded in winning Sultan Abdul Samad's approval. But there were others whose shortcomings in administrative ability or temperament endangered British–Malay relations. Speedy's regime in Larut had aroused criticism, and Sultan Abdul Samad had already been offended by Birch's abrupt manner at a meeting in 1871. Though experienced in colonial government, Birch had been employed mainly in Ceylon and was never comfortable in speaking Malay. It was in fact with some reservations, and only after some delay, that Governor Clarke had posted Birch to Perak as Resident.[5]

His misgivings were justified. Birch soon aroused the hostility of the Perak chiefs not merely because he had come to initiate the new system of tax revenue and centralized collection, but because he employed public humiliation to enforce his authority. What Birch called 'a good dressing down' aroused as much resentment among recalcitrant chiefs as the burning of their homes and the forced surrender of arms. The resident's attitude to slavery and his willingness to provide a sanctuary for fugitive debt slaves, especially women, was regarded by Malays as simple theft. The Menteri of Perak, Ngah Ibrahim, although a signatory to the Pangkor Treaty, was in the forefront of the nobles critical of Birch and the new state of affairs. He was especially humiliated because his territory of Larut was now administered by his former employee, Captain Speedy. This displacement of an established chief, the Menteri argued, augured ill for Perak's future. In a conversation with Sultan Abdullah the Menteri reportedly said:

'I think bye and bye Mr Birch will keep many many Europeans to take charge of the country and have stations and sepoys and police.

After a few years they will surely drive us out of the country . . . I have considered many days upon this case. It is improper for Your Majesty to follow the Resident, for his rank is only that of a Dato'.[6]

The tension was heightened by the animosity between Birch and Abdullah. The delay in Birch's appointment had allowed the Perak ruler to function virtually independently, and he resented the restrictions imposed by the Resident's presence. The manner in which he tried to resolve the situation is a curious mixture of traditional and modern which helps highlight the cultural changes taking place. On the one hand, Sultan Abdullah addressed a formal petition to the Singapore Governor asking that the Resident be placed under him; on the other, he called in the services of a spirit medium to help rid himself of Birch and other 'light-eyed men'.

For his part, Birch considered Abdullah 'eminently silly and foolish . . . an arrant coward'.[7] Far from supporting Abdullah, Birch's missives to his superiors maintain that Ismail was more widely acknowledged as ruler and was therefore a more legitimate successor. By early August 1875 the situation had become so serious that the new Governor, Sir William Jervois, believed some kind of formal control might now be necessary. 'Everything,' he wrote, 'seems tending to render it inevitable that Perak must become part of the British dominions.' Rumours flew wildly around Penang and Singapore, rapidly spreading to the Malay states, and the Perak princes and chiefs were convinced that annexation was imminent.

It was not long before their fears appeared confirmed. In October a decision was made which would provide for British administration over judicial matters, with the concession that Abdullah would be consulted 'whenever possible'. This measure, a fundamental departure from the terms of the Pangkor Treaty, seemed to Jervois necessary because Perak was already indebted by $18,000 to the Straits Settlements treasury. In his view, there was little chance of regaining this sum unless the British tightened their control. This exposure of the fiction of Malay rule by British advice was the final insult, and it was the unpopular Birch who bore the brunt of Malay anger. On 2 November, while posting notices of the controversial enactment, Birch was killed; Swettenham, who was also in Perak, escaped downriver.

The precise motives for Birch's murder are still debated. Popular interpretations of his death have seen it as an outburst against British authority, the first stirrings of an incipient nationalism. Certainly, the sense of being Malay against a European, an infidel, did play a part, as had attacks on Dutch officials in Kedah and Perak in the seventeenth century, and in Siak in the eighteenth. More significant is what the British represented: a departure from tradition and custom, a new and alien government which would destroy established privileges. But though the Perak ruling class presumably envisaged a return to something resembling the old order, the anger and resentment the British had aroused was not a Malay preserve. In 1878, for instance, members of the Ho Seng secret society killed the superintendent of the Dindings district as a reprisal for their loss of revenues.

On hearing of Birch's death, the British authorities anticipated a general uprising, and steps were immediately taken to quash any possible resistance. In Johor Raja Mahdi of Selangor, who had purportedly been planning an attack on his old appanage of Kelang, was arrested. Skirmishes occurred in November—December in Sungai Ujung, where British troops supported the Dato Kelana against his rivals who were bitterly hostile to those who had 'brought the white men into the country'. On one occasion armed bands were seen carrying the Turkish flag, a counter to the Dato Kelana's Union Jack and a reflection of the Pan-Islamic movement being sponsored by Turkey in the Middle East. The greatest attention was focused on Perak, but here the British clearly overreacted. The call for troops from as far afield as India and Hong Kong proved quite unnecessary, and one observer commented that there were probably no more than three hundred Malays under arms. However, for several months those pronounced guilty of conspiracy against Birch, including Sultan Abdullah and Sultan Ismail, were pursued. For the individuals captured, justice was summary. Three were hanged, while Abdullah, Ismail and several major chiefs were exiled.

In retrospect, Swettenham regarded this harsh retribution as having served the new order well. By removing most of the first-ranking chiefs, the British had eliminated the principal obstacles to the changes they proposed to make. For over fifteen years these positions remained unfilled, allowing for the creation of a very different type of administration. 'The state of Perak,' Swettenham wrote, 'gained in twelve months what ten years of "advice" could hardly have accomplished.'[8] But for Malays, the punishment meted out was a blatant demonstration of European ability to enforce their demands. Sultan Abdullah was never permitted to return to Perak, and years later the Sultan of Kedah stressed his anxiety to remain on good terms with the British because he well remembered the Perak ruler's fate. In Malay society where rebellions were traditionally led by some chief or anak raja, the British power to punish even the highest-born coupled with the knowledge that open resistance had little hope of success goes a long way towards explaining Malay quiescence in later years.

For those who co-operated with the British, the rewards were high. Raja Yusuf of Perak was appointed Regent since he had been absolved of implicaton in the conspiracy. Despite his known unpopularity with Malays, he was installed as Sultan by the British in 1887. In Sungai Ujung the new Dato Bandar, successor to the old enemy of the British, accommodated himself so successfully to the changed order that the British began to favour him above the Dato Kelana.[9]

The events of 1875–6 also meant that what has been called the British 'forward movement' received a temporary check. In London the Colonial Office was appalled, and its recriminations stilled for the moment any talk of further annexation which would entail increased expenditure. But expansionist feelings in the Straits Settlements remained undaunted. Although Birch's death was a timely reminder of the need to tread carefully and choose Residents wisely, it was not long before the attention of Jervois and his supporters turned to the Melaka hinterland. Here it is not easy to locate a straightforward economic motive for expansion, and indeed no British official ever argued that control in this area would bring great financial rewards. One study of the period has spoken of the imperialists' desire to quell the 'turbulent frontier' so close at hand,[10] and certainly politics in what later became Negeri Sembilan were nothing if not turbulent. British assistance to the Dato Kelana of Sungai Ujung had merely introduced an added complexity into the already protracted disputes among the leaders of Sungai Ujung, Jelebu, Johol and Rembau. In order to restore peace while strengthening British influence, Governor Jervois resorted to a device which had been considered successful in other areas of the British Empire — the use of a friendly and influential chief who would act as a medium through which subtle pressure could be exerted on his peers.

Abu Bakar, the Maharaja of Johor, seemed ideally suited to this role. He himself was ambitious and, as his previous involvement in the Pahang Civil War suggests, was anxious to extend his hold over territories that had in centuries past acknowledged the suzerainty of the old kingdom of Riau-Johor. In addition, he was already regarded with respect by most leaders in the quarrelling states. As far as Jervois was concerned, his prime qualification was his reputation as a willing recipient of Singapore's advice. So convinced was the Governor of the Maharaja's suitability as Singapore's representative that he aimed eventually to make Abu Bakar overlord of the entire Negeri Sembilan area. In 1876 Jervois was even willing to see not the British choice but Abu Bakar's own client, Tunku Antah, assume the contested position of Yamtuan over a number of small states (Sri Menanti, Jempul, Terachi, Gunung Pasir, Ulu Muar, Johol and Inas) which would now become the Sri Menanti confederacy. The Sri Menanti group agreed to permit peaceful trade through their territories and to refer disputes among themselves to Abu Bakar. The underlying assumption in Singapore was that the Maharaja would then consult British authorities over any future course of action. The following year a similar arrangement was made with the Penghulu of Rembau and with Jelebu. When Sultan Ali of Johor died soon afterwards, Abu Bakar was made guardian of

Muar, Sultan Ali's fief, in preference to either of Sultan Ali's sons. By 1878 Abu Bakar had thus become adviser to all the Negeri Sembilan states except Sungai Ujung.

The manoeuvring which this had involved on the Maharaja's part, the maintenance of credibility both in Singapore and the Negeri Sembilan states, is a testimony to Abu Bakar's political dexterity. While his achievement brought him an enhanced status and a prestige enjoyed by no other Malay ruler, it also served the Singapore government which in effect hoped to exploit Abu Bakar as a substitute Resident.

From the 1880s the 'forward movement' gained further momentum, a development attributed to the growing fear in London of threats to Britain's paramountcy in the peninsula. German activity in the Pacific was disturbing, while the French continued to consolidate their hold over Vietnam, Cambodia and Laos. The future of Siam, now caught between British Burma and French Indochina, was not at all clear. King Chulalongkorn's recruitment of specialists from all over Europe to assist in his modernizing programme was a source of unease, and the possibility of Siam falling under French or German control could not be discounted. In London, therefore, officials began to listen more seriously to arguments advocating an extension of British power in the Malay region.

Simultaneously a number of strong personalities were emerging as guiding forces behind public opinion in the Straits Settlements and the tiny European population in the Malay states. One of the most forceful was another of Raffles's admirers, Frank Swettenham, who throughout his life argued that expansion was not only in British interests but would also benefit Malays. Another influential figure was Frederick Weld, Governor from 1880 to 1887, who fully expected Malay rulers lacking advisers to be so convinced of the value of a British Resident that they would voluntarily ask for one. Weld's stated ambition was to extend British control as far as possible over the peninsula south of Siam during his term of office. In the Negeri Sembilan states, such men were far less amenable than Jervois to sponsoring Abu Bakar's influence. The Maharaja's loyalty and dedication to British interests, they claimed, were suspect, and he seemed unwilling or unable to settle the recurring quarrels between Negeri Sembilan chiefs. The peace of the protected Malay states stood in marked contrast to the Melaka interior, where a complex system of inheritance and succession, adapted from Minangkabau custom, imparted a unique character to local disputes. What would happen, it was asked, when Abu Bakar died? Would his heir be able to claim the same standing as his father?

With London's encouragement, Governor Weld began to press his views by slowly whittling away at Abu Bakar's position in Negeri

Sembilan. There was, however, a distinct difference between 1874 and 1880 in the manner in which the Residents were posted. In the former case, speed was essential in order to seize the long-awaited opportunity in the major tin areas. Now, because of the lack of significant tin deposits, the belief that any possibility of foreign intrusion in this area was slight, and the inability of most of these states to support a full Residential system, Weld could afford to bide his time. A process which took just months in Perak and Selangor was in Negeri Sembilan stretched over years. In 1881 Weld met the Sri Menanti heads and spoke of the advantages of dealing directly with Singapore rather than through the Maharaja. Then, between 1883 and 1887, British officers were appointed in Jelebu and Rembau, their powers slowly extended to resemble those of Residents elsewhere. There was sufficient time to ensure that the local chiefs were men who would willingly accept British advice, even if this entailed a manipulation of the electoral system.

The difference in Perak and Selangor is well illustrated when one realizes that the requests of Yamtuan Antah of Sri Menanti for a British Resident were in fact rejected until Weld considered the time appropriate. In 1885 a British officer was stationed in Sri Menanti, without any treaty basis, and performed duties similar to those of a Resident. Supervision over external affairs was also transferred to the British government. Four years later, in 1889, a new confederacy of Negeri Sembilan was formed, excluding only Sungai Ujung and Jelebu, which were eventually included in 1895. In 1898 the British were able to bring about the election of Yamtuan Antah's son as Yamtuan Besar of this reconstructed Negeri Sembilan, under the Resident's overarching authority. Despite the persistence of many local customs traceable to Minangkabau, the new administrative unity contributed to a gradual lessening of the differences in government and *adat* which had characterized the small Negeri Sembilan states prior to colonial control.

In contrast with Negeri Sembilan, the extension of British control into Pahang is a prime example of the way in which economic concerns could shape policy. Malay memories of Pahang as a land of gold, combined with its relative isolation, had given rise to stories depicting it as 'the richest and most favoured state in the peninsula'.[11] These legendary accounts were widely accepted, though the reality was less exciting. There were known gold and tin deposits but they were limited to small pockets in the interior near the Selangor and Trengganu borders. However, reports of Pahang's 'great wealth' from Swettenham, who travelled across the peninsula in 1885, simply served to reinforce general belief. In this context, London's growing sympathy with the ambition of colonial expansionists did not go unnoticed in Singapore. As the price of tin rose to unprecedented heights, so too did the sense of urgency among the Straits business community. Weld's conviction that Pahang's touted storehouse of minerals should be brought under British control established a major goal for his administration.

Commercial appetites were whetted because Bendahara Ahmad of Pahang now seemed more receptive to the notion of closer relations with Singapore. Previously his dealings with colonial officials had been limited and attempts by both Clarke and Jervois to extend Singapore's influence into Pahang had been rebuffed. From 1880, however, Ahmad made several trips to Singapore as the guest of Abu Bakar, whom he had since forgiven for supporting Ahmad's brother Mutahir in the Pahang War of 1858. Entertained during these visits by Weld and other Europeans, the Bendahara was not slow to draw a connection between Johor's impressive development and Abu Bakar's association with Singapore. The example of Johor apparently convinced him that European investment need not necessarily entail surrender of sovereignty. Ahmad subsequently sold mining concessions to a number of individuals and companies in Singapore, many of whom were merely speculators hoping to profit from a predicted treaty between Pahang and Britain. The personal nature of these transactions was to have serious implications. There was no legal safeguard to control transference of concessions, and some were later bought up by the Pahang Corporation, whose directors included some prominent men in London, one a member of Parliament. Furthermore, several concessions were apparently sold without any consideration of the territorial rights of Pahang chiefs or recognition of the fact that areas were often already being worked by local Malay or Chinese residents.

To Weld's disappointment, Ahmad did not ask for a Resident; on the contrary, he sought to prevent British political intervention following hard on commercial investment. In a move clearly intended to strengthen his authority in Pahang, Ahmad assumed the title of Sultan in 1881 and was acknowledged as such by his chiefs. From a Malay point of view he could now claim an even higher position than Abu Bakar of Johor, still only a Maharaja. The most persuasive arguments in favour of a British alliance put forward by Weld and his silver-tongued spokesman Swettenham met strenuous resistance. In 1885 Ahmad stated pointblank that he simply did not want a Resident. But by October 1887 the combined influence of Weld's nephew, Hugh Clifford, and the mediation of Abu Bakar finally persuaded Ahmad to sign a treaty with the British similar to one concluded two years before between Britain and Johor. Allowing for a British agent to reside in Pahang to help open the country to 'commerce and civilization', this treaty also acknowledged Pahang's standing as a 'sovereign state'.[12]

While the latter qualification was of immense significance to Ahmad, to Weld it was merely a sop to Malay pride. Hugh Clifford, the first agent, shared Weld's view and found the restraints on his powers a constant irritation. He could not introduce desired reforms, especially regarding slavery, nor control the granting of concessions. Pahang's government at the time, he afterwards claimed, was 'a disgrace to the peninsula'. Neither Ahmad nor his chiefs would willingly relinquish their rights, and the former even said he would rather see Pahang revert to a jungle than let it be governed by the British. He himself was determined to govern 'as long as life lasted'.[13]

The atmosphere in the royal capital, Pekan, grew ugly and verbal intimidation more blatant. Rumours circulated of a possible British shelling of the ruler's palace, causing panic-stricken Malays to hark back to the action by a previous British governor against Kuala Trengganu in 1862. Given the generally held belief in Singapore that Pahang was a land of untold wealth, Weld's own ambitions, and the financial involvement in Pahang of powerful commercial interests able to manipulate Colonial Office apprehension of German or French speculators, extension of British control into Pahang was a foregone conclusion. In 1888 the murder of a Chinese British subject provided the Straits government with the excuse to act. Under the threat of possible armed intervention, and with the memories of what had happened in Perak, Sultan Ahmad was finally induced to write a letter in which he asked for a British Resident who would help govern Pahang in the same manner as the other Malay states. His only conditions were that his own privileges and powers be protected and that old customs which had 'good and proper reason' be guaranteed. The Resident was duly appointed, but no guarantees were made. As one study of the period has pointed out, the request and the accompanying proviso were incompatible.[14]

Realizing the extent of opposition, the first Resident moved slowly, but historical circumstances and the methods used to introduce British control made conflict almost inevitable. Even before any British agent arrived, the political system in Pahang was undergoing considerable strain. Some of the interior chiefs, whose territories included rich mining districts, had gained their positions not through inheritance but as rewards for helping Bendahara Ahmad come to power. There were other nobles who resented the royal favourites and in 1884 had demonstrated their resentment by conspiring with Ahmad's brother Mansur in an abortive attempt to attack Pahang through Selangor. In addition, the interior chiefs enjoyed a large degree of independence, strengthened by Ahmad's frequent and often prolonged visits to Singapore. Some were more closely linked by blood, marriage or economic interests to Selangor and felt little sense of allegiance to the distant capital in Pekan.

Among these chiefs Ahmad's agreements with the British aroused considerable hostility. When representatives of European and Chinese firms to whom Ahmad had sold mining and timber concessions arrived to stake their claims, they were confronted by angry chiefs who regarded these areas as their rightful holdings. Changes subsequently introduced by the British Resident created further grounds for discontent. The new Resident set up courts of justice, a small police force and a state council, but the issuing of jungle passes, restrictions on carrying weapons, corvée duties for road building, registration of slaves and the centralization of finances met considerable resentment.

Some Pahang chiefs were willing to co-operate with the British, notably Tengku Mahmud, Sultan Ahmad's son, who hoped to succeed to the throne. But other chiefs strongly objected to the payment of salaries which denied them the right to collect revenue in their districts. The omission of some chiefs from the new 'civil list' effectively left them without any source of income, while other chiefs found their revenue dropped substantially. The Syahbandar, for example, had previously raised about $1,200 annually, but now received only $720. The Orang Kaya (district chief) of the *ulu* district of Semantan, Abdul Rahman, was so enraged by the decline in his revenue that he even asked for Semantan to be transferred to Selangor. It was Abdul Rahman, commonly known as Dato Bahaman, who was the spearhead of opposition to the changes the British had introduced. In 1891, as punishment for his continued defiance, the Resident persuaded Sultan Ahmad to sign a decree depriving Bahaman of his title. Towards the end of that year the latter declared his open rebellion, setting in motion a protracted series of skirmishes, ambushes and occasional engagements which became known as the Pahang War.

In terms of British policy, these disturbances strengthened the uneasy feeling that extension of control into Pahang might have been a mistake and forced a reassessment of Pahang's real worth in relation to Britain's interests. But for modern Malays the Pahang War, like that in Perak, has come to symbolize the struggle to safeguard Malay tradition, Malay values, the sense of Malay independence, against outside intrusion. The rebellion of the Orang Kaya of Semantan and his allies created the opportunity for leaders to emerge and legends to be created. Stories still abound of the famed fighter, Mat Kilau, whose exploits in the Pahang War gained him a place in popular memory as one of the heroes of Malay nationalism.[15]

Throughout the war, the rebellious chiefs always claimed that they were defending the ruler's interests. Initially Sultan Ahmad gave his tacit support, and the strength of the resistance also owed much to the role of Bahaman's *orang asli* supporters. Bahaman's own origins are obscure but he was reported to be partly Jakun, and his own knowledge of the jungle and ties with the interior *orang asli* enabled him and his followers to elude capture for some time. Another tradition claims that Bahaman was descended from a royal family of Sumatra.

The perception of Bahaman and his allies as guardians of the Malay heritage was heightened during the dying stages of the campaign when the remnants of the rebels became associated with a Trengganu holy man whose presence imbued their cause with the spirit of *jihad*, a holy war against infidels. The resistance, however, had already begun to weaken when Sultan Ahmad was pressured by the Resident into aligning himself with the British. It was his Malay following which pursued the rebels and only when the situation seemed more serious were small companies of Sikh troops brought in from Selangor and Perak. A general amnesty was issued in 1892 and the majority of the chiefs and their following surrendered. The remainder fled to Trengganu where they were treated sympathetically by local Malays. In 1895 a force led by Hugh Clifford crossed the Trengganu boundary and chased the rebels as far as Kelantan. In November of that year most of the leaders were arrested in Kelantan by the Siamese authorities and taken to Bangkok. Soon afterwards Tengku Mahmud's co-operation with the British was rewarded when he was confirmed as Sultan Ahmad's heir.

The Pahang War represented only a brief setback to the British 'forward movement'. Johor was now encircled by the Protected States and from the 1890s Abu Bakar's support in Singapore and even in London declined as the existence of a state governed completely by Malays came to be considered an anomaly. Prior to 1880 Abu Bakar had been able to maintain his high standing through his mutually rewarding relationship with the British authorities. While personally disapproving of many aspects of British policy along the west coast, Abu Bakar had become the linchpin of British influence in the Negeri Sembilan region, and had been instrumental in the extension of the Residential system to Pahang. However, Weld's suspicions of Abu Bakar came to be shared by others. Rather than being held up as a model government, Johor was now suffering by comparison with Perak and Selangor. It was claimed that the administration of justice in Johor was haphazard and the revenue unregulated, with far too much spent on Abu Bakar's 'extravagances' such as overseas travel. In London too the feeling grew that indirect rule as exemplified in the Residential system more effectively promoted 'peace, commerce and civilization'. Abu Bakar's insistence on Johor's status as a foreign state aroused particular concern because it raised the bogey of French, Dutch or German intervention. A Resident had been appointed in Pahang, ostensibly to protect the rights of a Chinese British subject: what would happen, it was argued, if the French should do the same on behalf of a Chinese from Saigon?

Abu Bakar was fully aware of the attitude of Weld and his circle. Two centuries earlier Johor rulers had not hesitated to appeal to Batavia, bypassing the Melaka governor, in order to present their case.

Heirs to this tradition of political astuteness, Abu Bakar and his advisers seized every opportunity to use friends in London as a counter to complaints from Singapore. In 1885, during Weld's absence, Abu Bakar invited the Acting Governor to inspect Johor. As a result of the visit a report praising government in Johor and Muar and commending the Maharaja's receptiveness to British suggestions was submitted to the Colonial Office. Abu Bakar himself went to London the same year and received a personal assurance that no Resident would be placed in Johor. A new treaty was negotiated granting him the title of Sultan and recognizing Johor as a sovereign state.

Although the treaty did little to change the existing situation, it nonetheless hinted at future developments. Johor's foreign affairs were to be under Singapore's control, and Abu Bakar agreed not to interfere in the affairs of other states or to grant concessions to foreign Europeans. One clause in the treaty also made provision for the appointment, should the need arise, of a British agent. Admittedly this agent was to have only consular powers, but events in Pahang three years later showed how easily such functions could be converted into a more stringent type of 'advice'. In 1888, when an agent was in fact proposed, Abu Bakar had to call on all his political adroitness and personal charm to convince Weld's successor of the value of direct relations between Johor and Singapore. Though he was successful, the treaty remained, and among many British officials there was a quiet assumption that the situation would be re-evaluated when Abu Bakar died.

In his final years, Abu Bakar attempted to ensure that Johor's special status would in fact endure. In London he instituted a Johor Advisory Board made up of several prominent Englishmen to communicate directly on his behalf with the Colonial Office. In April 1895 he promulgated a written constitution which spelt out Johor's separate identity. Islam was specified as the state religion; the duties of the cabinet ministers and the legislative council were laid down; and most importantly, it was stipulated that no part of Johor's territories could ever be alienated to any European power.

The Johor leaders who were to live on after Abu Bakar's death to become advisers to his son realized the strength of the expansionist lobby in Singapore. Despite Johor's long record of economic prosperity and sound administration, the Singapore Governor in 1893 claimed that 'progress' there was less than in any state under a British Resident. When Abu Bakar died in June 1895, Johor's position was less secure than twenty years earlier. Its independence was now under increasing threat as advocates of a 'British Malaya' that would include the whole peninsula gathered strength. Yet Abu Bakar's reign had bequeathed to Johor a tradition of sovereignty which was not easily set aside. Skilled diplomats, like Johor's Chief Minister Dato Ja'afar,

whose forbears had served the Temenggung family since Singapore's
founding, realized that this tradition must be reconciled with reality.
As the twentieth century dawned it was obvious that the relationship
between Johor and Britain would have to be reshaped to meet the
demands of a changing political environment.

The Residential System

The cornerstone of the Residential system was the concept of indirect
rule, vigorously enunciated by Frank Swettenham in 1876: 'To
preserve the accepted customs and traditions of the country, to enlist
the sympathies and interests of the people in our assistance, and to
teach them the advantages of good government and enlightened
policy.'[16] As it evolved in the protected Malay states, the Residential
system owed much to Hugh Low (1824—1905), whose successful
administration of Perak (1877—89) became the yardstick by which
other Residents and their achievements were measured. Low had spent
thirty years in the Borneo region and was a close friend of both James
and Charles Brooke. He admired their creation of a government which
seemed eminently suited to the local scene, being shaped by a genuine
respect for many indigenous customs and by a limited budget which
precluded a large European establishment. A modified version of the
Brooke model became the basis for Low's administration and through
his example influenced the nature of colonial rule in the four Protected
States.

The co-operation of the Malay ruling class, initially the most hostile
towards the British arrogation of power, was essential for the success
of indirect rule. If the British, like the Bugis before them, were to
justify their presence by pointing to a 'request' from Malay rulers,
they needed to maintain the appearance of Malay goodwill. As important as the rulers themselves were the nobility, and Swettenham later
acknowledged that one of the principal British goals had been to 'conciliate or overawe' the chiefs, many of whom were more powerful than
the rulers.[17]

A primary means of gaining the desired co-operation was to compensate the rulers, princes and leading chiefs for income they had lost
by the abolition of slavery and the introduction of a central treasury.
The major beneficiaries were unquestionably the Sultans, who were
given liberal allowances enabling them to live in a state far surpassing
other members of the ruling élite. They also gained in other ways.
Though they lost most of their former powers, British support gave
them security from potential challengers. In the protected Malay states
the days of civil war were gone, for no *anak raja* could now muster the
strength necessary to topple a British-backed Sultan.

Co-operative princes and important chiefs were also rewarded.

Large numbers were incorporated into the bureaucracy in positions such as native magistrate, and state allowances for this type of work relieved many from dependence on the all too fickle royal bounty. They thus gained a degree of independence previously denied to princes without their own appanage. As another generation grew up under the British umbrella and the immediate benefits of complying with the system became apparent, murmurings of discontent faded away. In 1878 Raja Bot, son of Raja Juma'at of Lukut, accused the Residents of 'usurping the position of rulers, acting so as to make the rajas small and of no account in the eyes of the people', but in 1890 he sent his son to the newly established Selangor Raja School for an English education.

The appearance of indirect rule, of British advice to a ruler and his court, was maintained by the institution of a State Council, which became the sole legislative body. It consisted of about ten individuals: the ruler, selected princes and chiefs, a restricted representation from the Chinese community and the Resident. But it was the Resident who nominated the members, who were then approved by the Governor and then formally appointed by the Sultan, usually for life. The Resident was the effective ruler since the Council met only about seven times a year. On these occasions, while the Regent or Sultan formally presided, the Resident prepared the agenda and, after consultation with the Governor, proposed the legislation to be discussed. Although the Council did provide a useful sounding board for public opinion, especially on matters affecting the Malays, its direct influence on legislation was limited. Furthermore, as time went on and administration became more involved, even the consultative function of the Council was ignored. Once the government had decided on a particular course of action, there was little the Council could do. Increasingly, the Councils simply approved decisions which had already been made. By the 1890s agendas for Council meetings were more detailed and meetings fewer; anything but the most perfunctory discussion would have been impossible. The process of governing was thus very different from the traditional assemblies, where several hundred members of the ruling class would gather in a meeting open to the public and decisions were reached after debates which could last several days. The only area which remained under effective Malay control was the administration of religious law and the appointment of religious officials, responsibility for which was left in the Sultan's hands. Even here the definition of what was 'religious' was not uncommonly redefined when the British felt it intruded into the sphere of civil law.

Local administration was under the general supervision of British District Officers, a post apparently modelled on the examples of Sarawak and British India. The District Officer functioned as a Resi-

dent on a smaller scale, and the area under his control could reach up
to 3,800 square kilometres or even more in Pahang, and include as
many as 20,000 people. The District Officer was responsible for such
matters as the district treasury, land rents, justice, revenue collection,
law and order, public health and the supervision of the Malay establishment. The latter was based on the *penghulu*, who were in charge of
mukim, an administrative division consisting of a main village or town-
ship and a smaller number of other hamlets or villages. The *penghulu*
under the British were drawn principally from well-connected families
and received a state salary and perquisites. As agents of government,
with jurisdiction over 500—3,000 peasants scattered through several
villages, they were charged with the collection of rents, the administration of local justice, and the maintenance of order.

Despite the retention of a shell of the traditional governmental
structure and the heavy reliance on Malay officers at the local level,
the nature of British rule was very different from that of the former
Malay administration. Those most obviously affected by the changed
order were the commoner chiefs, who unlike the extended princely
class were not accorded the privileges the British felt were due to
royalty. Only a few chiefs could be included in the new-style Councils
or be appointed as *penghulu*. The authority they had once held in the
countryside had been relinquished to the District Officers, and the
chiefs had thus lost control over the peasants from whom they had
formerly exacted labour and revenue. Many found it impossible to
live within their state allowances, and without rights of taxation were
perpetually in debt. The maintenance of a large following, previously
a sign of high status, was no longer possible because from 1882
measures were taken to abolish slavery and debt bondage. Corvée was
henceforth restricted to state works, and was limited to a few days a
year which could be commuted to a monetary payment. In removing
these practices, the colonial government removed the credit relationship between chief and villager which, with all its inequities, had in the
past created a mutual dependency between the two. The traditional
role of the chief as a link between ruler and village was also undermined.
While the *penghulu* still owed fealty to the Sultan, he was no longer
directly responsible to a chief but to his British District Officer.
Furthermore, those chosen as *penghulu* were no longer the chief's
clients but were recommended by the District Officer and appointed
by the Resident and Council.

A more subtle change was the widening gap between the topmost
levels of the Malay ruling class and the rest of Malay society. British
rule entailed a continuing association between the colonial power
and members of the Malay élite. Traditionally the life of the Sultan
and court had in most essentials paralleled that of the peasants, with
whom they shared the same perception of the world and interacted

at the most mundane levels. In the eighteenth century a Dutch envoy to Perak had chanced across the Raja Muda personally supervising the laying out of new rice fields. A hundred years later observers commented how Sultan Abdul Samad of Selangor mingled freely with his people, whether watching a cock-fight, chatting in the market or taking his daily walk. Now, however, the ruling class was slowly drawn into an alien Western ambience with values and a life-style totally foreign to that of a Malay villager. In the *kampung*, boys still sought to excel at *sepak raga*, Malay football, but the new generation of Malay aristocrats played tennis and polo. While village lifestyles remained unchanged, many members of the Malay ruling class were adopting Western dress, living in Western houses and even taking trips to London in emulation of the colonial official. By its very presence the new regime had helped foster a major cultural cleavage between the Malay élite and the peasants which weakened the unity of the society.

To a considerable extent this association between the Malay ruling class and the colonial authorities served to disguise the fact that real power ultimately resided with the British. Though the latter were in theory teaching Malays to administer their states, the nature of colonial rule did not encourage political initiative or provide an education in concepts of popular government that by the late nineteenth century had taken root in England. The state councils were never seen as a transition to a greater Malay voice in the administration. Weld, indeed, expressed the general British view that the *status quo* should continue indefinitely.

Nothing we have done has taught them to govern themselves; we are merely teaching them to co-operate with us ... I doubt if Asiatics will ever learn to govern themselves; it is contrary to the genius of their race, of their history, of their religious system, that they should. Their desire is a mild, just and firm depotism.[18]

The 'Plural Society'

Weld's comment opens up another perspective on the colonial period, for what the British had done was to introduce their own perception of what constituted the 'Melayu'. To the administrators of the Protected States, overwhelmingly middle-class, there was much in Malay society which touched an empathetic chord. A whole genre of literature grew up, vignettes of 'life in the East', reinforcing the British stereotype of the true Malay. Swettenham wrote:

The real Malay is courageous; ... but he is extravagant, fond of borrowing money and slow in repaying it ... He quotes proverbs

... never drinks intoxicants, he is rarely an opium smoker ... He is by nature a sportsman ... proud of his country and his people, venerates his ancient customs and traditions and has a proper respect for constituted authority ... He is a good imitative learner ... [but] lazy to a degree ... and considers time of no importance.[19]

By contrast, there developed a whole list of 'unMalay' qualities which were exemplified by other races. In British eyes the foremost of the unMalay traits was industry. Malays, it was widely accepted, were lazy, unwilling to work for wages and therefore could not be considered a potential pool of labour in the colonial economy. The measure of their lack of industry was provided by the Chinese who laboured in tin mines and on plantations and operated the tax farms. As a rule of thumb, the British believed, the rate of Chinese migration and the numbers of Chinese settlers were a reliable index of economic progress. In 1890, indeed, the Chinese indirectly provided 89 per cent of Selangor's revenue. The Chinese continued to come as labourers to the Malay states under the credit ticket system, but there was an ever-growing number of assisted migrants sponsored by family or friends especially after the Chinese government abolished restrictions on emigration in 1893. Until the twentieth century no attempts were made to stem this flow and despite the relatively high death rate and the numbers returning home, the Chinese population grew steadily. In 1891, when the first official census was taken, about half the total population of Perak, Selangor and Sungai Ujung was Chinese.

Many factors served to maintain the cultural and economic gap between Malays and Chinese. Unlike the rural Malays, the Chinese had become an urban group since it was in the Chinese-dominated mining areas that new towns were developing. Thus in 1891 Kuala Lumpur, with a population of 43,786, was 79 per cent Chinese. Demographic divisions were reinforced because administratively the British set the Chinese apart from the Malays. To a great extent the Chinese community already existed as a self-contained unit, and the famed Kapitan China Yap Ah Loy, closely associated with Kuala Lumpur's early development, reputedly had 4,000 men employed in his various mines, plantations and shops. Lacking the personnel necessary for controlling the Chinese community, the British depended heavily on the co-operation of men like Yap to maintain law and order. Initially, the goodwill of secret society leaders was also essential, and in Perak the leaders of both the Ghee Hin and Hai San were appointed to the state council. Gradually, a more formal means of dealing with the Chinese was established. In 1877 a Chinese Protectorate was set up in Singapore under William Pickering, and in the following years other officials fluent in at least one Chinese dialect and familiar with Chinese customs were appointed to the Malay states. It became accepted that a Chinese could more readily appeal to his 'protector' than to his District Officer, who usually spoke only Malay.

Chinese secret societies, however, remained a problem. In the Straits Settlements even registered societies were suppressed after 1890, and in the Protected States secret associations were in theory illegal from the inception of British control. But mere legislation could not eliminate the practices which had become so deep-rooted in the local Chinese community. The Ghee Hin and Hai San remained strong and in the Kinta district (Perak) in 1896 it was estimated that about 70 per cent of the Chinese mining population of nearly 14,000 were members. Nevertheless, the role of the societies was undergoing change, principally because they no longer had a monopoly on force. British access to superior arms, including the awe-inspiring Sikh police, quickly brought society-inspired riots under control. In addition, Chinese leaders themselves were interested in helping to keep the peace because their co-operation was frequently rewarded by a grant of profitable state revenue farms. While the societies did not disappear, many of their activities were diverted into more socially acceptable forms, and in the late nineteenth century there was a blossoming of dialect associations and mutual aid societies which filled many of the functions formerly the preserve of the secret *hui*.

With the gradual demise of the Kapitan China system, the Chinese Protectorate became the medium through which the Government hoped to reach the Chinese community. One of Pickering's original briefs had been to address himself to abuses of the credit ticket system, the living conditions of Chinese labourers and their exploitation at the hands of mine owners or plantation managers. Ordinances were introduced to register labour contracts, to explain the law to new arrivals, and to make undue cruelty a punishable offence. Further steps were taken later in the century to limit the number of days any labourer worked and to restrict his working day to nine hours. Laudable though such enactments were, it is difficult to assess the effectiveness of enforcement despite periodic inspections since the recruitment and supervision of Chinese labour remained largely in Chinese hands. Many iniquities persisted. Labourers were often paid by the truck system, by which goods, especially liquor and opium, were given in lieu of money. Addiction to alcohol and opiates among Chinese workers was high, and the cycle of constant indebtedness all too common. Reforms were hindered because the government was always open to pressure from employers and mine owners who presented the worker in a poor light. Government officials themselves were not anxious to change the cost structure and thus endanger the supply of cheap labour for the mines, plantations, and public works like roads, railways and canals. With economic development many of the ordinances, like those penalizing absconders, were intended to keep

Chinese workers from moving to areas such as Sumatra outside British jurisdiction.

The British assumption of responsibility for the Chinese also tended to lessen meaningful contact between Chinese and Malays. Increasingly, both groups became bound by stereotyped perceptions. For the Malay villager, the Chinese was a shopkeeper or a moneylender, often a man to whom he was indebted. The Chinese saw the Malays as a race submerged by others more energetic and sophisticated, which caused one Malay-language Chinese newspaper in 1894 to ask, 'Why are the Malays inert?' Nor were the upper-class Malays and Chinese drawn together in government service. Although some Chinese were employed in the lower ranks of the administration as clerks, surveyors and interpreters, there was no active involvement in the process of government apart from the inclusion of prominent Chinese on State Councils. The British continued to view them as transients, notwithstanding the increasing numbers who elected to stay in the Malay states.

Pickering, like most Englishmen, considered the Malays incapable of governing Chinese; to the latter, he said, it would seem 'like the white settlers of America submitting to the rule of Indian chiefs'.[20] Yet the success of Chinese–Malay relations in Johor belies such statements. Abu Bakar, recognizing that Johor's population was largely Chinese, incorporated Chinese into the highest levels of the bureaucracy. The Ghee Hin was permitted to function openly, despite British objections, because it was a useful means of maintaining order. In 1894 the Manchu Emperor even awarded Abu Bakar a decoration for his services to the Chinese. But in the Protected States the introduction of the Chinese Protectorate meant it was far less important for Malay chiefs and rulers to interact with the Chinese leaders.

The British creation of a dual system of government to administer the two major ethnic divisions provided no role for the growing Indian community. Indians had been migrating steadily to the Malay areas for generations but under the British the rate quickened as moneylenders came to the towns and clerks familiar with British administration arrived to fill minor bureaucratic posts. Most of the newcomers, however, were labourers. A fall in tin prices towards the end of the century led to a decline in Chinese migration, and the consequent shortage of workers pushed wages higher. Prior to this the Government of India had attempted to restrict the movement of labour to the Malay areas, but with the demand for cheap labour in the Straits Settlement and the Malay states steps were made to reach a compromise. Indian migration to the Straits Settlements was legalized in 1872 and to the Protected States in 1884. It was then that the flow began. While Chinese migrants still surpassed all others in total numbers, between 1891 and 1901 the Indian population in the Protected States rose to 58,211. This represents an increase of 188 per cent, relatively far greater than that of the Chinese in the same period (83·4 per cent).

Most of these migrants came from the Tamil areas of South India. Many of the European planters in Malaya had previously worked in Ceylon, and they had found Tamil workers particularly suited to their requirements. Recruited from the lowest levels of society, Tamils were considered more accustomed to British rule, more amenable to discipline than the Chinese, and more willing to work for wages than were Malays. These views were shared by the government, which also needed a constant supply of workers for public works, municipal services and road and rail construction. South India came to be regarded as a 'natural source' of labourers for the Malay States.

Indians came to Malaya by two means, the indentured and the *kangani* systems. By the former, the organization of migrants in India was in the hands of private recruiting firms in Madras or Nagapatnam. This system was never popular, either with Indians themselves or with employers. For Indians, the poor working conditions on many Malayan plantations, the prevalence of disease and the distance from home made Malaya far less attractive than either Burma or Ceylon, especially as the minimum contract was three years. Large numbers of recruited Indians were urban dwellers, unaccustomed to estate work, and there was a high rate of sickness and desertion. While government ordinances stipulated that an estate must provide medical care, enforcement of such measures was frequently resented by planters and seen as interference.

The indentured system was maintained in principle until 1910 but it did not succeed in attracting sufficient workers to satisfy the demand. Towards the end of the nineteenth century coffee planters, again drawing from the Ceylon experience, initiated a 'free' labour system by which the *kangani* (overseer) became the recruiter. The *kangani* signed up men from his own village in India and was paid a commission for each labourer. This personal association was more popular and after 1884 the net increase in the Indian labour force was rapid. With the growth of rubber plantations, virtually the sole source of Indian labour was via the *kangani* system. In 1907, through the co-operation of government and planters, the Tamil Immigration Fund was set up to subsidize Indian migrants who were then free to sell their labour where they wished.

Malaya's access to the continuing supply of cheap labour provided by Indian migration ensured the later success of the rubber industry. But this new Indian migrant, unlike those of past centuries who had often found high places in Malay courts, was given little chance to venture outside the narrow boundaries imposed by his social and economic status. As a group, they exercised little influence. No outstanding Indians emerged during this period to represent the interests of estate labourers, and although the government made sporadic efforts to improve working conditions on the plantations, planters usually raised objections when reforms involved additional expenditure. Without leadership, and with wages strictly controlled by agreements between government and private enterprise, it was not possible for Indians to exploit even the chronic shortage of labour or the competition between plantations and public works. They were probably relatively better off than in their villages at home, but poverty among Indian estate workers remained high, a depressing contrast to the wealthy Indian trader or merchant found in the urban centres.

At the turn of the century even the term 'Indian community' may be misleading. The category 'Indian' included not only Ceylonese (Sri Lankans) but disguised a whole range of different castes, as well as language and occupational groups from different areas of the subcontinent whose historical cultural links were often minimal. The history of Indians as an ethnic group in twentieth century Malaya/ Malaysia has been the struggle to attain a measure of unity and to assert themselves against the more dominant Chinese and Malays.

The plural society which evolved to service the developing colonial economy thus consisted of three generalized ethnic divisions: Malay, Chinese and Indian. Though simplistic and ill-defined, these were the categories by which the British administration perceived and governed local society. No real thought was given to many of the marginal groups, the men of mixed blood whose skills had often gained them positions of honour in traditional Malay society. British suspicion of the 'half-breed', Malay–Indian (*Jawi Peranakan*) or Malay–Arab, excluded them from the upper levels of the Malay administration. In urban areas like Penang and Singapore, however, they assumed a prominent role in vernacular education, in the Malay language press, and in local Islamic leadership. Another significant marginal group, ignored by British categories, was the Eurasians. Usually of mixed Portuguese or Dutch descent, they filled positions such as senior clerks, overseers and engineers in the state administration.

The very simplicity of the British categorization of Malayan society served to extend the boundaries of Melayu. While a stereotype of the 'real Malay' was being created, census figures using language and religion as an index of 'Malayness' inevitably included some *orang asli* closely associated with Malays as well as migrants from elsewhere in the archipelago. Large numbers of Javanese, for instance, were brought in as coolie labourers on government schemes such as canal or road construction. The migration from Sumatra was also high, and in some areas recent arrivals – Minangkabau, Rawa, Mandailing, Acehnese and Batak – could even outnumber the older population. The first generation clustered together and for a time preserved something of their own identity as testified by the numerous Kampung Jawa, Kampung Bugis, Kampung Kerinci and so on scattered through the peninsula. Malays distinguished between foreigners from the Netherlands East Indies, the *anak dagang* ('child of commerce') and the locally born, the *anak negeri* ('child of the country'), but the distinction disappeared for the migrants' descendants. The British tendency to group 'Malays' together was encouraged because a basic similarity of appearance, the use of Malay as a common language, and above all a shared religion continued to facilitate the absorption of Indonesian migrants into Malay society. The limits of Malayness were cultural and emotional rather than ethnic. When a man of Bugis origin saw himself as Malay, then that indeed he was.

Differing Rates of Development in the Protected States

Within the Protected States, British interest focused on Selangor and Perak, where an infrastructure was developed around the mining centres. Roads were built to the mining towns and later the plantation areas. In 1885 the first railway line was opened in Larut between Port Weld and Taiping, and in 1893 Ipoh and Teluk Anson were connected. By 1910 railways joined Johor Baru to Province Wellesley (Prai) on the mainland opposite Penang. Simultaneously, existing towns grew larger. It was here, where population was concentrated and where the revenue was largest, that social amenities were introduced. The first Government hospital, for example, was opened in Taiping in 1878. In the towns other innovations – paved roads, lighting, sanitation, the piping of water – continued to improve the quality of life. Already the disparity between the urban environment and that of the village had become marked.

On a wider scale, a similar disparity was seen in the contrast between economic development in Perak and Selangor and that of Negeri Sembilan and Pahang. A prime reason for the latter's failure to demonstrate the same material progress was the lack of resources, especially widespread tin deposits. Negeri Sembilan, by virtue of its proximity, did participate to a limited degree in the wealth of its neighbours, but Pahang's economy continued to flag. Specific geographic problems, such as the closure of the coast during the northeast monsoon and the high range separating Pahang from the west coast, impeded development. Only through bitter experience did European mining companies realize the greater difficulties involved in mining Pahang's lode tin as opposed to alluvial deposits on the west coast. The importation of sophisticated machinery which would have facilitated mining was impracticable because of poor communications. Rivers were still the main means of transport, and a trip from Pahang's new capital of Kuala Lipis to Singapore took over a fortnight by boat. Even when a road was built from Kuala Lumpur over the mountains to Kuala Lipis, the 130-kilometre journey could only be made by bullock cart. Until the introduction of the motor car Pahang was effectively cut off from the other British-ruled areas.[21]

Contending against such disadvantages, Pahang's production could not begin to equal that of Perak and Selangor. At no time did the mining revenue exceed 5 per cent of the total from the four Protected States, and it was never sufficient to meet Pahang's needs. It is not surprising, therefore, to find that in 1895 Perak had fifteen hospitals, Selangor fourteen, but Pahang only two. Finances showed no signs of improvement and fiscal difficulties were exacerbated by the uprising of 1891–5. By the time peace was restored, Pahang's official expenditure was two and a half times greater than its income. The development of local rubber plantations at the beginning of this century did bring financial benefits, but by then in terms of economy and social services Pahang had been far outstripped by the west coast states.

Demographically, too, Pahang was far more similar to Kelantan and Trengganu. Because tin and gold deposits were not widespread, only limited numbers of Chinese came to Pahang. The Malay character of the state remained despite strenuous efforts by successive Residents to encourage Chinese enterprise. The Chinese population, reckoned at about 6 per cent of the total in 1891, did reach 22 per cent by 1911 but Pahang could still be popularly described as 'the one real Malay state' under British influence.

The Federated Malay States

At the beginning of the nineteenth century the east coast of the peninsula had been more prosperous and more populous than the west. By the 1890s, however, the British had come to associate the largely Malay states of the east coast with lack of development. It was partly to lessen the differences between Pahang and the west coast that the four Protected States were grouped into a Federation in 1896. But the notion of a common purse which would, it was hoped, solve Pahang's indebtedness was only one reason behind the Federation decision. Proposals for some kind of union had been made through the 1880s, reflecting a trend towards larger administrative units already apparent in Negeri Sembilan and elsewhere in the British Empire, notably Ceylon (Sri Lanka). Advocates of Federation, like Swettenham, also propounded the advantages of administrative efficiency. Although administrative differences between the states were probably exaggerated, the call for uniformity in such matters as communication, taxation and justice found many supporters. In 1895 Swettenham, then Resident of Perak but with ambitions of gaining a higher post in the new Federation, was assigned the task of obtaining the rulers' approval of the scheme. It seems fair to say that the implications of the scheme were never fully explained to them. The longest discussion between Swettenham and a Malay ruler took only four hours, and there was no consultation with the leading chiefs or princes. The Treaty of Federation was worded so ambiguously that years later Sultan Idris of Perak complained he could not understand how Federation functioned. But Swettenham's arguments were persuasive, and in July 1896 the Federated Malay States (FMS) came into being with the capital at Kuala Lumpur in the heart of the tin mining region. The Federal Secretariat was to be headed by a Resident-General with jurisdiction over all the Residents and authority to represent the Federation's interest to the Singapore Governor, who was also High Commissioner for the Malay states. Departments of police, public works, posts, telegraph and railways were now placed under a single director; a unified civil service was set up, and tentative proposals were made for a common treasury. To assure uniformity, all laws except those of a purely local nature and all financial measures were drawn up in Kuala Lumpur.

The British had thus brought together four states in an administrative entity which had no historical antecedents. A significant step had been made in the centralizing process and the creation of what was to become British Malaya. It had, however, little obvious effect on Malays at large. Despite plaudits from the British, Federation brought no tangible benefits to the people and was a disappointment to the rulers who had hoped they might regain some of their lost authority. In a grandiose fashion, the Federation Treaty had guaranteed that they would 'not in the slightest degree be diminishing the powers and privileges which they now possess nor be curtailing the rights of self-government which they now enjoy'.[22] In fact, after 1896 more administration than ever before was carried out by the Residents in consultation with the Resident-General, without any reference to the ruler or the state council. Official conferences of rulers, or Durbars, were convened in 1897 and again in 1903 to bring the four rulers together, but despite the panoply surrounding them the Durbars had only vague advisory powers. The creation of the Federation must surely have eliminated any lingering belief that the Sultans were ruling with the 'advice' of their Residents. It was the realization of the true extent to which Malay rulers had relinquished their powers to outsiders which prompted Sultan Idris to express public concern of the loss of state individuality and the lack of Malay participation in government. The very real possibility that Malays might one day become 'strangers in their own land' led, as we will see in the following chapter, to the establishment of a Malay College at Kuala Kangsar in Perak.

In 1909 a further move towards centralization and uniformity was made with the creation of a Federal Council. It was to be headed by the High Commissioner based in Singapore, assisted by the Resident-General in Kuala Lumpur. The Sultans had agreed to the Council on the condition that their prerogatives were reduced no further, but the Council proceeded to assume the few financial and legislative powers still remaining in the hands of the state councils. The Sultans had no power of veto and in reality the Council, which included Europeans and Chinese representatives of planting and mining interests, became a vehicle for an extension of the authority of the High Commissioner/ Governor of Singapore. Governor Anderson (1904–11) was known to favour an amalgamation of Singapore and the Malay states, so that income from the FMS could help shore up Singapore's finances at times of recession. Since the FMS made use of Singapore's facilities, it was felt that they should also make a contribution to its revenue. Anderson's own goal of reinforcing Singapore's position in relation to Kuala Lumpur was achieved when the position of Resident-General was formally changed to that of Chief Secretary. But from the stand-point of the Malay rulers, the rivalry between Singapore and Kuala Lumpur merely diverted attention from a further diminution of states' rights.

The Expansion of British Interests in Borneo

The reality of British control in the newly Federated Malay States was clearly visible in the extent and growing complexity of the colonial administration. In Borneo, on the other hand, the British Government seemed far more reluctant to become directly involved. The only Malay sultanate along the northwest coast was the weakened state of Brunei, and until 1868 Sarawak had been able to push northwards, absorbing Brunei's territory in return for agreed payments. This created a dilemma for Britain, which was at least partly committed to Brunei because the 1847 treaty provided that any territorial cessions should be approved by the British government. In order to obviate the possibility of future intervention in conflicts between Sarawak and Brunei, Britain in 1868 invoked the 1847 treaty and refused to permit Sarawak to purchase the Baram district from Brunei. The second Raja, Charles, who succeeded his uncle the same year, was not easily deterred and for several years continued to press for the Baram cession. Eventually Britain agreed, basically because after 1881 it became involved in sponsoring an equally expansionist Trading Company in North Borneo and could not logically permit it to expand without granting the same approval to Sarawak.

The emergence of this Trading Company was a relatively late development. Until the 1870s there had seemed no necessity for the British to assert their position along the far northern coast of Borneo, which had remained under the nominal control of the Sultan of Sulu. From fortified coastal villages high ranking Sulu chiefs, who had been granted revenue rights over local jungle and sea products, wielded a fragmented and intermittent authority over the region. By the last quarter of the nineteenth century, however, this area was attracting greater interest in Britain. The passage between Sulu and North Borneo was important because it provided a trading route between Australia and China. It was therefore necessary to ensure that it would not fall under the control of any other European power, especially as France was moving to consolidate its position in Vietnam and thus dominate another flank of the sea route to China. Furthermore, the Dutch had for several years been expanding in southwest Borneo and there was also some British apprehension of intrusion by Spain, the United States, Germany and even Italy into the Borneo region. In the peninsula such fears had already given an impetus to Britain's 'forward movement', and in a less direct fashion they were also to influence developments in Borneo.

In 1877, an Englishman, Alfred Dent, advanced capital enabling the Austrian Consul-General in Hong Kong, Baron von Overbeck, to purchase the unexploited American concessions in North Borneo, soon due to expire. With the active support of William Treacher, the young acting governor of the British colony of Labuan (and later second Resident-General of the FMS), Overbeck negotiated a new cession of 17,252,000 hectares from the Brunei Sultan for an annual payment of $15,000. A significant feature of the agreement was that North Borneo would be in all essential respects independent of Brunei. Shortly afterwards, followed by Treacher, Overbeck went to Jolo where the Sultan of Sulu also ceded his rights in North Borneo for a rent of $5,000 yearly and made Overbeck 'supreme and independent'. Under Treacher's supervision a treaty was drafted with Sulu stipulating that this territory could not be alienated to any other nation without Britain's acquiescence. In February 1878 a Resident was appointed in the port of Sandakan, where the Union Jack was hoisted alongside Dent's own standard. Other representatives of the Dent–Overbeck partnership were subsequently landed along the west coast.

Officially, Britain could disclaim any responsibility for this activity in North Borneo but, though unofficial and personal, the links between London and the new order in North Borneo were real. Treacher did not act simply from a sense of patriotism, but had received indirect intimations from the Foreign Office as to how the North Borneo grant should proceed. Dent, who soon bought out Overbeck's share in the venture, had an influential friend in the Foreign Office, the Permanent Under-Secretary. Protests from Singapore and Sarawak against the grant of such a large block of land to a private concern met the response that it was 'truly a British undertaking'.[23] When the Philippine authorities attempted to raise the Spanish flag near Sandakan, a British warship with Treacher aboard was sent to forestall any future intrusion. Dent's London connections also helped him gain support for the formation of a company under Government auspices. In 1881, after protracted discussion, a British North Borneo Company was chartered in London and thus gained from the British Crown a degree of protection. The Company was bound to remain 'British in character', to relinquish foreign relations to Britain, and to submit the names of proposed governors for London's approval. In the same year Treacher was seconded from the Civil Service to become North Borneo's first governor. In 1885, England, Germany and Spain signed a convention recognizing Spanish sovereignty over Sulu; in return, Spain withdrew its former claims to North Borneo. Thus, though the British Government had somewhat reluctantly felt compelled to stake its claim along Borneo's northern coast, it had avoided the unwelcome adminstrative expense and deflected expected objections from other European countries by the useful expedient of a chartered company.

Both Sarawak and North Borneo were eager to expand their territories further. Charles Brooke's publicly stated goal of incorporating all Brunei into Sarawak expressed both his personal ambitions and economic reality, for much of Sarawak's revenue came from jungle produce, requiring still greater tracts of forest. Company officials in North Borneo justified their expansion because the large land areas ceded by Brunei were not all coterminous. In some districts Company concessions were separated by rivers controlled by independent chiefs, and these the Company was anxious to acquire. At the same time it also hoped to expand southwards, persisting in the belief that the forbidding jungle interior of Borneo was a storehouse of untapped wealth. Each additional river brought under Company control, it was felt, was a source of revenue — immediate in terms of taxes and customs duties, and potential in terms of land sales and possible mineral exploitation.

This expansion could take place only at Brunei's expense. Already the Sultan of Brunei could see the effects of the cessions made to Sarawak and North Borneo. 'Formerly,' he wrote to Charles Brooke in 1881, 'the territory of Brunei was united like unto a man with all his members complete. At present his arms are lost to him, leaving only his head and feet.'[24] The appointment of a British Resident to Brunei would have stopped its dismemberment, but although this proposal was discussed several times in the 1880s, it was for the time set aside. Ironically, in view of later oil discoveries, opinion in the British Foreign and Colonial offices was that Brunei could not support the cost of a European establishment. Another common belief was that Brunei could not long survive as an independent state and that the best solution was to partition it between Sarawak and North Borneo. Only rarely did the British government raise objections to cessions by the impecunious Brunei Sultan and his nobles, for continued encroachment by Sarawak or North Borneo at least excluded the intrusion of any other nation. From the outset, therefore, both Brooke and the Company saw themselves as engaged in some kind of contest to absorb as much territory as possible, often using highly questionable methods to gain or force Brunei's consent. Some of the North Borneo's Company's most valuable acquisitions were along the west coast, like the Putatan area and the Klias peninsula, both rich rice growing areas, and by 1901 Company territory included most of the modern state of Sabah.

At the same time Brooke was attempting to anticipate the Company. In 1882 and 1884 he acquired the Baram and Trusan Rivers, and in 1890 he seized the Limbang River, Brunei's last remaining territory of importance. In 1905 the final cession was made when the North Borneo Company transferred the small district of Lawas to Sarawak. In the following year a British Resident was appointed to Brunei as an alternative to total absorption by Sarawak, ending for ever the Brookes' cherished ambition. Nonetheless, Sarawak was now over twenty times its original size and its dominant ethnic group, the Ibans, had come to occupy many areas traditionally inhabited by other groups such as the Kayans, Kenyahs and Muruts.

The rivalry between Sarawak and North Borneo, the question of Brunei's future, and the possibility of foreign intrusion in Sarawak after Raja Brooke's death all served to fuel discussion of a closer association between the three states and Britain. Singapore was the obvious point of linkage, and even in 1881 Weld spoke hopefully of one day becoming High Commissioner for Borneo and the Malay states. Seven years later, in 1888, protectorate status was negotiated with all three states, by which they surrendered to the British Government responsibility for foreign policy and were in turn guaranteed protection from the threat of outside attack. The Brunei Sultan, Brooke and the Company all welcomed the security promised by the new arrangement, symbolized in the person of the Governor of the Straits Settlements who was now also High Commissioner of the Malay states and Consul-General for the Borneo States. An agreement between Britain and the Netherlands in 1891 settled disputed border claims, although the boundary between Dutch and British Borneo was not surveyed until 1912. This became the frontier between modern Malaysia and Indonesia. By the last years of the nineteenth century, northwest Borneo was so closely linked to British interests that an official in the Colonial Office could anticipate a future administration in North Borneo and Sarawak 'on much the same principles as the native states of the Malay peninsula'.[25]

Such predictions made little allowance for the very different character of the Borneo territories, not only from the peninsula but from each other. The development of Sarawak and North Borneo had followed separate paths despite some superficial similarities. Though the North Borneo Company was a governing concern, and not directly involved in commerce, it developed no real administrative policy to match the often perceptive views of the Brookes. Whereas the latter justified the lack of economic development by arguing that the spread of Western 'civilization' would be harmful to indigenous society in Sarawak, the lack of Western influence in North Borneo was more a function of faltering Company finances. There were scattered settlements along the coast, but only Jesselton (Kota Kinabalu) on the west coast and Sandakan on the east showed any signs of growing into large towns similar to those on the Malay peninsula. For the first decade of its existence, indeed, London fully expected the North Borneo Company to collapse. It was only saved from bankruptcy by revenue and export taxes derived from the local collection of jungle and sea products destined for the China trade. However, with the development of timber and tobacco in the 1890s, North Borneo's income steadily improved. The revenue rose from £37,075 in 1895 to £62,392 in 1900, and the flourishing timber and rubber industries in the early years of this century established the economy on a healthier footing.

Nonetheless, North Borneo was not as yet considered a wealthy state, and over-ambitious projects such as a west coast railway absorbed much of its income. Of necessity, the civil service remained small, numbering only twenty-eight Europeans in 1895, and thus limiting the effectiveness of Company government. Apologists for Company rule point to the gradual abolition of slavery following edicts in 1881 and 1883, an improvement in communications and medical services, the establishment of vernacular schools after 1911. But evidence that the Company was slowly assuming the responsibilities of a 'colonial' government was apparent only in the towns. Thirty years after the inception of Company control, the mass of inhabitants in North Borneo had received few tangible benefits apart from the effective elimination of headhunting.

The Company also had less success than the Brookes in fostering a general recognition of a white overlord. The administrative structure which existed, adopting numerous aspects from both Sarawak and the peninsula, had little meaning to the local populace. At the apex was the Governor, responsible to the Court of Directors in London, but with his brief term of office no Governor could ever assume the charisma of a Charles Brooke. From 1895 to 1910 the most dominant figure in North Borneo affairs was not a man on the spot but the Company's Managing Director in London, W. C. Cowie. While Sarawak could point to some local participation in government through the Council Negeri, in North Borneo the Governor's Advisory Council included no non-whites except an occasional Chinese merchant. Residents and District Officers adminstered the outlying settlements but many did not speak Malay, the only lingua franca along the coast, until several months after their arrival. Until 1892 knowledge of Malay was not required for promotion, and Hugh Clifford remarked at the time that not a single European in Company employ knew the language of any of the interior or coastal tribes. Undoubtedly some individual Residents administered wisely, but local distrust of alien rule was widespread. At the time the Company was chartered, one young chief in the Putatan area commented that he 'had heard dreadful accounts of the white man's government, that the police interfered in everything and that men were shut up in prison and that revenue was required in cash instead of kind'.[26] A generation later such suspicions still had not been laid to rest.

Although Charles Brooke himself always emphasized the difference between his style of government and that of Brunei, he did exploit many elements of the old system to the advantage of his regime. The North Borneo Company was impressed by the cheapness and effectiveness of Sarawak's administration but was far less successful in adapting pre-existing forms of authority to its own ends. Until the second decade of this century the Company relied heavily on the assistance of traditional leaders such as the Sulu chiefs who were recruited as native officers. However, by depending on feudal-type relationships between these leaders and their retainers, the Company was perpetuating the fragmentation of North Borneo society. A monthly salary of five Straits dollars might claim a headman's support in the short term, but it could not guarantee his lasting loyalty when his new duties conflicted with the traditional obligations of a local leader.

The lack of any heritage of wider loyalty beyond the purely local scene was exacerbated by the multitude of tribal and ethnic divisions within North Borneo which Company administrators only vaguely understood. The interior peoples were divided into two general categories 'Dusuns' and 'Muruts', but both subsumed a large number of groups whose language and culture were often very different. A further distinction was made between these generally animist inland peoples and the Moslem-influenced coastal groups, but the latter category also included several distinct ethnic communities. From necessity or ignorance the Company frequently placed native officers from one group over others with whom they had little in common, which in itself could be the basis of conflict. The influx of Chinese, Indians, peninsular Malays and other groups from elsewhere in the archipelago compounded the demographic complexity of the local population.

In both Borneo territories, as in the peninsula, revenue collection was a common cause of complaint against white rule. Yet in Sarawak, while many an Iban legend lauds the resistance of those who refused to pay the White Raja's dues, Charles Brooke was relatively successful in perpetuating the notion that tax remittance symbolized service to the ruler. Those who failed to pay, he said, were in a state of rebellion and justly deserved punishment. Without a personality like Brooke, and without access to a fighting force like the Ibans, the Company found the collection of taxes difficult, and yet they were an important source of revenue. A particular local grievance was the poll tax and the rigidity of its application. As one Bajau remarked, 'Although the Brunei *pangiran* [nobles] fine people tens and hundreds of piculs, it is all mere words, they can give what they have, but the white man's two dollars is two dollars and no less.'[27] So often, it seemed to the interior people, the acquisition of a river by the Company simply meant an increase in revenue collection. Established economic patterns were also changed by the Company's trading posts which often diverted commerce away from a previously prosperous river.

Although some Residents overcame these obstacles and fostered harmonious relations with the local population, the Company encountered recurring resistance which generally took the same form as responses in the past to encroachments by Brunei or Sulu overlords. Sometimes involving a few hundred people, sometimes widespread, such disturbances reflected the fragmented nature of North Borneo's population. Through the 1880s the Company usually reacted by sending an expedition to bring rebellious chiefs to heel, although by the turn of the century there was a growing willingness to negotiate.

It is often difficult to see the reason behind individual uprisings; perhaps it was a disputed judgement of a native magistrate, some European officer's ignorance of a past agreement, rumours of some new tax, a bad harvest, changes in land registration, resentment at the imposition of corvée or simply a generalized fear of change. One of the more intriguing of these occurred among west coast Muruts in the Padas and Tenom districts in 1891. Called the Malingkote Revolt, it was initiated by an individual who dreamed that an angel had given him powers of flight and invulnerability in return for the destruction of animals and crops. Spreading across large areas of the interior, the cult united many groups across traditionally hostile lines and sustained its hold on them for nearly a year. Years later, a similar pattern could be seen in the so-called Rundum Revolt among the interior Muruts in 1915 which was a direct outcome of the adverse effects of social and economic innovation.

The only indication of any unified movement against the Company was the Mat Salleh rebellion, which erupted in 1895 and was not fully quelled until 1905. Mat Salleh's grievances were never totally clear, although it seems that the introduction of a new tax on imported rice and another to help finance a cross-country railroad exacerbated a general discontent. Mat Salleh himself was an impressive man who, of mixed Bajau and Sulu parentage, could draw on a combination of Muslim and indigenous symbols of authority. His mouth, it was said, produced flames and his *parang* (curved cleaver) lightning; Moslems saw him as the Mahdi, the coming saviour. His use of flags, Islamic standards and the umbrella of royalty gave him a prestige and mystique lacking in more localized uprisings. Although Mat Salleh was eventually killed in 1900, jungle warfare continued for another five years and today he is still regarded as one of Sabah's great heroes.

By the first decade of this century the effects of Western penetration in northwest Borneo reflected the nature of the separate administrations. When Charles Brooke died in 1917 he left behind an economically undeveloped Sarawak but one in which there was some sense of allegiance to a central authority. However, in creating this entity he had assigned specific functions to the three major communities, Malays, Ibans and Chinese. In a society already ethnically fragmented, this policy merely heightened the natural tendency of the local peoples to view themselves communally.

In North Borneo, the Company had been unable to instil among the disparate population any significant feeling of loyalty to a greater political unit beyond individual groupings. Yet officials in the British Colonial Office remained undaunted by these realities and already there was talk of extending colonial control in the area. A Resident had been posted in Brunei, and one official commented confidently that 'British North Borneo, possibly also Sarawak, will fall to us within a measurable time'.[28]

The Incorporation of the Northern Malay States into British Malaya

Separate though they were, North Borneo, Sarawak, the FMS and the Straits Settlements at least shared some experience of Western rule, something which did not apply to the northern Malay states under Siam's suzerainty. Towards the end of the nineteenth century Siamese overlordship here became more formal, reflecting not only the development of a modern bureaucracy in Siam itself but also Siamese awareness of Britain's expansion in the peninsula. Siamese leaders and the European advisers they employed realized that the division laid down in the 1826 treaty was being questioned by British expansionists. Consequently, Siamese interest in all the northern Malay states became more pronounced, one indication being the compilation during the 1880s of various chronicles (*phongsawadan*) describing Siam's dealings with its Malay vassals since the eighteenth century. The contrast between the detailed Siamese knowledge of nineteenth century events and the vagueness of information relating to anything before about 1800 clearly shows the changed tenor of Siamese–Malay relations.

A further sign of renewed Siamese interest in the northern peninsula were several royal visits made by Chulalongkorn to the Malay states, the first ever made by a Thai king. In the 1890s there was a general reorganization of all provincial government in Siam, and this included the Malay states. The latter now fell under the direct control of the Ministry of the Interior and were grouped into circles (*monthon*), each with a Superintendent Commissioner (Khaluang Thesaphiban) appointed by the ministry. Under this new system Patani was under Ligor, Kelantan and Trengganu were controlled jointly from Phuket, while Kedah, Perlis and Setul were drawn into one circle under the Sultan of Kedah, Sultan Abdul Hamid (reigned 1879–1943).

In contrast to the British, the Siamese placed no great value on uniformity and the differing degree of centralized control reflected Bangkok's view of local politics. Kedah, by the 1826 treaty a 'territory' of Siam, had since 1842 been relatively free of Siamese control. A potential dynastic crisis and possible Siamese intervention in 1879 had been averted when three princes had agreed to act jointly as Regents for the young Sultan Abdul Hamid. The position of trust later given to Abdul Hamid in the Thesaphiban system indicates the value Bangkok placed on his diligent maintenance of peace. Kedah had also fulfilled its role as a loyal vassal by sending guns to assist Siam in a border dispute with the French in Laos. Links with Siam were reinforced through frequent trips to the Bangkok court by Kedah princes, some of whom pursued their studies there. Of all the Malay states finally ceded to the British in 1909, Chulalongkorn regretted most the loss of Kedah.

Kedah's excellent relations with Siam are all the more remarkable because Kedah was increasingly involved with the British. Sultan Abdul Hamid actively sought to incorporate many aspects of Western government, and in 1885 he visited Perak and Singapore to examine their administration. In Kedah itself he established the nucleus of a bureaucracy, including departments dealing with posts and telegraphs, lands and a treasury. Kedah was also fortunate in possessing several able court officials, among whom was the Chief Minister Wan Mat Saman, still considered one of the state's most outstanding administrators. As an observer remarked in 1900, 'It is interesting to see how a purely Malay government without European interference or guidance has endeavoured to model the adminstration on colonial lines, even to the appointment of an Auditor General.'[29]

Economically, too, Kedah was closely linked to the Straits Settlements, for the economy of Penang and Kedah had been basically integrated from the early nineteenth century. Kedah's revenue farms were controlled by Hokkien merchants in Penang, and from 1887 the same concern leased the principal farms, opium and spirits, in both places. Canals were built with loans from Penang, the most successful stretching for thirty-three kilometres connecting Alor Setar and Kedah Peak and opening up new areas for rice production. With Penang serving as an outlet to outside markets, Kedah began growing some commercial crops such as tapioca, nutmeg, cloves and coffee in addition to the staple crop, rice. Land registration was introduced in the 1880s, giving rise to a wealthy Malay peasant class, while the Chinese were beginning to develop rice milling and marketing.

Thus, in the face of potential intervention from Siam and the British, Kedah had succeeded in maintaining considerable freedom of action, establishing a reputation for responsibility and initiative. Even an avowed advocate of British expansion like Swettenham considered Kedah 'exceptionally well-governed'. By contrast, Siam had considered it necessary to assume much tighter authority over Kelantan. Quarrels among the royal family had been a characteristic of Kelantan politics, although the long reign of Sultan Muhammad II (1838–86) had brought some increase in royal authority. From 1891 disputes again developed, with rivals from three generations vying for power. Twice, in 1894 and again in 1900, Bangkok intervened to support one or another candidate for the throne. As a result, evidence of Siamese control became more visible. In the early 1890s the first of a series of Siamese commissioners took up residence in Kota Baru, the capital. Shortly afterwards a Siamese flag was hoisted and a party of Siamese soldiers was stationed there. Under this more direct supervision, efforts were made to reorganize Kelantan's finances and to strengthen central hold over village administration. Such measures were intended to prevent disturbances and, by rationalizing Kelantan's government, to forestall any potential British intervention. The ruler of Kelantan was himself amenable to administrative innovation, and following his visit to Johor and Singapore in 1896 a Land Office was set up in Kota Baru and a Public Works Department established. Sikhs recruited from Selangor made up a small police force, and other signs of 'progress' were apparent in the small printing press for government notices and the beginnings of a telephone service.

Unlike Kedah, however, there was relatively little economic development in either Kelantan or Trengganu. Rumours of great mineral wealth in this region circulated in the Straits Settlements, but the few Europeans who did penetrate into the region found that they were not welcome. Possibly on Siam's instructions, the rulers of both states refused to permit white men entry. Demographically, Kelantan and Trengganu were heavily Malay, and even at the time of the first official census in 1911 the Chinese here numbered less than 14,000, or about 2 per cent of the peninsula's total. The traditional economy had altered little during the nineteenth century, and despite limited mining and some pepper and gambier growing, Kelantan and Trengganu were barely rocking in the wake of changes along the west coast. If anything, the power of the aristocracy was more entrenched than ever, and most of the land was locked up in concessions to leading families who continued to present a challenge to royal authority. In Perak and Selangor, a communication network was slowly lessening the historic and geographic separateness of the upriver (*ulu*) areas; but in Kelantan and Trengganu roads outside the principal settlements were virtually non-existent, the only access to the interior being rivers and jungle tracks.

It was not by the criteria of economic development, which to the Westerner represented 'civilization', that the Malays of Kelantan and Trengganu measured their great achievements; rather, it was by the standards of an Islamic state famed for learning and scholarship. Travel to Mecca and study in the Middle East became increasingly common in the late nineteenth century, strengthening an established tradition of religious education. Islam in these states had undoubtedly benefited from Asian rather than Western overlordship, for unlike the British, the Siamese perceived no division between the secular and the religious. The influence and vitality of Islam had not been dissipated by the British partition of 'civil' and Islamic courts found in the FMS. In Kelantan and Trengganu, efforts to enforce Moslem precepts and eliminate 'unIslamic' practices were given continuing priority. Legal administration was brought more closely under the supervision of Moslem law courts, presided over by experts in Islamic law. Compliance with the outward forms of Islam, such as mosque attendance, were made obligatory, while stress was also laid on correct dress and strict observance of the fasting month. Admittedly, the enforcement of such enactments in areas away from the capital was difficult. The *Hikayat Sri Kelantan*, for instance, acknowledges that in the villages old customs were still current. But even if ineffectual, bans on popular amusements such as *menora* and *makyong* dance-dramas gave rulers a widely respected reputation for piety.

Even within the Siamese ambit, therefore, differences between the east and west coast were apparent. Although the Kedah court also assumed a leading role in the sponsorship of Islam, its economic association with Penang and its decision to emulate a Western-style bureaucracy, combined with a centuries-old relationship with Europeans, made it more similar to Johor than Kelantan or Trengganu. But one thing which all the northern Malay states had in common was a sense of pride in having preserved their independence under Siamese overlordship.

It was this very independence, and Siam's relatively loose hold over the northern Malay states, that concerned British observers in the late nineteenth century. Singapore Governors had long entertained ambitions of extending British power further, and in 1893 the Governor visited Kelantan and Trengganu without reference to Siam. In the face of new rumours of German and French interest in the Kra Isthmus London began to talk of a possible occupation of the northern states should Siam be threatened by the French. Even the 1896 Anglo-French Convention guaranteeing Siam's neutrality did not still anxiety for the future.

The leaders of Siam were in two minds about their relationship with the Malay vassals. In the words of King Chulalongkorn, 'We have no particular interest in the Malay States . . . if we lost them to England we would miss only the *bunga mas*. Apart from this there would not be any material loss. However, it is bad for the prestige of a nation. That is why we have to strengthen our hold over this territory.' In 1897 the Siamese were given a secret assurance that the British would recognize their suzerainty over the northern Malay states on the condition that no territory be alienated to a third power. Accordingly, when German firms applied in 1899 and 1900 to develop concessions off the Kedah coast, the Siamese bowed to British pressure and refused permission.

To Bangkok the national prestige derived from suzerainty over the Malay states became less important than using them as a bargaining point with the British government, especially regarding the touchy issue of British extraterritorial rights in Siam. Unbeknown to the Malay rulers, secret discussions between these two powers about an eventual transfer of sovereignty of the northern Malay states were being conducted even at the turn of the century. In this context, any small crisis could justify intervention by either Britain or Siam.

One recurring problem for the northern Malay states was monetary. Whereas Johor had been able to finance much of its development through Chinese revenue, neither Perlis, Trengganu nor Kelantan had a sizeable Chinese population and even in Kedah the Chinese numbered less than 8 per cent. Unlike the FMS, there was no watchful British Resident with his budget carefully monitoring income and expenditure, nor was there a ready source of credit which in time of trouble could shore up the treasury. A glance at Pahang helps make the point more clearly. Here, even with the most stringent fiscal controls the expenditure between 1904 and 1908 still exceeded revenue by 100 per cent, and the state was heavily dependent on loans from its FMS neighbours. There was no such safeguard for the states outside British control. In Kedah during 1904 the expense of five royal weddings brought the state to the brink of bankruptcy with its debts reckoned at four times the annual income. Kedah's credit in Penang was exhausted and as a final resort the ruler turned to Siam. A substantial loan was made, but on the condition that he agree to the appointment of a financial adviser who would, it was intimated, be withdrawn as soon as the debt was repaid. The discussion between the Siamese government and the British about who should fill this role demonstrates the intensity of British interest. The first adviser, an Englishman in Siamese employ, arrived in Kedah in 1905 but was replaced soon afterwards by a British officer seconded from the Indian Civil Service.

Meanwhile, financial problems in Kelantan had also provided the opening for the appointment of a British agent. In 1900 a certain R. W. Duff, newly retired from the state administration in Pahang, came to Kota Baru with the aim of acquiring mining concessions. He had already gained support from several companies in the Straits Settlements and was able to reach an arrangement with the Raja of Kelantan without any application to Siam. By the terms of his grant, Duff secured an absolute monopoly of mineral, trading and other rights over 777,000 hectares (about one third of Kelantan), together with an assurance that no further land would be alienated to Chinese. In return, the Raja received $20,000 and 2,000 shares in the Company.

Receiving news of this transaction, Bangkok not unreasonably judged it an indirect extension of British influence, aided, it was suspected, by active Malay collaboration. In July 1901 the ruler of Kelantan, Sultan Muhammad IV (1900–20), was summoned to Bangkok to explain his action at a meeting also attended by the rulers of Kedah and Patani. The British government, anxious to retain Siam's goodwill, was not at all willing to lend Duff any official support but after extensive appeals and litigation, Bangkok finally agreed to the Duff Company's concessions. Duff, however, continued to press for greater British involvement, even threatening to float his Company in some other European capital. If Britain did not seize the opportunity to move into Kelantan, he said, 'the rich commercial advantage to be gained in the development of the state would fall to the Germans'.

Among proponents of British expansion over the entire peninsula, Duff's argument found a ready response. In 1902 Swettenham, now Governor, proposed to Bangkok that in return for a clear definition of Bangkok's suzerainty over Kelantan and Trengganu the two states should accept a Siamese advisor employed by Bangkok but of British nationality. A principal factor in Siam's acceptance of these conditions was the influence of the American General Adviser to the Siamese Government, who regarded the Malay states as the cause of 'irritations and difficulties' and thus of little value. In 1902 an Anglo-Siamese treaty was signed, and in 1903 an Adviser, W. A. Graham, was sent to Kelantan. In the following years, between 1903 and 1909, his staff was increased by the posting of other Englishmen.

No Adviser had yet been appointed in Trengganu, and Kelantan still remained under Siamese suzerainty; but the links with the British administration were already tightening. Graham always saw himself as an employee of Siam, but his duties were defined in precisely the same terms as the FMS Residents, and the small bureaucracy he built up was modelled on that of Perak and Selangor. Judicial reforms were introduced, the powers of the Islamic court delineated, roads constructed, the treasury regulated and some secular education introduced. As in Kedah, however, state finances were insufficient to fund even fairly modest reforms, the situation being aggravated by the debased currency. In 1906 further loans were necessary to ward off impending bankruptcy.

Several factors served to hasten the final transferral of the northern Malay states to Britain in 1909. In Bangkok, Chulalongkorn still felt humiliated by the terms of the 1897 Secret Convention, which had essentially placed Siam's dealings with the Malay states under British control. Another source of shame was British extraterritorial rights in Siam which prevented the Siamese from bringing to court any Asian or European claiming to be a British subject. There was also a growing suspicion of Malay loyalty. According to rumours current in Bangkok, certain chiefs were deliberately cultivating the favour of the British agents, and in 1902 a serious rebellion broke out in Patani. On the British side, men like Swettenham were simply impatient at delays to what they considered the inevitable extension of British control. The British were also concerned about the growing numbers of Germans working in Siam, especially in departments dealing with railways. An *entente* between France and Britain in 1904 resulted in a decision to support Siam as a buffer state and to resist German influence in the region. To undermine German interests in Siam, the British agreed to relinquish their extraterritorial rights there and to provide a generous loan from FMS revenues for railway construction. In return, the Siamese should withdraw from the northern Malay states.

Even by 1907 it was clear that plans for a legal transfer were in the wind, for in that year the Duff Company was advised to remain in Kelantan rather than withdrawing as it had threatened. No formal discussions were ever conducted with the Malay rulers, although rumours had been circulating for some time. In 1908, through his Penang lawyers, Sultan Abdul Hamid of Kedah specifically asked the British to be consulted on any future changes. In Kelantan, the ruler sent a special deputation of ministers to present his case in Bangkok, while the Trengganu ruler despatched the *bunga mas* to Siam as a reminder of the long-established ties. It was clear that the more exacting nature of British control was not something they welcomed, and in Siam itself objections were raised at the loss of prestige which the surrender of territory entailed. A treaty, nonetheless, was concluded in March 1909, and in November of that year a probably bemused Edward VII was presented with the time-honoured symbols of overlordship, the *bunga mas dan perak*, from Siam's former Malay vassals.

The Treaty of 1909 was seen by many northern Malays as a betrayal, and the ruler of Kedah purportedly said that his country had been 'bought and sold like a buffalo'. In drawing an international boundary between Siam and 'British' Malaya, the 1909 Treaty finds a direct parallel in that between Britain and the Netherlands in 1824. Patani, which had been one of the most important Malay kingdoms in the seventeenth century and had remained a centre of Islamic scholarship, was now severed from the rest of the Malay world. Britain, in fact, had initially pressed for the cession of Patani as well, but the Siamese considered this too great a sacrifice. By insisting on the retention of Patani, Siam bequeathed to future governments the problem of absorbing the ethnically and culturally distinct Malay Moslems into the modern Thai state.

In Kedah and Kelantan, where British agents had already paved the way, the appointment of a British Adviser went relatively smoothly, although in each case any suggestions of incorporation into the FMS were vehemently opposed. Kedah in particular attained a reputation for the independence of its Malay Council, and in Singapore it was said that Kedah was a state 'where the black man rules the white'.[30] Resistance in Trengganu was more difficult to overcome. Sultan Zainal Abidin (1911—18) bitterly condemned the Siamese as thieves, who gave away what did not belong to them. He was only persuaded to agree to the 1909 Treaty after an assurance that the British agent assigned to Trengganu would only have consular powers. For the Sultan, the difference between an agent and adviser was an important legal distinction which he jealously guarded as a guarantee of his kingdom's independence and of the few freedoms still remaining to him. In 1911 he promulgated a state constitution modelled on that of Johor which allowed for a cabinet, a state council, ministerial departments and district officers — the outward trappings of a modern sovereign state. But the economy could not support the expenses involved in this degree of change, and in 1914 the Trengganu government was forced to request a loan from the Straits Settlements. The British agent also complained about other factors, such as the judiciary, the nature of land concessions, currency problems and above all lack of access to the treasury. The discovery of wolfram, a valuable component in some alloys, intensified the argument for extending the agent's powers. Had it not been for the outbreak of the World War I in August 1914 an Adviser might have been forced on Trengganu much earlier. As it was, the declaration of war and the Malay belief in an impending victory by Turkey, still regarded as the champion of Islam, hardened resistance. However, it was only a matter of time before Trengganu succumbed to unrelenting pressure from Singapore. A British commission, despatched in 1918 to investigate local administration, the police and the granting of concessions, predictably recommended the appointment of an 'Adviser' whose counsel 'must be asked and accepted in all matters except religion'. The new ruler, who had been one of the most forthright opponents of the British agent, publicly demonstrated his refusal to involve himself in the changed order by abdicating.

The Inclusion of Johor under British Rule

The extension of British control into Johor occurred about the same time as in the northern Malay states. During the late nineteenth century Abu Bakar had repeatedly diverted any attempts to modify the relationship between Singapore and Johor. Realizing the changes his death might bring, he had introduced a constitution in 1895 which expressly forbade the alienation of Johor to any European power, a pointed comment on Britain's ambitions. His death two months later brought to the throne his son Ibrahim, then a young man of twenty-two. Though inexperienced in administration, the new Sultan was at ease in Western society, had been educated in English and was a good horseman, cricketer and tennis player. But he acceded at a time when colonial authorities were increasingly anxious to expand Britain's hold over the entire peninsula. It is unlikely that any Malay ruler could have held out against the imperialist conviction that direct political control of Johor was vital to British interests in the area.

Maladministration of Johor could not be a justification. Anxious though he was to oversee the formation of 'British Malaya' before his retirement as Governor, Swettenham could find no reason for intervention during a tour of Johor in 1903. Abu Bakar's legacy was evident in a well-ordered government and an economy which, like the road system, was integrated with that of Singapore and the FMS. However, Ibrahim's personal life and attitude towards the colonial power provided ready arguments for advocates of intervention. Unlike his father, Ibrahim never gained the friendship of powerful individuals in the British government, and his lavish lifestyle, depleting a treasury already drained by Abu Bakar's frequent travels, aroused considerable criticism. Swettenham also objected to the influence in Johor of 'clever' Malays like Ibrahim's English-educated secretary who was accused of encouraging German and Dutch financiers. More serious in British eyes were the number of occasions when Ibrahim ignored colonial wishes, thus rejecting the implicit assumption that Johor should effectively operate as part of the FMS. The most contentious issue was Ibrahim's determination to maintain control over proposed railway links between Singapore and the FMS which was only settled when the FMS took over construction in 1904. In exasperation, Swettenham criticized Ibrahim for lacking 'good Malay qualities'.[31]

By 1905 Ibrahim had lost much of the privileged position for which his father had fought. Colonial Office opposition to private enterprise in Johor thwarted his efforts to found an independent Johor State Corporation for economic development. Even members of the Johor Advisory Board in London were working closely with the British government, and Ibrahim's efforts to constitute a new Board in 1907 were blocked. Under the constant threat of British intervention, he finally agreed to consult the British government on important matters and to obtain permission before making any trips abroad. Although the administration was functioning well enough, Ibrahim was gradually made aware of the seriousness of Johor's debts, something his ministers had recognized for some time. In 1909, after the Siamese cession of the northern Malay states, Ibrahim became more conciliatory, and himself proposed that a financial adviser be appointed to Johor. A British officer duly arrived the same year with instructions obviously not limited merely to financial affairs.

The expansion of the British presence was soon felt. More Europeans were appointed to the growing Johor administration, and after 1912 all such officers were seconded from the FMS. To those anxious for the 'ripe plum' to fall into British laps, the delay in assuming full control was irritating in the extreme. Ibrahim struggled to protect his shrinking independence, but several matters, notably his alleged extravagance and the condition of the Johor prison, finally provided the British with sufficient justification for intervention. In March 1914 Johor's General Adviser was legally made responsible to the High Commissioner (that is, the Singapore Governor) rather than the Sultan. But in the last weeks of Johor's independence, Ibrahim showed that he was still his father's son. His final acceptance of an Adviser with extended powers was made with the proviso that certain privileges be maintained in Johor, such as the wearing of a Johor uniform and the preference for Johor Malays in government appointments. Something of the unique place gained for Johor in British Malaya has lingered to the present day.

Hardening of Ethnic Divisions in the New 'British Malaya'

The process which can be seen as stretching back to the early nineteenth century had thus reached its conclusion. Though the peninsula was divided into the Straits Settlements, the FMS and the Unfederated Malay States (the four northern states plus Johor), though Borneo consisted of three protectorates, and though there was an uneasy division of power between Singapore and Kuala Lumpur, British political control was to all appearances complete. The borders then laid down, with the exception of Brunei and Singapore, have become the boundaries of modern Malaysia. However, the creation of this political unit, while absorbing much of previous empires such as Melaka and Johor, excluded some places which were culturally Malay and incorporated others whose association with the Malay world was peripheral. The boundaries reflected no sense of common allegiance to any centre, and the social and economic differences between the component parts were often extreme.

In other countries the colonial experience frequently served as the crucible in which a modern nation was melded. In the Netherlands East Indies, for example, young educated Sumatrans and Javanese learned to relate to each other as Indonesians. In Malaysia, on the other hand, reaction to the colonial presence was already serving to intensify the differences between the two major ethnic groups, Chinese and Malay. At the same time white attitudes were widening the gap between colonizer and colonized. The growth of the British community from the 1890s meant that they were no longer forced to associate with non-Europeans for relaxation or entertainment. Clubs reserved exclusively for whites had been formed, and in the major towns European residences clustered in recognized areas. The trend towards greater exclusiveness was apparent at more formal levels. During Anderson's term as Governor (1904–11), non-Europeans were excluded from the civil service, although in 1910 a separate arm was created for Malays.

A group hard hit by the closing of European ranks were the wealthy Chinese, whose association with high British officials had in the past often gained them special favours. After 1909 the practice of farming out revenue was ended, so that the Government itself now assumed responsibility for tax collection. The hold of leading Chinese over the mass of their countrymen had always been related to their position as fiscal agents, but now the son of Yap Ah Loy complained that if he went out on the streets other Chinese would not know him. The growing numbers of Chinese educated in English felt that avenues towards progress were denied to them and that professional qualifications would never compensate for the fact that their skin was not white. Inevitably many were disappointed and resentful at the dichotomy between the belief in equality acquired through Western education and the reality of inequality as practised in colonial society. Wealthier Chinese, drawn together by common interests, found solace among their own kind in clubs like the Weld Hill Club. The latter was modelled after the European clubs but was reserved for Chinese and had the highest subscription in the FMS. The lifestyle of upper-class Chinese had thus become an amalgam of Oriental and Western customs. Often it was men who had achieved some of the highest educational honours and had been sent to Britain for further study who were most active in sponsoring Chinese-language schools to ensure the survival of classical Chinese literature and culture. For these English-educated Chinese, a recourse to China's ancient culture proved an exhilarating antidote to daily reminders of the inferior status of the Chinese in colonial society. But another reason for the growing interest in Chinese culture was a new nationalism now sweeping through China.

In the late nineteenth and early twentieth century the whole question of what constituted a Chinese had come under fire because of challenges to the old order in China. In 1909 the Manchu government announced the principle of *jus sanguinis*, claiming as Chinese citizens all those of Chinese descent through the male line, irrespective of where they were born or how long their forebears had lived outside China. The struggle of the Manchu to retain power entailed extensive efforts to revive the loyalty of the Nan Yang Chinese, to encourage them to return to China for education and to remit funds for the imperial cause. Other groups in China also recognized the financial resource represented by the overseas Chinese. Royalist reformers exiled from China were active in soliciting support, and Sun Yat-sen, the revolutionary leader, visited Malaya eight times between 1900 and 1910 for the same purpose. After 1906 branches of the T'ung Meng Hui, the Chinese Revolutionary League, began to spring up, sometimes simply former secret societies in a new guise and thus fanning old feuds between clan and dialect groups. Cantonese were the most active revolutionaries, frequently fighting with other speech groups over such issues as discarding the queue as a sign of support to the revolutionaries. However, the formation of a Republic in China in 1911 engendered among overseas Chinese a widespread sense of pride in China's achievement and ideological divisions were submerged until the rise of the Chinese Communist Party in the early 1920s.

If events in China helped stimulate a pride in being Chinese, it is not surprising that it was within the Islamic context that the opposition between Melayu and the alien was most clearly expressed. From the Islamic heartlands of the Middle East notions of Pan Islam infused with the concept of *jihad*, the holy war, were filtering down to the village level in the Malay world. In Kelantan and Trengganu, where Moslem traditions were particularly strong, and where the population was heavily Malay, the imposition of colonial rule came as a rude shock. Branches of the Sarikat Islam, an Islamic association which in Indonesia provided a basis for later nationalist movements, developed all along the east coast, deriving support from a sense of Malay injury at increased taxes, changed tenancy regulations, interference with accepted agricultural customs, and the powers given to Malay officials imported from other parts of the peninsula.

In the past, peasant response to undue exactions or injustice had been flight, but there was no refuge in a peninsula dominated by a single colonial power. It is not surprising, therefore, that oppressed peasants, even lacking the traditional leadership of a chief or *anak raja*, occasionally resorted to rebellion. Two of the most well known of these are the To' Janggut uprising in Kelantan in 1915 and the rebellion in Trengganu in 1928. In both cases the leader could lay claim to spiritual powers, attracting followers who believed in his supernatural abilities and the invulnerability imparted by special objects such as a charmed kris. In Trengganu Haji Drahman went further and developed the notion that the land belonged to the people, for whom infidel government was improper and unnecessary. Though articulated in Islamic terms, many aspects of these rebellions are similar to peasant uprisings elsewhere and they may have been linked to the *haji*-led disturbances in Patani from 1910 to 1919. Such localized peasant rebellion was soon suppressed by the colonial authorities, the only lasting achievement being the creation of new heroes who had fought to preserve the honour of Malays.

More in tune with the mood of the twentieth century, more pervasive, and for that reason ultimately more influential was the response of the urban Islamic élite, who had begun to address the whole issue of the Malay condition. With a heavy component of Arab and Indian blood, their ties with the wider Islamic community were strong. Many saw a direct relevance for Malays in the teaching now emanating from the great universities of the Moslem heartlands, such as Al-Azhar in Cairo. According to this message, if Islamic society were to throw back the advance of the Christian West, Moslems everywhere must work to improve their situation. 'Verily, Allah does not change the condition of a people until they change their own condition' (Surah 13:11). Throughout the Malay world, wherever educated Moslems gathered, study clubs were formed to discuss some of the issues facing Moslems and particularly why Malays had apparently failed to attain *tamadun*, the newly coined word for a technological civilization. Similar questions were debated by the vernacular press. Because of their failure to grasp *tamadun* and acquire *ilmu* (knowledge), said a modernist Islamic journal published in Singapore, *al-Imam* (1906–8), Malays had been subdued by an alien white race. To meet the Western challenge, *al-Imam* urged the nurturing of a new generation of Malays through reforms in Islamic education which would incorporate the skills necessary to compete in a modern world.

In this chapter we have traced the political formation of British Malaya from its beginnings in indirect rule in the protected states to its final assertion of control over the entire peninsula. Northwest Borneo still stood somewhat apart, but in the Colonial Office the view that Britain would soon assume a more direct role there was frequently expressed.

Much has been written about the aims and motivations of British policy. It has been argued here that although there was never any blueprint for the extension of British control, a line of continuity does seem to stretch back beyond 1874 to the founding of Singapore in 1819. At the same time, the piecemeal nature of colonial expansion meant that some areas were always more directly exposed to the effects of Western influence. Within the Federated Malay States the development of Perak and Selangor, where tin deposits were rich, was very different from that of Pahang, from the outset an economic disappointment to the colonial government. In the Unfederated States the experience of Trengganu and Kelantan, many miles from any British-controlled city, bore little resemblance to that of Johor or Kedah, each separated from a Straits Settlements town by only a narrow stretch of water. The character of the Straits Settlements differed again, and the disparity between the Borneo states further complicated the picture. Despite the many differences so evident to a modern observer, the peninsula and in effect the Borneo protectorates had now been brought together under the colonial umbrella. Yet ironically, while uniting the disparate political units administratively, the British contributed to the hardening of ethnic divisions which was to plague all subsequent governments in Malaya/Malaysia.

6

The Functioning of a Colonial Society, 1919–57

By 1919 the entire Malay peninsula had come under some kind of British control. The Straits Settlements and the Federated Malay States (FMS) had been under British influence longest, and consequently their various institutions were more closely co-ordinated than those in the Unfederated Malay States (UMS). The latter continued to maintain their own system of governance but came under increasing British pressure urging incorporation into the FMS. Despite this pressure the unfederated states maintained their status till the outbreak of World War II.

The British failure to persuade the unfederated states to join the Federation had important consequences. In educational, economic and political policy, the unfederated states were always somewhat different from the FMS or the Straits Settlements. Since they also came to represent the most heavily Malay-populated areas in the peninsula, recent historical writings have tended to view them as the last bastions of Malay culture, successfully resisting European and other alien Asian incursions. This viewpoint has been unintentionally reinforced by scholarly research, which until recently has focused on the Straits Settlements and the FMS because it was here that substantial British records were maintained. There were, however, also significant developments occurring within the unfederated states which are essential not only to the story of British rule in Malaya but to an understanding of the evolution of the later independent Malaysia.

Once the British had succeeded in becoming the paramount power in the Malay peninsula, they continued a policy of 'conciliation' with the Malay rulers and of 'minimum interference' with the Malay peasantry. In keeping with their espoused intention of 'advising' the rulers and 'assisting' them to govern their realms, the British went about their business with utmost circumspection. Yet they could never ignore a basic consideration which had led to their presence in the peninsula: the maintenance of law and order so that British commercial interests would be able to exploit the area's wealth. Towards this end the British created a political and administrative machinery to mobilize the resources of the country.

Sources for the Colonial Period

For a historian one redeeming feature of colonial rule in Malaya is the extent to which government was conducted on paper. The Colonial Office records contain the ongoing correspondence between the Governor of the Straits Settlements (who was also the High Commissioner of the FMS) in Singapore and the Secretary of State for the Colonies in London, as well as private letters and departmental minutes. Correspondence between the Governor/High Commissioner and the Resident-General (later Chief Secretary, then Federal Secretary) in Kuala Lumpur and the Residents also provides a vast amount of material on the whole official colonial enterprise in Malaya. These are complemented by state files of correspondence to the Resident from federal and state departments and from private bodies and individuals. District and Land Office records contain details of local administration and are a useful supplement to those at the state and federal level. In addition, there are state annual reports, state and federal government gazettes, special reports and departmental studies on a wide variety of subjects, and other printed material which seem an integral part of any bureaucracy. Added to the official material are of course the records of private firms, individual reminiscences, newspapers and so on. It is thus possible to take almost any subject which attracted British attention – immigration, mining, agriculture, sanitation, education – and follow its history in considerable, sometimes exhaustive, detail.

Although in Borneo and the Unfederated Malay States there was not the mass of material available in the FMS, the British Agents' journals and reports, as well as records of the local Malay administration modelled after that of the British, contain sufficient material to be able to trace the development of these states in a manner not previously possible. Nevertheless, even in the twentieth century there are gaps in the records due to a variety of reasons. In Sarawak, for example, much of the already poor documentation for the 1930s was lost or destroyed during World War II.

During the colonial period many important works on early Malay history and culture were published by scholar–administrators, notably in the *Journal of the Malayan Branch of the Royal Asiatic Society* (*JMBRAS*). But invaluable as these studies were in recording many aspects of traditional Malay culture, they paid little attention to the contemporary scene. A more revealing gauge of local attitudes towards the changes occurring in Malaya in the first half of the twentieth century can frequently be found in personal interviews or in the numerous Malay- and Chinese-language newspapers and journals which were published during this period. As yet researchers into the history of colonial Malaya have made only limited use of these vital sources of information.

Establishing the Framework for an Export Economy

The almost unchallenged power of the new colonial rulers quickly set in motion the changes considered necessary to facilitate the development and continuing profitability of the export economy. They sought and achieved the 'congenial political and administrative framework' in which private enterprise could flourish. Unchallenged by any strong local interest groups, the British were free to embark on restructuring local society by regulating relations among groups of people and reorganizing resources for the greater aim of economic progress. By 1919 the Malay peninsula had witnessed a major transformation in its socio-economic landscape. It was appropriate that now the term 'British Malaya' began to gain currency, for Malaya had indeed become 'British' in terms of social and economic goals.

One contribution of colonial rule to Malaya's economic development was the assurance of security. The British official was within reach and could quickly bring the power of the colonial constabulary to enforce his authority. Since the frequent wars between Chinese secret societies and their Malay allies had been one of the reasons for intervention in 1874, the British were intent on justifying their presence by maintaining peace. No private entrepreneur, whether a European or a Chinese capitalist from the Straits Settlements, could be persuaded to invest in Malaya unless the colonial authorities demonstrated their ability to enforce the law. By 1919, despite occasional challenges, this ability was widely acknowledged.

Another British contribution to Malaya's socio-economic transformation was the establishment of an infrastructure, especially a communications system. Swettenham, as Resident-General of the FMS, stated in 1896 that it was Britain's duty 'to open up the country by great works: roads, railways, telegraphs, wharves'.[1] In the early days roads were built from tin mines, principally Chinese-owned and -operated, to navigable rivers where the tin was then transported to the coast. But between 1885 and 1895 four short railway lines were constructed, each connecting a coast port with a tinfield in west coast Malaya, and roads were then built to link mines with the new railways. In 1901 these lines were amalgamated to form the FMS Railways, known as the Malayan Railway Administration. Two years later a north–south trunk line joined the mining towns, and by 1910 it reached from Prai (Province Wellesley) in the north to Johor Baru in the south. The line was extended in 1918 from Prai to the Siamese border, and in 1920 from Gemas to Kuala Lipis (Pahang) and finally in 1931 from

Kuala Lipis to Tumpat (Kota Baru, Kelantan). It was also extended further southward from Johor across the causeway to Singapore in 1923. In this same period a direct road link, completed in 1928, was constructed between Johor Baru and the Siamese border. There was a spate of road-building in the east coast states and Johor in the 1930s, mainly in areas not served by railways, enabling many export products to be transported by road.

A third major change instituted by the British in their aim to develop a profitable colonial export economy in Malaya was the establishment of an effective legal and administrative system. One of the first acts of the colonial government was to repudiate Malay customary land rules and to formulate a Western-type land tenure system. To realize its vision of vast plantations replacing the virgin forest of Malaya, favourable land regulations were enacted between 1887 and 1904 to encourage Western planters to open up and settle the country. The government conducted land surveys so that leases could be accurately demarcated and information on mineral deposits made easily available. Regulations were also introduced to expedite export activities. In the early days these dealt principally with tin mining because of the large amounts of water and tin tailings involved. The government regulated the use of streams and watercourses, the disposal of tailings and the treatment of silt. Clearing rivers, repairing railway lines and roads and providing adequate port facilities all became the duty of the colonial government.

But perhaps the most significant of the services provided by the colonial government was the organization of manpower. As indicated in the previous chapter, it was to assist the various export industries that first Chinese and later Indian migrant labour was allowed to enter Malaya. Between 1911 and 1931 the government encouraged unrestricted immigration from India, China and the Netherlands East Indies to provide much needed workers for the still considerable tin mining enterprises and especially for the booming rubber industry. Only when world prices in tin and rubber fell during the Depression of the early 1930s did the government favour the repatriation of alien labour. A restricted immigration policy was in force between 1931 and 1947, and was then relaxed for the next decade as production was restored to pre-World War II levels. Over the years the colonial government thus successfully adjusted its immigration policy to cater to the labour needs of the export industries. The government's willingness to use its power to guarantee a ready and cheap source of labour was a strong inducement to private entrepreneurs to invest in British Malaya.

In a number of other ways the colonial government assured British Malaya's economic development. It linked the Straits Settlement dollar to the sterling in 1904, providing the stability needed for currency exchange, and introduced banking and insurance facilities to assist foreign capital entering Malaya. Over the years it continued to maintain European investors' confidence by establishing institutions of scientific research and technical training, excellent communication facilities, harbours, public utilities and a stable government. These measures were rewarded by a vast infusion of European capital, enterprise and management skills without which the rapid economic development of Malaya in the twentieth century would not have occurred.

A spectacular instance of entry of European capital and expertise into Malaya's economy occurred in the rubber industry. Rubber estates had at first been developed by individual planters, usually those who had earlier experimented with other crops such as sugar and coffee. After the rubber boom in 1905 these planters sought the help of British merchant firms already established in the Straits Settlements which used their reputations to raise capital and float joint stock companies in London and Shanghai. European investors were willing to support these ventures because of the experience and expertise associated with such prestigious firms as Guthries, Sime & Darby, and Harrisons & Crosfield. The merchant firms developed the agency system in which an agency house was responsible for supervising a number of companies and a large number of plantations. By concentrating management in the hands of an agency house, vast amounts of capital could be committed to a new industry and scarce management and administrative skills utilized to benefit all concerned. A manager and staff were appointed to oversee production in a particular estate, but technical and financial matters were left in the hands of the agency house with its expertise in wide-scale operations. Each company could therefore enjoy the facilities offered by a large agency house at a fraction of the cost. In return, the agency houses, now responsible for the export of the rubber and the import of consumer goods for the estates, benefited from the export—import trade and the economies in finance achieved in their large-scale operations.

Large European firms with substantial financial world-wide commitments were also a feature of the tin industry. As with rubber, the presence of a strong and sympathetic colonial government connected to the financial circles of London served to internationalize Malaya's tin industry. In 1913 the Europeans owned only a quarter of Malaya's tin mines, but by 1937 the proportion had grown to two-thirds. At first numerous groups were involved, but from about the mid-1920s a process of consolidation began. Though about eighty separate European companies were still registered in 1937, as well as hundreds of incorporated Chinese concerns, many of the European businesses were financially linked. A third of the entire tin output, for example, was owned by Anglo-Oriental (Malaya) Ltd, a subsidiary of London

Tin Corporation.[2] The European mines were controlled from abroad and managed by central agencies. The organization and administration of the European mines paralleled those of the rubber estates, although here international mining groups rather than agency houses ran the operation.

The Tin Industry

Although tin had been mined by Malays for centuries to satisfy the changing demands of India, China and Europe, production had been limited and carried out principally by *dulang* washing or panning of alluvial tin. It is estimated that only about 500 tonnes annually were mined by Malays up to the middle of the nineteenth century. A major development in the industry was the discovery in Perak of a major tin field in Larut in 1848 and another in Kinta in 1880. By the end of that decade there were some 80,000 Chinese in Perak who had arrived from China and the Straits Settlements as indentured labourers. These mining ventures were in the hands of Straits Chinese entrepreneurs, some of whom were backed by European capital from European merchant firms in the Straits Settlements. In the first half of the nineteenth century the Chinese introduced small but significant innovations, such as the chain pump to keep tin mines free of water. However, with the discovery of major tin deposits new mining techniques were developed, patterned after Western tin-mining enterprises elsewhere. The steam engine and centrifugal pump, introduced into Perak as early as 1877, solved the problem of flooding in the mines and enabled operations to occur at greater depth than hitherto possible. Hydraulic sluicing and gravel pumping were two other extractive methods which had come via Australia. The new techniques were readily adopted by Chinese miners, and by 1898 the FMS, with a total output of 40,000 tonnes, became the world's largest tin producer.[3]

Although Europeans had participated in a minor way in the tin industry in Perak in the 1880s, the entry of large European capital occurred only with the introduction of the bucket dredge in 1912, a method of mining which had proved especially profitable in New Zealand. Dredges expanded mining operations because they were effective in swampy areas and could also more profitably extract tin from ground with a lower ore content. Since this method of mining required large amounts of capital, a high technical knowledge and an extensive management capability, it could not be profitably employed unless a large area of tin-bearing ground could be leased. The colonial government was well able to accommodate such needs, since the major tin areas were in Perak, Selangor and Pahang within the FMS. The government also provided the tin miners with land surveys which contained information on tin areas and enabled leases to be accurately made. Because of the substantial capital expenditure required, only the large international mining companies had sufficient resources to make the bucket dredge method worth while. A principal source of finance and specialized skills was found in the Cornish tin industry which sought new areas of exploitation after the depletion of the Cornish tin fields in the late nineteenth century. In the early twentieth century an increased demand for tin for tinplating for the canning industry contributed to a rapid rise in tin production in Malaya.

World purchases of tin, however, did not continue to grow. Between 1870 and 1900 consumption trebled; between 1900 and 1930 it doubled; but between 1930 and 1960 it increased only slightly.[4] The USA has been a major market for Malaya's tin, but since the 1920s its demand has remained constant at around 2,540 tonnes because of more economic use of tin and better recovery methods. Large fluctuations in world tin prices between the world wars led tin-producing nations to adopt the Tin Control Scheme, which aimed at restricting exports by quota. Signed in March 1931, it was renewed in 1934 and 1937, and again resurrected in 1956. After the heady days of the late nineteenth and early twentieth centuries, the Malayan tin industry experienced some difficulties as tin prices fluctuated and restrictions were imposed on production. By the time Malaya became independent in 1957, tin as an export commodity was a poor second to rubber which accounted for 85 per cent of British Malaya's gross export earnings.[5]

Early Plantation Crops

In the nineteenth and early twentieth centuries, prior to the successful introduction of rubber to Malaya, several agricultural crops were grown commercially. Chinese planters had acted as pioneers, favouring crops which would yield returns within a short time of planting, grow well in most localities, and require no specific skills or undue outlay of capital for equipment and processing. Large Chinese-owned gambier and pepper plantations under *kongsi* direction had developed in Johor, Melaka, Negeri Sembilan and Selangor, while tapioca was generally restricted to Melaka and certain adjacent areas of Negeri Sembilan and Johor. These Chinese plantations proved a greater success and involved a larger land area than any other form of export-oriented agriculture prior to the introduction of rubber. At one time or another in the nineteenth century at least 200,000 hectares were affected by the shifting agricultural patterns of these Chinese commercial farmers.[6] Around the turn of the century, however, Chinese interest in gambier, tapioca and pepper declined as prices fell and experiments were made in growing tea, coffee and rubber. The colonial government's attitude to the established Chinese agricultural practices was also instrumental in encouraging them to move away from their traditional crops. Chinese farming methods were condemned because they led to soil exhaustion and a depletion of forests for use as firewood in numerous small factories. The government therefore considered Chinese plantations to be inimical to the larger interests of Malaya. While moving to suppress this type of agriculture, the authorities expressed their desire for the land to be more permanently cultivated.

In colonial eyes, any hope of achieving this lay with a group of Europeans involved mainly in trade who indicated a strong interest in developing export crops that had proved profitable in other parts of the world. Though early European plantations were experimental, since little was known about tropical conditions, they satisfied the colonial government's desire for more stable agricultural entrepreneurs. Europeans had access to much greater capital than the Chinese planters and could employ an experienced labour force. Furthermore, Europeans viewed their agricultural ventures as a long-term investment which would provide a future source of income for their families. They therefore wanted legal titles to their lands. The colonial government was not only willing to oblige, but actively encouraged European planters by importing pepper, cloves and nutmeg for the early plantations.

Of all the crops planted by the Europeans, only sugar and coffee had some degree of success. Early Chinese efforts in growing sugarcane and the participation of experienced sugar planters from Mauritius assured the success of this crop as a commercial venture. Malayan sugar became a highly capitalized European-controlled industry and appeared to have a bright future. However, by 1905 sugar planting declined rapidly in Province Wellesley and Perak. In 1911 the total area planted in sugar-cane in the FMS was concentrated in the Kerian district of Perak and consisted of only 8,400 hectares. Two years later in Province Wellesley the area under sugar had fallen to a mere 12·4 hectares. An important cause of the decline, particularly in the Kerian, was a change in government policy towards agriculture. During the 1890s the colonial authority had decided to expand *padi* (wet rice) production by financing irrigation schemes, but unfortunately areas suited to such schemes coincided with lands planted in sugar. There were other reasons for the sugar industry's decline, but the *coup de grâce* was the increasing profitability of rubber as an export crop.

The only other crop which proved to be moderately profitable in the nineteenth and early twentieth centuries was coffee. Large-scale coffee planting in Selangor, Negeri Sembilan, Perak and Johor in the last quarter of the nineteenth century was entirely a European effort with a number of former coffee planters from Ceylon participating. Coffee, as the first commercial crop which could be grown successfully in much of Malaya, brought planting capital, management personnel and imported Tamil and Javanese labour to many parts of the peninsula. Since coffee plantations appeared to satisfy the official goal of establishing large-scale stable European agricultural enterprise, the government sought to facilitate the industry's operations. Coffee planters received good land terms and large planting loans which, combined with a favourable labour situation, encouraged large-scale investment. Consequently, proprietary estates were rapidly replaced by those owned by companies. Despite these advantages and the 1891–6 coffee boom, by the first decade of the twentieth century Europeans had largely abandoned coffee planting for rubber. During the shortlived and unsuccessful efforts at establishing a coffee industry in Malaya, the government had adopted certain measures and European planters had gained specific knowledge of local conditions which together contributed to the early success of the rubber industry.

The Rubber Industry

Rubber's phenomenal rise as the pre-eminent export crop in Malaya is the more remarkable when one considers that at the end of the nineteenth century almost the total world production of natural rubber came from the wild rubber-producing plants in the Amazon Basin in Brazil. In 1820 world consumption of natural rubber was about 100 tonnes but in the following decades demand rapidly grew with a series of technical developments. Charles Goodyear's discovery of the vulcanization process in 1839, the growth of the electrical industry and especially the expanding uses of pneumatic tyres for bicycles and later motor cars in the late nineteenth and early twentieth century all contributed to the growth of the world market for natural rubber.

Malaya's involvement with rubber began with seeds of the rubber-producing plant, *Hevea brasiliensis*, which had been collected in Brazil in 1876 and sent to germinate in Kew. Some of those which were successfully germinated were sent to Ceylon and a few to Singapore, but these died. A further consignment of seedlings was sent the following year to Singapore and towards the end of 1877 nine of these were planted at the side of the Residency in Kuala Kangsar. Early plantings were unsystematic and intended principally for scientific observation. In the 1880s the interest of European planters in coffee diverted attention away from the doubtful rubber tree. Planters were apprehensive because the rubber tree had never been grown on plantations, it was indigenous to another part of the world, its maturity period was a long six to eight years, its productive life was unknown, areas in Africa were also growing the tree and the future of the market was uncertain. The individual who did most to encourage the growing of the rubber tree was H. N. Ridley, who arrived in Singapore in November 1888 to become the Director of the Botanical Gardens. Through his own experiments and personal persuasion he succeeded in having a number of trees planted on estates. His enthusiasm for popularizing this tree earned him the nicknames 'Mad Ridley' and 'Rubber Ridley'. Yet he was ultimately successful because of continuing experiments with the rubber tree, the increase in rubber prices and the collapse of the coffee market.

Rubber was first planted commercially in Malaya in the mid-1890s on estates previously opened for other crops. The coffee planters, with their ready source of capital, management personnel and labour supply, were the first to experiment with the rubber trees because of the low coffee prices. But by the beginning of the twentieth century, interplanting of rubber became commonplace on almost all existing estates, and even new land was being used solely for this crop. Rubber seemed the ideal crop to fulfil the government aim of long-term land use by Europeans, and in 1897 special land regulations were introduced in the FMS to encourage rubber cultivation.

The first rubber boom occurred in 1905–8 with the expansion of the motor car industry, and during this period the total area planted in rubber increased almost five-fold. By 1908 rubber was planted in every state of Malaya, occupying some 109,000 hectares, an area greater than that planted with any other previous crop. Government measures favourable to rubber planters in terms of land alienation, flow of capital, and labour regulations established the bases for the expansion of the industry. There were numerous small rubber planting companies formed in the period up to 1908, and the floating of these companies was undertaken mainly by large merchant houses of Singapore, the most important of which were Guthries, and Harrisons & Crosfield.

Another rubber boom period characterized the years from 1909 to 1912, and European companies expended large sums to buy up Malay lands and old Chinese sugar, gambier and tapioca plantations where crops had been interplanted with rubber. Many Malay and Chinese smallholders began to plant rubber with the hope of eventually selling the land to Europeans. Thus between 1909 and 1912 rubber acreage in the estates rose by 110 per cent, the number of rubber estates doubled, and the total area alienated for rubber on estates rose by about 291,000 hectares. By 1913 rubber in Malaya covered some 322,000 hectares, and by 1916 rubber passed tin as Malaya's chief export earner,[7] a position which it held until 1980.

The rubber boom was especially noticeable in the west coast states because it was here that an infrastructure established for the tin industry also came to benefit the rubber industry. The absence of railway lines, an adequate road system, and suitable year-round ports in the east coast states deterred any major European investment in rubber estates there. It was precisely these reasons which in earlier years had convinced nineteenth-century European entrepreneurs to concentrate their activity along the west coast. But to smallholders rubber seemed an ideal cash crop. It was hardy and thrived almost anywhere in Malaya because of its suitability to the various types of soils and growing conditions found on the peninsula. Although a rubber tree could not be tapped until about its eighth year, it could successfully be interplanted with more rapidly maturing crops. Once the tree was ready to be tapped, its productive life was about thirty years. The smallholder was therefore assured a steady source of income from his rubber trees which required little care and minimal cost in the preparation of the latex for market.

The extent of smallholder participation in the rubber industry only became apparent when the Stevenson Scheme came into effect in late 1922, setting a quota on rubber production which discriminated against the native smallholders. There had been a general rubber depression in 1920–1, and most of the European companies involved in the industry were unable to cover their costs. The international Stevenson Scheme was primarily intended to protect European capital in the rubber companies of Malaya, Borneo and the Netherlands East Indies from competition by native smallholder producers. One serious outcome of the scheme was its damage to US customers in the motor car industry, which was just coming out of the post-World War I depression. As a result, the Americans decided to diversify their sources of rubber. Firestone opened rubber estates in Liberia, and Ford did the same in Brazil. Efforts were also made to economize in the use of natural rubber, and a rubber reclaiming industry was established.

The problems experienced by the industry remained unrelieved during the Depression of the early 1930s. In 1934 an International Rubber Regulation Agreement was signed among the rubber producers of Southeast Asia limiting production with a fixed quota per country for an initial period of four years. Like the Stevenson Scheme, this new agreement principally hurt the smallholders because it came at a time when they were expanding faster than the rubber estates. The estates easily switched to oil palm, just gaining popularity as an export crop, but the smallholders lacked the capital and expertise to make such changes. However, the rubber industry survived, and by the outbreak of the Pacific War in 1941 new high-yielding trees, fertilisers, mechanization of estates and methods of preserving and concentrating latex assured it a prosperous future.

During the Japanese Occupation of Malaya there was some destruction of rubber trees and equipment, but by 1946 Malaya's production was already up to 410,000 tonnes, only about 100,000 tonnes less than in 1941. By 1948 production was at 708,000 tonnes, some 150,000 tonnes more than the previous record in 1940.[8] Despite the difficulties faced in the Malayan Emergency (1948–60) rubber production until 1958 continued at a high level. Nevertheless, the rubber industry was no longer as attractive to European investors as it had been in the early decades of the twentieth century. The trauma of the Occupation years, the insecurity of the Emergency period, and finally the uncertainty of the policies to be followed by a newly independent Malaya government raised doubts about Malaya's future. Furthermore, synthetic rubber production had rapidly expanded in the USA in the war years so that by 1944 the US synthetic rubber production had reached 950,000 tonnes a year.[9] Although demand declined, natural rubber could still command a ready market. High-tear strength, resilience and properties of abrasion-resistance and heat dissipation made natural rubber preferable to synthetic rubber for certain products such as aeroplane and heavy-duty truck tyres, parts of ordinary car tyres, and numerous mechanical goods. While the rubber industry was not as buoyant as it had been earlier in the century, when Malaya became independent in 1957 it was still one of the country's chief export earners.

The Palm Oil Industry

In the period when rubber dominated the agricultural export scene, a few estates with an eye to overseas markets began growing a new crop, oil palm (*Elaeis guineensis*). It had been introduced into the peninsula in the 1850s but was mainly cultivated as an ornamental plant. Only in 1917 was the first plantation of oil palm begun as a commercial venture. Although palm oil was used in the manufacture of soap, candles, flux for the tin-plate industry, margarine, vegetable oils, grease, and fuel for internal combustion engines, there was little progress in the industry till the slump in rubber prices after World War I forced planters to search for alternative crops. However, no large-scale development occurred until 1924 when three rubber companies in the Guthrie group formed Oil Palms of Malaya Ltd. Their example was later followed by other firms. Because of the need for capital and special expertise, especially in the processing of the oil, the industry was confined to large plantations usually located near some rubber estate in order to take advantage of the existing infrastructure. Most of the oil palm estates were consequently along Malaya's west coast. The number of hectares planted with oil palm steadily increased, and in the 1930s palm oil production greatly expanded. From a production of 3,350 tonnes in 1930 or 1 per cent of world output, it had risen in 1939 to 58,300 tonnes or 11 per cent of world output.[10] This dramatic improvement in the industry was due mainly to technical advances in cultivation, extraction of the oil, and the delicate task of transporting the finished product. When the Pacific War began there were some 36,000 hectares under oil palm. During the Occupation much machinery was lost, but by 1948 palm oil production was four-fifths that of the pre-World War II figure. By the end of 1954 palm oil was established as an export commodity with some sixty-three estates and a total of 50,000 hectares devoted to the growing of that crop.

Padi (Wet-rice) Farming

While the colonial government was reshuffling manpower, reallocating resources and encouraging European investment and expertise to benefit the export economy, it continued to maintain the myth that it was there simply to advise the Malay Sultans in ruling their lands. British officials therefore felt justified in adopting a generally *laissez-faire* attitude towards the economic development of the Malays. Use of Malays in the tin mines had proved unsatisfactory, and it was easier to import foreign workers. Chinese, Indians and Indonesians provided a sufficient supply of labourers to satisfy the needs of the export industries. As trade to China and India grew less important, the demand for forest and sea products was insufficient to make collection efforts economically worth while for the Malays. Except for the planting of gambier, pepper, coconut, rubber and later oil palm to supplement their income, a large percentage of Malays remained tillers of the soil, *padi* farmers. There were also a few fishermen, but the bulk of the population were farmers mainly working the alluvial lowlands in the northwest and northeast coastal plains and the river deltas.

Initially, the colonial government was unconcerned with this subsistence rice cultivation, but as the tin mining and later rubber industries absorbed increasing numbers of migrant labourers, the authorities began actively encouraging greater Malay rice production to feed the growing population. Towards the end of the nineteenth century there was even an attempt to import Chinese and Indian farmers, but with little success. Most migrants, hoping to make a quick profit and return home, were unwilling to make the long-term commitment farming entailed.

Increased internal demand for rice, coupled with the decline of traditional occupations such as Malay crafts and coastal shipping due to foreign competition, resulted in the extension of rice-growing in established *padi* areas in the northwest and northeast. These two areas were especially favourable for *padi* since there were usually adequate water, good drainage (except for the Kerian), warm weather, and in some areas availability of manure. Beginning in the 1880s the Kedah aristocracy was at the forefront in encouraging the expansion of rice-growing areas in the northwest. While the colonial government introduced a massive irrigation scheme for the Kerian and the other smaller projects, it was Malay initiative which was mainly responsible for increased rice production and acreage. During the colonial period 60 per cent of the total rice area was in the northwest (Perlis, Kedah, Penang, Province Wellesley and Perak), and 23 per cent in the northeast (Kelantan and Trengganu).[11]

These developments are noteworthy because, except for restricted areas mainly in Kedah and Kelantan, *padi* farming had never been a profitable venture in Malaya. Though rice was widely cultivated in the villages, it was mainly for local consumption. For many Malays it could represent a real burden: first, they often leased the land and thus faced the problem of tenantry; and secondly, they lacked credit and could therefore never become totally free of debt. With the introduction of export crops by private entrepreneurs under British colonial rule, Malay farmers were at last provided with an opportunity to supplement their income by planting cash crops. The government, however, was uneasy at this development, not only since it hoped for an increased rice production to feed British Malaya's growing population, but also because it preferred to see the Malays remaining on the land to become a 'settled peasantry'.

After 1895, as such cash crops as tapioca, gambier and pepper declined in importance, the government actively discouraged Malays from planting other commercial crops, especially rubber. The government considered the rubber tree a plantation crop, and all research in the industry's early period was undertaken with the needs of plantation cultivation in mind. A 'no rubber' condition was imposed on certain lands to prevent Malay farmers from growing this increasingly profitable and convenient cash crop. In 1917 a Rice Lands Enactment and a Coconut Preservations Enactment were introduced to prevent these crops from being replaced by rubber. In addition, the Food Production Enactment of 1918 set aside specific land for food cultivation only. Other inducements and subtle coercions were intended to make the Malay farmer remain on the land to produce food and, above all, rice. A critical shortage of rice in Malaya between 1918 and 1921 gave these measures special urgency.

Yet there was a major shortcoming in British efforts to encourage Malay *padi*-farming. The colonial government failed to respond effectively to the need for rural credit at reasonable terms and therefore condemned the farmer to the ever-present threat of losing his land to his creditor or of eviction by his landlord. Instead, the available credit facilities were channelled principally to European firms involved with the extractive industries. Even rice research lagged far behind that devoted to the export crops. In any conflict of interests — whether in terms of funds, personnel or time — rice was always sacrificed to rubber and tin, the two pillars of British Malaya's economy. The colonial government wished to promote long-term land development, and

it was believed that no better way existed than by means of a plantation industry funded by European capital.[12] Rice production was
necessary, but it was the plantation crops and the tin mines which
were the major export earners for British Malaya. Throughout British
colonial rule the Malay farmer was allocated a specific place in the
scheme of economic development, and it was here that he remained.

The effects of colonial attitudes and policy on the Malay peasant
were somewhat softened by his ability to ignore the enactments by
growing and selling small quantities of cash crops. Furthermore, he
was able to engage in legitimate economic pursuits to supplement his
income, such as providing firewood to the various mines and plantations. But where the new economic developments came to seriously
undermine the world of the Malay farmer was in his traditional relationships with his lord. While he continued to pay allegiance to his ruler,
the factors which had contributed to the viability of the traditional
socio-economic pattern were now absent. No longer was the Malay
ruler seen as providing the services and protection to his subjects in
return for the latter's labour and loyalty. The conspicuous presence
of the British official and the great changes brought by the mines and
the plantation industries were sufficient witness to the Malay farmer
that a new power was present in Malaya. Yet British paternalism and
policy prevented his withdrawal from the old cultural and economic
system, itself increasingly devoid of meaning, in order to gain a greater
stake within the colonial socio-economic structure.

Economic Development in North Borneo and Sarawak

In North Borneo the early economic experiences of Malaya were
repeated on a smaller scale, with unsuccessful attempts in the nineteenth century to introduce such industries as sugar, tapioca, opium,
silk, soya bean, orchid and pineapple. Coffee was hesitantly attempted
and abandoned, while the initial success of pepper and gambier cultivation soon faded with the rise of the rubber industry in the twentieth
century. Tobacco was the only imported crop in the nineteenth century
which proved commercially successful. But by 1891 tariffs imposed
by the American government to protect its own tobacco industry
signalled tobacco's eventual decline in North Borneo. In the early
years of the British North Borneo Company, however, it was not these
alien crops but the indigenous products which proved the financial
mainstay of North Borneo. The swallow's nest for the unique Chinese
delicacy, 'bird's nest soup', was harvested under contract systematically from a number of caves on the east and west coasts and offshore
islands and sent directly to Hong Kong. Other local products from the
jungle, such as rattans, gutta-percha and damar, were gathered and
sent to Singapore where they were processed for the world market.

But the greatest success of all North Borneo's products was its timber. In February 1885 the first shipment of logs went to Australia, signalling the advent of what was to become a prosperous and controversial export item.

The timber industry grew substantially in the last decade of the nineteenth century, spurred on by the demands for rail sleepers for the railway expansion underway in China. The British Borneo Trading and Planting Company was by far the biggest of four concerns involved in the industry. Then in 1920 a new giant, financially assisted in its conception by Harrisons & Crosfield, was formed under the name British Borneo Timber Company. It obtained a monopoly for twenty-five years to log on state land and provided the capital needed to expand the timber trade. By 1937 timber exports reached a figure of about 178,000 cubic metres, and Sandakan became one of the most important timber ports in the world. But this expansion was achieved with very little regard for conservation. Despite advances made by North Borneo's Forestry Department, which with the help of the Forestry Research Institute of Malaya gained increasing expertise in timber culture and administration, it was powerless to prevent the generally indiscriminate logging of the jungle. In the immediate post World War II years, reconstruction in Japan created a vast demand for timber. A number of new companies were allowed to enter the once exclusive domain of the British Borneo Timber Company, increasing considerably the area being logged. By 1961 timber had passed rubber as the major export earner in the state, earning $102·8 million to rubber's $41·2 million.

In the first half of the twentieth century, however, it was rubber which dominated the economic landscape of North Borneo. Although the rubber plant arrived in 1882, as in Malaya it was a while before it became generally accepted as a viable commercial crop. By early the next century it became obvious to many that rubber had a secure future in light of the technical advances being made, especially in transportation and communications. Large areas linked by railway lines to the coasts were planted with this new crop. The story of rubber in North Borneo and Sarawak paralleled that in Malaya, moving from the boom periods prior to World War I to slumps and restrictions in the 1920s and 1930s, disaster during the Japanese Occupation, and recovery on a modest scale in the post World War II years. One difference from Malaya was the slower rate of recovery and adaptation to new post-war circumstances. Only through government pressure did the industry finally modernize to reach the standards set in Malaya. After North Borneo came under the British Colonial Office in 1946, copra, manila hemp (abaca) and cocoa rose in importance as commercial crops, but rubber and timber remained the chief revenue earners.

Sarawak's economic development appears to have been restricted by the personal philosophy of its White Rajas which regarded the preservation of the local (particularly Iban) way of life almost as a sacred trust. By the beginning of the twentieth century its revenue was derived principally from fees from antimony royalties and from farming out opium, local wine (*arak*) and pawnbroking. As in North Borneo and Malaya, attempts were made to introduce tobacco, sugar-cane, tea and coffee as commercial crops, with little success. Gambier and pepper were developed for a time by Chinese farmers but never did achieve a prominent place in Sarawak's economy. Oil was found at Miri in 1895, which continued to be a good revenue earner till the outbreak of World War II, but it never approached the scale of the oil finds just across the border in Brunei. Coal and mercury were leading mineral exports in the late nineteenth century and then declined in importance with the growth of the rubber and timber industries. Timber became a principal export commodity by the late 1890s, and by 1941 it ranked second to rubber as the chief revenue earner for Sarawak. At the forefront of most of these economic ventures was the Borneo Company, the one Western commercial enterprise Charles Brooke had permitted. It suffered losses in Sarawak in the nineteenth century but gradually succeeded in making a modest profit up to 1941 without upsetting the White Rajas' conception of their role as guardians of local culture.

In both North Borneo and Sarawak an attempt had been made to establish an infrastructure to enhance these economic developments. However, the governments of these two states never commanded the same confidence or the resources as the British colonial adminstration in Malaya. In Sarawak's case the ruling philosophy of the White Rajas was an additional factor which determined the pace and extent of economic development.

By the end of formal colonial rule in 1957, the British had bequeathed the new independent government of Malaya an export economy which was the envy of Southeast Asia. Through co-operation between colonial government and European and Chinese business interests, Malaya had been transformed from an economy based principally on subsistence agriculture and regional trade to one oriented to export commodities of great value in the world market, such as rubber, tin and palm oil. The colonial government harnessed its every resource, from education to government administration, to assure the financial success of its export economy. North Borneo and Sarawak reflected on a minor scale the type of developments occurring on Malaya. While their revenues were still relatively insubstantial by Malaya's standards, they were nevertheless an inseparable part of the economic and social changes sweeping through the British colonial empire in Southeast Asia.

Education under Colonial Government

The identification of ethnic group with a specific economic role affected early colonial policy towards education. Only a small local élite would be given the privilege of an English education to equip them for clerical duties within the colonial government bureaucracy or in European-controlled companies. For the vast majority of the local people, the government believed, it was enough that each group be educated in its own language and learn to accept its allotted role in life as conceived by the colonial rulers. Put crudely, the European was to govern and administer, the immigrant Chinese and Indian to labour in the extractive industries and commerce, and the Malays to till the fields. Underlying the government's desire to extend education to all was the philosophical stand then current in England that governments everywhere should provide some popular education. But once the colonial government had declared its intent and provided the initial impetus towards the creation of an educational system for Malaya, it relinquished much of the direction of non-English medium schools in the first few decades of the twentieth century to the respective ethnic communities.

Formal Indian education in Malaya was pioneered in the first half of the nineteenth century by missionaries who opened Tamil schools in Penang, Melaka and Singapore. These proved unsuccessful, and only after the 1870s did Tamil schools become established in these areas. The colonial government in 1900 opened Tamil schools in Perak and Negeri Sembilan, but they clearly expected the missionary societies and the coffee and rubber estates to be responsible for Indian education. Since the government had neither guidelines nor provision to enforce Indian education, the quality of the voluntary primary schools on these estates varied considerably. Few of the rubber estates were willing or able to hire a qualified teacher and to provide him with the necessary books and equipment necessary to run a school. The teachers were often the Indian labour recruiter (*kangani*), a clerk, or sometimes just a literate labourer on the estate with little or no training. Most of the schools were conducted in Tamil, though there were also a few where the language of instruction was either Thelugu, Malayalam, Punjabi or Hindi. Textbooks were imported from India and provided a knowledge of India's culture, history and geography but nothing about Malaya. Whatever learning occurred during the brief period that an Indian estate child remained in school was therefore almost wholly India-orientated.

Other factors served to undermine the value of estate education. Since the estates provided employment for children ten to twelve years of age, there was little incentive for children to prolong their school attendance. A reluctance to pursue further education was reinforced by the estate-owners themselves, who saw the desirability of retaining the children on the premises to add to the workforce. Only in 1923, when the Labour Code was promulgated, were all estates with ten or more children of school age required to provide education. However, there was no substantial change in the quality of instruction available. Not until 1937 was an official Inspector of Schools with a knowledge of Tamil appointed to the Department of Education. At this time, too, the colonial government initiated a scheme for training Tamil teachers. After World War II the government began to take greater interest in the curriculum of Tamil schools and teaching methods in accordance with its new aim of preparing Malaya for independence. Some books were now Malaya-orientated, although the main thrust of the schools continued to be towards practical skills, such as agriculture, handiwork, sewing and physical education.

There were four types of Indian schools by 1949: those run by the government (twenty-six schools, mainly urban), by estates (three-fifths of all Tamil school enrolments), by missions, and by committees of local residents.[13] The government's participation in Tamil education was still minimal, but it made known its desire to create a contented Indian labour force with a basic knowledge of agriculture and handicrafts. No Indian education beyond primary school was considered necessary. Any parent seeking higher education for his child had to turn to the English-medium schools, but fees were often prohibitively high for a common labourer. Moreover, the British saw no good reason to make English-medium schools freely available to any local group. Thus a division between the mainly urban middle- and upper-class Indians and the rural and urban poor Indians was perpetuated by the manner in which Indian education evolved under the colonial government.

Chinese education in Malaya remained for a long time in the hands of the Chinese communities themselves. Prior to the twentieth century traditional Chinese education had been based on a knowledge of the Confucian classics. But because of the nature of Chinese migrant society in Malaya, genuine scholars were hard to find. Often the only qualification of so-called teachers was an ability to read and write fluently, while many also combined their teaching roles with those of professional geomancers and fortune-tellers. The method of instruction was rote-learning, with greater value placed on recitation of texts than on any learned disquisition on their contents. Chinese schools fell into three different categories: those under a committee formed by a district, a clan association, or Chinese families in a particular town or district; those under one or more teachers who formed a committee from financial patrons persuaded to lend their names to the enterprise; those run by teachers who relied on a low fee from students. The varying organization of Chinese schools was reflected in their quality, with those privately run usually the smallest and most deficient in proper facilities. The willingness and the ability of the Chinese to provide schools for their own children relieved the British of any real educational responsibility. For a time at least the colonial government could hold fast to the belief that the Chinese population in Malaya was merely transient. But because the Chinese schools were orientated to China, they were affected by political and intellectual trends in their homeland towards the end of the nineteenth century. Their involvement in China's problems inexorably drew the British government in Malaya towards a policy of intervention in the schools and a reluctant admission of the need for greater control of Chinese education.

The intellectual debates between reformers and revolutionaries in China were followed closely by all Chinese overseas communities. Both sides sent representatives overseas to explain their programmes and to obtain finanical support. Under attack by these groups, the Confucian classical education now appeared politically bankrupt and, more damaging, associated with the foreign Manchu overlords of China. Chinese schools in Malaya became increasingly politicized, especially after the successful Republican Revolution in China in 1911. In 1917, in an attempt to increase literacy in China and undermine the value of a classical education, the *pai hua*, or written vernacular, movement was initiated. Three years later China's Minister of Education ordered a form of *pai hua*, known as *kuo yu* (National Language), a compromise between northern and southern Mandarin, to be used for primary teaching.

This development had important consequences for the Chinese community in Malaya. In the past instruction was given in the dialect of the particular Chinese community sponsoring the school. As early as 1829 Singapore had Cantonese and Hokkien schools, and other dialect groups quickly followed, providing education for their own children. The introduction of *kuo yu* (Mandarin) into Chinese schools in Malaya as the medium of instruction became a unifying element within the Chinese community with its numerous dialect groups. They could now communicate with each other in a neutral language by which they could also identify themselves with the new Republican government of China. Pride in being Chinese was reinforced by an influx of teachers firmly convinced of the righteousness of the revolutionary changes in China and eager to proselytize the new ideas to the overseas Chinese communities. These highly motivated teachers and their inspiring nationalistic literature disturbed British authorities in Malaya. School texts and other educational material were blatantly anti-foreign. The colonial government viewed this development with some disquiet since the British had been blamed for many of China's ills in the nineteenth and early twentieth centuries. From the late

1920s the increasing politicization of Chinese education grew even more dangerous in British eyes with the introduction of Marxist–Leninist ideas. Chinese schools in Malaya, North Borneo and Sarawak now became the battleground of two separate ideologies: that of the government in power in China, the Kuomintang (KMT), and that of the opposition, the Chinese Communist Party (CCP). Like the reformers and revolutionaries who in the past had vied for the support of overseas Chinese communities, the KMT and CCP exerted their own pressure, creating a battleground within the Chinese schools themselves.

Even before the introduction of Mandarin, the British had been concerned about the extent of KMT involvement in Chinese schools in Malaya. With the rapid rise of the CCP, the situation deteriorated further as ideology began to take precedence over all other considerations. The increasing politicization of the Chinese schools was distrusted, not only because of its growing anti-British orientation, but also because of its implicit threat to the colonial government's conception of the Chinese as a transient population fulfilling an economic role in Malaya. The government was finally forced to introduce measures with the aim of establishing some control over Chinese schools. In 1919 it passed the School Registration Enactment designed to curb political activities. Within the schools, however, this enactment did not prevent a further growth of political debates which became especially acrimonious with the onset of the KMT–CCP power struggle in China after 1927. In 1929 the British were compelled to take more drastic action. All xenophobic elements in Chinese texts were removed; Chinese-born teachers were restricted; more government officials were created to oversee Chinese education; federal grants (and thus British control) were extended not only to schools teaching in a Chinese dialect but also to those using Mandarin.

With these measures the British abandoned their earlier *laissez-faire* policy towards Chinese education and acknowledged that they were dealing with large numbers of Chinese who considered Malaya their home. The reversal of Chinese migratory trends was a result of of changes within the economic sector of Malaya. Since the introduction of bucket dredges, European tin mining companies in the twentieth century no longer found it necessary to employ so many Chinese labourers in the industry. By 1937 70 per cent of Chinese males were no longer in the tin industry. Instead, they had gravitated to agricultural and commercial occupations and had made greater commitments to Malaya as their homeland. In 1947 some 42 per cent of Chinese males were in agriculture, and there was an increasing pattern of permanent Chinese settlements in the FMS, a trend reinforced by growing numbers of females in Malaya's Chinese population.[14]

Despite British efforts, it was impossible to remove the KMT government's influence in Malaya's Chinese schools. To combat such interference from China, the colonial government resolved to take a stronger interest in Chinese education. In 1935 the Education Department was empowered to introduce constructive changes in Chinese education with the help of substantial subsidies. One major step was the introduction of a teacher-training programme; another was the formal recognition of Mandarin as a medium of instruction. While these measures were an improvement over earlier colonial attitudes, they were insufficient to overcome a basic Chinese distrust towards British involvement. Because the latter had for so long been unconcerned about Chinese education, the motives behind their financial measures seemed questionable. To avoid interference in their curriculum, some Chinese schools continued to reject grants-in-aid, electing instead to receive financial support and school inspectors from the KMT government in China. Many Chinese were unenthusiastic about the stress on Malaya in the colonial government's curriculum, and preferred their children to be educated about China so they would not be alienated from their homeland. For them, Chinese education was valuable precisely because it created an awareness of being Chinese. But as with Indian education in Malaya, Chinese-medium schools did not provide the means by which an individual could rise under British colonial rule. Since Chinese education did not lead to social or even economic advancement, there was little demand from parents for Chinese schools beyond primary level, even though Chinese secondary education was available in Singapore in 1919 and in the larger population centres from the 1920s.

British attitudes towards the education of Malays, as with the Chinese and Indians, conformed to their view of that particular group's role in British Malaya. Despite the official stance that the Malays were masters of their own lands, the extension of colonial control made apparent the surrender of effective power by the Malay aristocracy to the British 'advisers'. Only the Malay Sultans appeared to have maintained and in some cases even enhanced their prestige through their association with the British. By contrast, the numbers of Malay chiefs employed in the State Councils remained small, and the the creation of posts such as native magistrate, judges and superintendents of *penghulu* was insufficient to absorb all the displaced Malay élite. If the latter were to be incorporated into the new governmental structure the British were creating, a fundamental change in their attitudes and skills was required. It was in hopes of bringing such changes about that Malays of good background were first encouraged to attend British schools.

Stamford Raffles had earlier foreseen the need to educate 'the sons of the higher order of natives' and towards this end had established the Raffles Institution in Singapore in 1823. His vision, however, was not shared by his successors, and the school failed to live up to

Raffles's expectations. On the peninsula itself the government made a few attempts to provide an English education for Malay princes and sons of Malay nobility. Although two English schools were opened in Perak in 1878 and 1883, there is record of only two Malays of noble background who attended. It was still difficult to convince the Malay upper class of the value of an English education. One important exception was Sultan Idris who ascended the Perak throne in 1887. As Raja Muda, or Heir-Apparent, he had visited London in 1884 and was favourably impressed by England's strength and prosperity. This experience probably convinced him that modern education, preferably English education, held the key to Malay economic and social progress. Through his initiative a 'Raja Class' was formed in the palace at Perak's royal capital, Kuala Kangsar, in 1888. An arrangement with a British tutor lasted for only a little over a year, but the interest shown soon led to the establishment of the first government English school in Kuala Kangsar, which became known in 1927 as the Clifford School.

Following Perak's lead, the Raja Muda of Selangor requested British help to form a school for the young princes in his state. In December 1890 the new 'Raja School' of Selangor was inaugurated with an Oxford-trained English clergyman as tutor. The school, said the British Resident of Selangor, W. E. Maxwell, was intended to educate the 'sons of Rajas and Chiefs, whose hereditary influence we desire to be used to the advantage of the State'. Basically, Maxwell saw this education as a means by which Malay sons of rajas and chiefs could be employed as government clerks and other lower officials. The British could then benefit from a trained bureaucracy while fulfilling the goal of 'conciliating' the Malay nobility through increasing its participation in the new governing apparatus. A principal aim of the school, in addition to imparting a good knowledge of English, was to 'build character' as understood in Victorian England. The sense of fair play, loyalty, co-operation, and class which characterized many English public schools was inculcated in the Malay students, themselves no strangers to class and privilege in their own society. Now their traditional attitudes were reinforced by the British, and a common bond bred of similar social backgrounds grew between colonial officials and the Malay ruling classes. The Raja School in Selangor closed in January 1894 but any interested Malay student could now study at the Victoria Institution in Kuala Lumpur, which was established the year before.

Despite the interest shown by the Perak and Selangor royal families in English education, as yet the openings in government service were insufficient to convince other Malays that English education had any practical value. This situation changed in 1896 with the formation of the Federated Malay States. As a result, the four state civil services were combined to form the Malayan Civil Service (MCS), leading to an expansion of the administrative and specialist services officered by

Europeans. There was a growth in the local clerical and technical staff, most of whom were Jaffna Tamils, Indians, Eurasians and Chinese. Some concern was expressed among British officials because of the government's obvious failure to do more in fulfilling its stated intention of educating the Malay ruling classes in the governing of their lands. Consequently, scholarship schemes were introduced to provide better access to English schools for Malays 'of good birth'. Through these schemes Malays were able to study at first-rate English schools such as Victoria Institution in Selangor, Taiping Central School (later the King Edward VII School) in Perak, and St Paul's School in Negeri Sembilan. An attempt was also made to include some of the brightest commoner Malay boys from Malay vernacular schools in this programme.

Such measures were clearly inadequate. By the end of the century the numbers of English-educated Malays were still insufficient to fill the government's need for writers, clerks and interpreters. To supplement the scholarship scheme, it was decided in 1899 to create Anglo-Malay Departments at Victoria Institution and at Kelang Anglo-Chinese School. These departments were to assist in easing the boys into an English school by providing one part of their education in English and the other in Malay. On a small scale the scheme was successful, but any thought of extending English education generally to the Malay commoner was rejected. Governor-General Frank Swettenham instead proposed that a Malay college be established 'where the best boys from the vernacular schools can be taught to become Malay teachers; and an Institute where a boy can obtain an industrial and technical education'. Swettenham still echoed the early British dual conception of their task regarding the Malays: conciliation of the Malay nobility and minimum interference with the Malay commoners. Greater employment of Malays in government was desirable, but only Malays of 'good birth'.

Concern at the small numbers of Malays in government service surfaced at the Second Durbar or Conference of Rulers held in Kuala Lumpur in 1903. Of a Malay population of 310,000 in the FMS, only 2,636 were employed by the government, and of these 1,175 were policemen.[15] While it had been the intention, if not the avowed policy, of the British eventually to fill the most important posts in state administrations by Malay rajas and chiefs, there was little evidence that this was being effectively implemented. The ruling classes in the FMS, on the other hand, could point enviously to their brethren in Johor and the Siamese-controlled northern Malay states who had retained substantial control over their own affairs. Demands by the Malay rulers at the Second Durbar for greater involvement in government, combined with British realization of the increasing costs of employing a disproportionate number of Europeans, succeeded in overcoming most objections to the creation of a Malay residential school for the training of Malay administrators.

In January 1905 the Malay College at Kuala Kangsar was opened. Although it had originally been conceived as a special residential school to train Malay boys from royal and noble families for government service, R. J. Wilkinson, the Federal Inspector of Schools, advocated that some commoners should also be admitted. His idea was to cull the best Malays presently attending English schools in the FMS, whatever their rank. However, Wilkinson's removal from the Education Department in 1906 brought a change in policy. Only occasionally were commoners admitted to the College and they were from families closely associated with Malay nobility or royalty. The Malay College thus became an institution for the traditional élite only, giving rise to the term the 'Eton of the East' because of its English public school image and the aristocratic backgrounds of its students. But despite the cricket, rugby, prefects and other trappings of the English public school system, a sense of Malayness was retained by the requirement that students wear the *baju*, *sarong* and *songkok*, attend Koran classes and observe Moslem holidays.

The success of the Malay College in providing an English education for the Malay upper class forced the government to fulfil its promise of recruiting the better graduates into the administrative service. A scheme was thus drawn up in 1908 and implemented in 1910 tailored specifically to absorb Malay College graduates into the newly created Malay Administrative Service. Not surprisingly, a new nickname for the College gained popularity among Malays: 'Bab ud-Darajat', the Gateway to High Rank.

The opening of the Malay College and the subsequent flow of English-trained Malays into government service were tangible evidence to the Malays of all classes that English education did confer social and economic benefits. This realization was simultaneously reinforced by the expansion of European commercial enterprises requiring ever more English-educated clerks and other officials. As a consequence, Malay parents began to demand English education so that their children could gain employment either in the government or in some European firm. Several Malay *penghulu* asked for English schools to be established in their villages, and others for English classes in the Malay vernacular schools. But British administrators were reluctant to expand the number of English schools. To satisfy the new call for English-educated Malays, it was proposed to increase the intake into existing English schools of selected Malays who had completed four years of Malay primary school. This decision was responsible for a rise in the number of Malays in English schools in the FMS from 9 per cent of total enrolment in 1919 to 15 per cent by 1936. By contrast, in those two years Chinese in FMS English schools accounted for 48 per cent and

50 per cent of total enrolment, and the Indians 30 per cent and 28 per cent.[16] But English education continued to be exclusive, especially after 1924 when the British announced their wish to avoid producing more English-educated than there were places in the government.

What distinguished English-medium from vernacular schools was the provision for advanced education beyond the primary level. In addition to ordinary secondary education, English-educated students could obtain technical and trade skills following the establishment of the Federal Trade School in 1926, and the Agricultural College at Serdang and a technical school in 1931. The British, however, were not anxious to encourage a university education for the local population for fear of creating 'a literary class with no employable skills'. In 1923 the Director of Education for the Straits Settlements and the FMS, R. O. W. Winstedt, expressed a view shared by many of this colleagues that 'a university education for the few will not materially affect the difficult social problems of a community of mixed races or directly benefit the economic life of the many'. At the tertiary level, emphasis was therefore away from a university training to more vocational courses which would provide 'useful' skills in the society.

A distinctive feature of English education in the Malay peninsula was the mixed ethnic composition of the classes. Unlike the vernacular schools which catered almost exclusively to a particular ethnic group, Malays, Indians, Chinese, Eurasians and Europeans attended the same English-medium schools. The shared aspirations of the students and the conformity to certain ideals imposed by the English school system helped create a bond which to a considerable extent overcame some of the differences of ethnicity and social background. In mission schools religion could also play a unifying role, though Malays tended to avoid such institutions because of their reluctance to be associated with any religion except Islam. But in the government English schools, English language and education for the first time bridged the cultural and linguistic gaps that had separated the various ethnic groups in the peninsula. Nevertheless, in relative terms the percentage of Malays was still low, since these schools were located principally in the urban areas where the Chinese and Indians were concentrated.

The vast majority of the Malays lived in the countryside, and if they received any formal secular education at all, it was at the government Malay vernacular school. True to their commitment to 'minimum interference' in the affairs of the Malay commoner, the British had sought simply to provide a basic education as part of their task as a civilized, beneficent administration:

At present the large majority of Malay boys and girls have little or no opportunity of learning their own language, and if the Government undertakes to teach them this, the Koran, and something about figures and geography (especially of the Malay Peninsula and Archipelago), this knowledge and the habits of industry, punctuality and obedience that they will gain by regular attendance at school will be of material advantage to them and assist them to earn a livelihood in any vocation, while they will be likely to prove better citizens and more useful members of the community . . . [17]

In Swettenham's view Malay vernacular education was not merely providing basic literacy; through a reorientation of values and attitudes it was to prepare Malays to accept their place in colonial society.

Until the early twentieth century Malay vernacular schools had very limited success. With the transfer of the Straits Settlements to the Colonial Office in 1867, attempts had been made to introduce education in Malay, but by 1882 almost all government schools had closed through lack of attendance. Under Governor Frederick Weld (1880–87), there was a concerted effort to revive the whole concept of education in Malay. Education expenditure was increased and all teachers were required to be competent in teaching the Koran, literary Malay and simple arithmetic. These new criteria for teachers proved too demanding, and before long the British reluctantly approved the practice of using some of the older pupils to assist in the teaching. The pupil-teachers underwent a probationary teaching period of a year or two, and if they proved satisfactory, they were transferred to a school of their own.

A more serious problem less easily resolved was that of attendance. Despite free instruction and government-provided books and slates, it was difficult for Malays to see the relevance of secular education. The value of studying the Koran was unquestioned, but the need to read and write Malay or to do arithmetic appeared of very limited use to a village Malay. Moreover, many parents required their children's help at home or in the fields. Falling attendance finally convinced the British government to attempt to implement compulsory education in the 1880s and early 1890s. While there were some results from this policy, in general attendance remained erratic and the pupils spent only one and at most two years in school.

With the appointment of R. J. Wilkinson as the new Federal Inspector of Schools in May 1903, Malay vernacular education took on a new significance. Wilkinson argued that the whole system of public instruction should be devoted to combating what he believed was a deterioration of Malay life and culture. Through education, he argued, the foundations for a new culture able to deal with the modern age could be laid. As an amateur historian, Wilkinson saw the past as the period of Malay glory and to preserve this heritage he introduced to the Malay school system the study of Malay literature printed in Rumi (the Malay language in Latin characters). Wilkinson feared that these classical tales, until then available only in Jawi (Malay written in Arabic characters), might remain unread as a new generation of Malays grew up who were more comfortable with Rumi. Wilkinson hoped that studying Malay classics in Rumi would help to reinstil among Malays an appreciation of their culture. These publications would also become more accessible to the other ethnic groups who knew Rumi but not Jawi, and thus foster some common bond based on Malay culture. Such a viewpoint was not a radical divergence from the official British stance that the Malay peninsula belonged to the Malays and that the other ethnic groups were transient elements within the local population. To have Chinese and Indians reading Malay classics was seen as a logical development if they were to remain in the Malay lands and become part of Malay society. A major advance was the standardization of Malay in 1904 which provided a basis for all future Malay publications. The establishment of small school libraries to house these books allowed ready access to the Malay community at large and to other interested ethnic groups. Wilkinson therefore helped sow the seeds of an educational concept which was later pursued with greater vigour and urgency by the independent government of Malaya after 1957.

In November 1906 the Education Departments of the Straits Settlements and the FMS were amalgamated and Wilkinson's post as Federal Inspector abolished. With Wilkinson's strong influence removed, Malay vernacular education was neglected until 1916 when R. O. W. Winstedt was appointed Assistant Director of Education (Malay), a new post approved by the Colonial Office. His tenure as Assistant Director between 1916 and 1921 and as Director between 1924 and 1931 saw a revival in Malay vernacular education. In 1922 the Sultan Idris Training College (SITC) was founded in Tanjong Malim, Perak, with the hope of training 'all Malay teachers in gardening and elementary agriculture, so that they in turn may introduce scientific methods into the most remote villages'. There remained a strong belief in government circles that education should not encourage unattainable aspirations among the Malays. A more important aim in the opinion of British administrators was the preservation of Malay social structure and the modernization of Malay royalty to cope with contemporary challenges. This lofty goal suited the aristocratic Malay College at Kuala Kangsar more than it did the Malay-medium SITC, which served Malays of common backgrounds. Yet despite its founders' efforts to encourage a practical agricultural education, SITC almost from its inception until the outbreak of World War II became the centre of Malay literary activity.

One contributing factor towards this new role was the transfer in 1924 of the Malay Translation Bureau from Kuala Lumpur to the SITC. The Bureau published textbooks for Malay schools and introduced a Malay Home Library Service in 1929. Its staff of Malay translators also produced a fortnightly newspaper and the *Majallah Guru*, a teachers' magazine, which served as their platform for debating current issues, especially the place of the Malays in a changing society. Via its teacher trainees and its publications, the SITC was able to disseminate a new awareness among Malays of the economic and social problems now confronting them. A strong sense of Malay consciousness was thus encouraged which was only rivalled by the *pondok* schools in the Unfederated Malay States (UMS). Only Johor never really developed *pondok* schools since all secular and religious education was placed under Johor's own Education Department which was formed in 1885.

Pondok ('hut') schools were so called because pupils studying under a renowned religious scholar would commonly set up huts wherever the scholar taught, either at his home or at a central mosque. A particular *pondok* would take either the name of the area or the principal teacher to distinguish it from others. In the early nineteenth century, text books were usually in Malay written with Arabic characters (Jawi) and only a few were in Arabic itself. Only later in the century were Arabic texts used in classes with the teachers providing translations. As a religious teacher's fame spread, students from the Malay peninsula and abroad would come to study under him. Since the colonial presence was far less evident in the UMS than in the FMS, *pondok* schools were unchallenged by the educational developments occurring under British tutelage in the FMS. During the nineteenth century the *pondok* schools in the UMS provided a strong focus via Islam for the reaffirmation of Malay identity and unity against their Siamese overlord. After the transfer of the northern Malay states to Britain in 1909, the thrust of this Malay consciousness was directed towards the colonial power.

The vitality with which Islam imbued the *pondok* schools is well illustrated by the story of the famous To' Kenali of Kelantan, a member of the second generation of *ulama*, or religious teachers, of the *pondok* tradition. In the early twentieth century he established numerous schools which were to have far-reaching effects on Islamic education not only in Malaya but in neighbouring countries. He was born Muhammad Yusuf in about 1868 to a farming family near Kota Baru. His first encounter with Islamic doctrine was at the central mosque which attracted many religious scholars. At eighteen he went to Mecca to study, a venture made possible only through the generosity of friends. Despite straitened circumstances, he managed to continue his studies with several eminent religious teachers in Mecca and was also able to visit Cairo, a centre of religious scholarship and Modernist Islamic ideas. In 1908, after an absence of twenty-two years, To' Kenali returned to Kelantan and began to teach. Two years later the first 'Pondok To' Kenali' was established, but soon he was forced to teach at the central mosque as well in order to accommodate all the pupils wishing to study with him. So widespread was his reputation that at one point he had as many as three hundred pupils from all over the peninsula, Indonesia (especially Sumatra), Patani and Cambodia.

To' Kenali was characterized by his Socratic method of teaching and his stress on discussion of political issues. He read such journals as *al-Ahram, Qullaushai* and *Al-Muqattan*, which contained news on world affairs from an Islamic viewpoint. Instead of shying away from secular issues, he encouraged an examination of problems confronting not only Kelantan but Malay society in general. It was through his knowledge of Islam and the international scene that he made his greatest impact on his pupils. Several later went on to become leading religious teachers and writers, as well as social critics. Others established their own schools and helped foster To' Kenali's method of examining society and attempting to assess what was best for the Malays. The *pondok* schools in the UMS and the government Malay vernacular schools in the FMS were therefore at the forefront of Malay demands for reforms within the British colonial system in the early decades of the twentieth century.

In Kelantan there was another important educational development with the formation in 1915 of the Majlis Ugama dan Adat Isti'adat Melayu (Council of Religion and Malay Custom). Two years later it launched its education programme with the founding of a Modernist Islamic school, the Madrasah Muhammadiah, which eventually offered three language streams — English, Arabic and Malay. In 1918 the Majlis attempted to incorporate some of the *pondok* schools, but it was forced to abandon them in 1924 because of lack of adequate funding. The Madrasah itself prospered, and many of its students continued their education at the Malay College in Kuala Kangsar, at the Penang Free School or at the SITC.

The *madrasah* schools grew in popularity during World War I. Unlike the more individualistic style of education which characterized the *pondok* schools, the *madrasah* had a set curriculum and an organizational structure much more in keeping with the secular schools. Arabic was the medium of instruction, but every opportunity was provided for the learning of English as well as mathematics and science, the 'modern' subjects. Indeed, the very impetus for the formation of *madrasah* schools was the desire to preserve the 'Islamic-ness' of the Malays at a time when Malaya appeared to be succumbing in every respect to the British. The founders of these schools hoped to demonstrate to the youth that one could be Moslem and still be modern, that Islam was not incompatible with modern advances.

Instruction in all these religious schools was by no means confined to Islam, for attempts were also made to combine religious learning and vocational training. One school in Perak, for example, offered courses which included commercial subjects, maths, history, English, business, and techniques for *padi*-planting and making soap and *kicap* (a type of soy sauce).[18] But the principal purpose for their foundation was religious training, a training which reinforced the belief that to be a Malay was to be a Moslem. By the very nature of their education, graduates of *pondok* schools and *madrasahs* saw Islam as being more important in constituting 'Malayness' than did their contemporaries from the colonial government's vernacular schools. Graduates of the *pondok* and *madrasah* schools formed an important part of the Malay-educated intelligentsia of the 1920s and 1930s, alongside those from the vernacular Malay schools, the Melaka Malay College (1900–21), and the Sultan Idris Training College.

Education in Sarawak and North Borneo

The Borneo states had become British protectorates in 1888 but their educational development was more a result of the philosophies of their respective rulers, the British North Borneo Company and the Brooke family. In Sarawak a systematic approach to education was first intro-duced by Raja Charles Brooke. While he believed that Western educa-tion was worthwhile, he knew that it would also undermine the local cultures which he admired. In his view the British had suppressed, rather than built upon, the Asian civilizations which they came to dominate. To put his beliefs into practice, Charles Brooke established a 'Government Lay School' at the turn of the twentieth century in Kuching where Malay boys were taught in Malay and Chinese boys in Mandarin. From 1904 to 1911 similar schools, but sometimes separate Chinese and Malay ones, were set up in many outstations. After 1912 the government withdrew from the field of Chinese education, since independent Chinese schools began to proliferate. Government Malay schools continued, however, existing side by side with the traditional Malay schools taught by religious teachers. True to his philosophy, Charles Brooke refused to 'tamper' with the lifestyle of the indigenous groups, particularly the Ibans, by subjecting them to Western education. Instead, he left the missions to undertake their education, providing their schools with an initial subsidy for a building as well as an annual grant. The Anglican Society for the Propagation of the Gospel was given charge of all Iban education in the Second Division, and the Roman Catholic Mission of the few schools in the Third Division. Nevertheless, only a small proportion of the Ibans were enrolled in these mission schools. By 1936 the 2,086 students in the twenty-five government schools for Malays and Moslem Melanaus included only six Ibans and one Land Dayak. The mission school enrolment had a better record, with 339 Ibans and 296 Land Dayaks. In 1936, however, three-quarters of Sarawak's total school population of about 14,000 were Chinese attending independent Chinese and mission schools.[19]

In 1935 the Le Gros Clark Report appeared which proposed wide-

ranging changes in the education system. Among its suggestions were
the appointment of a Director of Education and an Education Board
composed of representatives from the missions and the people; an
upgraded *Madrasah Melayu* to groom village schoolteachers and native
officers for administration; and technical and agricultural instruction at
the village level. But there appeared little support for the Report's
assumption that there should be a gradual transfer of the administration
to the natives, and by 1941 the only results of the recommendations
were a Director of Education and a Malay Teachers' College.

After Sarawak became a British Crown Colony in 1946, the main
priority was to bring education to the large section of the Iban and
Dayak population who had never had any schooling. Although the
British authorities intended to introduce universal education, this
proved financially unfeasible. In 1955 a new system of government aid
was introduced, providing substantial capital grants for new school
building and placing teachers' salaries on a regular basis. With greater
resources and a different governing philosophy, the new colonial
administration in Sarawak finally extended education to a large percentage of its population.

Education in North Borneo under the British North Borneo Company prior to 1909 was principally in the hands of missions, though
there were a few Chinese and Moslem schools. In 1919, however, an
Education Department was formed with inspectors of schools appointed for both the east and west coasts. The government also continued
its grants to mission schools. The first government vernacular school
was established at Jesselton (Kota Kinabalu) in 1915 to train sons of
native chiefs in a three-year course given in Malay. But because there
was no Koran study, most of the Moslem chiefs soon withdrew their
sons. Only the Muruts of the interior continued to attend. To remedy
this situation the government in 1923 introduced instruction in the
Koran and in English, both of which helped restore the school's
popularity. Following the British lead in the Malay states, the Company
began to encourage Malay education as opposed to the English-medium
government-subsidized mission schools. By 1930 ten Malay vernacular
schools had been established, patronized principally by Moslems or
those sympathetic to Moslem culture. From 1935 onward, government Malay vernacular schools were run much more tightly than
previously. Students had to wear uniforms issued twice a year, while
physical education and a daily gardening routine were added to the
basic curriculum of Malay language study, arithmetic, geography and
hygiene. In the same period the number of English schools run by the
missions showed a corresponding rise. Block grants from the government helped ease their financial burdens without bringing interference
in curriculum planning. In general, the mission schools reached a
standard that enabled their students to pass the Cambridge University

Syndic examination instituted in 1933. Within a few years, however, the combined demands of Malay vernacular education and mission schools imposed such a financial strain on the government that it decided to channel most financial support to its own schools. The government of North Borneo was satisfied to leave Chinese vernacular education almost wholly to the Chinese communities, subject only to an annual inspection. By 1940 there was a total of 10,993 students enrolled in Malay vernacular, mission and Chinese schools throughout North Borneo.[20] When North Borneo, like Sarawak, became a British Crown Colony in 1946, the increased resources which then became available to the government enabled it to satisfy the great demand for education in the post-war years.

In neither North Borneo nor Sarawak was education of the indigenous peoples as widespread or as relevant as in the Malay peninsula. The few who did receive formal schooling were taught an alien language and culture, whether Malay or English. In short, the educational philosophy and practice of the Brookes in Sarawak and the Chartered Company in North Borneo did little to alter the state of affairs in indigenous society.

Every type of educational system within Malaya, with the exception of English-medium schools, emphasized a distinct ethnic culture and history which helped preserve the separate identities of the various groups. This development was not actively fostered by the British; on the contrary, it arose through British inactivity in the field of education. From the beginning of their involvement in peninsula affairs in the middle of the nineteenth century, the British naturally regarded the areas as Malay and dealt with them as such. With the influx of large numbers of Chinese and Indian labourers during the nineteenth and early twentieth century, the situation in the peninsula changed radically. But there is little indication that the initial British colonial attitude towards the area altered significantly to accommodate the realities of a new colonial Malaya. The Chinese and Indians continued to be regarded as transitory labouring communities whose ultimate goal was to return home with their hard-earned wealth. The fact that these communities lived apart from another, conducting their own affairs as separate nations on Malay lands with the protection of the British overlord, aroused little concern. The Malay ruling classes were reconciled to the conception/deception that, under British direction alien Asian communities were assisting to extract the riches from Malay soil for the ultimate welfare of the Malay community. These alien Asians – Chinese and Indian – were considered temporary phenomena whose immediate needs should be satisfied but for whom any long-term planning would be unnecessary. The British government thus adopted a *laissez-faire* policy towards the education of

Chinese and Indian children and only later became actively involved in Chinese schools in response to growing direct and disruptive political influences from China.

The formulation of long-term policy was confined to the Malays. With the exception of a few outstanding commoners, English education was limited to sons of royalty and nobility who were to fill administrative posts in government and industry. Malay vernacular education, on the other hand, was provided for children of Malay commoners with the aim of teaching them to be better farmers or fishermen and to be contented with their position in life.

Only in English education did the government condone the participation of all ethnic groups, notably after the creation of the FMS in 1896 and the subsequent demand for English-educated personnel. Nevertheless, the British were again guided by the practical needs of the colonial society which they had created. English education was not available to all; whatever their ethnic group, only a privileged few gained access to English schools and hence to lucrative and prestigious positions in government or in European firms. The élitist nature of English education bred a certain type of individual whose social and intellectual mores became the bond which united him with fellow students regardless of ethnic background. In the exceptional case of Malay College at Kuala Kangsar, where admission was restricted to well-born Malays, there was another positive outcome. For the first time royalty and nobility from throughout the Malay peninsula were educated together, fostering a belief in the unity of all the Malay states.

But the exclusiveness of English education should not be regarded as a principal factor in the ferment which arose in the early twentieth century among the vernacular-educated Chinese and Malays. To them, English education as the key to success in Malaya's colonial society seemed increasingly irrelevant. They were instead inspired by a pride in their own identity. The Republican Revolution in China in 1911, and the subsequent cultural and language developments in the following decade and a half, restored China's self-respect after almost a century of humiliation by Western powers. Increasing involvement by the KMT government and later the CCP in the education of overseas Chinese helped sustain the latter's interest in China and their awareness of being Chinese.

The Malays, too, were becoming much more conscious of their distinctive identity, as Arabic-educated Malay scholars returned from the Middle East propagating the modernist Islamic creed that Islam and change were not incompatible. Such teachings reinforced the essential element which had long distinguished Malays from almost all other ethnic groups in the peninsula, the sense of being at the one time Moslem and Malay. While these *pondok* schools and some of the modernist Islamic *madrasahs* actively inculcated this belief in their students, the secular Malay intelligentsia centred in the SITC agitated for greater Malay political rights. Their desire for change became a noble cause, dedicated to furthering the interests of all Malay people. The atmosphere of the times imbued their activities with a sense of purpose which assured their lasting reputations as leaders of Malay nationalism in the period of *perjuangan*, the noble struggle.

By the 1930s the British were deeply concerned by the radical ideas expressed in the vernacular schools, especially those of the Chinese. The colonial authority was then sufficiently powerful to have exerted greater financial and hence curriculum control. However, by the time the British had recognized the reality of permanent Chinese and Indian communities within Malaya and the corresponding need to adjust previous attitudes to education, world-wide events overtook the country. The Depression in the 1930s and the outbreak of World War II prevented the colonial government from reversing even slightly the divisive trends which had arisen in vernacular education in the Malay peninsula. The trauma of the Japanese Occupation and the Emergency in the post-war years highlighted the divisions within the ethnic communities in Malaya and the desperate need for an overall policy which would prevent what appeared a real possibity of violent confrontation among the ethnic groups in Malaya or, more specifically, between the two largest groups, the Chinese and the Malays. While politicians sought economic and political solutions, others believed that any hope for a substantial change in attitudes within the various ethnic communities necessitated a revolution in the educational system.

In 1956, on the eve of Malaya's independence, the Education Committee headed by Abdul Razak bin Dato Hussein, Minister of Education and later Prime Minister, issued the following statement, capturing precisely the role conceived for education in the new nation: 'We cannot overemphasize our conviction that the introduction of syllabuses common to all schools in the Federation is the crucial requirement of education policy in Malaya. It is an essential element in the development of a united Malayan nation'.[21] The Committee recognized that the separate educational systems which had developed under British Colonial rule were responsible for divergent and distinct outlooks on Malaya as a homeland. If the new nation were to survive and flourish, one of its top priorities would have to be the inculcation of common ideals and aspirations based upon the premise that Malaya could arouse the allegiance of all its population. This was a formidable goal, but vital if the country were to remain united. While the economic and educational priorities of the colonial government had served to compartmentalize Malaysian society, it was hoped that the political institutions the British had established would be able to withstand the strains of a divided society long enough for a united nation to emerge.

Colonial Government and the Decentralization Debate

Although in time the British Resident or Adviser came to wield great authority in the peninsula, the Malay rulers continued to exercise a strong influence among their subjects. What often occurred was a rule by consensus and persuasion, since forceful opposition from either the British official or the Malay Sultan could ultimately render any one-sided policy ineffective. Throughout the nineteenth and early twentieth centuries such a system of rule in Malaya proved satisfactory because the large migrant Chinese population was relegated to a separate administrative unit, the Chinese Protectorate. The colonial government could regard the Chinese presence as a temporary expedient but one which did not affect the legal political arrangements reached by the British and the Malays.

This neat social division between Chinese and Malay was shaken by the development of rubber in the early twentieth century. Vast tracts of jungle were gradually cleared for the industry, and a steady stream of Indian migrant labourers appeared in Malaya. Unlike the earlier Chinese, many of the new Indian arrivals lived on the rubber estates, essentially existing as wards of the plantations. The rubber industry's attitude towards its Indian workers, at best paternalistic and at worst exploitative, made government supervision seem imperative as an insurance against possible abuses. Greater government intervention also appeared desirable because of increased European capital tied up in the tin and rubber industries by the second decade of the twentieth century. The British were thus forced by new conditions prevailing in Malaya to reassess their rationale for the exercise of authority in the Malay states. Despite their professed adherence to the concept that Malays ruled and the colonial authorities advised, the new economic and demographic developments in Malaya made it increasingly impossible for the British to argue this convincingly or with any great conviction.

The first British response to these new developments was a move towards further centralization throughout Malaya. Preservation of European confidence in the tin and rubber industries demanded much greater uniformity of laws and government policies than had hitherto been considered necessary. The trend towards uniform colonial administration had already begun with the establishment of the Federated Malay States in 1896 and the Federal Council in 1909. The practical effect of these centralization efforts was to relegate the Malay Sultan and his state council increasingly to 'traditional' Malay affairs, which had been interpreted by the British as matters dealing with Islam and

Malay ceremonial. The loss of effective power wielded by the Malay Sultans had caused concern among some officials but only became a subject of debate in the Federal Council in 1922 when the post-World War I economic recession led to a re-examination of policy. What had prompted the debate on the Sultans' powers was the desire for greater administrative economy. The Federal administration in Kuala Lumpur was attacked for excessive expenditure, and there was a call for re-trenchment and decentralization. The obvious solution was to relinquish more governmental duties to the states.

The move towards decentralization gained momentum in 1925 when High Commissioner Sir Laurence Guillemard, acting with Colonial Office approval, announced his intention of abolishing the Chief Secretaryship. Its powers would then be gradually devolved to the state councils, Residents and Federal heads of departments. Guillemard's proposals were welcomed by the FMS Sultans, who regarded with dismay the marked contrast between their slowly dwindling control over state affairs and the powers retained by rulers in the UMS. In the latter states the British Adviser consulted the Sultan and his council before taking any decision and was reluctant to override concerted Malay objections. The apparently greater authority wielded by the UMS Sultans aroused considerable envy among the FMS Sultans, despite the latter's more extensive wealth acquired through the new export industries. On a visit to England in 1924 the Sultan of Perak had specifically requested the Secretary of State for the Colonies to transfer to the Malay states some of the federal government's powers.

The solution to the decentralization controversy, however, could not be based solely on political considerations. The very presence of the export industries in the FMS, the source of their great wealth, had entailed tighter control by the colonial government. The need for uniformity of laws, an efficient administration, and proper maintenance of the infrastructure were necessary for the export industries to flourish. The colonial government was under greater pressure to safeguard business investments in the FMS than in the UMS, whose economic importance to the British was considerably less. In the end it was the economic pressure groups represented by European and Chinese business interests which again determined policy in British Malaya. They feared a return to the insecurity of pre-Federation days, with a consequent drop in confidence among the all-important big capital investors overseas. They were also reluctant to see the abolition of the Chief Secretaryship, since they believed that their interests would then be subordinated to those of the colony of Singapore, the home-base of the High Commissioner. Guillemard bowed to these pressures by preserving the Chief Secretaryship and making only a few gestures towards decentralization. Increased financial responsibility was given to the state councils, and four more members were added to the Federal Council. But an unfortunate consequence of Guillemard's proposals was an agreement signed with all four FMS Sultans in 1927 allowing them to forgo attendance at federal council meetings and to be represented by the Residents. As a result, the Sultans of the FMS effectively relegated almost total powers over legislation to the British. Their official powers in government were limited to attaching their signatures to laws passed by the council and attending the Durbar, the annual meeting of rulers.

The question of decentralization again arose in 1931 reflecting, as on the previous occasion, the sober circumstances of the export economy. This time the champion of decentralization was High Commissioner Sir Cecil Clementi who came to office in 1930. He argued that the gradual extension of British control in the FMS was at variance with their treaties with the Malay Sultans. Furthermore, he stressed the importance of decentralization as a means of encouraging the rulers of the UMS to become part of a future Pan-Malayan Union. Although his proposals were very similar to Guillemard's, he added two new features which provoked heated debate. His proposal of a Malayan Customs Union with a protective tariff merely echoed familiar economic sentiments expressed by contemporary governments around the world, but it drew fierce criticism from those who supported the continuance of Singapore's traditional free trade. The other new recommendation for an eventual Pan-Malayan Union aroused protests from the UMS, especially from Kedah and Johor, who feared the same loss of authority they had witnessed among their fellow rulers of the FMS. There was also opposition from the business interests in the FMS who were satisfied with the *status quo* and were wary of any new, unknown administrative structure. Business circles were apprehensive of subordination to Singapore, whose economic goals often diverged from those of the FMS. The Chinese further objected that any move towards decentralization could be detrimental to Chinese interests which would then be in the hands of 'autocratic' Malay Sultans. Such arguments were to surface again after World War II when the old scheme of a Malayan Union was revived.

The central issue underlying all debates on decentralization was plainly stated in 1932 by Sir Samuel Wilson, the Permanent Under-Secretary of State for the Colonies, when he was sent to Malaya to investigate the whole question. He recognized that from an economic point of view 'it would no doubt be advisable in a country the size of Malaya to have one Central Government administering the whole territory'. On the other hand, he saw the necessity of decentralization because the Malay Sultans were clearly discontented with their rapidly diminishing authority. Wilson reiterated a stand which had always adumbrated official pronouncements whatever their practical outcome:

The maintenance of the position, authority and prestige of the Malay Rulers must always be a cardinal point in British policy: and the encouragement of indirect rule will probably prove the greatest safeguard against the political submersion of the Malays which would result from the development of popular government on Western lines. For in such a government the Malays would be hopelessly outnumbered by the other races owing to the great influx of immigrants that has taken place.[22]

On balance Wilson saw the necessity of decentralization, but at a much more gradual pace than hitherto advocated.

The decision to work towards decentralization raised a serious problem. Since the advent of the British Advisory system in the Malay states, the state councils had been relegated to 'traditional' activities which did not interfere with the colonial economic processes. As a result, very few Malays in the FMS had been trained in government. It was feared that with the devolution of power from the federal government to the states, the latter would lack the experienced personnel to deal with their new responsibilities. Should Europeans, Chinese or Indians be brought into the state councils to remedy this situation, there was a real possibility of the Malays being overwhelmed and again controlled by outsiders. The choice was one between 'a substantial amount of power conferred upon an enlarged and cosmopolitan state council, or a small amount of power conferred on the old type of state council'.[23] Clementi opted for the first alternative, and so the state councils were enlarged with additional Chinese, Indian and European members. Rulers and Residents were again allowed greater participation in the state councils.

While High Commissioner between 1930 and 1934, Clementi introduced one reform which in subsequent years had far-reaching repercussions within Malaya: the employment of Asians in government services. However, the recruitment of Asians into the Straits Medical Service from 1932, the establishment in 1934 of the Straits Settlements Civil Service and in 1937 of the Straits Legal Service created opportunities for non-Europeans only at low levels. These primarily clerical positions were traditionally dominated by Jaffna Tamils, Indians and Chinese. In the wake of Clementi's reforms, English-educated Malays began to demand a greater share of clerical posts. In response, Clementi created a separate clerical service for each of the FMS open to all ethnic groups born and educated in the FMS but with a preference for Malays. He also increased the number of Malays in the Malayan Civil Service. Since the Malay Administrative Service formed in 1910 was reserved only for Malays, Clementi's reform considerably expanded the opportunities for a government career for English-educated Malays.

Some progress had been made towards decentralization by the outbreak of the Pacific War. By 1935 the Chief Secretaryship had been abolished and by 1939 the departments of agriculture, education, forestry, medical services, mining and public works had been largely placed under individual state control. Legislative powers had been divided between the federal and state councils, although one clause gave the federal council the power to legislate on 'all projects of substantive law not otherwise enumerated which are intended to have force throughout the Federation', and on any other subject determined by the High Commissioner 'to be within his competency'. In financial measures as well, the federal council still retained substantial powers despite decentralization measures. Each state received an annual block grant from the federal council, but the latter supervised its expenditure. In practice, therefore, the federal council still retained vast powers despite a few bold gestures towards restoring power to the Sultans and the states.

The UMS, like the FMS, were 'juridically independent and practically dependent' on the British. But there was one significant difference: most of the ministers and administrative officers were Malays, and the opinions of the Sultans and his councils had considerable weight in the decisions of the British Advisers. The political evolution in these states, like those in the FMS, was affected by their economic developments. Johor had quickly become a valuable hinterland for Chinese 'pioneer' agriculturalists from Singapore who cleared virgin land to plant tapioca, pepper, gambier and, from 1910, rubber. Rail and road links between west coast states and Singapore brought Johor within the economic developments of this whole area. Chinese and Indian immigrants involved in the rubber industry added to those Chinese already engaged in agricultural pursuits. By 1931 Chinese and Indians comprised 52·3 per cent of Johor's population, making it the only unfederated Malay state where the Malays were not in the majority. Extensive agricultural and mining concerns transformed Johor to the same extent as the FMS, necessitating certain changes in the style of government. Unlike the FMS, however, the Johor rulers succeeded in retaining a considerable degree of independence due to the abilities of its rulers, particularly Sultan Abu Bakar and his son and successor, Sultan Ibrahim (1895–1959).

Of the four northern states which made up the rest of the UMS, Kedah was most similar to Johor. Like Johor, it became part of the economic developments on the west coast because of rail and road communication. As in Johor, Kedah benefited from the movement of Chinese capital and labour from another of the Straits Settlements, Penang. European and Chinese rubber estates arose in Kedah, but the extent of economic change undergone by Kedah never reached the proportions experienced in Johor. In another particular respect Kedah resembled Johor, in that it was governed by capable leaders who were responsible for limiting the degree of British control and thus preserving the state's Malay character. Perlis remained a basically agricultural rice-growing state highly dependent upon Kedah.

Kelantan and Trengganu were still the most inaccessible of the Malay states, with railway links to Kelantan being completed only in 1931 and to Trengganu a few years later. Furthermore, monsoon winds closed the seas to shipping along the east coast for several months each year. These difficulties, coupled with the fact that Kelantan and Trengganu were reputedly under relatively oppressive governments, discouraged large-scale capital investment. The pattern of *padi*-planting and small-scale sea and river fishing continued to characterize the economic patterns of their predominantly Malay populations at a time when the other peninsular states were experiencing rapid economic social changes wrought by the tin and rubber industries.

The divergent economic and political developments of the FMS, UMS and the Straits Settlements left the goal of creating a single centralized government for British Malaya still unfulfilled by 1941. Despite the general argument that a union for Malaya was ultimately desirable, the established interests within each individual administrative unit distrusted any change. The FMS did not want an expansion of their administrative unit, which they found sufficient for their purposes. They feared control by Singapore and the prospects of bearing the financial cost of assisting in the development of the poorer states of the UMS. The UMS were equally wary of losing their sovereignty and control, as well as their way of life, by the introduction of foreign capital and labour into their states. The Colony of the Straits Settlements saw little benefit in becoming a part of a union where it would lose its advantage of free trade. In theory many were in favour of a union, but the reality frightened the vested Malay, European and Chinese interests. There was thus little progress towards a unification of these separate political entities. In August 1941, four months before the Japanese invaded Malaya, the High Commissioner reaffirmed British intention to respect their treaties with the Malay Sultans and to maintain the Sultans' interests in their separate states.[24]

Final Years of Company and White Raja Rule in Borneo

In the early twentieth century there was a noticeable change in the style of government in both North Borneo and Sarawak. The death in 1910 of the Managing Director of the British North Borneo Company, W. C. Cowie, removed his strong hand from North Borneo's affairs, while the domination of Raja Charles Brooke in Sarawak ended with his death in 1917, being replaced by his less assertive elder son, Vyner.

In both Bornean states, the passing of these giant personalities heralded the end of individualistic rule and of isolation from major economic and political trends around the world. Their participation in the world economy made them prisoner to external influences far beyond their shores. Technological and administrative advances being introduced in British Malaya were soon brought to Borneo on a modified scale to accord with the local situation.

In North Borneo a revision of salaries and pension schemes brought them more in line with the British Colonial Service, and new Departments of Education and Forestry, and an Advisory Council for Native Affairs were established. Closer links between the Colonial Office in London and the Company directors were forged through an arrangement by which the latter received all general directives and circulars to the Colonial Service, all Acts of Parliament pertaining to the colonies, Orders in Council and Royal Proclamations. In North Borneo itself the administration tended to implement ideas and techniques introduced from Malaya and to rely on staff recruited from there. A Legislative Council was introduced in 1912 with seven official and four unofficial members to represent the Chinese community, business interests and planters on the east and west coasts. There was no attempt to increase political participation among the indigenous peoples or to awaken any sense of common purpose in North Borneo as a political entity. By 1941 the government was still dominated by the concerns of vested economic interests.

In Sarawak the Brooke government had operated on the principle of the allotted role of the Malay as administrator, the Chinese as trader and cash-crop farmer and the Iban as police and soldier. As a result, other indigenous groups such as the Land Dayak, Melanau, Kenyah and Kayan remained in general outside the scope of government policy. There was a tendency to force groups to fit one of the categories. The Moslem Melanau, for example, were encouraged to become 'Malay', while the other non-Moslem indigenous peoples were often grouped with the Iban despite their obvious rejection of Iban values. But one positive outcome of this simple logic of the Sarawak rulers was the nurturing of a sense of one Iban people, an ideal which eventually did overcome the reality of numerous divisive groups.

In 1915, only two years before his death, Charles had decided to weaken the authoritarian nature of government by introducing a new Committee of Administration composed wholly of European officials. It was to operate alongside the old Supreme Council, composed of the Kuching Malay chiefs, which was now regarded as an anachronism. Three years previously he had also organized a State Advisory Council in England to oversee Sarawak's finances. These measures were prompted in part by Charles's lack of confidence in the ability of his son and successor to maintain a stable government in Sarawak without help, and in part by the rapid economic and administrative changes in the other British colonies. Sarawak could no longer avoid involvement in events beyond its borders, and it was Charles's hope to assure the smooth transition of Sarawak into the twentieth century.

During the regime of the third White Raja, Vyner Brooke, these institutional innovations were neglected, and the Supreme Council no longer met after 1927. Nevertheless, Sarawak had become part of the world economy and was much more closely linked to the other British colonies than ever before. Administration in Sarawak became more bureaucratic and rationalized with a written criminal code based on the Indian Penal Code introduced in 1923 and a Legal Department in 1928. More departments were created, municipal administration introduced in Kuching and Sibu, and a Chief Secretary appointed in 1923 with a Secretariat in Kuching. Residents were now to consider the Chief Secretary as 'co-ordinator' and reminded that they were part of 'one united Sarawak'.[25]

Many of these changes occurred in spite of Raja Vyner, who spent much of his time in Europe. Government in the 1930s was principally in the hands of the Chief Secretary, and executive power gradually began to be assumed by the Kuching bureaucracy. There was a move toward centralization with little regard for the 'interests of the natives', the *raison d'être* of Brooke rule. Problems of succession, brought about by Vyner's lack of a son and an ambitious nephew, Anthony, coupled with a desire to provide long-term financial security for his family, led Vyner to think seriously of selling Sarawak to Britain or of having a British General Adviser appointed to govern while he was in England. Britain suggested in July 1939 that a General Adviser be appointed with the occasional secondment of officers to and from Malaya and Sarawak. One was indeed appointed in early 1940, but he did not stay long. Then on 24 September 1941, in the week celebrating the centenary of Brooke rule, Vyner proclaimed a Constitution for Sarawak which altered the individualistic nature of Brooke rule and remodelled the old Council Negeri and the Supreme Council to accord more with the legislative and executive councils of the British colonies. The Constitution was approved by the British government, and by October 1941 plans were well-advanced in the Colonial Office for assuming control over Sarawak's internal affairs. A British Resident was to be appointed whose powers were undoubtedly intended to equal those in Malaya. But before any of these plans could be effectively implemented the Japanese began the invasion of Southeast Asia in late 1941.

Japanese Occupation and the Immediate Post-War Years

Malaya was invaded by the Japanese on 8 December 1941 and quickly overrun. The 'impregnable' island fortress of Singapore capitulated soon after on 15 February 1942, and the Netherlands East Indies followed in March. The Japanese army reorganized the political units in the area by making Singapore, now renamed Shōnan, the centre of the regional military administration which incorporated the Straits Settlements, the FMS, the UMS and Sumatra. Melaka, Penang and the Malay states were placed under a Japanese governor, while Singapore, ruled as a colony, was under a mayor. Military governments were also established in Sarawak and North Borneo. After Thailand declared war on the United States and Great Britain in 1942, Japan rewarded its new ally by allowing it to annex Kedah, Perlis, Kelantan and Trengganu in August 1943. These states remained under Thai control for the duration of the war, but on 16 August 1945 the annexation was declared null and void and these Malay states once again reverted to their pre-war status.

Ultimately, the Japanese hoped to make Singapore a permanent colony and the Malay states a protectorate. But in the early years of the Occupation, these long-term aims were sacrificed for the more crucial question of how Malaya could best contribute economically to Japan's war effort. Only when the tide began to turn against them in mid-1943 did they pay greater attention to encouraging Malay nationalism. The Japanese now organized mass demonstrations, pan-Malayan conferences, language-training and administrative education. In this period Malays increasingly began to see themselves as belonging to a Malaya-wide entity, rather than to their individual states. Ironically, a major contribution to the growing sense of a united Malay nation was the weakened position of the Sultans during the Occupation. Although by early 1943 the Japanese had restored to the Sultans the privileges they had previously enjoyed under the British, they did not pay the same deference to the Sultans as did the British colonial rulers. The weakened status of the traditional rulers in the Occupation, combined with Japanese encouragement of Malay nationalism, contributed to the growing importance of a new Malay élite who had arisen in the 1920s and 1930s.

These new Malay leaders were the products of a nascent Malay nationalism which had originated in the early twentieth century in response to the growing influence and presence of both the British and the Chinese in Malaya. At first this nationalism was contained within state boundaries but later became Malaya-wide as its appeal transcended traditional political boundaries. Three new élite groups came to vie with the old Malay ruling class as leaders who could best protect Malay interests. The first of these arose from a religious reform movement which had its origins in an Islamic Renaissance in the Middle East during the late nineteenth century. Malay Moslems returning from Cairo or the Hejaz brought reformist ideas which saw the renovation of Islam as a means of providing Malays with the means to respond effectively to the radical changes brought by the Europeans, Chinese and Indians. Many had been exposed to anti-colonial ideas in Egypt and had even published political pan-Indonesian articles in Egyptian journals. The main strength of this new élite group was in the urban centres, especially in Penang and Singapore, but it did gain adherents among religious teachers and others in rural society. Their main obstacle was opposition from the more traditional Islamic hierarchy, of which the Sultan was the formal head. The traditional religious and secular establishments, reinforced by expressed British intention to maintain Malay religion and custom, had too great a hold on the Malays for any other Islamic élite group to offer any real challenges to their authority.

Another new élite group which resulted from the changed circumstances within Malay society was the English-educated administrators and public servants from the traditional Malay ruling classes. The Depression and administrative reforms of the early 1930s for the first time upset the ethnic roles in British Malaya. Falling world prices for rubber and tin brought unemployment among the estate and mine workers, mainly Chinese and Indians. While the government had resorted to the unpopular practice of repatriating many of these labourers, others remained to eke out a living from the land, previously seen as a primarily Malay occupation. But some Malays, too, were abandoning agriculture and through English education seeking employment in government services. Clementi's reforms opened the door to the inclusion of more Malays in lower government positions and thus brought them into direct competition in a field which was practically a monopoly of Chinese and Indians. Rivalry among the various ethnic groups engendered a proprietary feeling among Malays that they, as the 'indigenous' people of Malaya, deserved better. This feeling was tapped by the new English-educated Malay élite, whom the Malay people already regarded as legitimate leaders because of their noble birth. Able to move confidently in the white man's world, these young men seemed to many Malays the rightful spokesmen for the Malay community.

The third élite group which arose in the early twentieth century was the secular, Malay-educated intelligentsia, mainly teachers and journalists. Many of them, like their reformist Islamic counterparts, advocated some type of 'Greater Malaysia' or 'Greater Indonesia'. They were drawn almost wholly from the Malay peasantry and were therefore critical of the establishment, whether the British colonial government, the traditional Malay ruling classes or the English-educated intelligentsia of any ethnic group. These Malay-educated élite founded the Kesatuan Melayu Muda (Young Malay Union) in late 1938, an organization very similar to the cultural—political youth groups which had sprung up throughout the Netherlands East Indies. Because of its strong views, it failed to gain a large following among the conservative rural Malays but became the basis for radical Malay political movements after the war.

During the Occupation members of this third Malay élite group sought to use the Japanese to achieve their social and political goals. The Japanese, for their part, saw some value in encouraging them, if only to assure their co-operation for Japanese economic and military plans. The radical Malay intelligentsia were chosen to lead the youth movements and conduct publicity campaigns to encourage nationalism. Several became leading figures in the paramilitary youth group organized by the Japanese known as PETA (Pembela Tanah Air — Defenders of the Fatherland). While hoping to use the Japanese to gain independence, the radical movement led by Ibrahim Yaacob also sought to assure its success by seeking clandestine alliances with the Chinese-dominated Malayan Peoples Anti-Japanese Army (MPAJA) as well as the traditional Malay élite. Despite their ambitious plans, the radicals had little to offer to these groups since they lacked a strong power base and were geographically divided. In July 1945 the Japanese finally agreed to promote a Malay nationalist movement based on the 'Greater Indonesia' concept. A new political organization, KRIS (Kesatuan Rakyat Indonesia Semenanjung — Union of Peninsular Indonesians, but later changed to Kekuatan Rakyat Indonesia Istimewa — Supreme Strength of the Indonesian People) was formed under the leadership of Ibrahim and Dr Burhanuddin Al-Hemy, with the aims of achieving independence and effecting a union with Indonesia. However, the unexpected surrender of the Japanese on 15 August brought these plans to a premature end.

The Indians were not treated as well as the Malays during the Occupation but were never brutalized as were the Chinese. Some Indian estate workers were forcefully conscripted for Japanese projects from which many never returned. But the comparatively mild treatment generally accorded the Indians was doubtless the result of the ambiguous status of India itself as a British colony. Indian nationalism became a convenient vehicle for obtaining Indian co-operation for the Japanese war effort. In July 1943 Subhas Chandra Bose, a former president of the Indian Congress who had been living in exile in Germany, was brought back to Singapore. In October of that same year, he proclaimed a Free India (Azad Hind) government and succeeded in enlisting Indians throughout Southeast Asia in the Indian National Army. The participation of Malayan Indians in this and other Indian nationalist political organizations, all of which were strongly anti-British, made the Japanese adopt a relatively lenient stance towards the Indians in Malaya.

Of all the major ethnic groups in Malaya during the Occupation, the Chinese received the harshest treatment from the Japanese. The long and bitter Chinese struggle to oust the Japanese invaders from their homeland had been generously supported by funds from overseas Chinese. Furthermore, there were many active Kuomintang and Chinese Communist Party sympathizers in Singapore and Malaya who were violently anti-Japanese. To root out these enemies, the Japanese systematically rounded up all the Chinese male population of Singapore in the first week of the Occupation and massacred thousands, estimated between 5,000 and 25,000. While this mass punishment of the Chinese was never repeated, smaller but equally brutal atrocities were committed against the Chinese throughout the Occupation. Yet the Japanese were finally forced to rely on them to assure the functioning of the wartime economy. By mid-1944 clubs were even formed for the Chinese in the Straits Settlements to discuss problems in the economy. These co-operative efforts, however, never removed Chinese bitterness towards the Japanese.

While underground movements were formed by various Indian and Malay groups, the main anti-Japanese activity understandably came from the ranks of the Chinese. They comprised by far the largest component in the MPAJA, which was in turn dominated by the Malayan Communist Party (MCP). Although the MCP was only formally organized in April 1930 it had an earlier existence in the mid-1920s as part of the Kuomintang (Chinese Nationalist Party) and in the South Seas Branch of the Chinese Communist Party based in Singapore. The Depression years provided the MCP with the first real opportunity to gain mass support by voicing the grievances of workers, mainly Chinese, employed in the export industries. With the Japanese invasion of China in 1937, the MCP once again became the champions of the Malayan Chinese by leading the Anti-Japanese National Salvation Associations. The MCP was in a strong position when the Japanese invaded, and it offered its full assistance to the colonial government. Co-operation between the two was shortlived, however, because the Japanese advanced much more rapidly than expected. The MCP was forced once again to go underground to survive. In the first year of the Occupation the Japanese successfully destroyed the entire Central Committee of the Singapore Party and almost all of the Central Committee of the MCP, except for Lai Tek, the Secretary-General. The MCP nonetheless lived on to play an effective role as part of the MPAJA's general resistance movement.

The anti-Japanese resistance in the Occupation bore certain features which came to characterize the later communist insurgency period. First, the MPAJA had a hard core of MCP members, as well as large numbers of anti-Japanese individuals, mainly Chinese, armed Malay units principally from the radical groupings, and a percentage of pure bandit elements. Secondly, the MPAJA had a support unit in its civilian wing, the Anti-Japanese Union (renamed the Min Yuen during the insurgency), which helped provide supplies and recruits to the MPAJA.

Thirdly, the MPAJA developed an attitude of contempt and then hatred towards the police. Fourthly, it cultivated relations with the aboriginal groups. Fifthly, it combined a policy of friendship and intimidation to achieve its aims among the civilian population. And finally, it gained valuable experience in guerrilla warfare.[26] The MPAJA fought practically alone against the Japanese until the last few months of the war. With the end of hostilities, the MCP was able to bask in the glory of its role in the MPAJA's wartime activities. In line with Communist International (Comintern) policy enunciated in 1941, it had achieved the immediate goal of defeating the Fascist powers. Now it was free to devote its attention to its objectives of winning the 'national revolution' by expelling the colonial masters from Malaya and then creating a social revolution.

In the chaos of the immediate post-war years, the MPAJA was the only armed, well-organized group within Malaya. It took over regional government, and the British were forced to rely upon it in many areas to maintain law and order. The MPAJA used this opportunity to deal harshly with old enemies and collaborators. Because of the prominent role the Japanese had given the Malays during the Occupation, many Malays were classified by the MPAJA as 'collaborators'. The violence initiated by ideology, however, quickly became interpreted as an inter-ethnic conflict. The Malays organized themselves under their village secular and religious leaders to fight what they saw as the 'Chinese' MPAJA/MCP. Even after the British returned communal killings continued, and as late as 1948 complete order had still not been restored throughout Malaya.

Isolated clashes between Chinese and Malays had occurred periodically in previous decades, but never before with such intensity. Up to the mid-1920s the Malays expressed concern at their steadily weakening economic and social position in their own country. While they compared themselves unfavourably with the rapid advances of the migrant Chinese and Indian communities, Malays rarely voiced a violent antagonism towards these groups. But by the late 1920s and the 1930s certain political and economic developments were to radicalize Malay attitudes towards other Asian groups, but especially towards the Chinese. The Chinese in Malaya became more politicized through the activities of the Chinese Communist Party and the revived Kuomintang. There was an increase in Chinese schools in Malaya using *kuo yu* (Mandarin) and teaching subjects more orientated to China than Malaya. British measures towards decentralization further weakened Malay authority and coincided with attempts by the Chinese to increase their own participation in government. Malay fears of Chinese domination were accentuated by the census of 1931 which revealed that for the first time in British Malaya, there were more Chinese (1,709,392) than Malays (1,644,173). The world-wide Depression of the 1930s, which hit Malaya's vulnerable export economy especially hard, led to a greater competition among the ethnic communities for the economic tasks previously dominated by one or another group. All these factors transformed Malay attitudes towards the Chinese from one of envy but toleration, to distrust. By the late 1920s and the 1930s the Malay press carried articles attacking the Chinese, and Malay groups began to organize to safeguard Malay interests. Formed in various states, these Malay associations met in a Pan-Malayan Malay Congress in Kuala Lumpur in August 1939, and in Singapore in December 1940. The latter meeting was attended by eleven associations, including Sarawak and Brunei.[27] Even prior to the outbreak of World War II, therefore, the Malays throughout the peninsula and even in Borneo had acted jointly in face of what they considered to be Chinese threats to Malay rights and privileges.

During the Occupation the anti-Chinese feeling among Malays was further encouraged by the Japanese who used paramilitary units composed mainly of Malays to fight Chinese resistance groups. The communal violence of the post-war years can thus be regarded as a logical outcome of divisive ethnic policies and attitudes which had developed gradually over the period of colonial rule and reached a peak in the late 1920s and the 1930s. The implications of the post-war violence were not lost on the people of Malaya. While independence was a desirable goal, there were some who expressed doubts that any independent Malayan government would be able to restrain ethnic enmities once the mediating hand of the colonial power had been removed.

The concern for the future of a Malayan nation resulted in a new type of nationalism not associated with any particular ethnic group nor with any organization holding out radical solutions for society. The aims of this group of nationalists were '. . . to create a real and valid sense of loyalty to Malaya among all races by inspiring in the Malay a national loyalty over and above his natural loyalty to the Sultans, as symbols of his racial history and traditions, and educating him to an adult understanding of his place as a Malayan; and by weaning the non-Malay races from their nostalgia for the homelands of their ancestors, by putting into their hands the real basis of an enduring loyalty'.[28] This group, which became the basis of the Malayan Democratic Union party, consisted principally of English-educated, Malaya-born individuals of all groups who believed the future lay with a multiethnic united Malaya, including Singapore.

The appeal of such 'Malayan' nationalists was timely, since by October 1945 the British had rejected their pre-war policy of recognizing the sovereignty of the Malay Sultans, the autonomy of the Malay states, and Malay special privileges. Despite the fact that two Malay battalions had fought with the British at Singapore in 1942, the refusal of the Sultans to evacuate with the British during the Japanese invasion and the activities of the Malays in Japanese-sponsored organizations like PETA brought disfavour on the entire Malay community. By contrast, the British believed that the Chinese and Indian communities had remained generally loyal to the colonial power. Such attitudes contributed to the formulation of plans for a Malayan Union in the war years which reversed the previous policy of maintaining the primacy of the Malays over the other Asian communities in Malaya.

Malayan Union and the Federation of Malaya

In 1944 the British government adopted a plan by Edward Gent, the Assistant Permanent Under-Secretary for the Colonies, to incorporate the FMS, UMS, Penang and Melaka into a Malayan Union, while making Singapore a separate crown colony. Although the idea of a unified administrative unit for British Malaya had been proposed before, it was now given greater urgency by the need for centralized direction to oversee post-war economic recovery as a prelude to self-government. Britain felt bound to declare its intention of returning independence to Malaya because it was a signatory to the Atlantic Charter declaring the right of nations to self-determination. This was one of the principal tenets of American foreign policy, and British self-interest argued for conforming with the desires of their rich and powerful ally. The Malayan Union, therefore, was presented as a necessary step toward the granting of independence to a united nation in which each group would have equal rights.

In the Union plan it was considered best to maintain Singapore as a separate colony because of fears that Malayan opposition to Singapore would prevent acceptance of the Union. There was the traditional distrust among Malaya's business interests of being subordinated to Singapore's own commercial concerns. Furthermore, the inclusion of a liberal citizenship policy in the Union plans was bound to arouse suspicion among the Malay leaders who feared being swamped by Singapore's large Chinese population. In any case the British government saw the value of retaining Singapore as a naval base for its own strategic operations in the Far East.

In formulating the Malayan Union proposal, Gent had paid little attention to representations made by various Malayan groups operating in exile which generally favoured a federation including Singapore. But such ideas were not acceptable to the British government, which believed that the period of military administration in Malaya in the immediate post-war years would provide ample time to gauge the feelings of the population on such matters.

The Borneo territories had been included in an earlier plan but later omitted because of the added complications they would present to an already difficult Union proposal. In April 1946 civil administration was restored to Sarawak, and Vyner Brooke returned temporarily to rule the country. Military administration in North Borneo lasted slightly longer, but in July Sarawak and North Borneo, including Labuan, became crown colonies. Both Brooke and the British North Borneo Company agreed to this transfer of authority because the cost of post-war reconstruction in their respective territories was beyond their resources. Furthermore, Company rule in North Borneo was no longer adequate to meet the needs of a modernizing state. Many of its officials now simply became incorporated into the British Colonial Service. The situation in Sarawak was more complex because of opposition to the transfer which was led by two members of the Brooke family and some senior Malay officials. Only by a narrow vote were Raja Vyner's proposals approved, paving the way for Sarawak's incorporation as a British crown colony on 1 July 1946. Opposition within Sarawak never completely subsided, and in 1949 the British Governor was assassinated by opponents of Sarawak's new status.

In the final proposal for a Malayan Union, therefore, it was adjudged safer to confine it to the Malay peninsula. In the autumn of 1944 the Colonial Office invited Sir Harold MacMichael to undertake a mission to Malaya after the war to secure new treaty arrangements with the Malay Sultans incorporating the ideas of the Malayan Union. On 3 September 1945, as the British were reoccupying Malaya, the British Cabinet gave its final authorization to the new Malayan policy and agreed to MacMichael's mission. Obtaining the signatures from the Sultans for the new treaties was not as difficult as was envisaged, and by 21 December every Sultan or Regent had consented to the new terms. Some expressed grave reservations but were at the same time eager to demonstrate their loyalty to the British since their role during the Occupation had come under criticism. All previous treaties signed over the years in which the British had acknowledged the sovereign rights of the Malay rulers were annulled. The pretence that the British were merely assisting the Malay rulers to govern their lands was finally removed.

Having obtained these treaties, the British then revealed the Malayan Union Plan in a White Paper in late January 1946. The plan was to create a unitary state comprising the FMS, UMS, Penang and Melaka with a central government, a governor, and legislative and executive councils. The Malay Sultans were to retain their positions but sovereignty was to be transferred to the British Crown. All citizens of the new Malayan Union would have equal rights, including admission to the administrative civil service. Finally, Malayan citizenship was to be extended to all without discrimination as to race or creed.

Contrary to British expectations, the normally apathetic Malay population rose as one in strong protest to this new scheme. Nor were the Chinese and Indian communities particularly enthusiastic and in fact even criticized some of the provisions. Retired British members of the Malayan Civil Service and Malay leaders led the attack on the Union plan, accusing MacMichael of using 'methods of intimidation' to obtain the Malay Sultans' agreement to the new treaties. The Old Malayan lobby in Parliament joined with such important ex-Malayan Civil Service Officers as Swettenham, G. Maxwell, Winstedt, Clementi and Guillemard to write letters to national newspapers and to petition Downing Street. Such activity created the impression of a groundswell of opposition to the Malayan Union and proved ultimately successful in bringing about the repeal of the Union scheme.

In Malaya itself the rulers were swept up in the anti-Malayan Union feeling and protested at the manner in which MacMichael had obtained their signatures for the new treaties. They rejected the Union plan and proposed to send a mission to London to seek its repeal. But the Malay point of view was to be most effectively advanced by a new political force which arose to channel Malay opposition to the Union. In March 1946 some 200 Malay delegates representing forty-one associations gathered in Kuala Lumpur for a Pan-Malayan Malay Congress to discuss a Malay national movement and a co-ordinated campaign against the Malayan Union. At this Congress it was agreed to form the Pertubuhan Kebangsaan Melayu Bersatu, or the United Malays National Organization (UMNO). At the next Pan-Malayan Malay Congress held in Johor Baru later in May, UMNO was inaugurated and Dato Onn Ja'afar, Chief Minister of Johor, chosen as its first president. This Congress also declared the MacMichael treaties to be invalid and demanded the repeal of the Malayan Union. Despite strong Malay opposition, the British government initially refused to withdraw the Malayan Union plans. Instead, it pressed for an immediate implementation so that the British Military Administration, which had governed Malaya since the end of the Japanese Occupation, could be removed. But when the Malayan Union was inaugurated on 1 April 1946, the opposition was so effective that the plan was never brought into effect. It was finally revoked in its entirety after 1 February 1948 when the Federation of Malaya was created.

The substitution of the new concept of a Federation of Malaya for the unpopular Malayan Union scheme was accomplished principally through negotiations between the British, the Malay rulers and UMNO. In the Federation the sovereignty of the Sultans, the individuality of the states, and Malay special privileges were upheld. A strong unitary central government was established with legislative powers, though the states were assured jurisdiction over a number of important fields. Citizenship was made more restrictive than in the earlier Malayan Union scheme, requiring residence of at least fifteen during the previous twenty-five years, a declaration of permanent settlement, and a certain competence in Malay or English. A High Commissioner was appointed, rather than a Governor, as a symbolic gesture that authority derived from the Malay Sultans rather than the British Crown.

The Federation was a victory for the Malays and was greeted with some dismay among other ethnic groups. Those who opposed the Federation proposals, however, lacked the unity at home and the powerful Parliamentary lobby and other supporters in London which had been crucial in the revoking of the Malayan Union scheme. The Chinese in particular felt betrayed since they believed that they had sacrificed more and had been the most loyal towards the British during the recent war. Some of the discontented Chinese now saw their only hope for a just society in the promises of the MCP.

The MCP and the Emergency

The MCP had been in a good position to seize power in the interim between the Japanese surrender and the return of the British in September 1945, but it had decided against such an action for various reasons, among which the most compelling was the military one. First, the MCP's forces were small, ill-equipped and unprepared to oppose a returning British force. Secondly, the Japanese with their 100,000 troops were bound by the orders of Admiral Louis Mountbatten of the Southeast Asia Command and would not have hesitated to use force to suppress the communists, especially after their bitter encounters during the Occupation. Thirdly, the communist parties in Britain and China and the Secretary-General of the MCP, Lai Tek, had urged that the MCP adopt a moderate policy. It therefore postponed violent action and decided to conduct an 'open and legal' struggle. The arms which it had collected during and immediately after the war were hidden in the jungle for the future struggle, and the MPAJA was disbanded. In its place the MPAJA Ex-Comrades Association was created to maintain liaison with the former guerrillas.[29]

The MCP began its legal activities by becoming a member of the Governor's Advisory Council in Singapore in 1945 and by being involved with such groups as the Malayan Democratic Union and the Malayan Nationalist Party. But its greatest success came in its establishment of the General Labour Unions (GLU) in Singapore in October 1945 and later in all the states of Malaya. The principal strength of the GLU was among the Chinese, but there were efforts at involving more Indians and Malays. These were only partially successful. Indian radicals eagerly participated in the unions, but the Indian estate workers began forming their own Indian labour unions and only much later became part of the communist-dominated GLU. The few Malays employed in various industries were reluctant to become part of a Chinese-controlled union, especially in times of communal tension. The power of the

GLU was demonstrated convincingly in strikes and rallies in Singapore and Malaya, but the GLU was not in total control. There is evidence of spontaneous strikes and unionization independent of the GLU, especially in the first half of 1946. Nonetheless, at the height of its power in early 1947, the Pan-Malayan GLU, renamed the Pan-Malayan Federation of Trade Unions (PMFTU) in March 1947, directly controlled 80—90 per cent of the unions in Malaya.[30]

The activities of the labour unions with their unrelenting wage demands combined with a temporary drop in world rubber prices in the middle of 1947 caused employers to organize and seek government action to restrict union operations. Increasing violence, especially against European planters, convinced the government of the need to strengthen the already stringent law of 1940 governing trade union activity. New government measures were introduced at the end of 1947 requiring all unions to register and imposing as a condition for registration certain terms on the eligibility of union officials to hold office. In this way the government successfully weakened the authority of the PMFTU over the trade union movement. Re-establishment of police authority in the countryside, strict government supervision of union accounts, and the generally improved situation of the workers in 1947—8 were further factors in the diminishing influence of the PMFTU and hence the MCP in the labour unions of Singapore and Malaya.

The MCP was also experiencing serious difficulties within its own organization. In March 1947 the Secretary-General Lai Tek disappeared, and it was later revealed by the MCP that he had been a double agent. This revelation brought suspicion and recriminations within the MCP, crippling its ability to act decisively. One outcome of Lai Tek's disappearance was a strengthening of the faction which had consistently argued for an armed struggle. At the Fourth Plenary Session it was decided to prepare for this struggle by moving all party activities underground. Trade unions were encouraged not only to improve the welfare of workers but also to lead the workers 'to the road of violent action'. A spate of murders and attacks on European estate managers in June 1948 alerted the authorities to a change of direction in MCP policy. Already some concern had been expressed at the increase in communist propaganda and the growing number of violent incidents connected with industrial disputes. The High Commissioner seriously considered banning the MCP, regarding it as the root cause of these disturbances. Although neither side took the first step in openly declaring war, continuing murders of Europeans on the estates finally forced the government to proclaim a State of Emergency throughout Malaya on 18 June 1948.

In the first year of the Emergency the guerrilla main forces were initially successful against mining and estate personnel and government officials, but they soon lost the initiative and were forced to take refuge in deep jungle. In the first half of 1949, the MCP set aside its earlier policy of attack in order to regroup, retrain and concentrate on developing strong popular support through the Min Yuen, or mass organizations. In the beginning these Min Yuen provided supplies, intelligence and auxiliary fighting units, but as the situation became desperate in later years, the Min Yuen became increasingly involved in the fighting. The Min Yuen was especially active in the Chinese squatter rural settlements which had arisen in the Depression of the early 1930s and in the Occupation years on forest reserves, Malay reservations, and on privately owned mining and agricultural estates. While the Japanese policy of encouraging food production on all available land was responsible for some of these settlements, their proliferation reflects a land hunger among many Chinese which was already evident prior to World War II. Throughout the Occupation the squatter settlements had generously provided the MPAJA with food, shelter and recruits. When the British civil government was re-established in Malaya, the MCP championed the cause of the Chinese squatters against efforts by the authorities to evict or control them. Partly in gratitude, partly through fear, these same Chinese squatter settlements, principally in remote areas with little government authority, again provided the MCP with support during the Emergency.

Communist activity recurred with great ferocity in the middle of 1949, reaching its peak in the first week of September 1950 when a record sixty-five major incidents were recorded. This new offensive highlighted the difficulties the government faced in trying to eliminate the sources of communist support in the local Chinese communities. In addition, the various British-led police and military units were beset by problems of morale and organization. A fresh initiative was clearly needed, and thus in March 1950 the government announced the appointment of Lieutenant-General Sir Harold Briggs as the new Director of Operations in the Emergency. Briggs identified his principal goals as the elimination of the Min Yuen and the communist main forces known as the Malayan Races Liberation Army (MRLA). His plan was to establish complete security within the populated areas in order to instil local authorities with confidence. It was hoped that this confidence would lead to a flow of intelligence to the British, enabling them to destroy the Min Yuen and hence deprive the MRLA of any support. Without access to the Min Yuen for food, information, or recruitment the MRLA would be eventually forced to undertake bolder action and would be destroyed by the Security Forces fighting on their own grounds.

Implementation of the Briggs Plan was facilitated by wide-ranging security measures announced by the High Commissioner Sir Henry Gurney in mid-December 1950. Malaya was now effectively placed on a war footing. Conscription for the military and police force was introduced, employment controlled, and special powers created to regulate society and destroy any communist guerrilla support. Armed with these measures, the government began the relocation of Chinese squatter communities from areas of strong Min Yuen presence. The communist guerrillas were all too aware of the devastating effect such a programme would have on their activities, and they therefore stepped up their attacks on the resettlement areas. By the second half of 1951 guerrilla incidents had moved from individual terrorist acts to large-scale action involving about thirty to fifty men. What Briggs had envisaged was now coming to pass. The continuing isolation of the main force guerrillas from their civilian sources of support led them to attack targets in the homegrounds of the security forces and hence expose themselves to unfriendly populated areas. The guerrillas were unsuccessful in disrupting or preventing the resettlement of Chinese squatters, and by the beginning of 1952 the programme was four-fifths completed with some 400,000 settled in about 400 'New Villages'.[31]

Despite this setback, the communists struck a severe blow to the morale of the government and to those who had come to believe in the ability of the British to provide security. On 6 October 1951 the High Commissioner Sir Henry Gurney was assassinated by a platoon of guerrillas on the long, narrow, one-way road leading up to the small resort of Fraser's Hill, about 105 kilometres outside Kuala Lumpur. The authorities had barely recovered from the shock when a month later the guerrillas inflicted the heaviest weekly casualties ever suffered by government forces. Briggs's retirement in December, followed shortly by his death, and the departure in the same month of the Commissioner of Police, further contributed to the demoralization within the country.

The MCP, however, was unable to take advantage of the disarray in the government because it was undergoing severe internal strains over questions of leadership and interpretation of the Communist Party line. A new programme of action was adopted by the Central Committee of the MCP in October 1951 emphasizing the subordination of military activities to political goals. Selective attacks were to be made principally for purposes of morale, propaganda and securing arms. The more important struggle, however, would be the awakening of the revolutionary awareness of the masses and the guerrilla units. Unfortunately for the MCP, its new political initiative coincided with the forging of a political alliance in 1952 between UMNO and the Malayan Chinese Association (MCA). The MCA had only been established in February 1949, partially in response to UMNO's founding three years earlier. But as a result of the successful co-operation of the Selangor branches of both parties in a local election, a new political alliance was born which was increasingly viewed as the only hope for a viable independent Malayan government.[32] With the British announcement of their intention to grant independence to Malaya, the MCP programme lost its momentum and communist hopes for control quickly faded.

Independence

In April 1949 the British Parliament made a commitment to Malaya's independence which was reaffirmed the following March by the Prime Minister. When Lieutenant-General Sir Gerald Templer arrived in Malaya in early February 1952 as the new High Commissioner he declared that his immediate objective was the formation of a united Malayan nation. Towards this goal and that of undermining and eventually destroying the MCP, Templer introduced local elections, village councils and Chinese citizenship to over half the Chinese population; merged the War Council with the Executive Council; and enabled the Chinese for the first time to enter the Malayan Civil Service. In April 1954 Templer announced that an early election for the Federal Council would be held in 1955, thereby indicating that Malaya was drawing closer to independence. Towards the end of that year leaders of the major Malayan political parties were appointed by the government to the War Executive Council so that they would be able to view Emergency operation planning at first hand and contribute to the destruction of the MCP.

Political developments within Malaya itself had moved in an unexpected direction but one which pleased the British authorities. Since the government had stressed the need for a *united* Malayan nation, the creation of communal parties had been viewed with some misgivings. However, in the Kuala Lumpur municipal elections of February 1952 the Selangor branches of the UMNO and the MCA successfully contested the elections as a united front. From this local initiative grew a national policy in which both parties retained their separate identities and political objectives while acting as one body in determining the candidates and the party to contest a particular seat. The incorporation of the Malayan Indian Congress into the Alliance as a full-pledged partner in 1954 was viewed by the colonial government as a positive step towards the creation of a united Malayan nation. In the federal elections of July 1955, the Alliance demonstrated its overwhelming support by obtaining 81 per cent of the vote and fifty-one of the fifty-two contested seats.[33]

As a result of this victory, the Alliance Party's views were given prominence by the Reid Commission, formed in 1955 to prepare a constitution for an independent Malaya. Nevertheless, the final document was not totally satisfactory even to the Alliance. Among the most controversial features of this Merdeka ('Independence') Constitution were those dealing with citizenship and the special privileges of Malays. There was to be a single nationality, in which all persons in Malaya could qualify as citizens either by birth or by fulfilling requirements of residence, language and oath of loyalty. UMNO's acceptance of this provision was only obtained in return for a guarantee of Malay privileges. In the new Constitution the Paramount Ruler (Yang Dipertuan Agung) was given the special responsibility of safeguarding the special position of the Malays, as well as the 'legitimate interests' of the other communities. The latter clause reflects the Commission's dilemma of attempting to satisfy Malay demands while preserving the original principle of a single nationality with equal citizenship. The Merdeka Constitution also provided for a Paramount Ruler to be chosen by the Conference of Rulers (Durbar) on the basis of seniority for a term of five years; a parliament composed of a wholly elected House of Representatives (Dewan Rakyat) and an appointed Senate (Dewan Negara); an allocation of power designated in subjects under a Federal List, State List and Concurrent List; and a guarantee of civil rights and of judicial review. On 15 August 1957 the Legislative Council ratified the Constitution, and on 31 August the independence of the Federation of Malaya was proclaimed.

A State of Emergency still existed at the time of independence, but the critical stage had passed. The resettlement of Chinese squatters into New Villages, enforcement of strict food controls, and more effective intelligence had made it increasingly difficult for the communists to obtain support. The concept of 'White Areas' was introduced in September 1953 in which areas considered to be free of guerrilla influence were rewarded by having their food restrictions and curfews eased. There was, therefore, an inducement for people to co-operate with the government so that their area could also be declared 'white'. By the time of Templer's departure in July 1954, victory was in sight as large numbers of guerrillas were destroyed and their Min Yuen dismantled. From mid-1954 the government also gained the upper hand in jungle fighting as *orang asli* groups were weaned away from communist guerrilla units.

The difficulties faced by the MCP and the announced government intention of holding federal elections in July 1955 as a preparatory step towards independence had convinced the MCP leadership of the need to seek a meeting with the Alliance leaders. In December three MCP leaders, headed by Chin Peng, met Tunku Abdul Rahman, president of UMNO and the new chief of the Federation Government; Tan Cheng Lock, leader of the MCA; and David Marshall, Chief Minister of Singapore. The principal point which seems to have emerged from the talks was that legal co-existence between the communists and the other parties was impossible. MCP members would have to abandon the Party's goals and activities if they were to be accepted back into Malayan society. The MCP leaders refused to countenance an idea which was tantamount to surrender and thus destroyed any hopes in the Party of obtaining a political settlement before a military one.

The government delegation was secure in the knowledge that the war against the communists was being won. The government's programme of psychological warfare, food denial and the relentless pressure of the Security forces contributed to the disintegration of guerrilla organization and the lowering of MCP morale. In 1958 large numbers of guerrillas surrendered, and major guerrilla incidents were reduced to one a month. The MRLA as an organized military unit ended in 1958, and the few remaining guerrillas retreated to the Thai border or to inaccessible jungle areas. By the end of 1958, the government considered the communist armed threat to Malaya to have ceased and the State of Emergency was officially ended on 31 July 1960. The Alliance government, which had won another impressive victory in the second federal elections in 1959, could now devote its full attention to the creation of a united Malayan nation out of the divisions resulting from British and Japanese colonial rule and exacerbated by the communist insurgency.

By the end of British rule in 1957, the new Federation of Malaya had inherited a number of features from the colonial past which proved a mixed blessing. The economy appeared healthy with 85 per cent of the total gross export earnings coming from rubber and tin,[34] though fears were already being expressed at their disproportionate strength in the export sector. A large measure of Malaya's economic success in the export field was due to direct and indirect governmental influence. By establishing law and order, creating an infrastructure, legislating a labour policy favourable to industry and facilitating the movement of European capital and expertise into Malaya, the government contributed to the spectacular success of rubber and tin as export earners for the colonial ruler. But in the process of attaining this economic goal, the British had allocated specific economic tasks to the various ethnic groups in the society. The Europeans provided the managers and the skilled personnel to supervise the whole economic development; the Chinese were initially recruited for work in the tin-mining industry; the Indians were assigned the task of working on the rubber estates; and the Malays were directed towards providing food for the growing economic machine created by the colonial government. This simplistic conception was modified by the need for local English-educated clerks and administrators to staff the ever-expanding government bureaucracy and business enterprises, and by the government's dedication to 'conciliate' the Malay ruling classes by involving them in the governing of the New Malaya. These considerations allowed a few privileged members to rise above the economic functions allotted to their particular ethnic groups.

Having made these economic decisions for the colony, the British could then fulfil their self-conceived role as civilized rulers by providing a primary education in the vernacular for Malays and by overseeing similar education in the Chinese and Indian vernacular languages. Almost no attempt was made to go beyond primary schooling since the government viewed education as a means of assuring a people contented in their assigned lot. The exception was the privileged upper strata of the three ethnic groups who, through English-medium instruction, were similarly to fill their specific role in colonial society. Education in British Malaya was therefore the handmaiden of the colonial economy, maintaining, except for a few members of the élite, the ethnic divisions within the community.

A similar judgement could be made about the role of colonial government in Malaya. The ongoing debates on decentralization masked a heavy underlay of concern that the growing export industries within the colony would be ill-served by the different administrative structures within Malaya itself. The ability of individual state governments to manage the export commodities within their boundaries was the measure by which the British decided the extent of decentralization. It was no mere coincidence that the east coast Malay states with few export commodities were practically free of colonial interference. In later years the government was quick to respond to the needs of the tin and rubber industries by agreeing to various Malaya-wide controls to maintain prices and ensure their profitability.

With the undermining of colonial rule during the Occupation and the immediate post-war debates on self-determination of nations, the British began preparations for the eventual independence of Malaya. But the arguments over the form which this preparatory stage was to take, whether union or federation, provided a context in which the major ethnic groups began to jockey for a favourable position when independence came. The British had created a multi-ethnic society and had successfully maintained the individual groups within a colonial framework. The chances of this British-created unit surviving independence had seemed especially remote with the outbreak of the communist insurrection. The State of Emergency which was declared to deal with the danger revealed some of the serious ethnic divisions existing within the community. Although the government's eventual victory over the communists had not yet been achieved by 1957 when the independent Federation of Malaya was announced, the communist threat had all but disappeared. But the communal threat remained, a legacy of colonial rule, which would determine the survival or eventual demise of the new nation.

The Forging of a Nation, 1957–80

Since independence the principal preoccupation of Malaya's government leaders has been the preservation of the country's fragile unity and the welding of a truly united nation. The success of the Emergency measures in dealing with the communists removed one major threat to unity, but there still remained the task of reconciling the demands of the communal groups in the creation of their new nation. Under colonial rule the British had orchestrated a smoothly functioning political and economic entity in which each ethnic group was allotted a specific role. In this colonial world, the British saw themselves as supreme arbiters, acting impartially and dispensing justice throughout the land. To a considerable extent the British role had been accepted by the society, and some groups genuinely believed that given the existing situation the colonial presence was desirable. The years of political conditioning could not be overcome simply by the transferral of sovereignty to a Malayan government. With the dismantling of British hegemony, each ethnic group feared being pushed aside by the others, and the post-independence years witnessed a scramble for dominance in areas hitherto restricted to one or another group. Each ethnic community wanted a share of what the others had and yet there was insufficient mutual trust to believe that the sharing would be done equitably. All governments in Malaya (and Malaysia since 1963) have been concerned with solving this vexing problem, which has continued to pose a threat to the nation's survival.

Independent Malaya/Malaysia: Sources and Historiographical Problems

In looking at the sources from the mid-twentieth century to the present, a historian is confronted with an altogether different historiographical problem from earlier centuries. Events are often too recent to determine their true significance in the broad sweep of Malaysian history, even though the proliferation of studies in many different fields reflects the growing sophistication of scholarship. Highly specialized studies by political scientists, sociologists, anthropologists, economists, educationalists, ethnomusicologists and so on deal in detail with many aspects of Malaysian society. They are able to draw from an infinite variety of sources, such as voluminous government reports, newspapers, journals, radio and television broadcasts, gazettes, public speeches and private interviews. To a greater extent than ever before the purely national scene must also be considered in terms of international developments, as increasing improvements in communications gives events overseas an unprecedented impact and influence on local society.

This vast body of material, combined with the recentness of the events themselves, presents a formidable task to an historian writing about Malaysia's immediate past. Events chosen for discussion may ultimately be judged insignificant, while others mentioned only in passing may prove to be vital in understanding subsequent events. However, an historian's perception of the past can provide him with the justification for his selection and interpretation of contemporary events.

The Alliance

Because of the legacy of colonial rule in Malaya, the most important political parties are understandably communal ones representing the interests of individual ethnic groups. But to the credit of the young nation's leaders, the main communal political parties have managed to evolve a working relationship with each other which has become the hallmark of Malaysian politics. The first successful trial of intercommunal party co-operation was in the local elections of 1952, when the Selangor branch of UMNO joined with the MCA. From their electoral victory grew the concept of an alliance between the major ethnic parties which would create some consensus for government. The dangers of communal violence were too great to ignore, and the Alliance, as this loose political organization came to be called, appeared the ideal means by which each ethnic group could be heard and compromises reached.

The dominant group within the Alliance was UMNO, led by Dato Onn Ja'afar from its founding in 1946 until 1951, and by Tunku Abdul Rahman from 1951 to 1970. The initial success of the party among Malays was due to its ability to harness Malay opinion in the fight against the Malayan Union. This was done through Malays in government service, who were able to use the administrative structure in the states for political mobilization. Senior Malay government officials organized district level Malay officials, who in turn enlisted the help of the *penghulu*, the village heads, to arouse the villagers to action. Via the colonial administration, UMNO was thus able to use the traditional Malay leadership at the lower levels in order to emerge as a mass political party.

Although the majority of the Malays regarded UMNO as their spokesman, there were other groups vying for Malay allegiance. Various Malay radical groups had mushroomed, but they were often seen as too extreme and their earlier tendency to associate with the Indonesian nationalist movements and with some Chinese-dominated groups alienated the conservative rural Malays. One group which did appeal to the villagers and which came to challenge UMNO, especially in the northern Malay states, was the Pan-Malayan Islamic Party, or in Malay, Persatuan Islam Sa-Tanah Melayu (PAS). At first, as the All-Malaya Islamic Association, it participated as part of UMNO but later adopted the name PAS in order to contest the 1955 Federal elections as a separate political party. Its strength derived from its appeal to Islam as the basis of a Malay-dominated society and in its demands for the preservation of Malay privileges. The principal PAS stronghold has been in Kelantan and Trengganu, two states with the highest national percentage of Malays and with some of the lowest levels of modern economic development. In 1955 it gained the only seat not won by the Alliance Party, hence earning that lone PAS parliamentarian the dubious distinction of being known as 'Mr Opposition'. Unlike UMNO it relied upon the 'sub-élites' of teachers and pupils in Moslem schools and in the Malay primary schools to disseminate the party's ideas to the villagers. By the 1959 Federal elections PAS, under the leadership of Dr Burhanuddin, had made considerable inroads into UMNO's support by appealing to all Malays on religious and communal issues.

The MCA was the second major party in the Alliance. Its guiding principle has always been the maintenance of ethnic harmony through accommodation. It was felt that by retaining access to the top leadership in the government, the needs of the Chinese community could be made known and the MCA would be recognized as the defender of Chinese interests. As time went on, however, acceptance of the MCA as the representative of the Malayan Chinese considerably lessened. Initially, the MCA faced difficulties because it primarily expressed the views of small Western-educated business and professional Chinese and had to win the support of numerous other Chinese interest groups, such as guilds, clan associations and trade unions. Only the ability of Tan Cheng Lock, its founding president and a respected Straits Chinese, and other MCA leaders in effecting a working relationship with the principal figures in UMNO assured the survival of the Alliance. A common educational experience in English schools not only forged a bond among the leaders of the Alliance parties but also made it possible for them to communicate meaningfully with each other. But as the MCA sought to expand its political following, other individuals — the products of Chinese education — began to play a more active part in MCA politics. More strongly communally oriented, they were more representative of the concerns of the majority of Malayan Chinese.

When the MCA's ability to operate within the Alliance appeared threatened by the demands of this new faction, the old guard suspended its leaders.

A third faction arose from the power struggle within the MCA. While sympathetic to the communal demands made by the party's radical wing, it was also convinced of the need to maintain good relations with UMNO in order to keep the MCA's position in the Alliance. This third faction emerged in 1957 around Dr Lim Chong Eu and obtained the support of young left-wing Western-educated intellectuals in the cities of Kuala Lumpur, Penang and Ipoh. Small in number, it was nonetheless a highly motivated and effective group, and in 1958 Lim was voted president of the MCA over Tan Cheng Lock. Although Lim assured Tunku Abdul Rahman that the MCA would continue to co-operate with UMNO, the close personal friendship between Tan and the Tunku, a major factor in the two parties' smooth relationship, was now absent.

As the 1959 Federal elections drew near, the new MCA leadership fought hard to retain the favourable treatment the MCA had received in 1955. In the latter case, the MCA had been allocated slightly less than half the positions on the Alliance ticket, even though the Chinese then made up 11·2 per cent of the total electorate. Because of the new citizenship laws the Chinese electorate in 1959 had increased to 35·6 per cent of the total, but the Alliance National Council had informally agreed on only twenty-eight places for the MCA. Lim, pressing for forty positions, then made his demand public in such a way that it appeared tantamount to an ultimatum. The Tunku replied by announcing that UMNO would contest the election without the MCA. Unwilling to risk an election alone, the MCA leadership hastily reconsidered and succeeded in having the MCA retained within the Alliance. The price, however, was high. The extreme communal faction within the MCA lost influence, Lim resigned as president, and only MCA members acceptable to the Tunku appeared on the Alliance ticket for the 1959 elections. As a result of this 'July crisis' the Alliance became a much more unified body, clearly responsive to the Tunku's leadership, while the position of the MCA as the proponent of Chinese interests became more and more untenable. The Chinese now began to look elsewhere for the leadership which they believed essential to prevent their total submergence by the Malays.

The third member of the Alliance was the Malayan Indian Congress (MIC). It was the weakest of the three parties in the Alliance, not only because of the small size of the Indian electorate, which was only 7·4 per cent of the total in 1959, but also because it had little real support in the Indian community. A glaring weakness was its failure to establish links with the lower-class Indian labourers who comprised a large part of Malaya's Indian population. Since the Indian community is divided and comprises less than a quarter of the electorate in any constituency, the MIC's principal concern has been to remain in the Alliance in order to obtain whatever concessions it is able to extract from the dominant UMNO partner. Many Indians have expressed dissatisfaction with the MIC's lacklustre performance in championing Indian interests within the Alliance. At best the MIC is regarded as simply 'tagging along' with the UMNO and the MCA, and at worst, it is accused of sacrificing Indian interests to achieve the government's goals. As with the relations between the other two members, the success of the MIC in the Alliance in the early years was largely due to a close personal bond between the Tunku and V. T. Sambanthan, the MIC president, who was an estate owner educated in both Tamil and English. When certain more radical communal-minded members of the MIC threatened to jeopardize its relations with UMNO, they were removed from the party. After 1958 the old leadership maintained firm control over the MIC and worked harmoniously with the Alliance National Council.

By the time of the 1959 Federal elections the Alliance, registered in 1958 as a political party independent of its member parties, was centralized and responding as one to the directions of Tunku Abdul Rahman. Nonetheless, the Alliance had only become a viable political vehicle because of compromises which had been reached by the three parties on the sensitive issues of citizenship, education and Malay special privileges. The MCA had wanted the basis of citizenship to be the principle of *jus soli*, whereby all those born in Malaya would automatically become citizens. The UMNO agreed to this in return for an MCA agreement to an educational policy where the Malay language would be compulsory in all schools and a common 'Malayan curriculum' devised for all schools of whatever language medium. The MCA and MIC also accepted the existing four-to-one ratio of Malays to non-Malays in the Malayan Civil Service and the adoption of Malay as the national language. For these concessions the UMNO assured the other two parties that liberal economic policies would be pursued to enable non-Malays to engage in economic activities without fear of confiscation or discriminatory taxation. The Alliance therefore assumed, perhaps unjustifiably, but nevertheless effectively, the role of representing the interests of Malaya's three major ethnic groups. While the more communal-minded politicians probably accurately reflected the dominant thinking of each of these ethnic communities, the Alliance held the reins of power because of the political pragmatism of its leaders and their ability to submerge their differences during elections and work as a team. Similar educational and social backgrounds among the principal leaders contributed significantly to their ability to effect practical solutions to problems. Their methods were often individualistic in nature, involving a widespread use of personal persuasion in dealing with foreign and local financial interest, the bureaucracy, and local state power structures. As the Tunku remarked: 'There are no water-tight compartments in our policies. In my party we are right and centre and left according to what is needed and what we think best.'[1] No other rival political group could amass sufficient seats to challenge the united Alliance, which therefore claimed a mandate to mould a new society from the various competing and frequently antagonistic groups.

The Formation of Malaysia

The Alliance had succeeded in the face of determined opposition in establishing a *modus vivendi* among the three ethnic groups, but this was merely a short-term solution. The eventual aim of the government was to create a new Malayan citizen whose loyalties would be to the nation, and not to any particular communal group. Such a goal appeared formidable indeed even to the most optimistic of Malaya's leaders. It was something of a surprise, therefore, when the Prime Minister Tunku Abdul Rahman announced in 1961 the idea of an expanded Malaya which would include Singapore, North Borneo, Brunei and Sarawak. The idea itself was not new, having been broached on a number of previous occasions by the British and by various local groups seeking a 'Greater Indonesia' or 'Greater Malaysia'. One author has even suggested that the initiative for the 1961 plan had come from the British government.[2] Whatever the origins of this plan, what puzzled political observers was the willingness of the Alliance government to incorporate Singapore into the proposed union. Malaya had firmly rejected earlier suggestions to the same effect because of fears that Singapore's predominantly Chinese population would upset the ethnic 'balance' and that Singapore's economic interests would clash with those of Malaya. There was also a belief that Malayan politics might become radicalized through contact with Singapore's strong left-wing groups. But by 1961 political circumstances in Singapore had given the Malayan government cause to reconsider its attitude towards union.

Since the introduction of elections in 1948, Singapore's politics had become increasingly dominated by the communists and other radical groups. These groups, however, had been kept under control by the colonial administration. Even when Singapore was given internal self-government in 1958, the British retained the responsibility of maintaining internal security and defence. This transitional constitution was to expire in 1963 and it was expected that Singapore would then demand and obtain full independence with total charge of its own affairs. Such prospects were regarded with some apprehension in Malaya. Tunku Abdul Rahman openly expressed his concern to certain

UMNO officers that an independent Singapore might be controlled by communists, who would then use their independent base to aid their compatriots in Malaya. One way of preventing this was to incorporate Singapore into some federation with Malaya where more moderate forces could counteract the left-wing elements in Singapore. In addition to the concern for national security, the Tunku saw federation as necessary to advance their 'mutual economy'. The economies of these two political units were too closely tied to be working at cross purposes or left to the political vagaries of one or another government. Fears among UMNO members that Singapore's inclusion in the Federation would lead to a swamping of Malaya by Chinese were allayed by the proposal that North Borneo and Sarawak also join and thus restore the ethnic balance. In the event, the major indigenous groups of Borneo frequently saw their interests diverging from those of the Malays. Nonetheless, this argument did serve its political purpose in convincing sceptical UMNO members to approve Singapore's entry into the proposed Federation.

The government in Singapore at the time of the Malaysia Federation proposal was the People's Action Party (PAP) which, led by a young lawyer Lee Kuan Yew, had come to power in 1959. Although its election platform called for some form of union with Malaya in which Singapore would be an autonomous unit, a faction within the party feared that any such union could only be achieved at the expense of Singapore's Chinese. In August 1961 Lee Kuan Yew met Tunku Abdul Rahman to draw up a preliminary agreement for merger. This agreement reflected Lee's success in obtaining specific concessions essential for eliminating some of the more serious objections to union. Singapore would maintain its free port status, a major concession to the business community which envisaged tariff barriers erected to protect Malaya's export-orientated economy. Singapore would also be given special autonomy in education and labour policies as well as a large proportion of its revenues for expenditure in those areas. The way was now smoothed for acceptance of the merger among the more communally minded Chinese population in Singapore, who had feared losing control over Chinese schools and Chinese-dominated labour unions. Because the concessions would give Singapore a degree of political and financial independence, it was agreed that Singapore's representation in the Federal House of Representatives would be limited to fifteen seats, three or four less than would have been allotted proportionate to its population. Despite strong opposition to these proposals by the Socialist Front (Barisan Sosialis) and the United Peoples' Party, a referendum to determine public opinion in Singapore received an overwhelming vote (71·7 per cent) approving merger.

At the time of the Tunku's proposal for a Federation of Malaysia, neither Sarawak nor North Borneo was prepared for self-government. In Sarawak Brooke rule had only ended in 1946 when the British government took control in order to oversee the enormous task of rebuilding the state after the devastation of the war years. The guiding principle of Brooke rule had been the preservation of the indigenous people, especially its largest group, the Iban, from external shocks. As a consequence heavy European or American investment in the economy was discouraged and only minor economic developments permitted. Even in government the Brookes kept the civil service and social services to a minimum, considering these to be infringements on local life. Neither a constitution promulgated on the eve of World War II nor the transfer of sovereignty from the Brookes to the Colonial Office in 1946 led to any substantial changes to the style of rule in Sarawak.

The political situation in North Borneo was in many ways similar to that in Sarawak. In 1946 North Borneo and the island of Labuan were ceded to Great Britain for the same reasons as Sarawak: the cost of post-war construction was considered too daunting for the North Borneo Company to undertake. As a colony North Borneo was given representation in government, but it had not experienced a direct election.

The two Borneo states were initially reluctant to join the Federation because of widespread fears about an unknown future without the paternalistic rule to which they had been accustomed. To overcome this reluctance, Malaya agreed to grant them a number of concessions among which were:

1. Both states would be given authority over immigration, including that of Malaysian citizens from other states.
2. Malay would be recognized as the national language but English would continue as a medium of instruction and as the official language for state government until the State Legislature decided otherwise.
3. Islam would be the official religion but other religions could be propagated.
4. Indigenous peoples of these two states would enjoy special privileges similar to those the Malays enjoyed in Malaya.
5. Financial arrangements would be made to guarantee Federal funds for economic development.
6. A separate Federal Public Service for the two states would be created so that expatriate officers could be retained until sufficient trained local officers became available.

In the 1963 municipal elections the pro-Malaysia Sabah (North Borneo) Alliance and Sarawak Alliance won decisively, giving them the mandate to negotiate terms of entry into the Federation.

Brunei was the fourth state invited by Malaya to join the Federation.

From the middle of the nineteenth century it had steadily relinquished territory, both to the North Borneo Company and to the Brookes. Finally the British government intervened in 1906 by appointing a British Resident and thus guaranteeing the integrity of the small piece of territory still remaining from the once vast kingdom of Brunei. The Sultan of Brunei continued to exercise autocratic powers over his subjects, a task made easier in the early twentieth century by substantial oil revenues flowing to the royal treasury. Nonetheless, the Sultan promulgated a new constitution in 1959 and held elections in 1962 as the first steps towards a constitutional monarchy. But the situation in Brunei took an unexpected turn when a young Brunei Malay, A. M. Azahari, sought to restore the former glory of Brunei by reuniting its former lands now held by North Borneo and Sarawak. Once this was done he hoped to include Indonesia and perhaps even the Philippines into a 'Greater Malaya' with Brunei at its centre. To this end, he contacted political groups in North Borneo, Sarawak, Singapore, Malaya, Indonesia and the Philippines. From the latter two governments he received secret financial and material assistance because of their hostility to the idea of a Malaysian Federation. When Azahari failed to rally support or approval for his plans from the Brunei court, he decided to seize power. The so-called Brunei Revolt on the night of 7 December 1962 was quickly suppressed by British troops, although Azahari himself escaped detention since he was safe in Manila. In the midst of this drama, the Sultan of Brunei became disenchanted with certain financial and constitutional aspects of the Malaysia proposal which would have weakened his position. By joining the federation, the Sultan of Brunei would have to agree to share his state's substantial oil revenues. He also felt he was entitled to a more senior position among the hierarchy of peninsular rulers in line for the revolving post of Yang Dipertuan Agung or Paramount Ruler. Considering these concessions too great a sacrifice, the Sultan finally declined the invitation to become part of the new Malaysia.

In the week following the outbreak of the Brunei Revolt, Indonesia officially proclaimed its support for Azahari and his rebels. Then in January 1963 Indonesia announced a policy of 'Konfrontasi' (Confrontation) against Malaya. Despite Indonesia's attacks on Malayan fishing boats and repeated violations of Malaya's air space, the Alliance government felt no great cause for alarm. Malaya had a defence agreement with Great Britain and knew that it could call on the British for support, as it eventually did. Indonesia's threats to bring economic pressure on Malaya never really eventuated because of the mutual disadvantages such action would incur. Indonesia's diplomatic campaign, however, did arouse some concern. Directed especially at the Afro-Asian Third World nations, this aimed to isolate Malaya and bring about the collapse of the Malaysia Federation scheme. But even this aspect of Indonesia's Confrontation scheme ultimately proved ineffectual.

In early 1962 the Philippine government under President Macapagal also voiced opposition to the Malaysia Federation on the grounds that North Borneo properly belonged to the Philippines. According to Philippine claims, the original 1878 transfer of territory of North Borneo from the Sultanate of Sulu (now part of the Philippines) was in the form of a lease rather than a sale. This had been demonstrated by subsequent regular annual payments from the Company to the Sulu Sultan. Initially, the Malayan government regarded the Philippine claims as having been motivated by domestic political considerations. It adopted a conciliatory attitude but never intended to relinquish Sabah nor allow this claim to interfere in the formation of Malaysia. As the Philippines became more belligerently insistent, Malaya eventually made clear its determination to proceed with the plan of including North Borneo in the proposed Federation.

Because of steadily deteriorating relations between Malaya and its two neighbours, Indonesia and the Philippines, the three heads of government met in Manila in July—August 1963 in order to reach a settlement. At this conference both Indonesia and the Philippines declared their willingness to recognize Malaysia 'provided the support of the people of the Borneo Territories is ascertained by an independent and impartial authority, the Secretary-General of the United Nations or his representative'.[3] Indonesia and the Philippines later repudiated a UN survey demonstrating that North Borneo and Sarawak wished to become part of Malaysia. When the Federation of Malaysia was officially inaugurated on 16 September 1963 both countries broke off diplomatic relations with Malaya. Indonesia conducted a 'crush Malaysia' campaign, and attacks along the borders of Sarawak and Sabah from Indonesian Borneo (Kalimantan) increased in number and severity. Indiscriminate bombing and terrorist acts were also committed by saboteurs landed or dropped secretly into Malaya and Singapore. However, Indonesia's hostile activities were successfully contained by Malaysian and Commonwealth forces, and Malaysia at no time felt endangered by its much larger and more populous neighbour. Relations between the two countries improved after September 1965, when the communists were ousted from all positions of influence in the Indonesian government. In August 1966 a peace agreement was signed between the two nations formally ending 'Confrontation' and indicating Malaysia's intention to have Sabah and Sarawak decide in an election whether they still wished to become part of Malaysia.

The battle over the Philippine claim to North Borneo (renamed Sabah after Federation) was conducted at a diplomatic level. President Marcos's election in mid-1965 had aroused hopes in Kuala Lumpur that some settlement was near, since there were indications that he did not support the Sabah claim. At first, domestic political pressure prevented him from any disavowal of this policy, but by June 1966 the Philippines had extended recognition to Malaysia and simply expressed its intention of continuing to pursue its claims to Sabah.

At the August 1966 talks between Indonesia and Malaysia, the hope was expressed of resuming close and formal ties among the nations of the region. What was envisaged was an association which would incorporate a larger grouping than either ASA (the Association of Southeast Asia, founded in 1960 by Malaya, the Philippines and Thailand) or Maphilindo (an acronym of its member nations Malaya, the Philippines and Indonesia, formed in August 1963). Thus in August 1967 ASEAN (the Association of Southeast Asian Nations) was established, consisting of Malaysia, Singapore, Indonesia, the Philippines and Thailand. While one of the motives for ASEAN's formation was to establish the neutrality of Southeast Asia and thereby prevent World Power intervention, a more important consideration was the hope of regional cooperation. ASEAN's success in both these endeavours has allayed Malaysia's fears of encroachment by its neighbours and reaffirmed its status as a respected sovereign nation.

Maintaining the Unity of the Federation

Even before Confrontation and the Philippine claim to Sabah had been resolved, the new Federation of Malaysia had succumbed to the strains of welding a unity from such disparate states. On 9 August 1965 the Malaysian House of Representatives (Dewan Rakyat) passed a Constitutional Amendment Bill enabling Singapore to secede from the Federation. From the very inception of the Federation proposal, Singapore had posed a problem. The basic reason for Malaya's decision to include Singapore was the widely held view that a left-leaning Singapore outside Malaysia was more dangerous than one within it. But very shortly after the formation of the Federation, the wisdom of this view was challenged. In the Singapore elections of September 1963 and the Malaysian elections of 1964 the Singapore-based PAP did battle with the Malayan Alliance. The PAP concentrated on undermining the MCA's claims to speak for the Chinese, although it assiduously avoided any attack on UMNO. The latter, too, was circumspect and refrained from portraying the PAP as a dangerous foe. Nonetheless, in the political heat engendered in these elections, communal tensions rose and in Singapore serious inter-ethnic clashes occurred. Both the PAP and the Alliance won handily in their respective strongholds. In Singapore in the September 1963 elections the PAP won 37 of the 51 elected seats in the Singapore Legislative Assembly. Across the causeway, in the 1964 Malaysian Federal elections the Alliance government won

89 of the 159 seats in the Dewan Rakyat, undoubtedly helped by the Alliance's call for national solidarity in face of external threats.

As the political struggle between the PAP and the Malayan Alliance intensified, Singaporeans came to regard various economic and political measures taken by the Malaysian government not only as detrimental to their interests but as Alliance attempts to dislodge the PAP from power. In September 1964 discussions were held by the leaders of both parties to consider a coalition government, but the Alliance rejected any such arrangement. It was then that the PAP decided to fight for a 'Malaysian Malaya' as opposed to a 'Malay Malaysia' which it claimed was being imposed by the UMNO-dominated Alliance government. In order to challenge its formidable opponent the PAP organized an alliance of its own comprising a number of opposition parties throughout Malaysia under the banner of the Malaysian Solidarity Convention. The heavily Chinese composition of this new political union made the struggle increasingly appear as one between non-Malays and Malays. As the media on both sides of the causeway focused on the significance of the new alignments, the expression of communal sentiments grew more blatant. In the Dewan Rakyat itself debates were acrimonious, but the new coalition appeared determined to persevere in its chosen course, despite the growing danger of open conflict. It was the threat of communal violence which appeared to have been the crucial factor in the government's decision to separate Singapore from the Federation of Malaysia. In the Dewan Rakyat Tunku Abdul Rahman explained that the communal issue concerned him most 'because the peace and happiness of the people in this country depend on goodwill and understanding of the various races for one another. Without it this nation will break up with consequential disaster'. While the Alliance government had preserved the unity of the Malaysian Federation in the face of diplomatic and military pressures from Indonesia and the Philippines, it succumbed to the threat of violence among its own people. It therefore agreed to Singapore's secession despite protests from Singapore's leaders.

With the secession, the Alliance government could divert its attention away from the all-engrossing political battles with the PAP to resume the urgent task of creating a genuine unity among the remaining members of the Federation. The inclusion of Sabah and Sarawak had made the task much more difficult even though the Alliance had adopted realistic goals towards them by providing longer periods of time to effect integration with the policies in Malaya. Granting concessions to the two Borneo territories to encourage their entry into the Malaysian Federation gave them far greater autonomy than that exercised by the peninsular states. Nonetheless, the central government was wary of a further dismemberment of the Federation and eventually intervened to prevent the rise of any political group which would threaten the nation's unity.

Sabah's Chief Minister Donald Stephens championed the cause of the indigenous peoples of Sabah, especially his own numerically dominant Kadazans. In his efforts to have the central government implement the guarantees to Sabah which had been promised at the time of Federation, he awakened Kuala Lumpur's fears of separatism or an unacceptable degree of state autonomy. As a result, Stephens was eased out of office and replaced as Chief Minister in 1967 by Datu Mustapha. The latter, a Moslem Sulu chief, at first seemed much more willing to bring Sabah into line with the policies of the central government. In Sarawak, too, the Chief Minister Stephen Kalong Ningkan from Sarawak's largest group, the Ibans, fought to preserve concessions granted to the state by the Malayan government prior to Federation. But he suffered a fate similar to that of his Sabah counterpart and was replaced as Chief Minister in 1966 by another Iban, Tawi Sli, who was more amenable to directives from Kuala Lumpur.

Under the leadership of Tunku Abdul Rahman the Federation had survived an Indonesian Confrontation, a Philippine claim to Sabah, a Singapore secession and a Bornean assertion of state autonomy. But the ability of the Alliance government to overcome these threats could only temporarily divert attention from the ever-present problems of ethnicity within Malaysian society itself. The solution, argued the government, must be to plan for the future and mould a new Malaysian citizen whose loyalty would be to the nation instead of a particular state or ethnic group. Few would have disagreed in seeing this goal as the only guarantee of Malaysia's survival; it was, however, the interpretation of what should constitute the 'new Malaysian' which became the contentious issue. The UMNO-dominated Alliance government decided that the basis for creating this new citizen would be Malaya's traditional culture and heritage, meaning Malay language and culture. The other ethnic groups argued for a Malaysian identity which would reflect the country's multi-ethnic background.

The national language question was a crucial aspect of this general debate. When the Merdeka (Independence) Constitution was promulgated in 1957 it included a provision that after ten years Malay would be the sole official language. The Borneo states were to enforce this provision ten years after their entry into the Federation. Subsequently, in September 1973, Sabah made Malay — now termed the Malaysian language (Bahasa Malaysia) or the National Language (Bahasa Kebangsaan) — the sole official medium of communication. Sarawak decided in March 1974 to retain officially both Malay and English until 1980, when English would be dropped. In Peninsular Malaysia a National Language Bill was passed on 3 March 1967. This latter bill typically represented a compromise solution within the Alliance government. Although Malay became the national language, English could be used in an official capacity. Only after the May riots of 1969 did the use of Malay become widespread in government, including Parliament and the courts. Furthermore, there was a guarantee that teaching and learning other languages would be permitted. As with all previous Alliance compromises, the more communally-minded elements of each ethnic group were dissatisfied. For many Malays the use of the Malay language was seen as a way of obtaining the advantages they needed to keep pace with the increased rate of development in their society. But it was also a matter of ethnic pride that at least one aspect of their culture should be adopted by the other ethnic groups in the society. Some Malays felt that the government should apply even greater pressure to enforce the use of Malay on all occasions and at all levels of society. The language issue was equally important to many Chinese, who thought that the lack of encouragement of their own language would be yet another step in the disintegration of the Chinese cultural heritage.

The Alliance government regarded not only language but also educational policy as important instruments in forging an integrated united society assimilated to Malay cultural traditions. In the Barnes Report of 1951, the Razak Report of 1956 and the Rahman Talib Report of 1960, the government expressed its intention of having a uniform and nationalized education system. The Alliance government attempted to achieve this without provoking hostility from the various ethnic groups. In the 1950s the emphasis was on the extension of government control over all schools. Once effective government control had been established, the task of education as the government saw it was to devise a standardized curriculum with the aims of training a modern élite and creating a national community based on Malay cultural traditions. Implementation of these long-range educational goals was to be gradual to avoid strong reaction from the ethnic groups affected. In the 1957 ordinance implementing the Razak Report, the first national Malay-medium secondary schools were founded as part of the government's determination to enable Malays to learn modern skills in their own language. The establishment of the Dewan Bahasa dan Pustaka (Literary and Language Agency) in 1956 was intended to encourage this development by creating Malay terminology in such fields as commerce, higher education, technology and science. Co-operation between the Indonesians and Malaysians in the late 1960s and the 1970s resulted in some standardization of terminology and the adoption in 1972 of a uniform system of spelling in their basically common languages. These were necessary steps to add substance to the hope that Malay would be able to cope as a national language in a modernized society.

While the government fostered Malay-medium instruction in the

National Schools, it also permitted the continuing existence of National-type Schools. These latter institutions received full government assistance but were allowed to teach in a language other than Malay. The government, however, did not abandon its eventual aim of standardizing education. In the Education Act of 1961, implementing the recommendations of the Rahman Talib Report of 1960, Chinese-medium secondary education in National-type Schools was to be abolished leaving only those in English medium. The preservation of English-medium schools reflected the government's ambivalence towards English education. Since the colonial period it had been in these schools that integration of pupils of various ethnic groups had been most easily achieved. Indeed, for a long time it was this common educational experience shared by the national leaders of the various ethnic groups which made it possible for meaningful dialogues to occur and compromises to be effected at the highest levels of government. It was also generally recognized that the prestigious English-medium schools, then considered the best in the country, were the training ground for the future élite. For the present, therefore, English was retained as a medium of instruction in National-type Schools.

In 1965 the government announced major changes in educational policy. First, the Primary Six exam was abolished, allowing anyone who completed primary grades to enter the Lower Secondary Schools (Forms 1, 2, 3). Secondly, Cambridge School Certificate and Higher School Certificate exams to determine entry into the University of Malaya would no longer be exclusively in English but would also be conducted in Malay. After the May 1969 riots, the government took steps to assure the dominance of the Malay language in the educational system. In July it was announced by the Minister of Education, Datuk Patinggi Abdul Rahman Yakub, later to become Chief Minister of Sarawak, that there would be a specific timetable for the use of Malay in English-medium schools. Beginning in 1970, all subjects in Form 1 would be taught in Malay except for lessons in English, Tamil and Chinese. The next year Form 2 would follow suit, and so on until the conversion of Form 6 in 1982.

Even before 1969 the government's language and educational policies were a focus of discontent among non-Malay groups, who regarded them as an attempt to secure the schools as one more area for Malay special privileges. The Chinese in particular were fearful of total submersion by the Malays and felt that yet another aspect of their culture was being sacrificed at the altar of national unity. In blunt terms, the price seemed too high. Many Chinese began to despair of the MCA's ability to ensure the preservation of Chinese interests, despite its membership in the governing coalition. Among the Chinese and Indian communities the MCA and the MIC were increasingly seen as ineffectual. In the campaign for the 1969 Federal elections there was thus widespread response to the promises of a new party formed in April 1968, the Gerakan Rakyat Malaysia (Malaysian People's Movement). The Gerakan was a non-communal party campaigning on the platform of social and economic reforms providing, as its slogan proclaimed, 'equality, justice and equal opportunity for all'. Another political party which benefited from the Chinese community's disenchantment with the MCA was the Democratic Action Party (DAP), which was the old Singapore-based PAP now reconstituted as a Malaysian party to contest elections in Malaysia. Ethnic equality and cultural pluralism were the basic principles underlying its platform. More specifically, it wanted an end to the Malays' special privileges and the beginning of true equality in education, whether in the language medium of Malay, English, Chinese or Indian. The People's Progressive Party (PPP), with its strength among the Chinese and Indian communities in Ipoh, also capitalized on their dissatisfaction at what they regarded as pro-Malay policies of the Alliance government.

Ethnic Disturbances of May 1969 and Emergency Government

The Federal elections of 1969 were fought on the highly emotional issues of education and language, which masked a deeper concern regarding the role of each ethnic group in the new Malaysian nation. Ever since independence the nation had been confronted with either internal or external threats which had served to moderate ethnic demands for the sake of national unity. In 1969, however, no such factor existed. Each ethnic group saw the elections of that year as a means of preserving its interests against the encroachment of the others. The election results were a severe blow to the Alliance. Although it still held the majority of seats in the Dewan Rakyat, the number had dropped from eighty-nine in 1964 to sixty-six, and its popular vote had declined from the 1964 total of 58·4 per cent to 48·5 per cent. The Gerakan, DAP and PPP together won a total of twenty-five seats and PAS twelve seats, thus depriving the Alliance government of the two-thirds majority which had previously enabled it to obtain constitutional amendments with ease.

On 13 May, three days after the elections, the jubilant Gerakan and DAP supporters took to the streets of Kuala Lumpur in a victory celebration. A counter-rally that evening by UMNO supporters quickly deteriorated into uncontrolled violence in the city. A State of Emergency was declared under Article 150 of the constitution. All administrative powers were then centralized in a National Operations Council headed by the Deputy Prime Minister, Abdul Razak. Only after four days of bloody fighting was order finally restored to the city, but for two months after the 13 May riots incidents of communal violence persisted. The government finally threatened to take severe action against the militant Malay groups, especially those calling for the Tunku's resignation because of his accommodating policies towards the other ethnic communities.

The Malay leadership in the Alliance blamed the opposition's unrestrained attacks on Malay privileges for arousing the violent Malay response, though this claim was vehemently rejected. The government warned that if further political excesses continued it would not be safe to return to a parliamentary-style democracy. As in the immediate post-war years, the riots of 1969 had painfully revealed how strong were the undercurrents of distrust running through the various ethnic communities. Once again the old question was raised, but this time with a far greater sense of urgency: how was a united and enduring Malaysia to be forged? The emergency government took immediate action to address itself to this question. One of its first steps was the creation in July 1969 of a Department of National Unity to formulate a national ideology and new social and economic programmes. On 31 August 1970, Malaysia's Independence Day, the new ideology *Rukunegara* ('Articles of Faith of the State') was formally proclaimed:

> Our nation, Malaysia, being dedicated to achieving a greater unity of all her peoples; to maintaining a democratic way of life; to creating a just society in which the wealth of the nation shall be equitably shared; to ensuring a liberal approach to her rich and diverse cultural traditions; to building a progressive society which shall be oriented to modern science and technology;

> We, her people, pledge our united efforts to attain those ends guided by these principles:
> Belief in God
> Loyalty to King and Country
> Upholding the Constitution
> Rule of Law
> Good Behaviour and Morality

In January 1970 the National Consultative Council (NCC) was formed to 'establish positive and practical guidelines for inter-racial co-operation and social integration for the growth of a Malaysian national identity'. This body comprised representatives from Ministers of the National Operations Council, state governments, political parties, Sabah, Sarawak, religious groups, professional bodies, the public services, trade unions, employers' associations, the Press, teachers and minority groups. It was the government's wish that deliberations be frank and away from the eyes of the media. In this way a body representing all segments of society might be able to achieve a true consensus (*muafakat*).[4] A return to the traditional Malay practice of governing by *muafakat* in a general assembly was thus being reintroduced alongside a Western-style parliamentary democracy. The latter institution had proved vulnerable to ethnic divisions within the society, and the government's Malay leadership was ready to experiment with an earlier governmental device which had served Malays well in the past. This *muafakat* government was not intended to replace the Dewan Rakyat, but it was hoped that a frank discussion of such issues as the New Economic Policy, the *Rukunegara*, the National Language and Malay special privileges might go some way towards resolving the explosive problems within Malaysian society. Yet the government was fully aware that, important though consensus and national ideology might be, the battle for unity would be won or lost in the economic and social restructuring of the nation. It was to this problem that the government thus directed its greatest energies.

Economic and Social Restructuring: The New Economic Policy

Long-term economic planning with the express aim of restructuring society and creating a genuine unity among its people was a new experience for Malaya/Malaysia. After independence in 1957 the economic policies of the Malayan government were no longer principally determined by the concerns of overseas investors or foreign governments. In the First (1956—60) and Second (1961—5) Malayan Plans, economic growth and the elimination of economic disparity among the ethnic groups were cited as the government's main objectives. However, in implementing these plans it was the former objective which dominated, with the latter serving as a constraint. A third objective, that of greater employment opportunities, would, it was presumed, be achieved with greater economic growth. The First Malaysia Plan (1966—70) stressed these three main objectives and with the same order of priorities.

Economic growth received greatest attention because it was believed to be the key to achieving the other two goals. For a while, however, Malaysia's planners were uncertain of the country's ability to sustain its remarkable growth because of the bleak future which appeared to confront the two pillars of its economy: rubber and tin. The former suffered from competition from the synthetic rubber industry, which had made significant advances in technology, packaging, and marketing techniques. Equally serious was the threat to tin as a result of a growing worldwide economy in its use, better recovery techniques and decreasing production in Malaysia. A fortunate contrast to this gloomy picture was the success of the plan to diversify the economy during the period of the first three development plans. The palm oil industry boomed, aided by a large influx of capital after World War II, a sophisticated research programme and a buoyant overseas market. By 1966 Malaysia had become the world's largest producer of palm oil. Timber, iron ores and manufacturing also contributed to growing export earnings.

Despite the impressive economic growth and stability achieved by the newly independent Malaysia up to 1970, the problems of unemployment and poverty persisted, notably in the rural areas primarily occupied by Malays. Stated goals notwithstanding, the government had only limited success in reforming rural land tenure, credit and marketing which were considered the major factors contributing to rural poverty. In 1955 and 1967 the Padi Cultivators (Control of Rents and Security of Tenure) Ordinances were passed in order to protect the tenant farmer. These laid down that the maximum rental for crop sharing should be one-third of the crop, while fixed rentals should vary according to the quality of the land. Then as now, enforcement of such measures by the Federal government was problematic because land issues are constitutionally under state jurisdiction. Federal and state governments do not always agree on a course of action, and therefore finding solutions to land tenure problems remains difficult.

In 1956, in an effort to give farmers access to more land, the government set up the Federal Land Development Authority (FELDA). Between 1956 and 1966 this body opened up large areas of land, each consisting of 1,600–2,000 hectares. Rubber or oil palm was planted, and housing and other facilities provided for about 400 families. Some of the largest FELDA schemes are the Jengka Triangle Project, covering some 132,000 hectares in Pahang; the Johor Tenggara Project, with 148,500 hectares in Johor; and the Pahang Tenggara Project, involving one million hectares. The schemes have succeeded in reducing rural poverty, but at a slow rate. Between 1956 and 1973 about 174,000 people of a total rural population of about 7,065,000 were resettled on FELDA lands.[5]

Rural credit, too, has been a continuing problem, although the Federal government did succeed in making finance more readily available to farmers. One important measure was the creation of rural co-operatives. They were able to provide loans at reasonable rates but were incapable of satisfying the great demand. In 1969 the Federal government therefore set up the Agricultural Bank of Malaysia to strengthen and co-ordinate public sector credit programmes for agriculture. During the First Malaysia Plan (1966–70), Farmers' Associations were also established to extend credit for farmers. Nonetheless, rural indebtedness was, and still is, far from solved. Lengthy bureaucratic processes when dealing with the government can frustrate the Malay farmer, who often prefers a familiar non-Malay moneylender despite the latter's less favourable terms.

In rural marketing the government did achieve some degree of success. In 1966 the Federal Agricultural Marketing Authority (FAMA) was established to co-ordinate the whole range of marketing activities so that farmers could obtain a good return for their produce. For example, it has helped ensure more efficient landing, storage and trading of fish which has been of considerable benefit to Malay fishermen.

The ethnic disturbances of May 1969 forced the government to reassess the entire question of economic growth in relation to the now vociferous Malay demand for a greater share in the country's wealth. According to one study, in 1970 some 49·3 per cent of all households in Peninsular Malaysia (791,600) received incomes below the poverty line, estimated at $M33 *per capita* monthly. Of these, about 75 per cent were Malays.[6] A new economic initiative was thus launched, seeking to reconcile the vexed question of ensuring economic growth while eliminating economic disparity, which in Malaysia unfortunately tended to reflect ethnic divisions. The New Economic Policy (NEP), to be implemented over a period of twenty-five years, from 1971 to 1990, is an effort to satisfy the more immediate demands of the Malays for the reduction of economic disparity while maintaining long-term growth. The Second Malaysia Plan of 1971—5 was conceived as the first in a series of development plans aimed at attaining the NEP's two principal objectives: first, a reduction and eventual eradication of poverty, irrespective of race; and secondly, a restructuring of society so that identification of race with economic function would be reduced and ultimately eliminated.

The first objective, it was hoped, would be achieved by facilitating the access of the poor to land, physical capital, training and public amenities. The second would be brought about by reducing the dependence of Malays and other indigenous groups on subsistence agriculture. This would be achieved by increasing their participation in the modern rural and urban sectors of the economy. In aiming at greater Malay participation, the government attempted to allay fears among the Chinese that this would be accomplished at their expense. It reaffirmed the belief that this restructuring would be achieved through sustained economic growth and not through redistribution of existing resources. This, the government felt, would mean that 'no particular group experiences any loss or feels any sense of deprivation in the process'.

During the period of the Second Malaysia Plan (1971—5), Malaysia's economic growth of 7·4 per cent per annum was somewhat higher than the original target[7] and compared extremely well with other countries. But progress towards eradicating poverty was slow. Efforts in the rural sector were still concentrated on land development, better irrigation and drainage facilities to extend *padi* land, on increased electricity supply and so on, without, some feel, sufficient attention to the root causes of rural poverty: land tenantry, credit and indebtedness. Both FELDA and state-controlled land development schemes were continued, but by 1975 the percentage of Malay families selected to participate remained small.

Continuing rural poverty has exacerbated the problems of the urban poor. There has been some movement of rural Malays to the cities where they are finding refuge in previously established squatter settlements. In 1976 there were 153,000 squatters in Kuala Lumpur alone, of whom 45 per cent were Chinese, 41 per cent Malay, 4 per cent Indian and 10 per cent mixed. Since then the influx of rural Malays has increased, considerably raising the Malay percentage in the squatter areas. Initially the government attempted to remove the squatters, but recently official tolerance towards their settlements has grown. It is clear that accommodation even in the government's low-cost, high-rise flats (*rumah pangsa*) is beyond the means of most squatters, whose average income is between $M150 and $300 a month.[8] The government has therefore brought some amenities to these squatter communities, such as water supply, rubbish collection, electricity, community halls and even playgrounds. However, it refuses to grant temporary occupation licences for fear of encouraging others.

The second objective of the NEP, the restructuring of society, has also met obstacles. It was hoped to effect a restructuring by first establishing an employment pattern reflecting the ethnic composition of the population, which in Peninsular Malaysia in 1970 was 53·2 per cent Malay, 35·4 per cent Chinese, 10·7 per cent Indian and 0·8 per cent others; and secondly, achieving by 1990 the following proportion of the share capital in the commercial and industrial sectors: Malays and indigenous peoples or their interests 30 per cent, other Malaysians 40 per cent, and foreigners 30 per cent. By the end of the SMP (1971–5), there was some improvement in the employment pattern even though the majority of Malays were still in agriculture and the Chinese in manufacturing, construction, transport, and commerce.

To ensure greater Malay participation in commerce and industry, the government created the following public enterprises: the Majlis Amanah Rakyat (MARA – Council of Trust for Indigenous Peoples), which is the reorganized Rural and Industrial Development Authority, the Perbadanan Nasional Berhad (PERNAS – National Corporation Ltd), the State Economic Development Corporations (SEDCs), the Urban Development Authority (UDA) and the Malaysian Industrial Development Finance Ltd (MIDF). In addition to assisting Malay entrepreneurs to enter a mainly foreign- and local-Chinese-dominated business world, these large statutory bodies have engaged in business ventures with the intention of eventually relinquishing control to Malay private groups. One important function of these bodies has been the purchasing of shares on behalf of the Malay and indigenous peoples, or *bumiputra* ('sons of the soil'), though this latter term has in effect come to be equated with the Malays. To hasten the process of Malay ownership of 30 per cent of the corporate sector by 1990, the government established the National Unit Trust (Amanah Saham Nasional) in January 1981 run by the National Equity Corporation (Permodalan Nasional Berhad). The scheme aims to allow Malays to gain part ownership of some of Malaysia's leading companies, instead of simply having equity assets held nominally on their behalf by quasi-governmental institutions. To retain Malay ownership and prevent individuals from disposing of their units to outsiders, as has occurred in the past, units can only be sold back to the Trust. By offering tax relief on dividend income and a good return, it is hoped that many Malays will participate in the scheme. The need to resort to some form of trusteeship in order to attain the 30 per cent goal of corporate ownership has, however, raised doubts about the efficiency of public sector enterprises. The government has also embarked on a number of training schemes in order to provide trained personnel among Malays. Between 1966 and 1975 the MARA Institute of Technology alone produced nearly three thousand graduates. Other training programmes have been set up in the ministries, the MARA vocational colleges, the National Productivity Centre, and various other institutions.

Initially, the government depended on compliance with national policy by industry and commerce in order to achieve 30 per cent Malay employment in the corporate sector. The lack of progress in attaining this goal, plus the tendency of firms to hire Malays mainly at the lower levels, indicated that stronger action was necessary, especially after the events of 1969. In 1971 an amendment to the 1968 Investment Incentives Act, known as the Labour Utilization Relief, was passed, extending the period of exemption from corporate tax for any firm employing a certain number of Malay workers. Even this, however, was considered inadequate. In 1976 the Industrial Coordination Act came into force, making all medium and large-scale manufacturing enterprises subject to licence. With the implicit threat of revocation of licences for non-compliance, the government hopes to achieve its employment goals 'over a reasonable period of time'.

One of the difficulties the government faces in implementing the employment policy is the likelihood that increased Malay participation in the skilled industries and occupations may have to be compensated by increased Chinese and Indian employment in the lower income, less-skilled occupations. Should this compensatory increase among the non-Malay groups not occur, then the NEP employment target may have to be achieved either through higher unemployment rates for the Chinese and Indians than for the Malays (which is not what the NEP intended, but which occurred between 1970–75) and/or through emigration of Chinese and Indians to increase the Malay percentage of the workforce.[9] What may temper this analysis is the sustained economic growth which has been boosted since the late 1970s by the country's vast gas and oil supplies.

By forming and assuring the dominance of certain large quasi-governmental institutions in the economy, assisting Malay entrepreneurs, enabling Malays to acquire the necessary business skill, encouraging Malay ownership in the corporate sector, and applying pressure on businesses through legislation, the government has shown its determination to reduce the identification of Malays with the rural sector and thus partially achieve one of the NEP objectives. However, progress has been slow and the government's task remains a formidable one.

The Third Malaysia Plan (TMP), 1976–80, continued the policies of the preceding Five-Year Plan, with a few noteworthy changes. Poverty was given new emphasis, with 38·2 per cent of all development funds devoted to its eradication. In addressing itself to Malay poverty, the TMP placed strong emphasis on creating a modernized and progressive rural economy by building towns and industries in the least developed states and in the depressed areas of the more developed ones. But the problem of land tenure persisted, undermining some of the government's efforts in the countryside. The urban poor was also a concern of the TMP, though tax incentives continued to favour large-scale and capital-intensive industries. In response to the participation of large public corporations in the business sphere, the MCA encouraged the small family-based Chinese firms to establish large modern corporations with the necessary financial and skilled manpower resources. The MCA pioneered the way in 1975 by forming the Multi-Purpose Holdings Berhad, while planning for others in the future. The MIC, operating from a much more moderate political and economic power-base, also established a 'Multi-Purpose Co-operative Society' to achieve greater employment among Indians and greater participation in land settlement schemes. The goals of the Third Malaysia Plan were aided greatly by good commodity prices and substantial oil revenue.

The Fourth Malaysia Plan (1981–5) was unveiled in March 1981. There are no significant departures from the previous Five-Year Plans, but there is a greater sense of urgency. Though more than half-way through the NEP one of the two principal objectives, that of eradicating poverty, remains elusive. Too many factors beyond the reach of legislation serve to stifle Malay initiative in the rural areas and prevent the Malay farmer from breaking out of his poverty cycle. The only recourse, as with his forebears in the distant past, has been to flee the land and seek a more hospitable environment. This has occurred in a dramatic way in the flight to the cities and especially to Kuala Lumpur in the Federal Territory. Here is the home of the central government, the government which has been conspicuous in building roads, bridges and public edifices in the rural areas. Now many Malays have left their villages and come to the government, expecting it to fulfil its promises of a better life. By mid-1981 Malays already constituted one-third of all urban dwellers, rising from 14 per cent to 21 per cent of the total *bumiputra* population over a period of a decade. But their presence in the urban areas has intensified the problems of the mostly non-Malay urban poor, and a scramble for scarce employment opportunities could prove dangerous if converted to ethnic terms. The Malay unemployment rate has fallen faster than the national average, high-lighting the varying success in eliminating poverty among all ethnic groups. While it is estimated that in the first half of the NEP, the period from 1970 to 1980, rural (that is, mainly Malay) poverty has fallen from 68 per cent to 46 per cent, for the mostly Indian estate workers, the drop has been only from 40 per cent to 35 per cent. There are no statistics available for Chinese new villagers, but it appears that their position has not improved as dramatically as that of the Malays.[10] Some observers feel that providing the poor Indian estate workers and Chinese New Villagers with land for agriculture would go a long way towards reducing poverty among these two groups while achieving the other government aim of removing identification of ethnic group with economic function.

The other major objective of the NEP is the restructuring of society. Some restructuring in the Malay community has occurred in the move-ment of the rural poor to the cities where they have become factory workers. This trend has been encouraged by greater job opportunities in the cities for Malays as a result of government policy requiring employers to set their hiring standards to reflect the proportional ethnic composition of the population. Additional Malay employment has been provided by the various quasi-governmental corporations.

The slow growth of the corporate sector has made the NEP goal of 30 per cent *bumiputra* ownership by 1990 seem unattainable. To achieve that target the National Equity Corporation was formed. The Fourth Malaysia Plan aims to continue to acquire shares through government-funded agencies acting in trust for the *bumiputra*. Some have expressed concern that by 1990, should this trend continue, there could be in Malaysia a vast public corporation managing the interests of the *bumiputra*, while the private sector remains in the hands of foreigners and the other ethnic communities. But in late 1981 the government began to take specific steps to gain greater control over the country's economy and hence be in a better position to implement measures to hasten the attainment of its NEP goals. In early September 1981 the National Equity Corporation acquired control of the London-based Guthrie Corporation. This was followed within a month by acquisition of controlling interests in Dunlop Estates and Barlow Holdings by other Malaysian groups. Harrisons and Crosfield is the last of the major plantation groups in Malaysia to remain under British control. By means of these take-overs the government has not only gained control over its agricultural export crops, but it can now raise the export value of rubber and palm-oil products through processing, product development, and resource-based manufacturing and marketing. The subsequent development of the manufacturing sector should bring added benefits to the country and contribute further to the achievement of the NEP goals. As the NEP enters the final decade, the government appears to be in a stronger position to determine its own economic strategy than has been the case at any time since the inception of this major programme to restructure Malaysian society.

A Diversified Export Economy

Fortunately for the government, heavy expenditure on development plans has been possible because of a healthy economy with an annual real growth rate of about 8 per cent throughout the 1970s. It has been this sustained economic growth which has thus far helped to mute criticisms of real and perceived inequalities among and within Malaysia's ethnic groups. The main reason for Malaysia's enviable economic achievement has been high world commodity prices which have benefited an export trade that consists primarily of petroleum, rubber, timber, tin and palm oil.

The success story in the export field has been the petroleum industry. Its promise as an export earner was impressively demonstrated in 1976 when its first net foreign earnings made up 18 per cent of the total earning among export commodities. In 1978 export of crude oil was second in Malaysia's overseas trade, principally because the offshore Trengganu fields began production in March of that year. But by 1980 oil export earnings reached M$7·2 billion (US$3·2 billion), far outstripping the long dominant rubber industry which earned M$4·8 billion in that same year. The average oil production by August 1980 was about 180,000 barrels per day, double the domestic requirement. Officially oil reserves are placed at about 1·4 billion barrels, but even conservative estimates make it close to 3 billion barrels.[11] The low sulphur content of Malaysia's oil makes it more desirable than that of the Middle East to pollution-conscious industrial nations. As a result Malaysia sells its dearer oil and then satisfies much of its oil needs from the less expensive crude from the Middle East. The Malaysian government has been following a policy of limited extraction in order to lengthen the life of oil supplies. Liquefied natural gas (LNG) promises to boost the petroleum industry's share of total export earnings even higher. When the US$ 1 billion LNG project in the Bintulu fields off Sarawak comes on stream sometime in 1983, Malaysia will be among the world's largest producers of LNG. It should bring in another US$600 million in revenue per year.[12] There are also claims that natural gas fields off Trengganu are even larger than those in Bintulu. With continuing high oil prices the petroleum industry's future seems rosy indeed.

Natural rubber, though displaced by the petroleum industries as the chief export earner, has continued to be a principal source of export revenue for Malaysia, recovering from the shock of synthetic rubber's significant technical advances. Malaysia's rubber exporters have also mainly overcome synthetic rubber's earlier advantages in the quality and packing of the final product. Furthermore, the Malaysian Rubber Research institute has made important discoveries reducing the gestation period of rubber trees from about seven to four years and improving the clonal varieties to maximize yields in the initial years. While there will not be the spectacular booms of the past, natural rubber, especially from Malaysia, will at least be able to maintain a high percentage of the now less than 50 per cent market which natural rubber has in total world rubber consumption.[13] Since smallholders account for 67·7 per cent of Malaysia's total area planted in rubber, the continuing strength of that commodity would help ease some of the rural poverty which the NEP hopes to reduce substantially by target date 1990.

Tin is now only the third largest export earner in Malaysia. The 1970s saw a steady drop in production which fell to 58,709 metric tonnes in 1977, the lowest since 1961. Despite these problems, however, tin was still the second biggest export earner in 1976 bringing in receipts of about M$1.5 billion. Thus far almost all of Malaysia's tin comes from alluvial mines with only one conventional lode mine, Pahang Consolidated. Tin-bearing states, especially Perak with its still considerable tin deposits, may increase prospecting and production assisted by foreign companies. Through favourable production-sharing agreements, it is hoped that the states will open their doors to more extensive exploitation which will help revive the industry. There have already been reports of vast new deposits of tin, mainly in the Malay Reservation lands, which through special legislation had hitherto remained unalienated for tin exploration.

Timber lies fourth as an export earner for Malaysia, behind petroleum, rubber, and tin. There is, however, a serious lack of reforestation which could damage the industry in the long run if remedial measures are not taken soon. By the end of the 1970s a total of 272,000 hectares had been logged annually, but in the last twenty years only some 216,000 hectares of permanent forest reserves had come under a reforestation programme. At present Malaysia still has fairly large virgin forests which will continue to be a source of substantial revenue, at least in the immediate future.

Palm oil has brought a steady flow of revenue to the government, being the fifth largest export earner in Malaysia. By 1977 there were some 742,117·5 hectares under oil palm, producing about two-thirds of the entire world's supply. Nonetheless, it faces strong competition from other vegetable oils in the world market, especially from soya bean oil in the USA. After palm oil's exceptional year in 1977, with high world prices because of poor harvests among Malaysia's competitors, the industry witnessed a slow downturn in the following year and further hardships because of drought.

In addition to these commodities, Malaysia is also blessed with other minerals which will probably be exploited by production-sharing schemes between the state governments and foreign as well as Malaysian companies. Sarawak was expected to sign an agreement some time in 1980 or 1981 for coal and Kelantan for copper and lead. Pahang has rich lead deposits associated with copper and silver, and in all likelihood will follow Kelantan's example in any production-sharing agreement.

While the five major commodities in Malaysia — rubber, oil, tin, palm oil, and sawlogs and sawn timber — accounted for 73·3 per cent of total export earnings in 1978, manufacturing's share was about 19 per cent.[14] The government hopes to raise this percentage to 26·6 per cent by 1990. The rate of investment in the manufacturing sector slowed down in the 1970s because of the world recession and the scepticism expressed about the Industrial Co-ordination Act, created as an instrument of the NEP. The Act's licensing requirements, especially that concerning equity participation of *bumiputras* and *bumiputra* employment, caused a drop in domestic Chinese as well as foreign investment. However, the government's desire to fulfil its objectives in the manufacturing sector has led to certain changes in the Industrial Co-ordination Act, thus restoring some confidence among investors.

Political Restructuring: The National Front (Barisan Nasional)

Whatever the degree of success, the bold measures of the NEP would have been difficult to implement had it not been for UMNO's power in the government. This power was further augmented by constitutional amendments passed by the Dewan Rakyat after the resumption of parliamentary rule in February 1971. The amendments were aimed at removing 'sensitive issues from the realm of public discussions so as to allow the smooth functioning of parliamentary democracy; and to redress the racial imbalance in certain sectors of the nation's life and thereby promote national unity'. Any public discussion, even by parliamentary members, of topics dealing with the power and status of the Malay rulers, Malay special privileges, citizenship, Malay as the National Language and the status of Islam as the official religion was now considered seditious. The amendments also reserved a quota of places within institutions of higher learning for *bumiputras* as one means of redressing the ethnic imbalance in the professions. The intention was to reserve places for Malays and the indigenous people of the peninsula and Sabah and Sarawak in certain areas of study, but especially in the fields of engineering, medicine, and the sciences. As a result of this amendment, by 1975 some 58·5 per cent of all degree students in Malaysia's five universities were Malays, though the numbers in the scientific fields remained low.[15] Most importantly, by constitutional amendments restricting discussion of 'sensitive issues', the government was free to pursue its policies with greater freedom. The media and even parliament, instead of being critics of government actions, became the instruments of endorsement and consensus. The term *muhibbah*, meaning goodwill between one ethnic group and another, became the catch-cry of the post-1969 government.

Government policy increasingly reflected the ideas of UMNO's leaders since all effective political opposition had been silenced or muted after the ethnic disturbances in 1969. The MCA had been thoroughly chastened by its failure at the polls in the May 1969 election and by a subsequent reprimand by the Home Affairs Minister, Tun (Dr) Ismail. The latter had warned that it would be better for UMNO to dissolve the Alliance if the MCA and MIC remained 'neither dead or alive'. In response to this warning, a Chinese Unity Movement was formed in which initially Tun Tan Siew Sin and various other important MCA officials played a part. The Movement touched a responsive chord among the Chinese community and gained widespread support clearly evident in its mass rallies. So rapid was the Movement's growth that the government and the established MCA leadership soon regarded it as dangerous. By denying the Movement registration as a party, and by arresting two of its founding members on charges of sedition, the government effectively undermined the efficacy of this organization.

With the demise of the Chinese Unity Movement, some of its more active members decided to work within the MCA in hopes of reforming the party itself and arousing stronger grass-roots support. At first the UMNO leadership viewed the infusion of new blood into the MCA as a positive step. Soon, however, the reformist movement degenerated into a battle for control of the party, which culminated in the victory of the old leadership under Tun Tan Siew Sin. The effect of this struggle was to further weaken the MCA, making its claim to be the sole spokesman of the Chinese community even less convincing than before.

Under the leadership of Tun Abdul Razak, who succeeded Tunku Abdul Rahman as Prime Minister in 1970, UMNO maintained its dominant position in the Alliance. There was a new vitality under Tun Razak which saw the emergence of a young militant Western-educated élite having closer affinity with the Malay- and Arabic-educated wing of UMNO than with the old-style English-educated Malay aristocracy. After the Tunku's retirement, and as the old guard within UMNO weakened, Tun Razak could pursue an independent course with assurance of full backing from his party. From a position of strength he expanded the Alliance coalition beginning in 1971 to form the National Front or Barisan Nasional of ten political parties, including PAS (called Parti Islam between 1971 and 1973) to contest the 1974 Federal Elections. While the declared intent was to reduce divisive politicking in accordance with government policy and the 1971 constitutional amendments, this move had the further effect of demonstrating UMNO's ability to use any combination of political parties to further its aims. Tun Abdul Razak bluntly told the MCA that it was 'no longer the sole representative of the Chinese community in the National Front'. The MIC, too, became much more responsive to UMNO's directions when Razak intervened to resolve a prolonged leadership struggle, assuring the retirement of Sambanthan and the accession of his deputy V. Manickavasagam as the new president in June 1973.

In the August 1974 federal elections few believed that the National Front would survive the inter-party struggles over allocation of seats which had so often severely strained relations within the Alliance. But with Tun Razak exercising a strong hand in this delicate task, the National Front emerged unscathed. Its main opponent in the elections was the DAP led by Lim Kit Siang. The election results came as no surprise to anyone. Of 114 seats (ten more seats had been added to Peninsular Malaysia in the new electoral boundaries) contested, the National Front won 104 of which UMNO took 62.[16] The National Front also succeeded in winning all of the state governments, including Kelantan since PAS was now part of the coalition.

The decisive victory of the National Front in 1974 appeared to be a popular mandate, encouraging the government to continue its social and economic policies aimed at creating a united Malaysian nation. The functions of the Department (changed to a Board in October 1974) of National Unity became more precise. It conducted national solidarity classes throughout Malaysia with the emphasis on teaching the National Language (that is, Malay) and civics and on sharing cultural traditions. The Ministry of Information began to work closely with the National Unity Board by promoting national consciousness in its radio and television programmes. Much of the success of these efforts was attributed to Tun Razak himself, whose moderate policies helped to ease the tensions and suspicions among the ethnic groups. His death on 14 January 1976 aroused some fears that the new leadership would be less successful in balancing conflicting groups within UMNO and the society at large. Fortunately, his successor, Datuk

Hussein Onn, son of UMNO's founder Dato Onn Ja'afar, was no stranger to national politics. He soon laid to rest any doubts concerning his ability to deal with sensitive issues in Malaysian politics.

The political skills of the new Prime Minister were put to the test in confrontations with various powerful state chief ministers. The first of these was with Datuk Harun Idris, the Chief Minister of Selangor, who represented an increasingly militant communal wing of UMNO. Datuk Harun had been kept in check by the two previous prime ministers, but his activities became so blatant that in November 1975 the Prime Minister decided to press charges of corruption against him. Although twice convicted and consequently evicted from UMNO, Datuk Harun's influence within the party and UMNO Youth remained strong and he was later allowed to rejoin. He was finally sentenced to six years' imprisonment on charges of corruption and forgery in 1978, but this did not prevent his winning a seat in UMNO's Supreme Council in that same year. His influence has remained considerable in UMNO and, especially since his release from prison in 1981, he continues to be regarded as a serious force in Malay politics.

Another confrontation arose with the powerful Chief Minister of Sabah, Tun Mustapha. He had originally come to power with Kuala Lumpur's help because of his efforts to bring Sabah into line with national policies. Once in control of the state government, he had run Sabah as a personal fiefdom, a feat made possible by Sabah's immense revenues from timber concessions. It had even been alleged that he had entertained notions of separation from Malaysia and of forming a new nation consisting of Sabah and the three Philippine areas of Sulu, Mindanao and Palawan. To Kuala Lumpur's further embarrassment, claims that he had channelled arms to Moslem rebels in the southern Philippines and reports of his aggressive religious policy attracted international criticism. To undermine Tun Mustapha, Tun Abdul Razak had earlier appointed a Chief of Police and a head of the armed forces in Sabah who were loyal to Kuala Lumpur. When an opposition party Berjaya arose in 1975, Tun Razak quickly accepted it as a member of the National Front.

Tun Mustapha finally resigned in October 1975 but still dominated Sabah politics as leader of the United Sabah National Organization. After Tun Razak's death, Datuk Hussein Onn continued to apply pressure on Tun Mustapha and was finally rewarded by the latter's removal from power through Berjaya's victory in the Sabah elections of April 1976. But in an unforeseen quirk of fate, many of the leading members of the new government, including the new Chief Minister Tun Haji Mohammad Fuad (formerly Donald Stephens), were killed in an air crash two months after the election. Datuk Harris Saleh was then appointed the new Chief Minister of Sabah.

Between 1977 and 1978 Datuk Hussein was also successful in asserting federal domination over the powerful state governments in
Perak, Melaka and Kelantan, thereby enhancing his image and that
of his National Front Government. In the Federal elections held in
July 1978 the National Front, minus PAS which had withdrawn from
the coalition in 1977, was again the overwhelming victor, taking 131 of
154 seats contested throughout Malaysia. In Kelantan itself the
long PAS domination of the state government was finally ended with the
victory of UMNO-Berjasa in the state elections. Datuk Hussein interpreted this victory as a vote of approval for the goals of the New Economic Policy and the government's attempt to create by 1990 a 'new
Malaysian' whose foremost loyalties would be to the nation rather
than to any specific ethnic group. This mandate continued to guide
the policies of Datuk Seri Mahathir Mohamad, who succeeded Datuk
(now Tun) Hussein Onn as Prime Minister in 1981.

The New Malaysian

Despite some success in restructuring Malaysian society to NEP
prescriptions, it may be optimistic to expect the emergence of the
'new Malaysian' by the target year 1990. The immensity of the problem is suggested by one reporter, who sees the 'new Malaysian' as 'a
Malay who sees his position as secure in a country where migrant
Chinese appear (falsely) to be the economic overlords; a Chinese who
sees his acquisitive talents are not unfairly circumscribed by political
manipulations; an Indian who sees his minority status as not exploited
because he is defenceless; a Dayak [Iban] or Kadazan who sees his
distance from Kuala Lumpur as no reason to be neglected'.[17]
   Of all the groups, Malays have gone furthest along the road towards
this evolution and for good reason. The government has rejected the
idea of assimilation, of transforming everyone in Malaysia into a Malay.
It has instead stressed integration of the society into a 'Malaysian'
identity which has as its core the cultural traditions and language of
the Malays. Government land development programmes, economic
incentive schemes, and technical training programmes have all contributed towards giving Malays a greater stake in the country's economy.
It appears that the Malays may once again assume a significant role in
trade and commerce which foreign observers had admired in earlier
centuries and which they had temporarily lost with the establishment
of British colonial rule. But great numbers of Malays are still locked in

a cycle of rural poverty which is exacerbated by high birth-rates, despite an active family planning programme. As a result, many rural Malays have moved to the cities seeking employment. This trend has been encouraged by better road systems, including the expected completion in 1981 of the 60-kilometre east—west highway linking Kota Baru in Kelantan with Penang. Although the government has encouraged labour intensive industries, growth in this sector has not been sufficient to absorb the new pool of cheap labour from the villages. A growing Malay middle class has benefited from the new government policies, but a large majority of Malays still have a long way to go before achieving a sense of economic security.

The Chinese generally believe that the government's attempts to provide Malays with a share of the economy will be at their expense. The Chinese own approximately 20 per cent of the major share capital in Malaysia, while foreign concerns account for a massive 60 per cent. Yet the government in the 1970s appeared reluctant to take action against any foreign company lest it abandon Malaysia for some other country offering a more favourable climate for investment. The Chinese therefore feared that allocation of capital resources to the Malays could occur only at their expense. Such fears may have been allayed by two developments: (1) figures which indicate that, though Chinese and Indian ownership of corporate equity in the 1970s rose by 6 per cent to 40 per cent of the total, the increase was a result of a sharp drop in foreign shareholdings;[18] and (2) Malaysian acquisition in 1981 of controlling interests in all but one major British plantation group operating in the country. There is thus reason to believe that 30 per cent Malay ownership may be achieved at the expense of foreign holdings.

Perhaps Malay entry into what is commonly seen as a Chinese sphere of operations would be tolerable if there were compensations for the Chinese in areas long dominated by the Malays. Significantly, the MCA passed resolutions in 1975 requesting the right for Chinese to participate in government land settlement programmes, to be recruited in the security forces, and to obtain a percentage of university places in proportion to their population in the country. Nonetheless, the Chinese can see little prospect of this effectively occurring since Malay ownership of land is a sensitive issue which the government is loath to raise. Malay domination of the security forces had arisen during the colonial period, and in the aftermath of 1969 there is a reluctance among some Malay leaders to see this 'fist' of the government lose its strong Malay component. In regard to university places, the government considers the training of large numbers of Malays as essential for the success of the NEP and is therefore unwilling to remove the favourable quotas for Malays in tertiary institutions. In short, there is little indication that the government is ready yet to make these concessions to the Chinese. The Malaysian Constitution itself preserves a pro-Malay bias in citizenship requirements, preservation of rural over-representation in the electorate, and in the use of Malay as a sole official language. Furthermore, with certain government measures aimed specifically at strengthening Malay economic participation, many Chinese can see only minimal benefit to themselves in the government's objective of restructuring society to remove the identification of ethnic groups with economic function.

The Indians have never been at the forefront of inter-ethnic conflict because of their small population in the country. But their leaders have succeeded through the MIC in making their voices heard and have even acted as mediators in the heat of communal debate between the two major ethnic groups. The MIC 'Economic Blueprint' issued in response to the NEP reflected similar concerns as those expressed by the MCA. But two problems were of particular interest: obtaining greater Indian participation in government land schemes, and directing government attention to Indian unemployment, which was higher than any other ethnic group. There appears little hope for the former, but the Indians can perhaps take comfort that the NEP objective to eradicate the poor 'regardless of race' may eventually bring some relief to the large numbers of Indian urban unemployed. However, the influx of rural Malays to the cities has put a considerable strain on resources. The Indian national leaders fear that they may soon lose their credibility if they cannot obtain concessions for the Indian community as a whole.

For the Iban of Sarawak and the Kadazan of Sabah, distance from Kuala Lumpur was seen as a positive factor when the Federation of Malaysia was formed. The slower rate of economic and political developments in the Borneo territories compared to Peninsular Malaysia up to 1963 made it advisable to ensure that they would not be overwhelmed by their more powerful partner. But Federation did not significantly alter the paternalistic nature of British rule, as both states were initially governed by dominating personalities. When Sabah's resilient Chief Minister Tun Mustapha eventually lost power, he was replaced in 1976 by Datuk Harris Saleh who, within his own party, Berjaya, is equally regarded as the *pater familias*. In March 1981 Datuk Harris led his Berjaya party to an overwhelming victory, winning 60 per cent of the vote and gaining control of all but four of the forty-seven seats in Sabah's state assembly. The results have been interpreted as a triumph of Berjaya's multi-ethnic approach over the communal parties, a significant development which many hope will not go unnoticed in Kuala Lumpur. Ethnic divisions have been underplayed deliberately by Datuk Harris in an attempt to foster a more rapid integration with Peninsular Malaysia. With his approval the publication of the 1980 census statistics will mention only three ethnic groups in Sabah: *bumiputra* (indigenous peoples and Malays),

Chinese and others.[19] It is expected that the next five years will bring still closer relations between Sabah and the peninsula.

After a decade in power, Sarawak's Chief Minister, Datuk Patinggi Tan Sri Abdul Rahman Yakub, finally retired from his post because of failing health. He was succeeded by his nephew Datuk Amar Haji Abdul Taib Mahmud, who had been a federal minister in Kuala Lumpur. The former Chief Minister was then appointed the Yang Dipertuan (Governor) of Sarawak. In the process, Sarawak's cabinet was reshuffled not without blessings from Kuala Lumpur. Having spent twelve years in Kuala Lumpur, Datuk Taib's relations with the centre are expected to remain good and contribute to a faster integration with Peninsular Malaysia.

With chief ministers promoting integration, both the Iban and the Kadazan will eventually become just another of the various communities comprising Malaysia. It remains to be seen whether the years of grace, when adjustment of the Borneo states to the new political creation was to have been made, were sufficient to equip their people to survive and prosper in their new nation.

The road ahead is still fraught with problems but at the mid-way point of the NEP the country's strong economic performance in the 1970s has helped make at least some of the difficulties less pressing. If this performance can be repeated in the next decade — and indications are that they can, aided by vast oil revenues — enough time may be bought so that the 'new Malaysian' may yet emerge. The pragmatism of the Malaysian government and its people has assured the survival of the nation through a number of challenges in the past. It may yet again prove to be the critical element in the forging of the 'new Malaysian' and a united Malaysian nation.

Conclusion: Some Themes in Malaysian History

Certain dominant themes emerge in examining the span of Malaysian history. One of these is the self-confidence with which Malays have always greeted external influences, an attribute undoubtedly arising from their long and persistent contact with the outside world. From about the beginning of the Christian era, Malays living on both sides of the Melaka Straits were witness to a growing international seaborne traffic passing through this narrow waterway, which linked India, the Middle East and Europe on the one hand, and Japan, Korea and China on the other. Taking advantage of their ideal location on the Straits, the Malays became active participants in this international trade and were able to develop successful entrepôts which formed the basis of some of the earliest and most influential maritime powers in Southeast Asia. The most impressive of the early kingdoms was Srivijaya, whose traditions were continued in an almost unbroken line to Melaka, Johor and Riau. They were noted not only for their flourishing entrepôt trade but also for their patronage of religion, the medium for many of the intellectual trends in the world beyond the Straits. This area, then, was never a backwater but was exposed to a continuing progression of ideas from abroad, the most suitable of which were adopted and adapted by the local population to suit their own needs.

The British presence in Malaya in the nineteenth century was initially accepted by the Malays in the same spirit with which they had greeted earlier influences. Several rulers and chiefs, responding to the increased demands for raw materials by Europe's rapidly industrializing nations, reorganized traditional economic patterns of collection and redistribution of resources. Such a response was especially noteworthy in Johor and Kedah, but was also reflected in economic co-operation between Europeans and/or Chinese and Malay chiefs in other states. A broad historical perspective provides some grounds for the assertion that, given time and their own methods, Malays would have adjusted to and profited by this new external influence as they had done so successfully in the past. Indeed, there were indications that a number of Malay rulers and chiefs had already begun this process of adaptation. However, a major difference with the past was the pace of change which characterized the nineteenth century. The rapid technological advances and the insatiable demands of industrial Europe, first for raw materials and later for lands to colonize, soon overwhelmed the Malays. The formidable union of new economic forces and political power in the industrialized West, which confidently viewed the whole world as a field of exploitation, impatiently swept aside any real or perceived hindrance to its goals.

In Malaysia, as in other parts of Asia, Africa and Oceania, the local people fell victim to an economic and political imperialism which forced them to abandon their own slower but less disruptive mode of absorbing outside influences. Yet when Malaya finally regained its independence from Britain in 1957, Malay resilience and their genius for adaptation to changed circumstances were still strongly evident. They had adopted/adapted the language, skills and to some extent the philosophy of the European, but at the same time they had retained their earlier identification and intellectual and emotional links with the Islamic world. The British concept of 'civilization' did not overwhelm but coexisted with the Islamic *tamadun*. As self-confidently as in the past, the Malays had selected the most useful elements from two separate cultures during the period of colonial rule and had made them their own. Government, business, education and even leisure activities reflected the two ideological streams, now effectively wedded into a 'Malay way of life'. There was no fear of either Western or Islamic ideas, for both were seen as enriching Malay culture.

Another theme in Malaysia's history is the ongoing struggle of the centre to restrain centrifugal tendencies in outlying territories. An explanation for the existence of these centrifugal forces may be found in the geography of the area. Many of the states in Peninsular Malaysia are situated along logical geographical divisions, separated from their neighbours by mountain ranges and dense jungles. While the seas did unite such states, the point of unity was often only the estuary of a major riverine network, with a vast interior free of central control. Until the late nineteenth century very little attempt was made to establish a unified bureaucracy linking all outlying territories to the centre. Each individual area developed independently under its own leaders and was linked loosely to the centre through the occasional affirmation of allegiance and acknowledgement of subservience. With the influx of Chinese and Indian migrants in the nineteenth and twentieth centuries, the likelihood of separate development occurring in certain urban centres, such as Singapore, created another possibility for fragmentation. The inclusion of Sabah and Sarawak into Malaysia contributed still further to centrifugal tendencies since they were physically and, to a considerable extent, culturally separated from the peninsula.

One effective counter to centrifugal forces has been the important role played by the centre as the principal reception and redistribution point for goods and ideas. Many outlying areas in the past submitted to the loss of a degree of sovereignty in exchange for these benefits and for the added inducements of prestige acquired through association with a major centre and assurance of protection against enemies. At times force was used by the centre to maintain its economic dominance, but primarily that which sustained the unity was its ability to continue assuring specific benefits to its vassal states.

There were, nonetheless, areas which were never totally responsive to the centre. In the Srivijayan period it was Kedah and north Sumatra; in Melaka times it was Kedah and east coast Sumatra; and since the formation of the Federation it has been such states as Sabah, Sarawak. Singapore and Kelantan. The forces of fragmentation in Malaysia have at times been so great that both the centre and the component states have been forced to reconsider the arguments for maintaining the *status quo*. When the benefits no longer appeared to outweigh the disadvantages, a severance of ties between centre and periphery has occurred, as happened in Singapore's secession from the Federation in 1965. This secession made Malaysia's leaders more determined to preserve the unity of the remaining states of the Federation. Towards this end government policy has aimed at creating a united people through language, formal education and even the arts. By the early 1980s, the effort towards integration has shown some success, as Sabah, Sarawak and Kelantan have become more responsive to central direction. The centrifugal tendencies remain, but with strong and committed leaders in Kuala Lumpur dedicated to the preservation of the Federation and the primacy of the centre, there is every reason to believe that these tendencies will be effectively restrained.

A third theme which emerges in Malaysian history is the changing conception of what constitutes 'Melayu' or Malay. It has been suggested that one of the first uses of 'Malay' as an exclusive term appears in the early history of Melaka. The immigrants from Srivijaya proudly asserted their unique identity *vis-à-vis* the local population by referring to themselves by the name of their original homeland which, according to their tradition, was on the Melayu River near Bukit Si Guntang in Palembang. In the early Melaka period things Malay became the ultimate measure of refinement and acceptability. As the local population in Melaka gradually assimilated the language and culture of the newcomers, Malay retained its exclusive connotation but was used to distinguish a now famous Melaka from the various areas in the Malay–Indonesian archipelago emulating its language, styles, and customs. To be truly Malay was to be a Melakan, a definition which was expanded in the mid-fifteenth century to include Islam. Islam became a vital component in the definition of a Malay and served varying purposes in subsequent centuries. When the northern

Malay peninsula was threatened by the Thais, the term Malay was employed to underscore the identity of a people, an identity based not only on language and customs but also on religion. The perceived fear of cultural absorption into a Thai—Buddhist nation made the belief in a separate and distinct Malay people of great urgency.

Under colonial rule the term Malay was formalized by the British to distinguish the Malay-speaking Moslems residing on the peninsula and offshore islands from the large immigrant groups of Indians and Chinese. Migrant Indonesians who spoke Malay or Indonesian and were Moslems often became incorporated into the Malay category because the colonial power had created broad ethnic divisions for administrative convenience and to fill certain functions in the colonial economy. In the interwar period the anti-foreign attitudes of some Malays led them to expand the definition of Malay to include all the indigenous peoples of the Malay archipelago irrespective of religion. But generally the colonial government's categorization of Malay was retained until the granting of independence to Malaya in 1957, when in the first flush of enthusiasm it was suggested that the term be used to designate all those who wished to become citizens of the new nation. The suggestion was considered but rejected and the Constitution formalized colonial practice by defining a Malay as 'one who speaks the Malay language, professes Islam and habitually follows Malay customs'.

After the formation of Malaysia in 1963, the inclusion of large numbers of indigenous groups from Sabah and Sarawak necessitated a revision of the old ethnic categories. Although for political purposes the Bornean peoples had been classified with the Malays of the peninsula, they remained an anomaly since most were clearly not Malay in language, religion, or culture. To overcome this difficulty the term *bumiputra*, 'sons of the soil', was created to refer to the peninsular *orang asli*, the indigenous peoples of Sabah and Sarawak, and Malays. In practical administrative calculations regarding employment, education and economic quotas, the *bumiputra* category virtually replaced that of Malay. Nonetheless, the term Malay persists, and in late 1980 the government even discussed a stricter definition of the term to eliminate abuses regarding alleged 'Malay' economic ownership and participation.

Since the 1970s there has been an Islamic fundamentalist revival in Malaysia known as the *dakwah* movement, which has made Islam the crucial determinant of any true Malay. And by the early 1980s one faction began to advocate the use of Malay once again exclusively for those who are ethnically Malay, speak Malay and are Moslems, thus bringing the meaning of the term full circle. But more moderate and influential forces see the official use of *bumiputra* as an important step towards eliminating all categories and creating a united people with a single identity.

The attempt to incorporate migrant groups into local society is another recognizable theme in the history of Malaysia and of vital importance today. Whether Malaysia survives as a political unity may depend on its ability to make ethnic identifications redundant and to create an acceptable new identity. In the process of creating the 'new Malaysian', the government is not embarking on a novel idea but is simply employing methods used in centuries past. The founders of Melaka successfully established their language and culture as the basis of a new society composed of immigrant and local Malays, *orang asli* and *orang laut*. Subsequent centuries saw the Minangkabau, Bugis, Javanese and various other Indonesian groups conform to the standards of Malay society. What contributed to the ready absorption of these latter groups has been their basic similarity of lifestyles with the Malays and their common religion. No such commonality exists between Malays and the two largest minorities, the Chinese and Indians. They differ physically, culturally and frequently in religious belief. The task facing the government today is thus far more difficult.

But there is an even more subtle difference between these mainly nineteenth- and early twentieth-century migrants from the Indian subcontinent and China, and earlier migrants from Indonesia. When the latter arrived in the peninsula, they mainly entered lands governed by Malays and came to recognize Malay authority as legitimate. The vast majority of Chinese and Indian immigrants, on the other hand, came into a British-governed peninsula and in general acknowledged British authority. In a colonial society so efficiently compartmentalized, the Chinese and Indians understandably regarded the Malays as standing basically in the same relation as themselves to the colonial power. Each was assigned a role, and each performed it according to British prescriptions. The latter carried on the charade of sharing rule with the Malays, but the migrant communities did not distinguish between legalities and actualities. For them it was the British who were the true rulers of the land in which they resided.

It was these attitudes so naturally acquired in 'British Malaya' which proved a major obstacle to the creation of a united people in independent Malaya/Malaysia. At the end of World War II the British authorities proceeded to prepare for independence in which all groups would be regarded as equal citizens. But such a course of action aroused the sense of honour of certain British colonial officials who subscribed literally to the agreements which recognized the sovereignty of Malay rulers. The Malays, therefore, were restored to their former positions of authority, and the Chinese and Indians were now to regard the Malays, not the British, as their rulers. Fortunately for the young nation, there were Malay leaders who acknowledged the vast changes in Malayan society and the folly of advocating a style of rule which would ignore the rights and needs of the migrant communities. Yet the basic question remained: how were such large minorities to become melded into a new 'Malaysian' identity? What should this identity be? These questions were emotionally debated but remained unresolved until the tragic events of May 1969. The ethnic violence shocked the nation and made apparent the need for some resolution of these questions. The post-1969 Malaysian governments have, therefore, felt it necessary to create a 'new Malaysian' whose identity, espoused in the *Rukunegara*, will be based on Malay language and culture but which will also incorporate aspects of the migrant cultures.

Throughout Malaysian history migrant groups have come to the peninsula and have become part of the established society. In earlier centuries this assimilation was not a major problem because the numbers of migrants involved were relatively small. Though the situation of the Chinese and Indian communities in Malaysia in the early 1980s differs in scale and complexity from earlier migrant groups, the present Malaysian government believes that they can be intergrated into a basically Malay society. It is towards this goal that Malaysia's leaders have attempted to restructure the society by formulating a series of elaborate development plans known as the New Economic Policy. By target date 1990 the government hopes to achieve the 'new Malaysian'; but even if the objective is not met by that date, at least a start will have been made.

These, then, are some themes which have recurred throughout Malaysia's long and varied history. While they provide guideposts to a historian seeking to interpret the significance of past events, they may be equally instructive to Malaysia's present generation whose attitudes and outlook will help determine their country's future.

Notes and Further Reading

Introduction: The Environment and Peoples of Malaysia

Further Reading

A specialist geographical description of Malaysia can be found in Charles A. Fisher, *South-East Asia: A Social, Economic and Political Geography* (London, 1964). Ooi Jin Bee, *Peninsular Malaysia* (New York and London, 1976) covers the peninsula in considerable detail. There are several books dealing with the local peoples. A general cultural survey is N. J. Ryan, *The Cultural Background of the Peoples of Malaya* (Kuala Lumpur, 1962). A standard introduction to the demography of the Malay peninsula is still T. E. Smith, *Population Growth in Malaya: An Analysis of Recent Trends* (London and New York, 1952) and for Borneo, L. W. Jones, *The Population of Borneo: A Study of the Peoples of Sarawak, Sabah and Brunei* (London, 1966).

R. O. Winstedt, *The Malays: A Cultural History* (Singapore 1947) and later editions, and *The Malay Magician* (London, 1951) are useful studies, though the approach could be considered dated. Iskandar Carey, *Orang Asli: The Aboriginal Tribes of Peninsular Malaysia* (Kuala Lumpur and London, 1976) gives an informative and personal discussion of the various aboriginal groups. Frank M. Lebar, ed. *Ethnic Groups of Insular Southeast Asia* (New Haven, 1972) contains an authoritative discussion on indigenous Borneo peoples. For the Chinese, see Victor Purcell, *The Chinese in Malaya* (London, 1948; reprinted Kuala Lumpur, 1967), a standard work written by a former Professor of Chinese in Malaya. Sinnappah Arasaratnam, *Indians in Malaysia and Singapore* (Kuala Lumpur, 1979) is the most recent account of Indian migration and the present state of the Indian community.

There are various histories available, some of which will withstand the test of time. R. O. Winstedt, *A History of Malaya*, revised edition (Singapore 1962) and *Malaya and its History* (London, 1948) and subsequent editions are still basic reading although considerable new material has appeared since their publication. R. J. Wilkinson, *A History of the Peninsular Malays* (Singapore, 1923) is also an important early source. A collection of Wilkinson's essays, *Papers on Malay Subjects*, has been edited by P. L. Burns (Kuala Lumpur and London, 1971). Wang Gungwu (ed.), *Malaysia: A Survey* (Melbourne, 1964) is a collection of twenty-six essays on different aspects of Malaysia's history edited by a leading Malaysian historian. J. M. Gullick, *Malaysia* (London, 1969) concentrates on the modern period but is a very competent study of certain key topics such as education, the urban scene, rural development and so on. The most recent history is C. M. Turnbull, *A Short History of Malaysia, Singapore and Brunei* (Melbourne,

1980) which takes into account the research available at the time of going to press. The introductory chapters of R. S. Milne and Diane K. Mauzy, *Politics and Government in Malaysia* (Vancouver, 1978) give an overview of the current political scene.

Chapter 1: The Heritage of the Past

Notes

1. Paul Wheatley, *The Golden Khersonese* (Kuala Lumpur, 1961), p. 273. Colonel James Low (1791–1852) was a member of the Madras Army stationed at Penang, who was later civil officer of Province Wellesley from 1827 to 1837. Low studied both Thai and Malay, and wrote several academic papers describing his archaeological excavations in Province Wellesley and southern Kedah.

2. Peter Bellwood, *Man's Conquest of the Pacific: the Prehistory of Southeast Asia and Oceania* (Auckland, 1978), Chapters 5 and 8.

3. F. L. Dunn, *Rain Forest Collectors and Traders: A Study of Resource Utilization in Modern and Ancient Malaya* (MBRAS Monograph, no. 5, 1975), pp. 78–103. The Temuan are a proto-Malay group, numbering around 9,000 mainly found in Selangor and Negeri Sembilan. The settlement studied here was within a day's reach of Kuala Lumpur.

4. F. Hirth and W. W. Rockhill (eds), *Chau Ju-Kua on the Chinese and Arab Trade* (St Petersburg, 1914; reprinted Amsterdam, 1966), p. 32.

5. Hinduism, which grew out of a much earlier brahmanical religion in India, began to assume identifiable features about the first century of the Christian era. It evolved from a variety of beliefs, some Vedic in nature, and others popular cults. Although Hinduism incorporates a large number of gods and goddesses, a main feature is the concept of a trinity, with Brahma the Creator, Viṣṇu the Preserver and Śiva the Destroyer. While Brahma gradually receded into the background, the adherents of Viṣṇu and Śiva grew, both schools believing that its god represented the absolute.

   The Buddha, the Enlightened One, was born in about 566 BC. He abandoned his life as a prince in order to find salvation through meditation. He taught that salvation lay in achieving *nirvana* or extinction of desire and freedom from the endless cycle of rebirth. After the Buddha's death divisions developed, and a number of different sects emerged. The two major schools are the Hinayana (Lesser Vehicle), which claims to follow the original Buddhist doctrine more closely and from which Theravada grew, and the Mahayana, or Greater Vehicle, which has incorporated the concept of *bodhisattva*, one who forgoes *nirvana* to work for the good of mankind and whose assistance can thus be solicited by prayer and offerings. Mahayana Buddhism lost ground in Southeast Asia after the thirteenth century, when Theravada-Hinayana established itself as the more popular sect.

   Republics and kingdoms had begun to emerge in north India from about 600 BC, and by the fourth century BC a large empire controlled by the Mauryas had emerged. In South India various kingdoms began to develop at the turn of the last century BC. In northern India the classical age is represented by the Gupta period (*c*. AD 300–700), and in the south by the post-Gupta period, especially around AD 900—1300 when the Cholas were the dominant power.

6. J. G. de Casparis, *Prasasti Indonesia: Selected Inscriptions from the Seventh to the Ninth Century AD*, vol. II (Bandung, 1956), p. 20.

7. Alastair Lamb, 'Takuapa: The Probable Site of a Pre-Malaccan Entrepôt in the Malay Peninsula', in John Bastin and R. Roolvink (eds), *Malayan and Indonesian Studies: Essays Presented to Sir Richard Winstedt on his Eighty-fifth Birthday* (Oxford, 1964), pp. 76—86.

8. O. W. Wolters, *Early Indonesian Commerce: A Study of the Origins of Srivijaya* (Ithaca, New York, 1967).

9. Hirth and Rockhill, op. cit., p. 62.

10. Dunn, op. cit., pp. 105—6.

11. G. R. Tibbetts, *A Study of the Arabic Texts Containing Material on South-East Asia* (Leiden, 1979), pp. 112—14.

12. Wheatley, op. cit., p. 60.

13. Ibid., p. 255.

14. Ibid., p. 28.

15. Ibid., p. 254.

16. O. W. Wolters, *The Fall of Srivijaya in Malay History* (Ithaca, New York and London, 1970).

17. Paul Wheatley, *Impressions of the Malay Peninsula in Ancient Times* (Singapore, 1964), p. 85.

18. Hirth and Rockhill, op. cit., p. 23.

19. Wolters, *Early Indonesian Commerce*, op. cit., p. 187.

20. Hirth and Rockhill, op. cit., p. 60; Wolters, *The Fall of Srivijaya*, op. cit., p. 1.

21. Tibbetts, op. cit., pp. 43, 182; Wheatley, *The Golden Khersonese*, op. cit., p. 199.

22. Wheatley, *The Golden Khersonese*, op. cit., pp. 38, 57, 68, 84, 91; Hirth and Rockhill, op. cit., p. 31.

23. Wheatley, *The Golden Khersonese*, op. cit., p. 82.

24. Ibid., p. 200.

25. Ibid., p. 80.

26. Hirth and Rockhill, op. cit., pp. 155 ff.

27. Armando Cortesão (ed.), *The Suma Oriental of Tomé Pires* (London, 1944), 2 vols.

28. C. C. Brown, '*Sejarah Melayu* or Malay Annals', *JMBRAS*, 25, 2 and 3 (1952), p. 12.

29. R. J. Wilkinson, *Malay Literature* (Kuala Lumpur, 1907), p. 5.

30. Wolters, *The Fall of Srivijaya*, op. cit., Chapter 4.

31. Wolters, *Early Indonesian Commerce*, op. cit., p. 15.

Further Reading

Recent systematic archaeological work on early Malaysian history is limited, although several teams have made important contributions. In Borneo, the major studies have been undertaken by the late Mr Tom Harrisson and Barbara Harrisson with assistance from a number of colleagues, including Professor S. O'Connor of Cornell University. A general survey is Tom Harrisson, 'The Prehistory of Borneo',

Asian Perspectives, 13 (1970), pp. 17—45. A memorial issue, *JMBRAS*, 50, 1 (1977), gives some personal assessments of Harrisson's work by other scholars in the field. Dr A. Lamb and Mr B. Peacock have also excavated extensively on the peninsula. Their findings, which include some discussion of earlier archaeological work, are scattered through numerous articles, but unfortunately some of the most interesting ones appeared in the *Federation Museums Journal*, the *Brunei Museum Journal*, the *Sabah Society Journal* and the *Sarawak Museum Journal*, which do not have a good distribution outside specialist libraries. A useful volume is Alastair Lamb, 'Miscellaneous Papers on Early Hindu and Buddhist Settlement in Northern Malaya and Southern Thailand', *Federation Museums Journal*, New Series, 6 (1961). A basic bibliography is F. L. Dunn and B. A. V. Peacock, 'An Annotated Bibliography of Malayan (West Malaysian) Archaeology', *Asian Perspectives*, 14 (1973), pp. 43—8, although this only covers the period up until 1969, and does not include Sarawak and Sabah. John Miskie, 'Classical Archaeology in Sumatra', *Indonesia*, 30, October (1980), pp. 43—66 gives an overview of current findings in Sumatra. Peter Bellwood, *Man's Conquest of the Pacific: The Prehistory of Southeast Asia and Oceania* (Auckland, 1978) provides the regional context for Malaysia's prehistory.

A useful survey of jungle collecting, based on anthropological, geographical and archaeological studies, is F. L. Dunn, *Rain Forest Collectors and Traders: A Study of Resource Utilization in Modern and Ancient Malaya* (MBRAS Monograph, no. 5, 1975). D. Sopher, *The Sea Nomads* (Singapore, Memoirs of the National Museum, no. 5, 1965), gives a detailed description of the role of the *orang laut* in the collecting process. W. W. Skeat, *Malay Magic* (London, 1900; reprinted New York, 1967) contains valuable information on the attitudes of the local people to the natural environment.

The basic chronology for the first years of the Christian era is still provided by G. Coedès, *The Indianized States of Southeast Asia* (Honolulu, 1968), but it is not easy reading. Students may find it easier to consult D. G. E. Hall, *A History of Southeast Asia* (London, 4th ed., 1980). Paul Wheatley, *The Golden Khersonese* (Kuala Lumpur, 1961) gives a scholarly discussion of Chinese, Indian and Arab sources relating to the peninsula before the sixteenth century. For the general reader his views are synthesized in *Impressions of the Malay Peninsula in Ancient Times* (Singapore, 1964). Some readable primary sources are F. Hirth and W. W. Rockhill (eds), *Chau Ju-Kua on the Chinese and Arab Trade* (St Petersburg, 1914; reprinted Amsterdam, 1966) which describes the area in 1225; J. V. G. Mills (ed. and trans.), *Ma Huan. Ying Yai Sheng Lan: The Overall Survey of the Ocean's Shores* (London, 1970), an account of various countries in Southeast Asia written by the interpreter for the Chinese Admiral Cheng Ho in the mid-fifteenth century; W. P. Groeneveldt, *Notes on the Malay Archipelago and Malacca* compiled from Chinese sources (*Verhandelingen van het Bataviaasch Genootschap van Kunsten en Wetenschappen*, 7, 1896), pp. 113—34. G. R. Tibbetts, *A Study of the Arabic Texts Containing Material on South-East Asia* (Leiden, 1979) revises and expands his earlier articles on references to Southeast Asia in classical Arab texts.

A masterly introduction to the richness of early Indian history and civilization is A. L. Basham, *The Wonder that was India* (London, 1954). Romila Thapur, *A History of India* (London, 1966), vol. I, is also excellent for this early period.

Specialized work on Srivijaya is O. W. Wolters, *Early Indonesian Commerce: A Study of the Origins of Srivijaya* (Ithaca, New York, 1967). His other study, *The*

Fall of Srivijaya in Malay History (Ithaca, New York and London, 1970), is a controversial but stimulating reconstruction of the connection between Srivijaya and Melaka based on Armando Cortesão (ed.), *The Suma Oriental of Tomé Pires* (London, 1944), primary Chinese dynastic and travel records, and the *Sejarah Melayu*, the Melaka court text (ed. C. C. Brown, '*Sejarah Melayu* or Malay Annals', *JMBRAS*, 25, 2 and 3, 1952). Wolters also gives a synthesis of the present state of knowledge about Srivijaya in 'Studying Srivijaya', *JMBRAS*, 52, 2 (1979), pp. 1–32.

Chapter 2: Melaka and Its Heirs

Notes

1. Armando Cortesão (ed.), *The Suma Oriental of Tomé Pires* (London, 1944), vol. 2, p. 285.
2. I. A. MacGregor, 'Notes on the Portuguese in Malaya', and 'Johore Lama in the Sixteenth Century', *JMBRAS*, 28, 2 (1955), pp. 5–125.
3. Wang Gungwu, 'The Opening of Relations between China and Malacca, 1403–5', in John Bastin and R. Roolvink (eds), *Malayan and Indonesian Studies: Essays Presented to Sir Richard Winstedt on his Eighty-fifth Birthday* (Oxford, 1964), p. 101.
4. Cortesão, op. cit., vol. 2, pp. 241–6.
5. Ibid., p. 246.
6. A. Reid, 'The Structure of Cities in Southeast Asia, Fifteenth to Seventeenth Centuries', *JSEAS*, 11, 2 (1980), p. 239.
7. Virginia Matheson, 'Concepts of Malay Ethos in Indigenous Malay Writings', *JSEAS*, 10, 2 (1979), pp. 351–72.
8. *Hikayat Hang Tuah*: an epic of incidents in the life of the Malay hero, Hang Tuah, which probably existed in oral form long before it was written down during the seventeenth century. The first definite reference to a text occurs in 1736. A romanized edition is Kassim Ahmad, *Hikayat Hang Tuah* (Kuala Lumpur, 1964).
9. It has been suggested that 'Melayu' may have once been the name of the river now known as the Tatang. According to this view, when the author of the *Sejarah Melayu* mentions the Tatang, he may be referring to the lower part of the Musi River. W. J. van der Meulen, 'Suvarnadvīpa and the Chrysê Chersonêsos', *Indonesia*, 18, October (1974), p. 32.
10. This text is the *Hikayat Deli* from east coast Sumatra, discussed by A. C. Milner, 'The Malay Raja: A Study of Malay Political Culture in East Sumatra and the Malay Peninsula in the Early Nineteenth Century' (PhD thesis, Cornell University, 1977), p. 162.
11. C. C. Brown, '*Sejarah Melayu* or Malay Annals', *JMBRAS*, 25, 2 and 3 (1952), p. 54.
12. Ibid., p. 134.
13. Kassim Ahmad (ed.), *Kisah Pelayaran Abdullah* (*The Story of Abdullah's Voyages*) (Kuala Lumpur, 1970), p. 34.
14. B. Schrieke, *Indonesian Sociological Studies*, vol. 2 (The Hague/Bandung, 1957), p. 12.

15. A. H. Johns, 'Islam in Southeast Asia: Reflections and New Directions', *Indonesia*, 19, April (1975), pp. 41–2.

16. Malay verses in which the second couplet explains the hidden metaphor in the first.

17. Mark Dion, 'Sumatra Through Portuguese Eyes: excerpts from João de Barros *Decadas da Asia*', *Indonesia*, 9, April (1970), p. 143.

18. John Harris (ed.), *Navigantum Atque Itinerarium Bibliotheca I* (London, 1705), p. 748.

19. Three nineteenth-century recensions of this chronicle are extant; it probably dates from the seventeenth and eighteenth centuries but was recopied and adapted several times subsequently. Version A is an administrative document stressing the relationship between Ayudhya and Ligor, while B is more concerned with Ligor's religious history.

20. D. K. Wyatt, *The Crystal Sands: The Chronicles of Nagara Sri Dharramaraja*, Cornell University Southeast Asia Program Data Paper no. 98 (Ithaca, New York, 1975), pp. 108–9; Anker Rentse, 'History of Kelantan', *JMBRAS*, 12, 2 (1934), p. 56.

21. A. Teeuw and D. K. Wyatt (eds), *Hikayat Patani, The Story of Patani* (The Hague, 1970), p. 13.

22. 'Drums of sovereignty', the *nobat*, consist often of drums and wind instruments and are played at the installation of the ruler. To accept a *nobat* from a ruler is to accept his overlordship. It is an acknowledgement that one's sovereignty derives from that particular ruler.

23. Wyatt, op. cit., p. 146.

24. 'Phongsawadan Muang Trangganu', in *Prachum Phongsawadan* (*Collected Chronicles*) (Bangkok, 1963), vol. 2, part 2, p. 301. This text was kindly translated for the authors by Ms Orrawin Hemasilpin.

25. A Kedah text which incorporates much oral legend, the best-known recension having apparently been written down in the late seventeenth century.

26. *Dagh Register gehouden in 't Casteel Batavia* . . . (Batavia 1887 etc.), 1644–5, p. 71. The authors are grateful to Ms Anna Weidemann for this reference.

27. J. E. Heeres, *Bouwstoffen voor de geschiedenis der Nederlanders in den Maleischen Archipel*, vol. 3 (The Hague, 1895), p. iv.

28. Alexander Hamilton, *A New Account of the East Indies* (Edinburgh 1727/ London 1930), vol. 2, p. 45.

29. Paul Wheatley, *The Golden Khersonese* (Kuala Lumpur, 1961), p. 311.

Further Reading

For the period of the fifteenth- and sixteenth-century history of the Malay region, there are two works of great value. The first is the Malay court history, the *Sejarah Melayu*, which has been translated into English by C. C. Brown in '*Sejarah Melayu or Malay Annals*', in *JMBRAS*, 25, 2 and 3 (1952). The other is a work by a sixteenth-century Portuguese apothecary, Tomé Pires, translated into English by Armando Cortesão under the title, *The Suma Oriental of Tomé Pires* (London, 1944). These two contemporary works provide an interesting Malay and European view of events in the fifteenth and sixteenth centuries, though the latter work appears to have incorporated Malay material.

A detailed account of the trade patterns in the Malay—Indonesian archipelago prior to the fifteenth century and during the period of the Portuguese and early Dutch presence in the area is found in M. A. P. Meilink-Roelofsz, *Asian Trade and European Influence in the Indonesian Archipelago between 1500 and about 1630* (The Hague, 1962). Another worthwhile study of the sixteenth century and early seventeenth century is P. A. Tiele's series of articles in Dutch entitled 'De Europeers in den Maleischen Archipel' ('The Europeans in the Malay Archipelago') in *BKI* from vol. 25 (1877) to vol. 36 (1887). C. R. Boxer's *The Portuguese Seaborne Empire, 1415–1825* (London, 1969) and *The Dutch Seaborne Empire, 1600–1800* (London, 1965) provide a readable and broad perspective of Portuguese and Dutch activities, not only in Asia but in other parts of the world.

On the story of the efforts of the descendants of Melaka's royal house to establish a kingdom on the Johor River and their conflicts with the Portuguese, see I. A. MacGregor, C. A. Gibson-Hill and G. de G. Sieveking, 'Papers on Johore Lama and the Portuguese in Malaya (1511–1641)' *JMBRAS*, 28, 2 (1955). L. Y. Andaya, *The Kingdom of Johor, 1641–1728* (Kuala Lumpur, 1975) discusses the Melaka period and gives an analysis of events in the Malay world in the seventeenth and early eighteenth centuries. An account of the sixteenth- and seventeenth century events in Perak, Kedah and Aceh can be found in B. W. Andaya, *Perak: The Abode of Grace, A Study of an 18th Century Malay State* (Kuala Lumpur, 1979). Denys Lombard's *Le Sultanat d'Atjeh au temps d'Iskandar Muda, 1607–1636* (Paris, 1967) is a study of Aceh under its greatest ruler and its expansion on both sides of the Straits of Malacca in the early seventeenth century.

There are also studies of the history, literature, and customs of a number of Malay states written by two of perhaps the greatest scholar—administrators in Malaya in the twentieth century, R. J. Wilkinson and R. O. W. Winstedt. Among Wilkinson's long list of works are *A History of the Peninsular Malays* (Singapore, 1923); 'The Malacca Sultanate' in *JMBRAS*, 13, 2 (1935); and in collaboration with Winstedt, 'A History of Perak', *JMBRAS*, 12, 1 (1934). Winstedt was even more prolific than Wilkinson, and among some of his studies are *A History of Malaya*, revised edition (Singapore, 1962); 'The Early Rulers of Perak, Pahang and Aceh', *JMBRAS*, 10, 1 (1932); 'A History of Johore (1365–1895 AD)', *JMBRAS*, 10, 3 (1932); 'A History of Negeri Sembilan', *JMBRAS*, 12, 3 (1934); 'A History of Selangor', *JMBRAS*, 12, 3 (1934); and 'Notes on the History of Kedah', *JMBRAS*, 14, 3 (1936). See Lim Huck Tee and D. E. K. Wijasuriya (eds), *Index Malaysiana* (Kuala Lumpur, 1970) for a listing of all the works written by Wilkinson and Winstedt in the *JSBRAS* and *JMBRAS*.

For a discussion of the political nature of certain Malay states, see the following articles in A. Reid and L. Castles (eds), *Pre-Colonial State Systems in Southeast Asia* (MBRAS Monograph, no. 6, 1975): L. Y. Andaya, 'The Structure of Power in 17th Century Johor'; V. Matheson, 'Concepts of State in the Tuhfat al-Nafis'; B. W. Andaya, 'The Nature of the State in 18th Century Perak'; and D. Lewis, 'Kedah — The Development of a Malay State'.

A brief but competent discussion of the history and society of Brunei is given in D. E. Brown, *Brunei: The Structure and History of a Bornean Malay Sultanate*, Monograph of the Brunei Museum Journal, vol. 2, 2 (1970). For early historical relations between the southern Philippines and North Borneo, see C. A. Majul, *Muslims in the Philippines* (Quezon City, 1973).

Material on early Thai—Malay relations can be found in Charnvit Kasetsiri, *The Rise of Ayudhya: A History of Siam in the Fourteenth and Fifteenth Centuries* (Kuala Lumpur, 1976). It is especially valuable in its discussion of the various types of vassals subject to Ayudhya and its manner of dealing with them. D. K. Wyatt's *The Crystal Sands: The Chronicles of Nagara Sri Dharramaraja* (Cornell University Southeast Asia Program Data Paper no. 98, Ithaca, New York, 1975) is a useful study of the influence of Ligor (Nagara Sri Dharramaraja—Nakhon Si-thammarat), Ayudhya's southern provincial capital, on the northern Malay states. For an understanding of Patani's ambiguous position between the Thai and Malay worlds, see A. Teeuw and D. K. Wyatt (eds), *Hikayat Patani, The Story of Patani* (The Hague, 1970), 2 vols.

Chapter 3: The Demise of the Malay Entrepôt State, 1699—1819

Notes

1. The Ibans are the largest indigenous group in Sarawak (see Introduction). The term 'Iban' did not come into general use until after World War II, and in the nineteenth century the term 'Sea Dayak' was normally employed. The first ruler of Sarawak, James Brooke, introduced this to differentiate what he thought were coastal tribes from the inland people, the 'Land Dayaks'. Only gradually did it become apparent that these were actually distinct ethnic groups.
2. 'Phongsawadan Muang Trangganu', in *Prachum Phongsawadan* (*Collected Chronicles*) (Bangkok, 1963), vol. 2, part 2, p. 299. Kindly translated for the authors by Ms Orrawin Hemasilpin.
3. Raja Ali Haji, *Tuhfat al-Nafis* (*The Precious Gift*), ed. and trans. Virginia Matheson and Barbara Watson Andaya (Kuala Lumpur, 1982), p. 43.
4. SSR G34/6, Light to Shore, 23 Jan. 1794 (FWCP 1 Aug. 1794), fols. 128—30.
5. *Dagh-Register Gehouden int Casteel Batavia* . . . (Batavia, 1887 etc.), 1682, p. 68.
6. *Silsilah Melayu dan Bugis* (Johor Baru, 1956), p. 13.
7. KA 2522 OB 1745, Gov. de Laver's Report on Melaka, 27 Dec. 1743, fo. 73.
8. A. Teeuw and D. K. Wyatt (eds), *Hikayat Patani, The Story of Patani* (The Hague, 1970), p. 201. The *Hikayat Patani* is a court text written in the classical Malay style, probably dating from the early eighteenth century.
9. Matheson and Andaya, op. cit., pp. 359, 373.
10. Jennifer Cushman and A. C. Milner, 'Eighteenth and Nineteenth Century Chinese Accounts of the Malay Peninsula', *JMBRAS*, 52, 1 (1979), p. 24.
11. As note 4 above, fo. 127.
12. Although eighteenth-century Dutch sources mention Rembau 'with its nine *negeri* [countries] ', there is no further evidence of the nature of these divisions.
13. KA 3446 OB 1780 Gov. of Melaka to Batavia, 12 Feb. 1778, fo. 152; KA 3491 OB 1782 Gov. of Melaka to Batavia, 20 Feb. 1781, fo. 96; KA 3519 OB 1783 Gov. of Melaka to Batavia, 7 Dec. 1782, fo. 118.
14. SFR G35/15, King of Kedah to Gov. of Madras (FSGCP, 25 June 1772), fols. 101—2.

15. KA 3049, Secret, Gov. of Melaka to Batavia, 13 Oct. 1765, fo. 59.
16. 'Country' trade was port-to-port trade within the eastern seas, meaning east of the Cape of Good Hope. This was distinguished from 'Europe' trade between Europe and the East via the Cape. There could be both private country trading and Company country trading, but the links between the English East India Company and British private country traders were especially close. During the eighteenth century British private country traders outnumbered all others from Europe, and by the end of that period their activities had become professionally organized and financed.
17. R. Bonney, *Kedah, 1771–1821: The Search for Security and Independence* (Kuala Lumpur, 1971), p. 170.
18. Ibid., p. 79, fn. 4.
19. Ibid., pp. 180–1.
20. Ibid.
21. Cod. Or 7304, Leiden University (the 'Siak Chronicle'), fo. 540.
22. Cushman and Milner, op. cit., p. 32.
23. A. H. Hill (ed.), *Hikayat Abdullah (The Story of Abdullah)* (Kuala Lumpur, 1970), p. 272.
24. Carl Trocki, *Prince of Pirates: The Temenggongs and the Development of Johor and Singapore, 1784–1885* (Singapore, 1979), p. 47.
25. Cushman and Milner, op. cit., p. 52.
26. Hill, op. cit., pp. 158–9, 162.

Further Reading

There are a number of relevant Malay texts for the eighteenth century but unfortunately few of these have been published, and still fewer translated into English or historically annotated. The nineteenth-century work, *Tuhfat al-Nafis (The Precious Gift)* by Raja Ali Haji, deals with Bugis, Malay and Minangkabau relations. It has been translated and annotated by Virginia Matheson and Barbara Watson Andaya (Kuala Lumpur, 1982). E. U. Kratz's romanization and German translation of the Malay court notebook from Johor, *Peringatan Sejarah Negeri Johor* (Wiesbaden, 1973), listing events of note in the Johor court from 1677 to 1750, is a valuable example of the court notebook genre. It is very similar to a Bugis-influenced work, the so-called *Hikayat Negeri Johor*, which goes on to describe events in Riau and Selangor until the beginning of the nineteenth century. This has been romanized and edited by Ismail Husain, MBRAS Reprint no. 6 (1979), pp. 183–240. The *Misa Melayu*, an eighteenth-century court chronicle from Perak, was first edited and romanized by Sir Richard Winstedt, and has since been reprinted (Kuala Lumpur, 1962). A later text from Kedah, the *Al-Tarikh Salasilah Negeri Kedah* (Kuala Lumpur, 1968) was compiled in 1928 by the court archivist and despite its relatively recent date contains many fascinating legends relating to the eighteenth century. A well-annotated Malay work relating to the late eighteenth and early nineteenth century is *The Hikayat Abdullah*, ed. A. H. Hill (Kuala Lumpur, 1970), which gives a personal but perceptive view of Singapore and Melaka society at the beginning of the nineteenth century.

The basic history of Johor/Riau in the eighteenth and nineteenth centuries is still E. Netscher, *De Nederlanders in Djohor en Siak* (*VBG*, 25, 1870). An unpublished overview of the eighteenth century, based on Dutch sources, is Dianne

Lewis, 'The Dutch East India Company and the Straits of Malacca, 1700–1784: Trade and Politics in the Straits of Malacca' (PhD thesis, ANU, 1970). A more detailed study of Johor, attempting to balance European and Malay material, and bringing together information on the *orang laut* and Bugis, is Leonard Y. Andaya, *The Kingdom of Johor, 1641–1728* (Kuala Lumpur, 1975). Barbara Watson Andaya, *Perak, The Abode of Grace: A Study of an Eighteenth Century Malay State* (Kuala Lumpur, 1979) incorporates European and Malay material relating to Perak, and also covers some aspects of the history of Kedah, Selangor and the wider Malay world as they impinged on Perak. The history of Kedah from 1770 based on English sources is covered by R. Bonney, *Kedah, 1771–1821: The Search for Security and Independence* (Kuala Lumpur, 1971). A. Teeuw and D. K. Wyatt, *Hikayat Patani, The Story of Patani* (The Hague, 1970), 2 vols, contains a brief summary of what is known of Patani's history in the eighteenth century. Mubin Sheppard, 'A Short History of Trengganu', *JMBRAS*, 22, 3 (1949), pp. 1–74 depends heavily on the *Tuhfat al-Nafis*. Anker Rentse, 'History of Kelantan', *JMBRAS*, 12, 2 (1934), pp. 44–62 gives a short account of Kelantan's history incorporating material from H. Marriott, 'A Fragment of the History of Trengganu and Kelantan', *JSBRAS*, 72, 3–23 (1916), a translation of part of a Malay text now lost. The first chapter of Carl Trocki, *Prince of Pirates: The Temenggongs and the Development of Johor and Singapore, 1784–1885* (Singapore, 1979) deals with the background to the founding of Singapore, which is the specific focus of C. M. Turnbull, *A History of Singapore 1819–1975* (Kuala Lumpur, 1977); Khoo Kay Kim, *The Western Malay States, 1850–1873: The Effects of Commercial Development on Malay Politics* (Kuala Lumpur, 1972) provides a useful survey of the western Malay states in the first decades of the nineteenth century.

The material relating to Brunei, Sabah and Sarawak is severely limited. For an important study of Iban oral literature, see Benedict Sandin, *The Sea Dayaks of Borneo before White Rajah Rule* (London, 1967). The first chapters of Robert Pringle, *Rajahs and Rebels: The Ibans of Sarawak under Brooke Rule, 1841–1941* (Ithaca, New York, 1970), discuss Iban migration into present-day Sarawak and also contain an excellent geographical description. Nicholas Tarling, *Britain, the Brookes and Brunei* (Kuala Lumpur, 1971) brings together the relevant English material for the eighteenth and early nineteenth century; James Warren, 'Trade, Raid, Slave: The Socio-Economic (Patterns) of the Sulu Zone, *1770–1898*' (PhD thesis, ANU, 1975), draws on Spanish, Dutch and English archives to see Borneo's northwest coast in terms of its relationship to the Sulu Sultanate.

A translation of an eighteenth-century Chinese account of the Malay peninsula is useful in showing trading contacts with China in this period; Jennifer W. Cushman and A. C. Milner, 'Eighteenth and Nineteenth Century Chinese Accounts of the Malay Peninsula', *JMBRAS*, 52, 1 (1979), pp. 1–56.

There are several studies of the economic policies of the Dutch East India Company, but the most readable on the Company's role as a whole, setting it in the context of events in Asia and Europe, is C. R. Boxer, *The Dutch Seaborne Empire, 1600–1800* (London, 1965). Holden Furber, *Rival Empires of Trade in the Orient, 1600–1800* (Minneapolis, 1977) compares the VOC with its rivals, the other European trading companies. Nicholas Tarling, *Anglo-Dutch Rivalry in the Malay World, 1780–1824* (Brisbane, 1962) describes Dutch and British conflicts and relates these to events in Europe and the Malay areas.

Chapter 4: 'A New World Is Created', 1819—74

Notes

1. A. H. Hill (ed.), *Hikayat Abdullah* (Kuala Lumpur, 1970), p. 64.
2. Asa Briggs, *The Age of Improvement, 1783—1867* (New York, 1959), p. 3.
3. The estimates given by T. J. Newbold, *Political and Statistical Accounts of the British Settlements in the Straits of Malacca* (London, 1839; reprinted Kuala Lumpur, 1971), vol. 2, *passim*, and in P. J. Begbie, *The Malayan Peninsula* (Madras, 1834; reprinted Kuala Lumpur, 1967) are often quoted, but modern estimates of the peninsula's Malay population in the 1830s vary from around 200,000 to 425,000. See, for example, Ooi Jin Bee, *Peninsular Malaysia* (New York and London, 1976), p. 112, and R. D. Hill, *Rice in Malaya: A Study in Historical Geography* (Kuala Lumpur, 1977), p. 177.
4. KA 3858, Secret, King of Trengganu to Gov. of Malacca, 6 Oct. 1791.
5. The governors of the more important Siamese provinces and the Malay vassal rulers all bore the title Phaya, loosely translated as governor and second highest in the five grades of conferred nobility in Siam. For praiseworthy service a Phaya could be promoted to Chau Phaya.
6. Nicholas Tarling, *British Policy in the Malay Peninsula and Archipelago, 1824—71* (Kuala Lumpur, 1969), p. 30.
7. There is some discrepancy over the year when the Governor of Ligor received this title. Henry Burney's account indicates that it was before 1811, but official Thai sources give 1822. Lorraine Gesick, review of R. Bonney, *Kedah, 1771—1821: The Search for Independence* (Kuala Lumpur, 1971) in *JSS*, 63, 2 (1975), p. 409.
8. SSR F5, King of Perak to Gov. of Penang, 10 Sept. 1826, fo. 7.
9. Kassim Ahmad (ed.), *Kisah Pelayaran Abdullah (The Story of Abdullah's Voyages)* (Kuala Lumpur, 1970), p. 54; A. H. Hill, op. cit., p. 301. *Joget Melayu* is a Malay dance performed by two people keeping in step. Skill is judged by one partner's ability to copy the other's steps exactly.
10. Mohd. Taib Osman, 'Hikayat Sri Kelantan' (MA thesis, University of Malaya, 1961), p. 53.
11. See above, Chapter 2, p. 52. The term *sufi* was first applied to Moslem ascetics who wore coarse garments of wool (*suf*). In simple terms, Sufis aim to attain direct communion with Allah and claim that they reach a higher level of spiritual experience than can be gained through revealed religion, especially that codified in Islamic law and laid down in the sayings of the Prophet. A *tariqa* (Malay *tarikat*) was a way by which a student could be guided through stages to experience the divine Reality.
12. Tarling, op. cit., p. 67; 'Phongsawadan Muang Trangganu', in *Prachum Phongsawadan (Collected Chronicles)* (Bangkok, 1963), vol. 2, part 2, p. 307. Kindly translated by Ms Orrawin Hemasilpin.
13. A. C. Milner, 'The Malay Raja: A Study of Malay Political Culture in East Sumatra and the Malay Peninsula in the Early Nineteenth Century' (PhD thesis, Cornell University, 1977), p. 19.
14. Robert Pringle, *Rajahs and Rebels: The Ibans of Sarawak under Brooke Rule, 1841—1941* (Ithaca, New York, 1970), p. 129.

15. Wong Lin Ken, 'The Trade of Singapore, 1819–69', *JMBRAS*, 33, 4, (1960), p. 295.

16. Raja Ali Haji, *Tuhfat al-Nafis (The Precious Gift)*, ed. and trans. Virginia Matheson and Barbara Watson Andaya (Kuala Lumpur, 1982), p. 271.

17. James Warren, *The North Borneo Chartered Company's Administration of the Bajau, 1878–1909*, Center for International Studies, Ohio University, 1971.

18. C. M. Turnbull, *A History of Singapore 1819–1975* (Kuala Lumpur, 1977), p. 37; John Cameron, *Our Tropical Possessions in Malayan India* (London, 1865; reprinted Kuala Lumpur, 1965), p. 35.

19. Wong, op. cit., p. 122.

20. Figures calculated from Wong, ibid., pp. 207–10, 252–4.

21. Pringle, op. cit., p. 268; J. M. Gullick, 'Selangor, 1876–1882. The Bloomfield Douglas Diary', *JMBRAS*, 48, 2 (1975), p. 41; C. M. Turnbull, *The Straits Settlements, 1826–67* (Kuala Lumpur, 1972), pp. 276–8; F. L. Dunn, *Rain Forest Collectors and Traders: A Study of Resource Utilization in Modern and Ancient Malaya* (MBRAS Monograph, no. 5, 1975), p. 109.

22. SSR G34/6, Light to Shore, 25 Jan. 1794 (FWCP 1 Aug. 1794), fo. 120.

23. Carl Trocki, *Prince of Pirates: The Temenggongs and the Development of Johor and Singapore, 1784–1885* (Singapore, 1979), pp. 85–117.

24. Khoo Kay Kim, *The Western Malay States, 1850–1873: The Effects of Commercial Development on Malay Politics* (Kuala Lumpur, 1972), p. 218.

25. Turnbull, *The Straits Settlements*, op. cit., p. 292.

26. For a detailed discussion, see C. M. Cowan, *Nineteenth Century Malaya: The Origins of British Political Control* (London, 1961), pp. 43–54 and W. L. Blythe, *The Impact of Chinese Secret Societies in Malaya* (London, 1969), Chapters 1–4.

27. Khoo, op. cit., pp. 123–4.

28. Turnbull, *The Straits Settlements*, op. cit., p. 301.

29. Eunice Thio, 'British Policy towards Johor; from Advice to Control', *JMBRAS*, 40, 1 (1967), p. 3.

30. Trocki, op. cit., p. 204.

31. Barbara Watson Andaya and Virginia Matheson, 'Islamic Thought and Malay Tradition', in Anthony Reid and David Marr (eds), *Perceptions of the Past in Southeast Asia* (Singapore, 1979), p. 123.

32. C. M. Turnbull, 'Origins of British Control in the Malay States before Colonial Rule', in J. Bastin and R. Roolvink (eds), *Malayan and Indonesian Studies: Essays presented to Sir Richard Winstedt on his eighty-fifth birthday* (Oxford, 1964), p. 174.

33. Khoo, op. cit., p. 165, fn. 4.

Further Reading

The founding of Singapore and the development of the Straits Settlements in the nineteenth century are well covered in L. A. Mills, 'British Malaya, 1824–67', *JMBRAS*, 33, 3 (1960); Nicholas Tarling, *Anglo-Dutch Rivalry in the Malay World, 1780–1824* (Brisbane, 1962); C. M. Turnbull, *The Straits Settlements, 1826–67* (Kuala Lumpur, 1972); C. M. Turnbull, *A History of Singapore, 1819–1975* (Kuala Lumpur, 1977). All contain extensive bibliographies.

C. H. Wake, 'Raffles and the Rajas', *JMBRAS*, 48, 1 (1975) places the founding of Singapore in the setting of Malay politics. Wong Lin Ken, 'The Trade of Singapore, 1819–69', *JMBRAS*, 33, 4 (1960) gives a survey of Singapore's trade, with useful tables. Sophia, Lady Raffles, *Memoir of the Life and Public Service of Sir Thomas Stamford Raffles* (London, 1830), 2 vols, conveys a sense of Raffles's dreams for the extension of British power in the region.

British involvement with the Malay States and the events leading up to intervention are best analysed in C. D. Cowan, *Nineteenth Century Malaya: The Origins of British Political Control* (London, 1961) and C. N. Parkinson, *British Intervention in Malaya, 1867–77* (Singapore, 1960). Nicholas Tarling, *British Policy in the Malay Peninsula and Archipelago, 1824–71* (Kuala Lumpur, 1969) and *Piracy and Politics in the Malay World: A Study of British Imperialism in the 19th Century* (Melbourne, 1963), deal in some detail with British relations with neighbouring Malay areas. Khoo Kay Kim, *The Western Malay States 1850–1873* (Kuala Lumpur, 1972) discusses the commercial links between the Straits Settlements and the Malay States before formal British intervention. W. F. Vella, *Siam under Rama III, 1824–51* (New York, 1957) has a good section on Siam's relations with the northern Malay states.

The nature of Malay society in the period immediately before intervention is discussed in J. M. Gullick's classic, *The Indigenous Political Systems of Western Malaya* (London, 1958). There are a few studies of individual states, of uneven quality. For a bitter attack on Siam's treatment of Patani, see the scarce Ibrahim Syukri, *Sejarah Kerajaan Melayu Patani* (*The History of the Malay Kingdom of Patani*) (Pasir Putih, Kelantan, n.d.). An account of the civil war in early nineteenth century Kelantan is in C. Skinner, *The Civil War in Kelantan in 1839* (MBRAS Monograph, no. 2, 1965). M. C. Sheppard, 'A Short History of Trengganu', *JBRAS*, 22, 2 (1949) remains the most accessible account of Trengganu's history in the early nineteenth century. W. Linehan, 'A History of Pahang', *JMBRAS*, 14, 2 (1936), though lacking analysis, contains excellent material drawing heavily from the unpublished *Hikayat Pahang*. R. O. Winstedt and R. J. Wilkinson, 'A History of Perak', *JMBRAS*, 12, 1 (1934) is still a standard work; R. O. Winstedt, 'A History of Selangor', and 'Negeri Sembilan, the History, Polity and Beliefs of Nine States', both in *JMBRAS*, 12, 3 (1934) should also be consulted.

Johor is again well studied. R. O. Winstedt, 'A History of Johore (1365–1895 AD), *JMBRAS*, 10, 3 (1932) remains a basic work. A more interpretative study is Carl Trocki, *Prince of Pirates: The Temenggongs and the Development of Johor and Singapore, 1784–1885* (Singapore, 1979), which also contains a good bibliography for the period.

The literature on the Chinese is extensive. A contemporary account is J. Vaughan, *The Manners and Customs of the Chinese of the Straits Settlements* (Singapore, 1879; reprinted Kuala Lumpur, 1971). Victor Purcell, *The Chinese in Malaya* (London, 1948; reprinted Kuala Lumpur, 1967) gives a general overview. An exhaustive study of the secret societies is W. L. Blythe, *The Impact of Chinese Secret Societies in Malaya* (London, 1969). A useful article using Chinese material is Yen Ching Hwang, 'Early Chinese Clan Organizations in Singapore and Malaya, 1819–1911', *JSEAS*, 12, 1 (1981), pp. 62–92. Trocki, *Prince of Pirates*, op. cit., contains a section on *kongsi* organization in Johor which should be read in conjunction with A. E. Coope, 'The Kangchu System in Johore', *JMBRAS*, 14,

3 (1936), pp. 247–63. Chinese commercial agriculture is discussed in J. C. Jackson, *Planters and Speculators: Chinese and European Enterprise in Malaya, 1786–1921* (Kuala Lumpur, 1968) while Wong Lin Ken, *The Malayan Tin Industry to 1914* (Tucson, 1965) provides detailed information on Chinese tin mining in the nineteenth century. S. M. Middlebrook, 'Yap Ah Loy', *JMBRAS*, 24, 2 (1951) gives a useful though occasionally inaccurate account of one of the great Chinese leaders of the nineteenth century.

There are several contemporary Malay texts. A. H. Hill (ed. and trans.), *Hikayat Abdullah (The Story of Abdullah)* (Kuala Lumpur, 1970) contains perceptive contemporary material, as does Abdullah's *Kisah Pelayaran Abdullah (The Story of Abdullah's Voyages)*, ed. Kassim Ahmad (Kuala Lumpur, 1970) which describes his journey to the east coast of the peninsula. It is available in an English translation in A. E. Coope, *The Voyages of Abdullah* (Kuala Lumpur, 1967). Abdullah's son Ibrahim was employed by Maharaja Abu Bakar of Johor and also wrote an account of several trips on official business. It has been edited and translated by Amin Sweeney and Nigel Phillips, *The Voyages of Mohamed Ibrahim Munshi* (Kuala Lumpur, 1975). Amin Sweeney (trans.), *Reputations Live On: An Early Malay Autobiography* (Berkeley and Los Angeles, 1980) is a valuable contemporary account by another of Johor's Malay officials. Raja Ali Haji, *Tuhfat al-Nafis (The Precious Gift)* remains an important source, especially concerning developments in Islam. It has been translated and edited by Virginia Matheson and Barbara Watson Andaya (Kuala Lumpur, 1982). Mohd. Taib Osman, 'Hikayat Sri Kelantan' (MA thesis, University of Malaya, 1961), a romanization of a manuscript dated 1914 in the Royal Asiatic Society, throws considerable light on many aspects of Kelantan history, especially in the nineteenth century.

Numerous contemporary sources in English have been published, several of which contain transcripts of official documents since lost. The most important are: J. Anderson, *Political and Commercial Considerations Relative to the Malayan Peninsula* etc. (Penang, 1824; reprinted *JMBRAS*, 35, 4, 1962); P. J. Begbie, *The Malayan Peninsula* (Madras, 1834; reprinted Kuala Lumpur, 1967); J. Cameron, *Our Tropical Possessions in Malayan India* (London, 1865; reprinted Kuala Lumpur, 1965); T. J. Newbold, *Political and Statistical Accounts of the British Settlements in the Straits of Malacca* (London, 1839; reprinted Kuala Lumpur, 1971), 2 vols; G. W. Earl, *The Eastern Seas* (London, 1837; reprinted Kuala Lumpur, 1971). The *Journal of the Indian Archipelago and Eastern Asia*, ed. J. R. Logan (12 vols, 1847–59), contains many invaluable descriptions of contemporary customs and local history.

Borneo is less well served. A. L. Reber, 'The Sulu World in the Eighteenth and Nineteenth Centuries' (MA thesis, Cornell University, 1966) and James Warren, 'Trade, Raid, Slave: The Socio-Economic Patterns of the Sulu Zone, 1770–1898', (PhD thesis, ANU, 1975) place Borneo in the Sulu world. There are several studies of James Brooke. An early biography is Emily Hahn, *James Brooke of Sarawak* (London, 1953); the most recent is Nicholas Tarling, *'The Burthen, the Risk and the Glory': The Life of Sir James Brooke* (Kuala Lumpur, 1982) which includes new material and a good bibliography. A useful examination of links between Brooke and British interests is John Ingleson, *Expanding the Empire: James Brooke and the Sarawak Lobby, 1839–1869* (Centre for South and Southeast

Asian Studies, University of Western Australia, 1979). The only full study of Charles Brooke is Colin N. Crisswell, *Rajah Charles Brooke* (Kuala Lumpur, 1978). S. Baring Gould and C. A. Bampfylde, *A History of Sarawak under its Two White Rajahs* (London, 1909) is a semi-official history and therefore uncritical. The best book on nineteenth century Sarawak is Robert Pringle, *Rajahs and Rebels: The Ibans of Sarawak under Brooke Rule, 1841–1941* (Ithaca, New York, 1970) which although focusing on the Iban—Brooke relationship, covers numerous other topics. Benedict Sandin, *The Sea Dayaks of Borneo before White Raja Rule* (London, 1967) has incorporated much of the oral material of the Ibans. Hugh Low, *Sarawak: its Inhabitants and Productions* (London, 1848) and Spenser St John, *Life in the Forests of the Far East* (London, 1862), 2 vols, are interesting contemporary accounts. The development of Kuching itself is traced by Craig Lockard, 'The Southeast Asian Town in Historical Perspective: A Social History of Kuching, Malaysia, 1820–1970' (PhD thesis, University of Michigan, 1974). For the relationship between Brunei, North Borneo and Sarawak, the reader is directed to the suggested reading following Chapter 5.

Chapter 5: The Making of 'British' Malaya, 1874–1919

Notes

1. J. M. Gullick, 'The Tampin Succession', *JMBRAS*, 49, 2 (1976), p. 3.
2. Emily Sadka, *The Protected Malay States, 1874–1895* (Kuala Lumpur, 1968), p. 79, fn. 2.
3. Chai Hon Chan, *The Development of British Malaya 1896–1909* (Kuala Lumpur, 1967), p. 305.
4. Ibid., p. 8; Sadka, op. cit., pp. 3–4.
5. C. D. Cowan, *Nineteenth Century Malaya: The Origins of British Political Control* (London, 1961), p. 225.
6. P. L. Burns (ed.), *The Journals of J. W. W. Birch* (Kuala Lumpur, 1976), p. 178.
7. Ibid., p. 104.
8. R. O. Winstedt and R. J. Wilkinson, 'A History of Perak', *JMBRAS*, 12, 1 (1934), p. 116.
9. Sadka, op. cit., p. 279.
10. Eunice Thio, *British Policy in the Malay Peninsula 1880–1910*, vol. I, *The Southern and Central States* (Singapore, 1969), p. xix.
11. R. G. Cant, *A Historical Geography of Pahang* (MBRAS Monograph, no. 4, 1973), p. 29.
12. Thio, op. cit., p. 85.
13. W. Linehan, 'A History of Pahang', *JMBRAS*, 14, 2 (1936), p. 121.
14. Thio, op. cit., p. 91.
15. In 1969 an old man in Pahang identified himself as Mat Kilau and after extensive investigation by the state government his claim was confirmed. Khoo Kay Kim, *The Western Malay States 1850–1873: The Effects of Commercial Development on Malay Politics* (Kuala Lumpur, 1972), p. 192, fn. 1; Sa'ad Shakri bin Haji Muda *et al. Detik*[2] *Sejarah Kelantan* (Notes on the History of Kelantan) (Kota Baru, Kelantan, 1971), pp. 95–7.

16. Sadka, op. cit., p. 105.
17. Frank Swettenham, *British Malaya* (London, 1906), p. 282.
18. Sadka, op. cit., p. 17.
19. Frank Swettenham, *Malay Sketches* (London and New York, 1913), pp. 2–3.
20. R. Emerson, *Malaysia: A Study in Direct and Indirect Rule* (New York, 1937; reprinted Kuala Lumpur, 1964), p. 503.
21. Chai, op. cit., p. 65.
22. Emerson, op. cit., p. 137.
23. L. R. Wright, *The Origins of British Borneo* (Hong Kong, 1970), p. 147.
24. Colin N. Crisswell, *Rajah Charles Brooke* (Kuala Lumpur, 1978), p. 160.
25. Nicholas Tarling, 'Britain and Sarawak in the Twentieth Century', *JMBRAS*, 43, 2 (1970), p. 28.
26. Ian Black, 'The Ending of Brunei Rule in Sabah', *JMBRAS*, 41, 2 (1968), p. 185
27. Ibid., p. 187.
28. Nicholas Tarling, *Britain, the Brookes and Brunei* (Kuala Lumpur, 1971), p. 518.
29. Sharom Ahmad, 'The Political Structure of the State of Kedah, 1879–1905', *JSEAS*, 1, 2 (1970), p. 125.
30. J. de Vere Allen, 'The Elephant and the Mousedeer — A New Version: Anglo-Kedah Relations, 1905–1915', *JMBRAS*, 41, 1 (1968), p. 94.
31. Keith Sinclair, 'The British Advance in Johore, 1885–1914', *JMBRAS*, 40, 1 (1967), p. 100.

Further Reading

The literature on the first half of colonial rule is extensive and the bibliographies of works cited below should also be consulted.

British colonial policy in Malaya in its imperial setting is discussed by W. D. McIntyre, *The Imperial Frontier in the Tropics, 1865–75* (London and New York, 1967) and J. S. Galbraith, 'The "Turbulent Frontier" as a Factor in British Expansion', *Comparative Studies in Society and History*, II, 2 (1960), pp. 150–68. The account of political expansion after 1874 is discussed in the last chapters of C. D. Cowan, *Nineteenth Century Malaya: The Origins of British Political Control* (London, 1961). The first twenty years of colonial rule in the FMS is analysed in Emily Sadka, *The Protected Malay States, 1874–1895* (Kuala Lumpur, 1968). The story of political developments is picked up by Eunice Thio, *British Policy in the Malay Peninsula, 1886–1901*, vol. I, *The Southern and Central States* (Singapore, 1969). Chai Hon Chan, *The Development of British Malaya 1896–1909* (Kuala Lumpur, 1967) covers the same period but adds further detail on social measures using material obtained from annual reports.

The early chapters of W. R. Roff, *The Origins of Malay Nationalism* (New Haven and Kuala Lumpur, 1967) give important information on intellectual movements in Malay society, while the early sections of Lim Teck Ghee, *Peasants and Their Agricultural Economy in Colonial Malaya, 1874–1941* (Kuala Lumpur, 1977) discuss the effects of colonial rule on the Malay peasant in the Protected States.

Both Chai, *The Development of British Malaya* and Sadka, *The Protected Malay States*, op. cit., contain useful sections on the Chinese relationship to the colonial authority, and the reader is also referred to works cited in the bibliography to Chapter 4. Kernial Singh Sandhu, *Indians in Malaya: Immigration and Settlement 1786–1957* (Cambridge, 1969) deals in detail with Indian migration; a briefer overview is in Sinnappah Arasaratnam, *Indians in Malaysia and Singapore* (Kuala Lumpur, 1979).

British colonial society is described in a lively manner in John Butcher, *The British in Malaya, 1880–1941: The Social History of a European Community in Colonial Southeast Asia* (Kuala Lumpur, 1979). A selection of contemporary sketches about life in Malaya from the colonial viewpoint is W. R. Roff, *Stories by Sir Hugh Clifford* (Kuala Lumpur, 1966) and *Stories and Sketches by Sir Frank Swettenham* (Kuala Lumpur, 1967).

There are numerous contemporary commentators, and the journals of individual residents are particularly useful. P. L. Burns (ed.), *The Journals of J. W. W. Birch* (Kuala Lumpur, 1976); P. L. Burns and C. D. Cowan, *Swettenham's Malayan Journals, 1874–76* (Kuala Lumpur, 1975); Emily Sadka, 'The Journal of Sir Hugh Low, Perak 1877', *JMBRAS*, 27, 4 (1954); J. M. Gullick, 'Selangor, 1876–1882: The Bloomfield Douglas Diary', *JMBRAS*, 48, 2 (1975); Peter Wicks (ed.), *Journal of a Mission to Pahang, January 15 to April 11 1887*, by Hugh Clifford (Honolulu, 1978). Books of reminiscences and travel supply other interesting details. Isabella Bird, *The Golden Chersonese and the Way Thither* (New York, 1883; reprinted Kuala Lumpur, 1967) should be read in conjunction with Emily Innes, *The Golden Chersonese with the Gilding Off*, 2 vols (London, 1885). J. F. McNair, *Perak and the Malays; 'Sarong and Kris'* (London, 1878) is by a participant in the Perak campaign following the murder of Birch.

Work on the northern Malay states has tended to deal with selected topics, and is largely in article form. For an overall picture of the British advance, see Rupert Emerson, *Malaysia: A Study in Direct and Indirect Rule*, (New York, 1937; reprinted Kuala Lumpur, 1964). Some specific articles are J. Chandran, 'The British Foreign Office and the Siamese Malay States, 1890–97', *Modern Asian Studies*, 5 (1971), pp. 143–59; E. Thio, 'Britain's Search for Security in North Malaya, *JSEAH*, 10, 2 (1969), pp. 279–303; Ira Klein, 'British Expansion in Malaya, 1897–1902', *JSEAH*, 9, 1 (1968), pp. 53–68.

A useful collection of essays on Kelantan is W. R. Roff (ed.), *Kelantan: Religion, Society and Politics in a Malay State* (Kuala Lumpur, 1974). Clive Kessler, *Islam and Politics in a Malay State: Kelantan, 1838–1969* (Ithaca, New York and London, 1978) gives a background synthesizing nineteenth-century material. A good study of late-nineteenth-century Trengganu society and the 1928 uprising is Heather Sutherland, 'The Taming of the Trengganu Elite', in Ruth McVey (ed.), *Southeast Asian Transitions: Approaches through Social History* (New Haven and London, 1978). For further information, see J. de Vere Allen, 'The Ancien Regime in Trengganu, 1909–1919', *JMBRAS*, 41, 1 (1968), pp. 23–53 and S. T. Robert, 'The Trengganu Ruling Class in the Late Nineteenth Century', *JMBRAS*, 50, 1 (1977), pp. 25–47; W. A. Graham, *Kelantan: A State of the Malay Peninsula* (Glasgow, 1907) is a contemporary description by the first Adviser.

The only full study of Kedah in this period is Sharom Ahmad, 'Transition and Change in a Malay State: A Study of the Economic and Political Development of Kedah, 1879–1923' (PhD thesis, University of London, 1969). From this he has extracted several articles: 'The Structure of the Economy of Kedah, 1879–1905' *JMBRAS*, 43, 2 (1970), pp. 1–24; 'The Political Structure of the State of Kedah, 1879–1905', *JSEAS*, 1, 2 (1970), pp. 115–28; 'Kedah–Siam Relations', *JSS*, 59,

1 (1971), pp. 97–117; see also J. de Vere Allen, 'The Elephant and the Mousedeer – A New Version: Anglo-Kedah Relations, 1905–1915', *JMBRAS*, 41, 1 (1968), pp. 54–94.

Singapore's history during the late nineteenth century is well covered in C. M. Turnbull, *A History of Singapore 1819–1975* (Kuala Lumpur, 1977). For Johor in this period, see Thio, *British Policy in the Malay Peninsula* op. cit; Keith Sinclair, 'The British Advance in Johore, 1885–1914', *JMBRAS*, 40, 1 (1967), pp. 93–110; J. de Vere Allen, 'Johore 1901–1914; the Railway Concession; the Johore Advisory Board; Swettenham's Resignation and the First General Advisor', *JMBRAS*, 45, 2 (1972), pp. 1–28; Christopher Gray, 'Johore 1910–1941: Studies in the Colonial Process' (PhD thesis, Yale University, 1978). Amin Sweeney, *Reputations Live On: An Early Malay Autobiography* (Berkeley and Los Angeles, 1980) is a translation of the writings of Johor's Datuk Bentara Luar.

Pahang has been generally neglected and most studies of the FMS rely heavily on material from the west coast. Thio, *British Policy in the Malay Peninsula*, op. cit., gives the best coverage. Jang Aisyah, *Pemberontakan Pahang, 1891-1895* (Kota Baru, Kelantan, 1972) is a study of the Pahang uprising, while R. G. Cant, *A Historical Geography of Pahang* (MBRAS Monograph, no. 4, 1973) provides a geographer's view of the effects of British intervention on local society and economy.

Borneo in the context of European diplomacy is treated in G. W. Irwin, *Nineteenth Century Borneo: A Study in Diplomatic Rivalry* (The Hague, 1955). Nicholas Tarling, *Britain, the Brookes and Brunei* (Kuala Lumpur, 1971) and *Sulu and Sabah: A Study of British Policy towards the Philippines and North Borneo from the Late Eighteenth Century* (Kuala Lumpur, 1978) discusses the emergence of the Borneo territories in relation to changing British imperial policies. L. R. Wright, *The Origins of British Borneo* (Hong Kong, 1970) covers the late nineteenth century, with a somewhat different interpretation from Tarling. The works cited in the bibliography for Chapter 4 are also relevant for this period. To these can be added K. G. Tregonning, *A History of Modern Sabah; North Borneo, 1881–1963* (Singapore, 1965). Owen Rutter, *British North Borneo* (London, 1922) gives an uncritical but informative account of the early development of North Borneo. As yet unpublished is I. D. Black, 'Native Administration by the British North Borneo Chartered Company, 1878–1915' (PhD thesis, ANU, 1970), which contains valuable details unavailable in other studies. James Warren, *The North Borneo Chartered Company's Administration of the Bajau, 1878–1909*, Center for International Studies, Ohio University, (Athens, Ohio, 1971) provides disturbing evidence of the dislocating effects of Company policies on the Bajau.

Chapter 6: 'The Functioning of a Colonial Society', 1919–57

Notes

1. P. J. Drake, 'The Economic Development of British Malaya to 1914: An Essay in Historiography with Some Questions for Historians', *JSEAS*, 10, 2 (1979), p. 274.

2. G. C. Allen and A. G. Donnithorne, *Western Enterprise in Indonesia and Malaya: A Study in Economic Development* (London, 1957), pp. 153, 157.

3. Ibid., p. 152; Yip Yat Hoong, *The Development of the Tin Mining Industry of Malaya* (Kuala Lumpur/Singapore, 1969), p. 19.

4. Lim Chong-Yah, *Economic Development of Modern Malaya* (Kuala Lumpur, 1967), p. 39.

5. D. Lim, *Economic Growth and Development in West Malaysia, 1947–1970* (Kuala Lumpur, 1973), pp. 7–8.

6. J. C. Jackson, *Planters and Speculators: Chinese and European Enterprise in Malaya, 1786–1921* (Kuala Lumpur, 1968), p. 6.

7. Ibid., p. 249; Lim Chong-Yah, op. cit., p. 97.

8. C. Barlow, *The Natural Rubber Industry, Its Development, Technology and Economy in Malaysia* (Kuala Lumpur, 1978), p. 76.

9. Ibid., p. 76.

10. P. P. Courtenay, *A Geography of Trade and Development in Malaya* (London, 1972), p. 125.

11. R. D. Hill, *Rice in Malaya: A Study in Historical Geography* (Kuala Lumpur, 1977), pp. 196–7.

12. Jackson, op. cit., pp. 223–4; Lim Teck Ghee, *Peasants and Their Agricultural Economy in Colonial Malaya, 1874–1941* (Kuala Lumpur, 1977), pp. 46, 87–8.

13. S. Arasaratnam, *Indians in Malaysia and Singapore* (Kuala Lumpur, 1979), p. 185.

14. Phillip F. S. Loh, *Seeds of Separatism: Educational Policy in Malaya 1874–1940* (Kuala Lumpur, 1975), p. 93.

15. R. Stevenson, *Cultivators and Administrators: British Educational Policy towards the Malays, 1875–1906* (Kuala Lumpur, 1975), p. 175.

16. Loh, op. cit., p. 106.

17. Stevenson, op. cit., pp. 57–8.

18. Khoo Kay Kim, 'Malay Society, 1874–1920s', *JSEAS* 5, 2 (1974) pp. 188–9.

19. R. Pringle, *Rajahs and Rebels: The Ibans of Sarawak under Brooke Rule, 1841–1941* (Ithaca, New York, 1970), pp. 139–49, 339 fn. 3.

20. K. G. Tregonning, *A History of Modern Sabah: North Borneo, 1881–1963* (Singapore, 1965), p. 185.

21. F. H. K. Wong and Gwee Yee Hean, *Perspectives: The Development of Education in Malaysia and Singapore* (Singapore, 1972), p. 31.

22. L. A. Mills, *British Rule in Eastern Asia: A Study of Contemporary Government and Economic Development in British Malaya and Hong Kong* (London, 1942), p. 60.

23. Ibid., pp. 63–4.

24. A. J. Stockwell, *British Policy and Malay Politics During the Malayan Union Experiment, 1942–48* (MBRAS Monograph, no. 8, 1979), pp. xiv–xv.

25. Pringle, op. cit., pp. 335–6.

26. A. Short, *The Communist Insurrection in Malaya, 1948–1960* (London 1975), pp. 24–5.

27. Khoo Kay Kim, 'Sino-Malay Relations in Peninsular Malaysia before 1942', *JSEAS* 12, 1 (1981), pp. 98–106.

28. Cheah Boon Kheng, *The Masked Comrades: A Study of the Communist United Front in Malaya 1945–48* (Singapore, 1979), p. 5.

29. Ibid., pp. 23, 27.

30. M. Stenson, *Industrial Conflict in Malaya: Prelude to the Communist Revolt in 1948* (Kuala Lumpur, 1970), p. 124.
31. Short, op. cit., p. 293.
32. R. Stubbs, 'The United Malays National Organization, the Malayan Chinese Association, and the Early Years of the Malayan Emergency, 1948—1955', *JSEAS* 10, 1 (1979), pp. 85—6.
33. G. P. Means, *Malaysian Politics* (London, 2nd ed., 1976), pp. 163, 167.
34. D. Lim, op. cit., pp. 7—8.

Further Reading

There has been a number of excellent studies made on the period of British rule in Malaya in the twentieth century. British colonial administration is the subject of a penetrating analysis by R. Emerson in *Malaysia: A Study in Direct and Indirect Rule* (New York, 1937; reprinted Kuala Lumpur, 1964). Its critical view of the intent of British policy became the inspiration to a new generation of scholars writing about the post-independent period in Southeast Asia. Other studies of British rule are L. A. Mills, *British Rule in Eastern Asia: A Study of Contemporary Government and Economic Development in British Malaya and Hong Kong* (London, 1942); Virginia Thompson, *Postmortem on Malaya* (New York, 1943); and J. S. Sidhu, 'British Administration in the Federated Malay States, 1896—1920', (PhD thesis, University of London, 1975). An important study of the impact of British rule on the Malays is W. R. Roff's *The Origins of Malay Nationalism* (New Haven and Kuala Lumpur, 1967).

For accounts of colonial rule in the Borneo states, see K. G. Tregonning, *A History of Modern Sabah: North Borneo, 1881—1963* (Singapore, 1965) and Nicholas Tarling, *Sulu and Sabah: A Study of British Policy towards the Philippines and North Borneo from the Late Eighteenth Century* (Kuala Lumpur, 1978). Robert Pringle, *Rajahs and Rebels* (Ithaca, New York, 1970) is an excellent study of Brooke rule and its impact on indigenous society. Steven Runciman, *The White Rajahs* (Cambridge, 1960) presents a more personal look at the Brookes themselves. Robert Reece, 'The Cession of Sarawak to the British Crown in 1946' (PhD thesis, ANU 1977) deals with a little-studied period in Sarawak's history.

On the economic development of British Malaya, an indispensable study is G. C. Allen and A. G. Donnithorne's *Western Enterprise in Indonesia and Malaya: A Study in Economic Development* (London, 1957), which describes the manner in which government and Western capital co-operated in the development of Malaya's economy. A more recent and general study which traces the development of Malaya's economy from the early tin-mining days to the post-independent period is P. P. Courtenay, *A Geography of Trade and Development in Malaya* (London, 1972). Lim Chong-Yah, *Economic Development of Modern Malaya* (Kuala Lumpur, 1967) is another general study of economic conditions in Malaya with useful statistical information. The first European and Chinese ventures into agricultural export commodities is the subject of J. C. Jackson, *Planters and Speculators: Chinese and European Enterprises in Malaya, 1786—1921* (Kuala Lumpur, 1968). A valuable analysis of the effects of colonial policy on Malay farmers is Lim Teck Ghee, *Peasants and Their Agricultural Economy in Colonial Malaya, 1874—1941* (Kuala Lumpur, 1977). There are several studies on tin for this period, the most impressive being Wong Lin Ken, *The Malayan Tin Industry to 1914* (Tucson, 1965). For the story of the tin industry after 1914, see Yip Yat Hoong, *The Development of the Tin Mining Industry of Malaya* (Kuala Lumpur/Singapore 1969). For rubber in Malaya, the classic work is P. T. Bauer, *The Rubber Industry: A Study in Competition and Monopoly* (London/New York, 1948). John Drabble, *Rubber in Malaya 1876–1922: The Genesis of the Industry* (Kuala Lumpur, 1973), and Colin Barlow, *The Natural Rubber Industry, Its Development, Technology and Economy in Malaysia* (Kuala Lumpur 1976) bring the picture up to the modern period.

To deal with education in British Malaya, one is forced to examine various systems which applied to the different ethnic groups. A well-written study of education of Malays both in English- and Malay-medium schools is Rex Stevenson, *Cultivators and Administrators: British Educational Policy towards the Malays, 1875–1906* (Kuala Lumpur, 1975). An examination of the various types of schools available to those who wanted a Chinese-medium education is found in V. Purcell, *The Chinese in Malaya* (London, 1948, reprinted Kuala Lumpur, 1967). Indian education, which was basically Tamil-medium education, is discussed in K. S. Sandhu, *Indians in Malaya: Immigration and Settlement 1786–1957* (Cambridge, 1969) and in S. Arasaratnam, *Indians in Malaysia and Singapore* (Kuala Lumpur, 1979). For a general discussion of all of these 'systems' of education and their impact on the unity of Malayan society under British rule, see Phillip Fook Seng Loh, *Seeds of Separatism: Educational Policy in Malaya, 1874–1940* (Kuala Lumpur, 1975). Islamic education, especially in the northern Malay states, has been little studied. Some recent articles on the subject are Khoo Kay Kim, 'Malay Society, 1874–1920s', *JSEAS*, 5, 2 1974); Abdullah al-Qari b. Haji Salleh, 'To'Kenali: His Life and Influence', in W. Roff (ed.), *Kelantan* (Kuala Lumpur, 1974) pp. 87–106; and Abdullah Alwi Haji Hassan, 'The Development of Islamic Education in Kelantan', in Khoo Kay Kim (ed.), *Tamadun Islam di Malaysia* (Kuala Lumpur, 1980) pp. 190–228.

The story of the Japanese Occupation in Malaya has been discussed from a personal view, as well as from the view of national policy. Among the former are Chin Kee Onn, *Malaya Upside Down* (Singapore, 1946) which describes the life of a civilian in Perak under the Japanese, and F. Spencer Chapman, *The Jungle is Neutral* (London, 1949), an account of the organization of anti-Japanese resistance in the jungles of Malaya by a British army officer who remained behind when the Japanese invaded the peninsula. Tom Harrisson, *The World Within* (London, 1959) is an account of the author's experiences after being parachuted into Borneo during World War II. A discussion of the war years from those who participated at the planning level can be found in Lt.-Gen. A. E. Percival, *The War in Malaya* (London, 1949), Lt.-Gen. Gordon Bennett, *Why Singapore Fell* (Sydney, 1944) and Col. Masanobu Tsuji, *Singapore: The Japanese Version* (Sydney, 1960). Japanese policy in general towards expansion in Southeast Asia is the subject of W. H. Elsbree, *Japan's Role in Southeast Asian Nationalist Movements, 1940–1945* (Cambridge, Mass., 1953) and J. Lebra (ed.), *Japan's Greater East Asia Co-Prosperity Sphere in World War II: Selected Readings and Documents* (Kuala Lumpur, 1975). Specific Japanese Occupation policy within Malaya itself is discussed in Yoichi Itagaki, 'Some Aspects of the Japanese Policy for Malaya Under the Occupation, with Special Reference to Nationalism', in K. G. Tregonning (ed.),

Papers on Malayan History (Singapore, 1962). Another study on the subject by a Japanese is Yoji Akashi, 'Japanese Policy towards the Malayan Chinese, 1941—45', *JSEAS* I, 2 (1970).

On the Malayan Union there have been several important studies. The first is J. de Vere Allen, *The Malayan Union* (New Haven, 1967) which examines the negotiations towards the Union's formation, and the second is A. J. Stockwell, *British Policy and Malay Politics During the Malayan Union Experiment, 1942—1948* (MBRAS Monograph, no. 8, 1979). Stockwell's study expands on the earlier work by Allen as a result of new archival material which became accessible to scholars. A third study is Mohamed Noordin Sopiee, *From Malayan Union to Singapore Separation* (Kuala Lumpur, 1974) which attempts to place these political events within a theoretical framework on political unification.

The communist insurrection in Malaya between 1948 and 1960 has been discussed in a number of detailed studies. The origins of the insurrection are examined in M. R. Stenson, *Repression and Revolt: The Origins of the 1948 Communist Insurrection in Malaya and Singapore* (Ohio, 1969) and *Industrial Conflict in Malaya: Prelude to the Communist Revolt in 1948* (Kuala Lumpur, 1970). G. Z. Hanrahan, *The Communist Struggle in Malaya* (New York, 1954) focuses on aspects of guerrilla warfare. R. Clutterbuck, *The Long War: The Emergency in Malaya 1948—1960* (London, 1967) and *Riot and Revolution in Singapore and Malaya, 1945—1963* (London, 1973), and E. O'Ballance, *The Communist Insurgent War, 1948—1960* (London, 1966) are military accounts of the conflict. A. Short, *The Communist Insurrection in Malaya, 1948—1960* (London, 1975) is a study of the insurrection which began as an official government history and therefore contains considerable previously highly classified material. Han Su-yin, *And the Rain My Drink* (London, 1956) is a novel about life in the Emergency and particularly in a New Village.

Chapter 7: The Forging of a Nation, 1957—80

Notes

1. D. K. Mauzy and R. S. Milne, *Politics and Government in Malaysia* (Vancouver, 1978), p. 131.
2. S. Bedlington, *Malaysia and Singapore: The Building of New States* (Ithaca, New York, 1978), pp. 103—4.
3. G. P. Means, *Malaysian Politics* (London, 2nd ed., 1976), p. 316.
4. Mauzy and Milne, op. cit., pp. 90—1.
5. Radzuan Abdul Rahman, 'Agricultural Development Strategies Re-examined', in Cheong Kee Cheok *et al.*, *Malaysia* (Kuala Lumpur, 1979), p. 209; Frank Peacock, 'The Failure of Rural Development in Peninsular Malaysia', in J. C. Jackson and M. Rudner (eds), *Issues in Malaysian Development* (Singapore, 1979), p. 381.
6. Ishak Shari, 'A Study of Urban Poverty: The Kuala Lumpur Experience', in Cheong *et al.*, op. cit., p. 51.
7. David Lim, 'The Political Economy of the New Economic Policy in Malaysia', unpublished manuscript, p. 2.

8. Peter Pirie, 'Squatter Settlements in Kuala Lumpur', in Cheong *et al.*, op. cit., pp. 75, 99.

9. Donald R Snodgrass, *Inequality and Economic Development in Malaysia* (Kuala Lumpur, 1980), pp. 280–1.

10. *Far Eastern Economic Review*, 10 April 1981, p. 75.

11. *Far Eastern Economic Review*, 22 August 1980, p. 40.

12. *Asia Yearbook 1979*, Far Eastern Economic Review (Hong Kong, 1980), p. 45.

13. R. Thillainathan, 'Public Policies and Programmes for Redressing Poverty in Malaysia — A Critical Review', in Khoo Siew Mun and B. A. R. Mokhzani (eds), *Poverty in Malaysia*, essays presented to Prof. Ungku A. Aziz (Kuala Lumpur, 1977), p. 248; Colin Barlow, *The Natural Rubber Industry, Its Development, Technology and Economy in Malaysia* (Kuala Lumpur, 1978), p. 92.

14. *Asia Yearbook 1980*, Far Eastern Economic Review (Hong Kong, 1981), pp. 237–8.

15. Mauzy and Milne, op. cit., p. 339.

16. Bedlington, op. cit., p. 155.

17. *Far Eastern Economic Review*, 22 August 1980, p. 40.

18. *Far Eastern Economic Review*, 23 January 1981, p. 52.

19. *Far Eastern Economic Review*, 3 April 1981, pp. 12–13.

Further Reading

Post-independent Malaya developments are discussed in two excellent books. The first is G. P. Means, *Malaysian Politics* (London, 2nd ed: 1976) and the second R. S. Milne, *Government and Politics in Malaysia* (Boston, 1967). There is a new edition of the latter book written by Milne in collaboration with Diane K. Mauzy and entitled *Politics and Government in Malaysia* (Vancouver, 1978). The final chapters assess the success of the government's attempts to achieve the goals of the New Economic Policy. Other general works on the politics and the political process in Malaysia are M. E. Osborne, *Singapore and Malaysia* (Ithaca, New York, 1964) and S. Bedlington, *Malaysia and Singapore: The Building of New States* (Ithaca, New York, 1978). The latter is especially interesting with regard to Sabah which the author knew intimately after seven years of service there in the British colonial service.

On the ethnic aspects of politics in Malaysia, see K. J. Ratnam, *Communalism and the Political Process in Malaya* (Kuala Lumpur, 1965), R. K. Vasil, *Politics in a Plural Society* (Singapore, 1971), and Cynthia Enloe's stimulating *Multi-Ethnic Politics: The Case of Malaysia* (Berkeley, 1970). Karl von Vorys, *Democracy without Consensus: Communalism and Political Stability in Malaysia* (Princeton, 1975) attempts to demonstrate the viability of the democracy created by Malaya/ Malaysia's leaders based not on a national integrated community but a discrete communal one. John Funston, *Malay Politics in Malaysia: A Study of UMNO and PAS* (Kuala Lumpur and Singapore, 1980) discusses the evolution of these two Malay political parties, which represent two differing approaches to Malaysia's future, in the pre- and post-1969 period.

On the Borneo states, see R. S. Milne and K. J. Ratnam, *Malaysia – New States in a New Nation: Political Development of Sarawak and Sabah in Malaysia* (London, 1974); M. C. Roff, *The Politics of Belonging: Political Change in Sabah and Sarawak* (Kuala Lumpur, 1974); J. P. Ongkili, *Modernization in East Malaysia 1960–1970* (Kuala Lumpur, 1972); and Michael Leigh, *The Rising Moon: Political Change in Sarawak* (Sydney, 1974).

On the economy of independent Malaya, one of the most readable and useful studies is David Lim, *Economic Growth and Development in West Malaysia, 1947–1970* (Kuala Lumpur, 1973). His second book, now in press, takes the story up to 1980. A concise and penetrating analysis of the interrelationship among inequality, economic development and ethnicity in Malaysia is Donald R. Snodgrass, *Inequality and Economic Development in Malaysia* (Kuala Lumpur, 1980). In addition to those books mentioned in the economy section of the bibliography in Chapter 6, other books on the economy of modern Malaya are R. Ma and You Poh Seng, *The Economy of Malaysia and Singapore* (Singapore, 1966) and P. J. Drake, *Financial Development in Malaya and Singapore* (Canberra, 1969). There are also two volumes of essays which examine the government's efforts to achieve its economic and social goals through its various development plans. The first volume, B. A. R. Mokhzani and Khoo Siew Mun (eds), *Poverty in Malaysia* (Kuala Lumpur, 1977), consists of essays by Malaysian scholars discussing various aspects of the Second Malaysia Plan; and the second volume, James C. Jackson and Martin Rudner (eds), *Issues in Malaysian Development* (Singapore, 1979) contains essays by foreign scholars mainly based in Australia. Essays in the latter volume tend in general to be critical of the progress of the Malaysian government in eradicating poverty and removing inequities in the society.

On education in Malaya/Malaysia since independence, for a general straightforward account of educational policy and the changing curricula in Malaysia's schools see Francis H. K. Wong and Gwee Yee Hean, *Perspectives: The Development of Education in Malaysia and Singapore* (Singapore, 1972). Cynthia Enloe, *Multi-Ethnic Politics*, op. cit., examines educational policy in the wider perspective of multi-ethnic politics.

On the Federation of Malaysia in 1963, see W. A. Hanna, *The Formation of Malaysia: New Factor in World Politics* (New York, 1964); T. E. Smith, *The Background to Malaysia* (London, 1963); M. E. Osborne, *Singapore and Malaysia*, op. cit; Nancy Fletcher's *The Separation of Singapore from Malaysia* (Ithaca, New York, 1969); and R. A. Andersen, 'The Separation of Singapore from Malaysia: A Study in Political Involution' (PhD thesis, American University, Washington, DC, 1973). The reaction of Sabah and Sarawak to the Malaysia Federation is discussed in J. P. Ongkili, *The Borneo Response to Malaysia* (Singapore, 1967) and in B. Ross-Larson, *The Politics of Federation: Syed Kechik in East Malaysia* (Singapore, 1976). The latter book is about a Malay lawyer's influence on the politics of Sabah and Sarawak from the mid-1960s into the 1970s. The story of the opposition to the Malaysia Federation from the Philippines and Indonesia can be found in Marvin Ott, 'The Sources and Content of Malaysian Foreign Policy toward Indonesia and the Philippines, 1957–1965' (PhD thesis, Johns Hopkins University, Baltimore, 1971), M. Leifer, *The Philippine Claim to Sabah* (Hull, 1968) and J. A. C. Mackie, *Konfrontasi – The Indonesia–Malaysia Dispute 1963–1966* (Kuala Lumpur, 1974).

On the 1969 ethnic disturbances and post-1969 events, the works by von Vorys (1975), Means (1976), Milne and Mauzy (1978) and Bedlington (1978) cited above are useful. For a more detailed account of the events of 1969 itself, there is the official report published by the National Operations Council entitled *The May 13th Tragedy* (Kuala Lumpur, 1969). It describes the background of the riots, the riots themselves, and then discusses the future direction of the nation. Goh Cheng Teik, *The May Thirteenth Incident and Democracy in Malaysia* (Kuala Lumpur, 1971) provides a political analysis of the reasons for the outbreak of violence; whereas Mahathir b. Mohamad, *The Malay Dilemma* (Singapore, 1970) attempts to see a deeper cultural basis for the disharmony between the Chinese and Malays in the society. Two other studies of the event are J. Slimming, *Malaysia: Death of a Democracy* (London, 1969) and Felix Gagliano, *Communal Violence in Malaysia 1969: The Political Aftermath* (Athens, Ohio, 1970).

Glossary

adat	customs and traditions
adat katumanggungan or *adat temenggung*	customs and traditions associated with the law of the sultans
adat parapatih or *adat perpatih*	customs and traditions associated with the matriarchal law of Minangkabau and considered democratic in nature
akar bahar	black coral
anak dagang	resident foreign merchants ('child of commerce')
anak negeri	native ('child of the country')
anak raja	royal offspring
arak	fermented drink made from rice or from various types of palm trees
bahar or *bahara*	a measure of weight, about 170 kilogrammes
bahasa	literally 'language', but often used in the past to refer to the whole range of acceptable behaviour among Malays
baju	general term for a loose shirt or jacket
batu Sarawak	antimony ('Sarawak stone')
Bendahara	the principal official in the kingdom, often likened to a Prime Minister
berbisan	term used to describe a relationship between those whose children are married
bicara	deliberation; discussion
biduanda	page; palace orderly in the Melaka court

bumiputra	'sons of the soil'; a term employed by the Malaysian government to refer to Malays and all other indigenous groups in the country
bunga mas dan perak	'gold and silver flowers', but in reality a tree adorned with gold, silver and other precious ornaments sent regularly as tribute from vassal states to the Thai court
Daeng	a Bugis title of nobility
dakwah	to 'call' or 'invite', i.e. the duty of Moslems to call all mankind to Islam. In Malaysia the term is associated with a fundamentalist Islamic revival movement
Dato, Datuk	a title often associated with a great non-royal chief; in modern Malaysia the term 'Datuk' is conferred in recognition of outstanding service to the nation
daulat	often translated as 'sovereignty' but which in the royal context refers to the special spiritual forces surrounding Malay kingship
derhaka or durhaka	treason to the lawful authority, thus most often equated with treason to the ruler
Dewan Negara	the Senate, the Upper House of Malaysia's Parliament
Dewan Rakyat	the House of Representatives, the Lower House of Malaysia's Parliament
dulang	a tray or pan used for washing for gold or tin
Durbar	Conference of Rulers, referring to the periodical meeting of the rulers of the Malay states
fitnah	malicious rumour
gunung	mountain
Hadat	Advisory Council to the ruler in some Bugis kingdoms in South Sulawesi
haj	pilgrimage to Mecca

haji	one who has made the pilgrimage to Mecca
hamba Melayu	slave or subject of the Melayu, a term used during the Melaka period to refer to *orang asli* and *orang laut* peoples who had become associated with the Melayu migrants from Sumatra
hikayat	narrative, story, tale in prose
hui	Chinese society
ilmu	knowledge, science
Jawi	1. Malay language written in Perso-Arabic script 2. a term used in Mecca to refer generally to those from the Malay-Indonesian archipelago
Jawi Peranakan	locally-born Moslems of mixed Indian/Malay or Arab/Malay descent
jihad	the Holy War, which is an Islamic concept referring essentially to the spread of the faith through force of arms, but used commonly in the Moslem areas of Southeast Asia in earlier centuries as a cry for unity among fellow Moslems to destroy the Christian Europeans in the area
joget	Malay dance by two persons in step
kafir	infidel, unbeliever
kampung	a village; a compound of houses usually under the authority of an important individual
kangani	Indian labour recruiter
kangchu	title given to a Chinese river headman in Johor
kerah	corvée labour
keramat	saintly, miracle-working; can refer to people, animals or shrines
kongsi	Chinese business co-operative
kuala	estuary

kuo yu	National Language, adopted as the standard language in China which was a compromise between northern and southern Mandarin
kurnia	bounty of the ruler
Laksamana	an important official whose principal duty was to be in charge of the ruler's fleet, hence often equated with an admiral
madrasah	a Modernist Islamic school
makyong	a theatrical performance with obvious Thai influence originating in the northern Malay states
memberi 'aib	cause shame
menora	an operatic performance similar to the *makyong*, popular in the northern Malay states
Menteri	Minister
merantau	the Minangkabau tradition of going abroad to seek fortune or religious knowledge
mesyuarat bicara	deliberative assembly in which decisions are reached through consensus
Min Yuen	civilian support units for the Malayan Communist Party during the Emergency
monthon	Thai provincial administrative unit; 'circle'
muafakat or *mupakat*	agreement reached through consensus
muhibbah	a feeling of goodwill and brotherhood
mukim	administrative district around a common mosque
musim Ilanun	season of the Ilanun, that is 'pirate season'
Nan Yang	'Southern Ocean', a term used in Chinese imperial records to refer generally to the Southeast Asian region
nasihat	advice
negeri	settlement, state, country

negeri asing	a foreign country
nipa	thatch palm, *Nipa fruticana*
nobat	royal orchestra; in the Melaka period a *nobat* was conferred on the more important rulers who acknowledged Melaka's suzerainty
orang asli	indigenous groups living on the Malay peninsula, excluding ethnic Malays
orang hulu	upriver people, a term used for one of the indigenous groups in the Malay peninsula
orang kaya	literally 'rich man', but a term applied more commonly for nobility; sometimes used to refer to a district chief
orang laut	sea and riverine peoples in the western half of the Malay-Indonesian archipelago
orang tua	elders
padi	wet rice agriculture
pai hua	spoken Chinese vernacular, i.e. Mandarin
pangiran	In Brunei, a title for nobles
pantun	a quatrain made up of two parts, the first having a hidden meaning and the second rhyming with the first part and explaining it
parang	curved cleaver with a concave cutting edge widening out towards the tip
penghulu	headman; head of a village; district head
perahu	Malay boat without deck
perjuangan	struggle; in a nationalist context it has an even loftier connotation and should properly be translated as 'noble struggle'
phongsawadan	Thai chronicles
Phaya	Thai title, loosely translated as governor, second highest in five grades of conferred nobility. For praiseworthy service a Phaya could be promoted to Chau Phaya
phra cao	highest Thai title used for independent kings

pikul	a measure of weight, about 62·5 kilogrammes
pondok schools	'hut' schools, referring to the common practice in the past of pupils erecting huts for accommodation during the period they studied with an Islamic scholar; traditional Islamic education
pulau	island
Raja Muda	Heir-Apparent, but in the kingdom of Johor this title was appropriated by the Bugis in the early eighteenth century for their leader who often directed affairs of the kingdom on behalf of the Malay ruler
rantau barat	the western areas, used in the Melaka period to refer to outlying dependencies
Rukunegara	Articles of Faith of the State
Rumi	the Malay language written in Latin script
śakti	supernatural power associated with great men
sarong	a long loose cloth worn as a skirt by both men and women
sepak raga	a game played with a rattan ball
singkeh	literally 'new man'; a recent Chinese immigrant
songkok	a round cap made of cloth or velvet like a fez without the tassel
suku	clan; among Minangkabaus in the Malay peninsula, this term refers to a number of uterine families (*perut*); also used to refer to *orang laut* tribes
sungai	river
surat kuasa	letter of authority
surat sungai	a title deed giving authority over a river district
Syahbandar	harbour master, a post which gained in importance as international trade grew in Malay kingdoms

syariah	Islamic law, in contradistinction to *adat* which is law based on customs and traditions
tamadun	literally 'urbane' and 'cultured', but used increasingly by Moslems from the late nineteenth century to signify modern Islamic civilization as distinguished from Western civilization
tarikat	Islamic mystical brotherhood
Temenggung	Malay minister in charge of defence, justice and palace affairs
Tengku, Tunku	title for Malay princes
Thesaphiban system	a reorganization of Siamese provinces into circles (*monthon*) instituted in the 1890s
tripang	sea cucumber, bêche de mer, sea slug (holothurian)
tulin	inherited property
ulama	religious teacher
ulu	upriver
umat or *ummat*	the world community of Moslems
Yang Dipertuan Agung	Paramount Ruler
Yang Dipertuan Muda, or in the Johor Bugis version, *Yamtuan Muda*	title of the *Raja Muda*, Heir-Apparent
zaman mas	golden age

Index